A NOTE ON THE AUTHORS

Both Jack Northman Anderson and Ronald Walter May have know[n] McCarthy well. Their book is the product of more than a year [of] exhaustive research through files of back newspapers and records, a[nd] of numerous interviews that took them from city to city to talk [with] people whose lives have run tangent to McCarthy's career.

Jack Anderson is a veteran newsman. During World War II, he wa[s] a war correspondent in China, first for a string of newspapers, later f[or] the Shanghai edition of *Stars and Stripes*. Since 1947, he has been [a] staff reporter for Drew Pearson on the "Washington Merry-Go-Round[."] He is a member of the White House Correspondents' Associatio[n.] Anderson started his newspaper career as a reporter for the *Desere[t] News* of Salt Lake City, later worked on the city desk of the Salt Lak[e] *Tribune*. As a war correspondent, he traveled for two months behin[d] Japanese lines with the Chinese Nationalist guerrillas. He was wit[h] the guerrillas at the war's end when they began fighting the Chines[e] Communists. After the Japanese surrender, he covered the Nationalis[t-] Communist truce talks and General George Marshall's mission t[o] Chungking. Anderson first met McCarthy in 1947 after he came t[o] the Senate. They got to know each other so well that McCarthy at[-] [t]ended Anderson's wedding reception in 1949.

Ronald May has lived in Wisconsin for twenty years. He was [a] [r]adio news writer for the Madison office of the United Press, and chie[f] [r]ecord clerk of the Wisconsin State Senate. A graduate of the Uni[-] [v]ersity of Wisconsin, he also attended Marquette University in Mil[-] [wa]ukee, where McCarthy matriculated, too. May is a World War I[I] [v]eteran of more than three years' service with the Navy. In the cours[e] [o]f his research for this book, he lived for two months in McCarthy'[s] [h]ome town of Appleton, Wisconsin. He also quit his job in order to [s]pend his full time for six months working on the book.

Where conversations are reported in the book, they are based on [a]ctual dialogue or close paraphrasing. Behind the text are voluminous [f]act-files verifying the data.

McCARTHY

THE MAN, THE SENATOR, THE "ISM"

McCARTHY

The Man, the Senator, the "Ism"

By JACK ANDERSON *and* RONALD W. MAY

THE BEACON PRESS · BOSTON

Library of Congress Catalog Card Number: 52-11115

Printed in U.S.A.

Contents

v

McCARTHY

THE MAN, THE SENATOR, THE "ISM"

1. Portrait of a Senator

A WHISPER RUSTLES THROUGH THE SENATE GALLERY. THE spectators nudge one another and nod toward the Senate floor, where a dark figure suddenly appears at a side entrance. He pauses for an instant in the doorway; then, seemingly aware that all eyes are upon him, he strides toward his seat, browses through papers on the top of the desk, ambles to the back of the chamber to whisper earnestly into the ear of another Senator. Then he barges through the same entrance and is gone.

This is one of the rare appearances in the Senate of its most controversial member, Senator Joe McCarthy, the Man from Wisconsin who is too preoccupied with hunting headlines to spend much time on the Senate floor.

What kind of man is this who is called crusader by some, witch-hunter by others; and by still others a skillful camouflage artist for the isolationists' Congressional votes sabotaging concrete measures opposing the spread of Soviet power — such as *No* votes on the Marshall Plan, Point Four, and military aid to free nations? Who is this man whom newsmen have voted the "worst Senator of all 96," yet whose power has frightened and silenced many of his colleagues; whose name has entered the language in the word "McCarthyism"?

He's an ingratiating, friendly hail-fellow-well-met, called "Joe" by almost everyone who has known him more than five minutes. "He comes to you with tail wagging and all the appeal of a tramp dog," said one colleague. He is earthy and unpretentious in manner and dress, often with rumpled clothes (he presses his pants under the mattress at night) and unshined shoes; a big barrel-chested man with a large head, huge hands, and short, restless, muscular arms; a man with a constant tremor of the head; a ruggedly handsome man who is so aware of his stock resemblance to Pat O'Brien that he keeps the movie star's autographed picture on his office wall.

A man of furious physical energy and capacity for work, McCarthy treats each day as a new crisis — and a matter of life and death. He is tense, on edge, always in a hurry (except when bad health forces him to take periodic rests). He rushes through a paper, scanning for special items; gets up late, goes to bed long after midnight. Sometimes after a night at his desk, he just curls upon an office couch until his staff discovers him in the morning.

After an exhausting mental siege, he will let off steam in violent exercise out of doors. After the grueling Senate session and Republican convention of 1948, Joe took off for Lefor, North Dakota, and got a job as a farm hand. He pulled down ten dollars a day operating a combine; the other hired hands never knew that they were grappling grain with a United States Senator.

Like many another bachelor, he could use a woman to pick up after him — his pockets are stuffed with notes; he drops his clothes around his room wherever he happens to take them off, and hotels are constantly forwarding clothing he has forgotten. But "Joe has never even been close to getting married," says Urban Van Susteren, his former campaign manager. And Tom Korb, a close friend, says: "Joe has a strong respect for women. He wants to put women on a pedestal, but I don't know whether he could make the sacrifices involved in a marriage."

He's a successful bachelor in one domestic field anyway —
there's nothing he enjoys more than tying on an apron and
cooking a meal. His idea of a meal is a steak well-done, or
"cremated," as he calls it. But during the 1947 Christmas
season, he whipped up an exotic feast for a group of friends
at the home of Mrs. Francis Werner in New London, Wisconsin. A culinary work of art, it featured venison meat balls
wrapped in grape leaves, potatoes broiled in chicken broth,
and chicken browned in a skillet, roasted and served with
a dressing made from a secret McCarthy formula.

This is a brief profile of the man McCarthy. But what
is he like underneath? How he emerged, a shy, awkward
boy from the cocoon of an isolated Wisconsin community,
to his role as the most controversial and feared man in the
United States Senate — that is another story.

2. Humble Beginnings

ONE HUNDRED MILES NORTH OF THE BEER AND BUSTLE OF
Milwaukee, and 150 miles south of the once-thriving
gambling clubs run by the Capone gang in the woods along
the Wisconsin-Michigan border, lies a farmed-out stretch of
soil which once supported a forest of virgin hardwoods.

The land was settled by big-muscled, hard-swearing ex-
lumberjacks of German and Irish extraction, who swarmed
down from the pine country in the north to become farmers.
They were joined by Irish immigrants coming directly from
the old country, plus a scattering of other settlers from Holland, Germany, and England, who felled the trees and
planted corn, oats, wheat, barley.

The land in the three counties of Shawano, Outagamie,
and Langlade is mostly sandy loam. It had been rich and
fertile enough for the land-hungry settlers back in the middle
1800's when the government began selling it for $2.50 an
acre. But by the turn of the century it had become the kind
of soil that gave to the farmer only what he put into it. And
as farming became increasingly technical and competitive,
profits had a way of falling behind losses in the new-
fangled account books. Strong-backed farmers with single-
minded dedication to the soil could eke out a living by dint of
eighteen-hour days and seven-day weeks; others, less dedi-
cated, lived in the shadow of failure.

Barren of rich soil, the rural tri-county area was also
barren of rich ideas. There was no time for them, and the

6

section remained a semi-isolated, unto-itself segment of Americana, like William Faulkner's Yoknapatawpha County, where "The Idea" was important only when it concerned the everyday tools of survival — the livestock, the plow, the farm-yard well — but totally unimportant when it concerned society in the mass, living conditions or people in the great world "outside." It was the kind of intellectual vacuum that could produce a farmer like lanky Jim Heenan, who told the authors that most big-city folks were Leftists — but who was not sure what a Leftist was.

And it was the kind of intellectual vacuum that could produce Jim Heenan's neighbor — Joe McCarthy.

By the time Joseph Raymond McCarthy was born, on November 14, 1908, the family fortunes had taken a swing upward, because of father Timothy's ability to submerge himself in hard work. The first four McCarthy children were born in a log cabin; Joseph was born in an eight-room, white clap-board house on the 142-acre McCarthy farm, located in Grand Chute township of Outagamie County near the north shore of Lake Winnebago.

The farm was in the center of a section called "The Irish Settlement." There families were clannish, closemouthed, suspicious, thrifty — but, above all else, good Catholics. And unlike the legendary Irishman, they were not easy talkers, except among themselves. They were imbued with a profound suspicion of outsiders, a distrust of outside ideas and new ways of doing things; and father Timothy McCarthy was no exception. He taught his seven children that the only important things in life could be found on their rolling acres, in the crops and cattle that took all of Timothy's time. Tim and his wife Bridget were industrious, frugal, and devout; their life was a continuous round of work, relieved only by an occasional visit with the neighbors and by Sunday worship at St. Mary's Church in Appleton, seven miles away.

Into this all-work-and-no-play atmosphere, Joe McCarthy

was born; and he adapted to it like all the other McCarthy children. His neighbors say that young Joe wore overalls instead of diapers, shucked corn instead of playing with blocks, and learned to pitch hay long before he learned to pitch baseballs.

"Joe worked like the devil," a neighboring farmer recalls. "I remember one day when he was helpin' Tim load hay into the barn. We was usin' a team of horses and a rope and pulley to hoist the hay up. Joe's job was leadin' the horses. He had to lead them across the yard and through a ditch and clear to the road. The ditch was near fulla water, but Joe plowed right into it, up to his knees, leadin' them horses. Never even slowed down. One of his boots came off in the mud and I remember he didn't go pick up that boot till all the hay was in. Joe was always like that — a hard worker."

There were dozens of old Timothy's prime virtues that his son Joseph neglected in later years; but the principle that man is made to work, and work hard, the boy never forgot. There was an eleventh commandment in the McCarthy home — "Thou shalt live by the sweat of thy brow" — and young Joe obeyed. His father was a demanding taskmaster who wanted more than anything else to see his sons become successful farmers and respected churchgoers. And old Tim wasn't inclined to spare the rod to achieve these objectives, especially when the boys acted defiant and rebellious. Tim demanded strict Old World obedience from his children; perhaps that is why many of them left home at early ages — and perhaps that is what drove young Joe to seek solace from a cruel world in the warm glow of his mother's love.

To Bridget McCarthy, the entire universe revolved around her blue-eyed, gawky, fifth-born child. It was she who kept telling him to "get ahead" and "be somebody." Young Joe was an ugly duckling, and his shaggy eyebrows, blue eyes, and lips that turned downward at the corners gave him a serious, brooding look. Big-chested and short-armed, he reminded his older brothers of a cub bear, and they took pleasure in telling him so. Sometimes when he had taken more kidding than he could stand, he would challenge his older brothers to boxing matches. And when they beat him up, he would run crying across the yard to the house — to his mother — for comfort and protection. Then Tim would scold his wife for mothering Joe.

When he grew older, his family says, he turned more and more to books. His oldest sister, Olive, now recalls: "He was always reading library books. Sometimes he'd read till late at night — and then get up at five-thirty to do his chores in the barns."

The neighbors remember Joe as a shy lad, seen-but-not-heard. One woman recalls that whenever her family visited the McCarthys, Joe would be nowhere in sight. Once, she remembers, on a hot Sunday afternoon in August, the grown-ups took their chairs outside to sit in the shade. She was surprised, she says, to spy Joe hiding under a wagon. Upon being found out, he quickly darted into the barn. Another time, the boy shut himself in his room and wasn't seen or heard until his mother dragged him out for supper. "He was so uncomfortable," the neighbor recalls, "that he squirmed around and didn't hardly say a word. And as soon as he had gobbled up his food, he ran off."

This shyness followed McCarthy to the Underhill Country School, a mile from home, where all eight grades studied and recited together in a single small, bare room. Although he did well in his early school years, and even skipped a grade, young Joe never felt comfortable under the teacher's gaze, nor enjoyed frolicking on the swing and teeter-totter at recess with the other children. And he was so self-conscious that he could hardly find his voice when it came his turn to recite.

Often, as a long afternoon wore on, he would raise his hand for permission to go outside. Then he would flee home to his mother. This illustrates a characteristic that still shows up in the man known today as Senator Joe McCarthy. In the company of people who are not his close associates he fidgets with his tie, squirms restlessly on his seat, gulps his food and drink, and is unable to control a nervous twitch of his head. More often than not, he will bolt away at the first opportunity.

It was fortunate for young Joe that he lived in a society in which shyness was no serious fault. The McCarthy family almost never left the farm. Their only visits were to the homes of other Irish families on the neighboring farms, and Joe would play outside the house while the visit was going on, so that he wouldn't have to talk to any of the grownups. His former playmates say he entered into their games (kick-the-can, hide-and-seek, tag) only with reluctance, and his feelings were easily hurt. They say that, as long as they knew him, he never really learned how to play.

Joe viewed the world beyond the farm through the adventure novels and the Sunday supplements which he read incessantly, and through the grade-B movie thrillers which he saw occasionally in Appleton.

In his early teens, he thought for a time of becoming a great inventor. One Sunday afternoon he worked for hours rigging a parachute out of sticks and an old blanket. When the time came to try out his invention with a jump from the haymow, he called over his younger brother Howard, who had been watching.

"Look, I'd make the jump myself," Joe explained with scientific detachment, "but I want to study the whole thing from below in order to make adjustments later." He helped his brother put on the harness. "Now, when I say the word, jump." Flattered, Howard jumped.

When he struck the ground, he was knocked out cold.

3. The First Chickens

JOE MCCARTHY GRADUATED FROM THE UNDERHILL COUNTRY School at the age of fourteen — a stubby, morose child, strong for his age, who shunned the company of others. Bullied by his brothers, cowed by old Timothy, the young boy found refuge only in his mother.

Further schooling, under the circumstances, held no appeal for him. History and arithmetic and geography might have interested him once, but now they seemed to add no bricks to the grandiose castles he was building in the air. And at school the teachers noticed that he paid less and less attention, and sulked in a world of daytime reverie.

Once, according to his sister Olive, he could look at a page in a book and know it almost by heart in a few minutes. Now he lost interest in schoolbooks, and quit school after finishing the eighth grade. Still obsessed by an undirected ambition, he went to work on his father's farm. After a few months under the heavy hand of Timothy McCarthy, young Joe began to display outwardly an antipathy toward his father. By now old Timothy could be called a success. He was raising potatoes, corn, barley, and oats, and he had a contract to raise acres of cabbage for a sauerkraut plant in New London. There was good money, too, in the gallons of milk he sent off to market each day. Timothy was the fountainhead of the family's blessings.

Working under his father's domineering hand, Joe began to evolve a plan. Its end was to prove to his mother that he

11

was also a grownup, that he could be as successful as his father. If his plan had worked out as he wished, it is doubtful that he would have become, finally, a United States Senator. But he failed by the thinnest of margins, and the frustration of failure only doubled the drive that was to take him down the road to national prominence and power.

Joe's plan took shape after he had made $65 by doing part-time work for an uncle. He took the money to old Timothy, as one businessman to another, and announced that he wanted to rent some land. His father grudgingly allotted him one acre, charging the standard amount; and the Joseph R. McCarthy chicken farm began.

It took Joe exactly two years to build his small investment into 2,000 laying hens, 10,000 broilers, a chicken house (part of which is still in use on a neighboring farm), and a truck for hauling his poultry to market. McCarthy became something of an authority on poultry diseases, feed, and marketing, and his business was talked about all over Outagamie County. All this Bridget McCarthy watched proudly, even though young Joe remained a child to her. When he first began driving his products to the Chicago markets, his mother insisted that the city of gangsters was not a safe place for her innocent young son to visit. So to show his mother how he stood in the world of men, Joe put her in his truck and took her to Chicago with him: a sixteen-year-old boy, driving a man's truck, doing a man's job, taking his mother across the Wisconsin state line for the first time in her life. It was the high point of Joe's young life; but the triumph was to be short-lived.

One day the over-ambitious young McCarthy figured he could make even greater profits by loading more chickens on his truck. Swaying around a bend on the road to Chicago, the top-heavy truck tipped over, and scattered chickens, feathers, and splintered crates over the roadside. Joe cursed and fumed, and swore he would quit the chicken business.

But back on the farm, he upped his work schedule to twelve and fourteen hours a day, seven days a week. Every dollar he made was plowed back into the poultry farm. In a desperate struggle to build up the business, he over-extended himself, saved no money for emergencies — and consequently met disaster when bad times came.

It began one cold night when he emerged from the hot, moist chicken house, his chest bare and sweat pouring down his face, and walked across the barnyard to the house. He took a chill, and two days later was on his back with influenza. He had no savings to pay for a professional poultry-man to care for his chickens; and he was too proud to ask his father for help. Besides, from the start Timothy had made it clear: "You want to run your own poultry farm? Go ahead. But remember — I got no time to help you. I got my own work to do."

In desperation, Joe hired a couple of inexperienced neighbor boys to care for the chickens until he was back on his feet. The farm boys, underpaid and uninterested, let most of the flock die, and five years of work died with them. One chronicler of McCarthy's life has described the dramatic moment when young Joe sat down and wept at the loss of his poultry empire. But the truth is that by this time he was growing tired of the society of chickens; the poultry market was declining; it was getting harder and harder to make profits.

Besides, he began to feel an irresistible attraction to the big cities, with their crowds and bright lights and opportunities, and he decided to break away. As a local poultry king, he had met some of the "worldly" people in the countryside — bartenders, gamblers, young-men-about-town. Now he circulated among them, looking for an empty rung on some new ladder of success.

It was only a thirty-mile drive from Grand Chute to Manawa, Wisconsin, but for Joe McCarthy it was one of the longest journeys of his life. He made the break away from home and — without taking a backward look — plunged into a new life.

His first stop was the boarding house of Mrs. Frank Oster-loth, a 74-year-old widow, who reminded him of his mother; later he was to refer to her tenderly as his "second mother." Joe liked the convivial atmosphere in the house, where he associated with other young men like himself who had come from near-by farms to work in town.

One of these boys, now a farmer, recalls: "Joe was steamed up when he came to Manawa. I never saw anybody so steamed up. He just couldn't ever relax; he worked at every-thing he did. He was pushing all the time."

The once-shy but now brash young Joe McCarthy obtained a job as manager of the Manawa unit of the Cashway chain grocery stores. Now, away from the stern discipline of Tim-othy McCarthy, he could flex his muscles in public and make his first real jabs at the world.

The limited world of Manawa (5,000 population) was ideally suited to the 19-year-old McCarthy. Its people lived in the conviction that the north-country folk were more in-dependent, more practical, more "American" than those who lived in the stultifying atmosphere of the big city. And one aspect of this conviction was to be seen in the exaggerated pride of the youths in their manhood. They asked but one thing of a newcomer — that he qualify on their terms.

A group of young men whom McCarthy was anxious to impress invited him to go swimming one day. He couldn't swim, but he eagerly accepted. They drove up to the Chain of Lakes, shed their clothes, and one by one sprang into the water from a twelve-foot diving board. When Joe's turn came, he wrapped an inner tube around his waist and jumped. Arms flailing, legs splashing water, he looked as if he would drown. But when the others swam to help him, Joe came up, spouting water, and yelled at them to stay away. He strug-gled to shore, clambered back onto the diving board, and again leaped into the water. He was deathly afraid of water, as well as of height; but stronger than his fear was his determination to prove himself. For hours he kept jumping — then diving — from the board into the lake, attacking the water as if it were a human enemy. Long after the others had quit, he was still diving, his sides black and blue from the impact of the rubber tube. But he learned to swim and dive, and was accepted. His tremendous perseverance in whatever he tried made him a man to be reckoned with.

Joe had little trouble fitting into his new life. He found it easy to accept the outlook on life of the Manawa crowd, to adopt their strong distrust of big-city ways and their feeling that the big-city man was somehow a dandy. The cracker-barrel philosophers of the region considered city dwellers as "know-it-alls" who used big words to impress and confuse their listeners, and whose involved, drawn-out methods of thinking were suspect. The north-country people held that any subject could be summed up in one or two short sentences. They liked the kind of talk that comes "straight from the shoulder" and goes "straight to the point" — without any complicated foolishness. It bothered them little that some subjects were complex. The complex they simplified; the confusing they ignored.

It was into this intellectual climate that Joe plunged at a crucial point in his development. At Mrs. Osterloth's boarding house he took the lead in wide-ranging discussions; and he brought to his job as manager of the new Cashway store some of the enthusiasm for country conversation that he displayed at the boarding house.

McCarthy's career as a storekeeper started off with great velocity. A noisy, smart-alecky kid in many ways, he brought to the Cashway a momentary air of excitement and drama. He joked, flattered, and praised outrageously, playing always to his audience. And his methods paid off: the store made a larger profit than most others in the Cashway chain. Joe

encouraged his customers to wait on themselves, a revolu-
tionary principle in those days. He made the Cashway into
a sort of community center, kept it open nights, and listened
to a constant tune on the cash register as counterpoint to the
hum of conversation in the store. Joe also became the hero
of a diarrhea epidemic that struck the town's chicken population: He went from coop to coop at nights, applying his
special talents in the field of chicken care.

Meanwhile, McCarthy was acquiring a social magnetism;
wherever he went he became the center of attention, the
focal point of activity. In the afternoons, he would stand at
the door greeting everyone who passed, trading wisecracks
and pleasantries — a cheerful "Good day" to the women, the
latest fast joke with the men. And soon the whole town was
talking about him. Local spit-and-argue clubs would adjourn
their meetings in front of the tavern to saunter over to "Joe's."
The McCarthy-created atmosphere of good humor and excitement became so infectious that even rival grocers dropped
in at times and helped wait on customers. This was no problem for them, since their own stores closed at night — and
their customers were in the Cashway. Young McCarthy was
the town's leading personality, and Manawa was almost as
proud of him as the Cashway management was.

But Joe was not content to idle on the road to success.
He was now twenty years old, and he had never attended
high school. The realization was slowly taking hold that he
would have to swallow his pride and cram his heavy frame
into the tiny desks of Little Wolf High School.

In Louisiana, a man named Huey Long had completed law
school in a single year. History would show a parallel between the two — one from the South, the other from the
North.

4. Back to School

A MOUNTAINOUS OBSTACLE STOOD IN THE PATH OF JOE MC-
Carthy's future — his lack of education. It would take more
than eight grades of schooling to get where he wanted to go.
So he talked the matter over with his Manawa "mother,"
Mrs. Osterloth. "You'll never go far without a high-school
diploma, Joe," she said, "and you'd best start getting it this
fall."

The following September, Joe strolled over to Little Wolf
High School and announced to his friend, Principal L. D.
Hershberger, that he wanted to register. So, from the
cracker-barrel sessions at Cashway store, he transferred to
the classroom discussions of Little Wolf High. And his new
companions were 13- and 14-year-olds.

Of course it was a little embarrassing. "The day I first
walked into that classroom and sat down with those kids,"
McCarthy recalls, "I would have sold out for two cents on
the dollar. But they all knew me pretty well, so I got along
all right." And after making some degree of adjustment to
his young classmates, "I got rolling and finished first-year
algebra in six weeks, and Latin in seven. The teachers were
swell; they gave me special instruction after school and
nights."

From the start of his belated high-school career, young Joe
had at least two people in his corner: Mrs. Osterloth and
Principal Hershberger. For her part, the elderly widow kept
Joe studying long into the night. There was always a pot of

17

coffee on the stove; when Joe emptied it, Mrs. Osterloth would brew more. And where the widow supplied the drive, Hershberger supplied the Open Sesame. For hours at a time, the principal or a faculty member would help Joe cram. As fast as he could finish one course, he was handed another; and by the time six months had gone by, he was already a junior.

Then he discovered that he needed advanced mathematics in order to clear the hurdle into college; but the Little Wolf curriculum offered no such course. Joe solved that problem by enrolling in a correspondence course of the University of Wisconsin. Two weeks before school let out for the summer, Hershberger gave Joe the final correspondence-school examination. His grade was 93.

Meanwhile, business at the store had taken a dive, despite the clerking help of his sister Olive, who had loyally come up from Appleton to help him out. Not long afterward, Joe was fired. But he got another job ushering in the local movie house at night, which not only provided living expenses but permitted him to see the movies free. With the rest of the townspeople in the dark theater, he gazed hungrily at the adventurous life of the big city: the glittering, tinsel world of the "outside" as portrayed by Hollywood. Sometimes he would bolt out of the back row and into the tiny theater office, throw open a book, and gobble down a chapter of history in a few minutes, perhaps feeling that he was hastening the day when he would be part of the world he saw on the screen. More and more he was filled with the sense of hurry: the need to get things done, and fast.

By the time the school year came to a close, young Joe had finished the curriculum of a full high-school course — with one exception. A pert young teacher, still full of the ideals of normal school, refused to give him a final examination. She disapproved of the crusade to push Joe through school in a year, and charged openly that the teachers were cutting corners to do it. She held that education was something that cannot be hurried, and therefore she refused to give the test.

The teacher was only a few years older than Joe. So he began saving his warmest smile for her, and asking her advice on minor points in the regular classroom assignments she handed out. Finally he invited her to the annual prom. Perhaps it was in the middle of a dreamy waltz that she revised some of her old ideas about education. Joe was allowed to graduate.

Many accounts have been given about McCarthy's high-school feat. In his campaign literature in later years, the accomplishment grew and grew.

The story is told that McCarthy studied around the clock, that he quadrupled the speed of the educational process by denying himself all outside activity. He had not needed to do this. George Kelly, a schoolmate, recalls that McCarthy found time to try out for the basketball team, although he didn't make it. "He was always awkward," Kelly recalls. "He was too rough and couldn't work with the team. And he couldn't seem to learn the rules."

When he could no longer use basketball as an outlet, McCarthy built up an excess of nervous energy. In the late afternoons he would work off this energy by giving boxing lessons to the younger students. Hershberger recalls: "He would take 'em on at five-minute intervals — any and all, whoever wanted to put on the gloves." But after a few months, the younger students grew tired of being used as punching bags and stopped showing up. When that happened, Joe would crawl into a sweatsuit and run three or four miles, along roads and through fields. Then he would take a bath, eat, and begin memorizing the next week's homework in one night.

The end result was a graduation ceremony that centered around the 21-year-old McCarthy. Hershberger told the townspeople: "We never graduated a student more capable of graduating." He extolled McCarthy as "the irresistible force who overcame the immovable object." But to the proud Joe, sitting straight and erect and aware of the admiring eyes upon him, this was just the first step. The next object on his list was Marquette University, a Jesuit college in near-by Milwaukee. Marquette required four years of high school from its entrants; a one-year cram course would not have been acceptable. But Joe wrote for entrance papers anyway, and to the question "Did you attend four years of high school?" he answered "Yes."

"He meant to tell them the truth later," says Hershberger, "when they'd got to know him better."

The north-country folk saw their conquering hero off to Marquette with mixed emotions. But no matter what they thought of him, they had to admit that for almost two years he had brought a little zest and spice into their back-country routine.

As for Joe, he hit the hilltop campus at Marquette with something less than a dull thud. Brashness in Manawa was impressive; in Milwaukee it was annoying. And anyway, Joe didn't look or act like other college men. He looked older, a circumstance only partly due to the fact that he was losing his hair; and his bucolic manners and eager-dog approach repelled the more sophisticated co-eds. Altogether, he was too loud and too rough to fit easily into the campus atmosphere.

Enrolled in the engineering school, the 21-year-old Joe plunged into a crowded routine of study and work. During the next few years, he worked as a short-order cook, washed dishes, sold tires, tended a filling station, worked on a construction gang, drove a truck, parked cars at the Wisconsin Club — and developed poker techniques that enabled him to make a killing at the expense of some alumni on a football trip to Pittsburgh.

If this didn't impress his fellow students, at least the newspapers took notice. A feature story in the Milwaukee *Sentinel*

told about the north-country student: the-young-man-who-
seizes-America's-opportunities-and-works-his-way-through-
college. (This was a slight inaccuracy in Joe's case, since
he leaned heavily on old Timothy — who at his death left
Joe no money because "I have expended a rather considerable
sum for his education.")

It may have been a coincidence that Joe happened to be
dating the reporter who wrote the story. His former roommate, Jack Walters, recalls that Joe dropped the girl, then
suddenly started dating her again. It was shortly thereafter
that her story about him appeared. Joe secretly bought a
stack of the papers and hid them under his bed. When his
roommates wandered in for the night, Joe asked casually:
"Anything special in the paper tonight?"

"Not much," shrugged one. "Just a piece about you."

Joe feigned indifference, glanced at the article nonchalantly when it was handed to him, then carelessly flipped it
to the floor. A dozen times that night, he subtly steered the
conversation back to the article. But one roommate finally
spotted the stack under the bed, and chided: "Joe, you big
ham. How many newsstands did you buy out?"

Meanwhile, his old friend Hershberger had been promoted
to a larger school at Hortonville, near Appleton; but he had
not forgotten his prize pupil. The two had kept in frequent
touch, and McCarthy had complained about his trouble ad-
justing to the campus life. He just didn't seem to make an
impression, he confessed, and the co-eds put a strange stiff-
ness in his tongue. But Hershberger thought he had a
solution; he invited collegeman McCarthy to speak to the
Hortonville student body — to tell them how they, too, could
trade hayseed and plowshare for culture and learning. At
the same time, Hershberger hoped public speaking would
cure Joe's stage fright.

Joe sat uncomfortably on the stage, listening to Hershberger extol him in an introduction. His throat dried out;

he tried to swallow, and he couldn't. And as he arose to speak, there might have come to him out of the past the bellowing voice of old Timothy and his brothers, reminding him of his own inferiority. Joe looked offstage at the big red light — "EXIT" — and he thought of running toward it. Then he heard a whisper from Hershberger: "Go ahead. You're on!"

Shakily, Joe walked to the podium. He had memorized a speech, word for word and gesture for gesture. But now it was lost in a sea of bored young faces. Joe blurted out a few words; to this day, he doesn't remember what he said. And then he bolted offstage. The entire performance, from introduction to conclusion, lasted only a few minutes. All the way back to Milwaukee, McCarthy cursed himself for his failure. And he applied for membership in the Franklin Club, a debating society. Once again, the inner tube would make his sides black and blue; but once again he would learn to swim.

Joe began as a poor debater: awkward when he had the floor, over-emotional, and weak on facts. Even in those days, McCarthy laid great stress on words like "America," "loyalty," "patriotism," and "the principles our forefathers died for." He sprinkled them into his debates with abandon. In his early debating career, Joe was strongly anti-Hoover, blaming the GOP administration for the Depression. He also defended the Democratic platform for world peace, and' his best-remembered debate was his affirmative stand on the subject: "Resolved, that the way to bring about world peace is through disarmament."

It was just a few months after he joined the debating society that he decided to take a bold step: he ran for president of the club. There were long, loud complaints from Franklin Club old-timers, who felt a newcomer shouldn't be so presumptuous as to run for such a high office. But Joe politicked hard. He bought "cokes" and coffee for club members; he buttonholed them in the school corridors and made lavish promises.

When election day came, it was Joe McCarthy versus Charles Curran. Joe sat in the back of the room, wearing a turtle-neck sweater. Nervously, he played mumblety-peg on the floor with a knife, and as the votes were counted, the knife flashed faster and faster. Finally the results were announced. Curran had won by an overwhelming majority. Joe stabbed his knife deep into the floor, jumped up, and walked out. But he determined to stay in the Franklin Club, to perfect his own speaking techniques, and some day to impress the same voters who had rejected him.

In the meantime Joe went out for boxing as a vent for his emotional steam. At first, he was clumsy and awkward. He was a wild slugger who would rush out of his corner at the first sound of the bell and start raining gloves on his opponent. He never left the offensive unless he was knocked to the canvas. He fought as if he were still taking on the high-school boys back in Manawa, but once in a while he would run into an experienced boxer who cut him to ribbons. A Madison, Wisconsin, pharmacist who used to watch McCarthy in the ring at Marquette recalls that Joe would take some terrible beatings. But even when he was against the ropes with blood dripping and both eyes blackened, he kept smiling, almost as though he liked it — a fact which left the druggist feeling that there was something strange about the rough young man.

Joe's ring techniques were rough and rampageous, the same techniques that he brought later to the political ring. It is an axiom in the fight world that a total disregard for health and safety can carry one toward the top — that sheer guts, or sheer recklessness, can substitute for skill in the ring. So it was with young McCarthy; by virtue of a driving courage and a hard head, he achieved campus fame as a boxer. In his senior year, when the boxing coach quit, McCarthy

managed to get the job. And he probably would have gone
professional, had it not been for a bad sinus condition and
some wise words from Fred Saddy, later secretary of the Wisconsin State Athletic Commission, who was then a boxing
instructor at the Milwaukee Eagles club gym. He warned
young Joe that he would end up punch-drunk and cauli-
flower-eared unless he learned to cover up —something
McCarthy knew he would never learn.

But his boxing career brought to McCarthy the campus
popularity he sought. Eventually, his room became a gathering place, like the Cashway store in Manawa; and his blunt
opinions found receptive ears. But — sweetest victory of all
— the young ladies began to appreciate him in spite of his
coarse exterior. He went out with dozens of them, flitting
from one to another, until he met Mildred Byrnes. One of
McCarthy's closest college friends said later that Joe fell
head over heels in love with the Byrnes girl. It was the first
time that love had entered his life. Although she has since
married, divorced, and remarried, the same close friend says:
"I think he's still trying to impress her, wherever she is, whatever she's doing." If McCarthy had possessed any money
in those days, he might have married Mildred Byrnes. But
instead the romance foundered, and he began seeking other
friendships, shaking hands, and slapping backs in a never-
ending search.

5. Budding Lawyer

AFTER TWO PLODDING YEARS IN COLLEGE, JOE MCCARTHY seemed to be making no academic hay. Like many another young engineer, he discovered that the memorizable formulas of an engineering course were not the easiest route to a diploma. He came face to face with the fact that he couldn't build an engineering career on the meager mathematics crammed into his head at Manawa. In later years, his campaign literature boasted that he had led his engineering classes. But in fact he didn't. He followed them, well down on the list. And then he switched to law.

From the first, Joe had inclined toward the company of law students — boisterous, congenial, garrulous individuals with a flair for the bizarre and a taste for politics. The boarding house where they lived was run by John Kuhn, a stocky German with a thick accent, who wore boots and admired Prussian ways. His wife was a gentle, soft-spoken woman who dispensed advice and comfort to her young boarders. Joe fondly called her his "second mother" — an honor that he had already conferred on his Manawa landlady, Mrs. Osterloth.

Alive with the clamor and oratory of young lawyers, the house was proudly hailed by its boarders as "the famous house of Kuhn." And sprawled over its furniture, the young students weighed the problems of the day. The two favorite topics at their bull sessions, recalls one former boarder, were girls and politics — subjects in which the law students con-

sidered themselves well-versed. Into this convivial atmosphere, Joe easily blended; there was no question but that law
was his dish.

Scholastically, a law course also had its advantages. To
begin with, Joe's fellow law students in the Delta Theta Phi
fraternity house kept a supply of "canned" briefs and files
of examinations for years back. Before a test, Joe would hole
up in his room and cram entire pages into his sponge-like
brain. He cut classes freely, missed the finer points of law,
and became a source of dismay to his teachers. But at examination time he always passed.

One of his professors remembers McCarthy as a man who
"knew very little when he got here, and very little when he
left, but got through on his memory." Another professor says
McCarthy showed little ability to understand theories or
follow involved reasoning but had an almighty capacity for
remembering — a talent which he still shows today except
when it becomes convenient to forget, as under cross-examination in his sundry law suits.

The lowest mark he ever scored was in legal ethics, taught
by a popular old priest, Father McMahon. The priest, now
dead, had a speech defect that tied his tongue in knots when
he got excited; in order to stir him up, Joe would ask trick
questions; and afterwards the boys would get together and
roar with laughter at the priest's sputtering, halting explanations. And because Joe could mimic Father McMahon's
flustered speech almost perfectly, he developed a law-school
reputation as a "card." Among the extroverted young men of
the law school, this was no mean accomplishment. To it was
added his old ability to make others feel important, and the
result was inevitable: popular Joe McCarthy ran for president
of his class.

His opponent was Charles Curran, the man who had defeated him for president of the Franklin Club. This time
McCarthy vowed he would win. He let his homework slip,

cut school for days at a time, and devoted night and day to politicking. But he also agreed publicly with Curran that each would vote for the other at election time, in a spirit of good will and friendship. When the votes were counted, the two had finished in a dead heat. Curran suggested cutting cards for the presidency, but Joe insisted that they campaign for another week and have another go at it. In the new elections, McCarthy won by two votes. A single person had switched his ballot, and Curran thought he knew who it was.

"Joe," he asked McCarthy, "did you vote for yourself?"

McCarthy smiled. "Sure," he said. "You wanted me to vote for the best man, didn't you?"

But Curran, now a successful lawyer in Mauston, Wisconsin, bears McCarthy no malice, because of something that happened later. "My father died in 1933, while I was in school," Curran recalls. "Just before the funeral, Joe drove all the way to our house in an old Model A he'd borrowed. He cut classes, left his job, and borrowed money to get there. He did that for me, and he'll always be my friend."

Now that he was class president, McCarthy began to acquire an appetite for the power and prestige that went with politics. One morning he took off from his classes and went with a fellow law student to the Milwaukee City Council chambers. They heard long speeches about paving and sewerage and street lighting; but to young Joe these seemed especially empty. He turned to his companion and remarked: "If that's the best they can do, they ought to be kicked out." Later that morning, the companion remembers, Joe mused about politics, and commented that some day he would like to be Governor or a Senator. He was far away on some distant political cloud, until he was interrupted by his friend, who reminded him that it was time to return to his part-time job — washing dishes. And that day, over the steaming sink, McCarthy decided on another plunge: politics.

On a debating trip later into the north country, driving his

old black Chevrolet, Joe baffled his fellow students by stopping in small towns along the way to meet the local judges.
"Might do me good later," he explained. Joe McCarthy, law
student, already was hitting the campaign trail.

With a clearer objective once again in mind, he redoubled
his cramming. And among his college mates, he developed a
ready handshake and a fast line of patter. In short, he took
on the loud-talking, fur-coat-wearing appearance of a big-
man-on-campus.

6. Law, Poker, and Speeches

SIX HOURS AFTER JOE MCCARTHY HAD BEEN SWORN IN AS A member of the Wisconsin bar, he opened a law office in Waupaca, thereby setting up shop ahead of a classmate and collecting a bet. It was a one-man law firm; McCarthy preferred to lone-wolf it.

The day after he hung out his shingle, he was pleased to see three people sitting in the waiting room when he burst in promptly at 9 A.M. "Good morning, good morning," he said cheerfully. "I'll be with you in a minute." He took off his hat and coat, and stepped back into the waiting room. But only two people remained.

"Where'd the elderly gentleman go?" asked McCarthy.

"Into the dentist's office," said a woman. "And that's where we're going too."

McCarthy had forgotten that he shared the waiting room with a dentist. The rest of the day, business streamed in and out; but the customers' troubles were dental, not legal. It gave him plenty of time to ponder the wisdom of his plunge into the unfamiliar town of Waupaca, when he could have returned to his old haunts in Manawa or Appleton.

He had chosen Waupaca because it was small enough for him to gain a wide acquaintance in a short time, and because it was a county seat, offering political possibilities for a newcomer. And although Waupaca was only thirty miles from Appleton and Grand Chute it sported many big-city attractions. On the outskirts of town, back in the deep woods near the Wolfe River, roadhouses thrived behind darkened shades. County police staged infrequent raids on lonely houses of gambling and prostitution, which flourished and lapsed as the law-enforcement temperature varied.

About a mile west of town, on Highway 10, stood Ben Johnson's bar (now called the Oakwood and under different management). It was before Ben's bar that Joe did most of his practicing. He became a poker-playing fanatic, sitting in Johnson's back room until early in the morning, sometimes leaving his law office unoccupied for a whole day while he tried to run up his winnings. One week end he invited a girl up from Milwaukee. He took her to Johnson's, got into a poker game, then ignored her except for mumbled "thanks" whenever she brought him a drink from the bar. The others suggested that he quit the game and devote his time to the visitor, but Joe only shrugged: "She knows the way home."

A fellow Waupaca lawyer remembers that McCarthy "had the guts of a burglar" in his poker sessions. "He was brutal," the lawyer relates. "He'd take all the fun out of the game, because he took it so seriously. We never knew when we had to cover anything he put up. Sometimes we'd win. Funny thing about Joe, you could usually beat him with a pair of jacks. But whenever you'd come up with a full house or a flush and bet your wad on it, he'd come up with something better."

McCarthy played "big-pot" poker. He bluffed so much that his opponents could never tell whether he had a good hand or a bad one. Hence, when he did end up with a power-house hand, he would often rake in $100 or $200 at a time, taken largely from players who thought he was bluffing.

It was a good thing that his poker winnings were high; he needed them to make up for the steady mediocrity of his law business. The county-court records show only four cases credited to the young lawyer in his entire nine-month stay in

Waupaca. The file on his first case shows an out-of-court settlement of $5,125 to a McCarthy client whose husband had been killed in an auto accident. In his second case, he helped foreclose a mortgage on a farmer who later paid up, thus erasing the foreclosure. His other two cases were dismissed.

But while he eked out a living from his poker winnings and his small clientele, McCarthy was slowly building toward his ultimate ambition — a successful political career. To this end, he became a joiner and a speechmaker. He joined the Junior Chamber of Commerce, the Lions Club, the county bar association, and a local businessmen's group. He took on all sorts of outside chores in the interest of gaining a reputation as a community leader. When anyone had tickets to sell or dances to promote, Joe jumped up to volunteer. He was in charge of ticket sales for Waupaca's third annual President's Birthday Ball in 1936; he helped arrange a gala bridge party for Lions and Lionesses on New Year's Eve (Joe won the booby prize); and — pleasantest task of all — he was elected chairman of the Lions Club Harvest Day Committee, thereby earning the right to judge all the pretty girls competing for Harvest Day Queen.

Although he still carried his boxing gloves around in his car, McCarthy got little chance to show off his ring skill. Instead, he found another release for his nervous energy: he joined a softball team. But as an outfielder he lacked coordination; he was still the awkward, off-form athlete. Most of the players didn't much care whether they won or lost; McCarthy was the single exception — he always played hell-bent for victory. This made him the laughingstock of the town on one occasion. It was Waupaca's annual benefit ball game, a raucous, happy-go-lucky affair in which the players had to ride animals. The batter would hit the ball, then mount and ride to first base. The fielders had to ride after the ball, and they weren't allowed to dismount until they were within a single stride of the ball.

One of the opposing players smacked a long fly deep into McCarthy's right-field bailiwick, and Joe and his mule were off at the crack of the bat. But about ten strides away from the ball, Joe's animal lost its zest for the game, slammed to a halt, and began munching the outfield grass. McCarthy slapped the mule's rump, cursed and fumed, and finally kicked the mule in the leg. But the animal wouldn't move. By this time, the crowd was laughing at his frustration. So he grabbed the mule around the midsection, lifted it off the ground, and carried the animal bodily over to the ball.

But Joe was not to linger long in Waupaca. One day early in 1936, a successful Republican lawyer from nearby Shawano, Mike G. Eberlein, dropped into the small McCarthy office. He and Joe sat down and had a talk, and McCarthy painted a picture of himself as a brilliant young lawyer with an ever-widening reputation in the county. Eberlein listened with an indulgent smile, knowing full well the truth about Joe's practice.

Finally, he interrupted: "Why don't you close up this dive and come to work for me?"

Joe shot back: "Why don't you close up that dump of yours and come to work for me?"

To Lawyer Eberlein, this impudent young man was just what he was looking for. He laughed, shook hands, and said: "Think it over, Joe."

The next morning at 8:00 A.M., Joe announced to Eberlein's surprised receptionist in Shawano: "I'm your new boy. You watch; in a few years I'm going to be on the top of the heap around Shawano."

McCarthy was right; he was to stride quickly to the top. And, on the way, Mike Eberlein's political dreams would be crushed under the ambitious heel of his own hired man.

7. First a Democrat

GRUFF, HEAVY-SET MIKE EBERLEIN HAD TAKEN MANY A SPIN on the political merry-go-round in his long and lucrative law career, but he had never been able to grab the brass ring. He had keynoted a handful of state GOP conventions, and he was considered a Republican "power." But in both his attempts at election to public office, he was roundly defeated — the first time for attorney general of Wisconsin, the second for U. S. Senator. Now that he was mellowing with the approach of his middle years, he had but one dream left — election to the bench, an honor he felt he had coming to him. Almost from the first day young Joe McCarthy entered the firm, the two got together and planned far ahead, to the day when Mike would become a Wisconsin circuit judge and McCarthy would inherit the law practice.

At first, the Eberlein-McCarthy relationship seemed like a mixed marriage to the citizens of Shawano, a town of about 5,000 population some forty miles north of Waupaca. Old Mike was the north country's "Mr. Republican"; but his young helper had never made any bones about his antipathy toward the GOP in general and Herbert Hoover in particular. The Waupaca County *Post* took due notice of this apparent difference between the two lawyers in a squib published February 20, 1936, just before McCarthy left to join Eberlein:

"When I move to Shawano," murmured Joe McCarthy, "I'll have to make a hasty transition from a young Democrat to a young Republican." So, just to add a dash of zest in the life of Mike Eberlein's new hired man, we carefully padded his brief case with a couple copies

33

of the *New Masses*, a recent edition of the *Daily Worker,* and a vest-pocket sized *Das Kapital.*

To the political pundits of the north country, it seemed an odd move for Mike Eberlein to bring a Democrat into his Republican stronghold. But Joe McCarthy had a persuasive way with people and, at heart, he was neither Republican nor Democrat; he was *political.* And during his early development the donkey was moving faster than the elephant.

Mike Eberlein saw the political promise in the ambitious young McCarthy; he nursed it along, and acted like a father to Joe, perhaps hoping that McCarthy would eventually follow the political winds to Republicanism. And one of the first problems confronting the fatherly Eberlein was how to keep McCarthy in money. Joe's starting salary was $200 a month, more than adequate for a single man in the 1930's. But he was always broke. Eberlein explains: "He had a poor business head. He never could save. It went as fast or faster than he got it. If he ever saved a cent, it would be a surprise to me."

Since Joe could never make his $200 stretch out across the month, Eberlein worked out a special arrangement for Joe's own protection. The old lawyer suggested: "I'll pay just half your salary — $100 — at the beginning of every month, and hold the other half to give you in a lump sum of $1,200 at the end of the year." Joe agreed.

"But apparently even that didn't work out too well," Eberlein recalls. "Joe somehow always seemed to be able to get hold of more money when he needed it. I've heard — though of course I don't know it for a fact — that he managed to get advance credit on the money that was coming to him from me at the end of the year."

Some of the money was dissipated in a constant attempt to buy political prestige. Joe picked up the tabs at luncheons, and he kept in the public eye by promoting speaking engagements whenever he could. The Shawano County *Journal* of

April 8, 1937, reported that McCarthy addressed the Lions
Club in the Murdock Hotel. The paper said:

> Mr. McCarthy described certain types of legal procedure and named
> several cases where men had been convicted of crimes, but later had
> been proved innocent. He said that the problem of rectifying miscar-
> riages of justice was one of the great problems of the legal profession.

Later, he gave a talk to the Shawano Junior Women's Club
on one of his favorite subjects, "Americanization." He also
spoke about a trip he had made to Canada, his ideas on dairy-
ing — and any other subject that came to mind. He once
confided to a friend that he could become an expert on any
subject in one night at the public library by using his college
cramming habits.

McCarthy had been in Shawano less than a year when
he took his first serious plunge into politics. In August of
1936, he was elected president of the Young Democratic
Clubs of Wisconsin's Seventh District, which includes ten
counties. Thus equipped with a campaign organization, Joe
announced his candidacy for district attorney of Shawano
County. He redoubled his speaking pace and set a new
handshaking record for the area. And he became an outspoken advocate of a plan that on the surface seemed a great
money-saver to the taxpayers, but in actuality was a means
which would enable the district attorney to go into a higher
salary bracket. McCarthy's plan was reported, on August 4,
1936, by the Shawano *Evening Leader,* under a somber picture of the young candidate wearing dignified rimless glasses
(which he didn't need) and a black suit:

> Placing the district attorney on a part-time basis and salary is ad-
> vocated by Joe McCarthy, candidate for the office on the Democratic
> ticket, he announced today. Under the set-up as advocated by Mc-
> Carthy . . . the salary that goes with the office would be reduced by
> about 50 per cent. While he would be required to be available, as now,
> at all times for county work, he would be allowed to take care of his
> own private practice when he had no county work to do.

Of course, the system would also enable the district attorney to use the prestige of his office to line up clients who would pay for the privilege of being represented by the county's top prosecutor. But if Joe knew this, he never mentioned it to the voters.

The primary-election date was September 17, 1936, and McCarthy was to learn on that day that the Democratic mule was a political liability in Wisconsin. Louis Cattau, the Progressive candidate, polled 3,014 votes; Republican Ed Aschenbrenner, 692; and Democrat McCarthy, a mere 577. Thus it became clear to Joe that he hadn't a prayer of winning the general election two months later. He decided to use those two months to convince the voters that he was a self-sacrificing young man who didn't mind losing so long as the county gained. So on October 14, he addressed a Democratic rally:

The candidate for a county office has a duty to the voters above and beyond selfish promotion of his own candidacy. The candidate has a duty to help clear away the smoke screen and help every voter to base his vote upon facts and reason rather than unreason and fallacy. If, when the morning of November 4th dawns, I know that I have in any way helped the voters to cast a vote based upon the facts as they are — distorted neither one way or the other — then the question of whether or not I personally am elected will, in my mind, fade into insignificance.

When Joe sat down, the assemblage in Joe Casetta's bar at Almon, Wisconsin, gave him a standing ovation. He was compared to "Fighting Bob" La Follette, and his political fortunes veered upward. In the general election in November, he wound up ahead of the Republican Aschenbrenner, and he polled seven times as many votes as his showing in the primary. The final vote: Cattau, 6,175; McCarthy, 3,422; Aschenbrenner, 2,842.

The handwriting was already beginning to show on the voting-booth wall.

8. Teaching an Old Judge New Tricks

FOR THE HUNDREDTH TIME, YOUNG JOE McCARTHY WAS LISTEN-
ing to old Mike Eberlein pour out his heart on the subject
of his political ambitions. "Joe," Eberlein confided, "I'm
going to run for circuit judge next time. And I think I can
make it."

McCarthy jumped up, shook Eberlein's hand, and told
him the tenth circuit deserved a man of Eberlein's caliber.
But it was several months before Eberlein would make a formal announcement, and during that time Joe McCarthy was
a much-preoccupied young man. In his mind, a plan was
taking shape. "You know," McCarthy remarked to a friend,
"Mike has one of the finest legal minds in the state. But he's
probably the world's worst politician."

The next day, Joe McCarthy announced for circuit judge.

When the news reached Mike Eberlein, it caught him with
his political pants down; and his outrage knew no bounds.
McCarthy's announcement had taken the form of a letter to
the voters of Shawano, Outagamie, and Langlade counties.
It read, in part: "The present judge, Edgar V. Werner, was
born in 1866. Even though he is willing to sacrifice himself,
the job of circuit judge is far too exacting . . . for a man of
his age."

Eberlein had pride. What was he to do now? Repudiate
McCarthy and run? Or sit this one out, the way he had sat

out other campaigns most of his life? Reluctantly, Eberlein decided not to run; the only move he made was to announce that young Joe and he were no longer associated. "I simply told him it would be better if he left," the old lawyer told his friends. And sadly, Mike Eberlein tucked his ambitions back into mothballs.

Nowadays, Eberlein won't discuss the rift, because later he won the judgeship with McCarthy's backing. As for Joe, he explains that he left Eberlein because "I had to campaign night and day, and I didn't think it would be fair to stay on the payroll." And so the old wounds have healed on the surface. Eberlein, when asked about Joe, confines himself to the comment that Joe "has one of the finest legal minds I have ever known." And, in what could be one of the terms of peace between them, McCarthy pays the same formal compliment to Eberlein.

McCarthy's campaign for the judgeship could well serve as a classic battle plan for any ruthless politician who wants to parlay hard work and native cunning into a brass nameplate in the Senate Office Building. He became a whirling dervish, zipping from town to town and from farm to farm, speechmaking, backslapping, milking cows, changing babies, jollying farmwives, and having heart-to-heart talks with the menfolk. His line changed whenever necessary: "Yes, Mrs. Brown, apple pie is my favorite." "Yes, Mrs. Frost, I like lemon meringue best." "Yes, Mr. Jones, La Follette has helped the state." "Yes, Mr. Smith, La Follette has gone too far and should be beat."

A grizzled old farmer, who prefers to be known as "Bill Cummings" in these pages, remembers the first of two campaign visitations McCarthy paid him. "He didn't know me from Adam," the farmer remembers. "But somehow he had learned my name, and my wife's name, and our kids' names, and our dog's name. When I first noticed him, he was outside petting the dog. By the time I got to the front door, he was handing my daughter a lollipop, and then Indian-wrestling with my boy."

Farmer Cummings says he first pegged McCarthy as a salesman, "but when he grabbed my hand and introduced himself, I remember his name from a letter he sent me, saying he wanted to beat old man Werner 'cause the judge was too old for the job."

Farmer Cummings says Joe stayed miles away from the subject of the judgeship. What he was interested in, the farmer remembers, was the farm — its livestock, poultry, and crops. "He wanted to know if I'd let him milk a cow; said he wanted to keep his hand in. He milked good." But what nearly floored Farmer Cummings was a remark McCarthy dropped out of a clear blue sky. "Say, Bill," McCarthy said, "how's that sick mare of yours? Any better?"

The pair went out to the barn to examine the animal. "He treated that mare like his own flesh and blood," Farmer Cummings says. "He acted as if it was the saddest thing in the world that my mare was sick. And he promised he'd do all he could to help."

The next week, Farmer Cummings got a letter from the young candidate, outlining all the various ways to cure sick horses, and wishing all good luck to Farmer Cummings, his family, his dog, his crops, and his livestock.

"Did I vote for him?" Cummings says. "Sure, I voted for him. Wouldn't you, after that?"

Of course, Farmer Cummings might not have voted for McCarthy so readily had he known what he learned after the election. He was talking cross-fence with his neighbor. "Funny thing about that McCarthy," the neighbor told Cummings. "He came to my house a while back. Wanted to know how you cure a sick mare. I told him all the ways I could think of, depending on what was wrong with her, and he wrote it all down. Said he was interested in animals."

Every responsible politician in the three-county area labeled McCarthy's candidacy a farce. He had barely turned thirty; he was probably the least experienced lawyer in the district, and he lacked the dignity a judge should have. Bouncing around from town to town in his old white car with a loudspeaker on top, he looked like anything but the prototype of a staid, respectable circuit judge. And those who knew him well laughed when they saw him in action. "He's just a backslapper," they said. "He'll never get any-where in the big time."

But Joe had a true picture of politicking in the backwoods; he knew, better than most, that it was a matter not so much of issues as of persons. Election times brought the north-country folk a close-up of the men who sought office. For months, the meeting rooms of Appleton, Shawano, and the outlying villages would ring with the eloquent oratory of politicians. Their speeches would deal with God, honor, progress, patriotism, and the price of milk. The typical cam-paigner's platform usually consisted of blaming the local ills on Eastern bankers, the railroads, and the British. So the candidate who could adapt to this framework would be on a par, ideologically, with all the others. Then all he had to do was take off down the dusty roads of his district and visit the voters in their fields and barns, presenting himself for ap-proval while pitching in with the work. And such a candidate was McCarthy.

To hold down his political fort while he was in the field, Joe recruited a small army of campaign workers. The first to check in, both physically and financially, were some of his relatives, who sat long into the night writing postcards to the voters, signed "Joe McCarthy." They were joined later by volunteers, mostly housewives, who had been stirred by Joe's campaign oratory and impressed by his slogan, "Justice Is Truth in Action." With the help of this hand-writing corps, Joe assailed the tri-county voters via R.F.D. Russell J. Earling, probate register of the county court in

Appleton, recalls that Joe sent out thousands of postcards before the election; and he knew most of the addressees by their first names.

As for his opponents, they were lackadaisical about the whole campaign, standing instead on the predictions of local writers that McCarthy didn't have a chance. The incumbent, Judge Edgar V. Werner, had spent twenty-four years on the bench, and had easily defeated everyone who had ever run against him. A third candidate, A. M. Whiting of Antigo, figured to win in Langlade, his home county. In the other two counties, Outagamie and Shawano, McCarthy and Whiting were expected to split the vote, thus returning Judge Werner to office in a landslide. But Joe didn't diagnose it that way. Later, he was to say: "Whiting is a swell fellow and if I had thought that my candidacy would have hurt him, I would have withdrawn. But I figured I could win."

Before the election, McCarthy was probably the only citizen of the north country who thought he would be the next circuit judge. The others felt that nothing could upturn the faithful and conscientious Werner. Feeling for Werner was best summed up in an Appleton *Post-Crescent* editorial of March 31, 1939:

> Concerning Judge Werner, who has lived in this community so long, words of praise would be mere surplusage. But a reminder to the voter that in Judge Werner this judicial district has a judge of unassailable integrity is material to the election. The people of this county should hardly be in a mood to dispense with the services of one who has proven so dependable for so long.

But it was in Judge Werner's long career that young Joe McCarthy found the chink in the old man's armor. He began hammering. In his campaign speeches, he carelessly referred to "my 73-year-old opponent" (Werner was 66). He compared Werner to "the nine old men of the Supreme Court," thus twanging a national chord that was in harmony with the times. But for all this, he was saccharine-sweet about

Werner. He called him "my distinguished opponent" and "that fine jurist." He sought to create the impression that Werner was a man who had worked so long and so hard for the three counties that now he had earned a rest, that the voters owed this much to "my worthy opponent."

And happily for McCarthy, Werner fell into the age trap. He began devoting half his speeches to justifications for elderly persons, and the papers carried his rambling descriptions of himself as a man "old only in years." When Mc-Carthy finally succeeded in getting Werner hot under the collar, the elderly jurist demanded a public retraction on the age issue. But Joe, instead, seized on the opportunity to run an ad on the general subject under the heading "WHAT ABOUT THIS AGE QUESTION?" In the text, he slipped in this telling blow: "I further pointed out that my only reason for calling attention to the number of years he had served and to his age was to suggest that after he had served over 35 years in public office, at a total income of $170,000.00 to $200,000.00, it might be well for him to retire."

McCarthy had totaled up Judge Werner's lifetime public income, thrown in a few thousand extra, and presented it as the impressive sum of "$170,000.00 to $200,000.00." Simple arithmetic would have shown that Judge Werner, even by McCarthy's mathematics, had made only an average lawyer's salary in the employ of the people — $4,800 to $5,700 a year. But McCarthy knew that few north-country folk would think their way through this simple problem, and the result would be a characterization of Judge Werner as one who had slopped through life at the public trough.

The results were devastating. Judge Werner, regarded as a "shoo-in" by the political experts, polled 11,154 votes; Whiting got 9,071; and McCarthy won handily with 15,160. At the age of thirty, three years out of law school, green, raw, and ambitious, Joe McCarthy had pulled Wisconsin's political upset of the year.

But he was not yet out of the woods. Judge Werner's backers did some totaling of their own. They figured the cost of McCarthy's thousands of postcards, which added up to big money even at a penny apiece. They threw in the price of his jaunts into the back country, the posters he tacked up, the newspaper ads he bought. And they went to the authorities with what they thought was a prima-facie case of violation of the state's corrupt-practices law. They charged that McCarthy overspent the statutory allowance and misrepresented Judge Werner's age. After a year of investigation, during which political strings were pulled, Governor Heil announced: "I have examined the petition and do not find any material allegations." Joe was in.

But although the problem "Where did the money come from?" no longer had any legal meaning, it remained interesting. Obviously Joe McCarthy, who couldn't make ends meet and had borrowed against his salary all his life, had found some financial angels who thought his election to the bench was a good investment. The McCarthy campaign had been, for that area, a tremendously expensive one, begun at a time when his own finances were recorded in red ink. And yet, after the election Joe still had enough capital to finance an ad in the Appleton *Post-Crescent*, telling the voters he would like to meet each of them personally to thank them for electing him. And he had enough money to "get away from it all" for a three-week vacation in the South. So the question was raised that still haunts him today: "Where's all the money coming from?"

The answer, found later in these pages, is a chapter in itself.

9. Justice on the Double

JUDGE McCARTHY BREEZED INTO THE COURTROOM FULL OF VIM
and vitality, like a strong west wind blowing through the
moldering halls of justice. And the strength of his breeze
blew order and decorum out the courthouse window.

There were about 250 cases in backlog when McCarthy
took over. The wheels of Wisconsin justice had been grinding
too painstakingly to suit Joe's pace. Within a few months
he was caught up, and from that day on, he was never behind
in his court calendar. In one stretch of forty-four days, his
court remained in session past midnight twelve times. His
court reporter, Pat Howlett, a balding, harassed gentleman
who took many a ribbing from the judge in open court, recalls: "Joe always drove himself hard. Sometimes I couldn't
keep up." And an Appleton lawyer, Gus Keller, says: "Joe
wanted to try every case in the United States."

In Wisconsin, circuit judges interchange positions once in
a while and sit in each other's places. From the start, Joe
began making these trades wholesale, thus providing himself
with an expense-paid means of becoming known from one
end of Wisconsin to the other. And whenever he went to a
strange area, he would look up lawyers, judges, and newspapermen. He kept a black book of all political bigshots in
every city he visited; and, traveling through, he would call
them and pass the time of day. But it was to newspapermen
that he was most cordial. Some reporters kept a careful watch

44

on the court rosters to see when their friend Joe McCarthy would arrive to pick up the tabs at the swankiest places in town. He became known all over the state as the most generous, dynamic, nose-to-the-grindstone judge on the bench. And perhaps all this glare made it hard to see through to the clear picture of his judicial record.

He built up his reputation exactly as he had in the past — quantitatively instead of qualitatively. He tried five cases for for every one his colleagues tried; divorce trials were sometimes knocked off in five minutes; manslaughter trials took a little longer. Justice took off her robes and put on a track suit.

Joe was so determined to establish new records that he sometimes left his court reporter far behind. One night he finished a case in Antigo in the evening, and then announced to Reporter Howlett that they would drive to Racine overnight to hear cases the next morning. Howlett refused. He told Joe he wasn't leaving Antigo until he had had a good night's sleep, even if it meant his job. "I haven't got time to argue," Joe snapped. He made the 300-mile drive to Racine in a raging blizzard, borrowed a court reporter, and was on the bench trying cases at 9 A.M.

In order to continue his gallivanting around the state, McCarthy would agree to hear cases in other courts even though his own cases were scheduled at the same time, and then call in other judges to take over cases in his court. Ironically, most of this backstopping fell to Circuit Judge Hughes, who bore McCarthy no great measure of good will, having once threatened McCarthy, the lawyer, with a contempt-of-court citation.

McCarthy's courtroom manner was carefully contrived to impress the spectators; he could be cheerful to the point of slapstick, or judicially stern, depending on the effect he wanted to create. Once, when he thought it time to put his foot down, he arose from his chair, pointed a finger at a lawyer in the back row, and barked: "Bill, if you want to win a case in this court, put out that cigar!" It was the last time Lawyer Bill Green ever smoked in McCarthy's court.

But on another occasion, seeking to create a different effect, he turned whimsical. A doctor had just testified that his patient had been seriously injured in a traffic accident and that the doctor's bill had been "reasonable." Joe turned to the plaintiff's attorney and observed: "Every time a doctor comes in here, he tells me his patient was seriously injured and his bill was reasonable. I'm still waiting for the day when a doctor comes in and says, 'No, my patient wasn't hurt so bad, and my bill was way too high.'" The lawyers laughed, and the audience went away feeling that here was a judge with human qualities.

Thanks to Judge McCarthy's bourbon-and-banter press relations, reporters on small-town papers tended to magnify his virtues and overlook his defects. So, little by little, the fledgling judge convinced the north-country residents, via the newspapers, that he was indeed endowed with all the homey virtues and that his judicial record could bear microscopic scrutiny. Of course, this reputation might have bubble-gummed in his face had the press taken the trouble to examine one McCarthy case.

But if the newspapers weren't talking, Wisconsin's lawyers were. To this day, the merest mention of the Quaker Dairy case will bring to the minds of the state's legal fraternity a sour recollection of Judge McCarthy. The case has since been held up to young lawyers as an object lesson in misconduct on the bench.

Quaker Dairy, a milk distributor, had been making life difficult for Appleton-area farmers, who found their profits squeezed by the company's pricing practices. When the situation reached its worst, the Wisconsin Department of Agriculture stepped in and made an investigation. It found that Quaker Dairy was violating laws put on the books to protect the farmers from price undercutting. And, almost immediately, the Agriculture Department filed suit in Mc-Carthy's court, asking for an injunction against the company to make it obey the law.

From the beginning, the legal machinations emitted a slight odor. Quaker Dairy was badly in need of time to prepare a defense for its obvious violation of the law. Yet not even friendly Judge McCarthy could be depended on to postpone the trial for the six or eight weeks the company figured it needed. So Quaker hit on a novel scheme. There was an obscure law on Wisconsin's books that allowed a judge to postpone any trial involving an attorney who was also a state legislator until the current session was ended. And so company representatives hastened to Madison, the state capital, and persuaded Assemblyman Mark Catlin to take their case. Judge McCarthy promptly postponed the trial date six weeks until June 6, when the legislature was to adjourn. And after the six weeks were up, Proxy Catlin bowed out in favor of the firm's regular lawyer, assisted now by a close friend of McCarthy, Andrew Parnell.

Meanwhile, Judge McCarthy had signed a temporary injunction preventing Quaker Dairy from violating the law. But three days later, for some unrecorded reason, he whirled in the other direction and suspended his own injunction. When the case finally came to trial, McCarthy manifested a touching regard for the problems of the lawbreaking dairy, and complete contempt for the farmers who had elected him. He announced that it was true the law was being broken and that the Agriculture Department's lawyer, Gilbert Lappley, was right. A smile crossed Lappley's face as the judge continued his rambling verdict, but it soon dissolved when McCarthy added a long, sonorous "however." What followed the judge's "however" was to be the beginning of the end of Lappley's promising law career. McCarthy went on to void the injunction against Quaker Dairy — on the interesting grounds that the law the company was violating would be off the books anyway in six months. McCarthy said that enforcement of such a law would work "undue" hardship on the company. Thus began McCarthy's career as a law-maker; in voiding the injunction, he had in effect revised the statute — a function that constitutionally belonged to the legislative branch.

Lappley was stunned. He asked McCarthy to repeat, but the words came out the same. Still flabbergasted, Lappley countered: "Well, that seems to take care of the future. But how about our charge that the company violated the law in the past?" McCarthy's answer was a short shrug of the shoulders and a boyish grin. Lappley, angered by this breezy interpretation of the law, demanded an early trial of the charges that Quaker Dairy had engaged in illegal practices. Judge McCarthy replied that, in view of his decision, such a trial would be a "waste of the court's time." He dismissed the entire case.

When Lappley couldn't find justice in McCarthy's court, he hustled over to the state Supreme Court in Madison and asked for an order forcing McCarthy to try the case. As a matter of course, the high court sent to Appleton for the recorded transcript of McCarthy's verdict and his ruling. But, mysteriously, a vital part of the transcript had disap-peared. McCarthy's lawyer promised that it would turn up within a few days; when it didn't, Judge McCarthy was asked for an explanation. Blandly, Joe wrote that he had ordered his court reporter to destroy the notes. Why? "Be-cause they weren't material." This was, perhaps, the first and the last time in American judicial history that a trial judge admitted that his verdict and explanation were im-material.

Later Joe — with the shoe on the other foot — would be able to work up considerable indignation in accusing others of destroying relevant records.

Wisconsin lawyers felt that McCarthy's conduct would

have resulted in immediate disbarment for a judge of less popular appeal, but the Supreme Court contented itself with a scathing denunciation of McCarthy's blind-flying on the bench.

"A judicial officer is required to administer the law without respect to persons so long as it is enforced," the court observed. "Any other course would constitute an infringement upon the powers and functions of the legislature, interfere with the operation agencies . . . and result in advantage to persons who disobey the law."

McCarthy's ruling, the Supreme Court held, "constituted an abuse of judicial power."

As for the convenient disappearance of the stenographic transcript, the court said: "Ordering destruction of these notes was highly improper. In this proceeding this court is the judge of the materiality of the notes . . . It should not be necessary to belabor the point that the trial court in ordering destruction of the notes misconceived his function and mistakenly arrogated to himself the powers of this court."

And if anybody had any doubts as to the Supreme Court's convictions about why the notes were destroyed, Chief Judge Rosenberry added: "The destruction of evidence under these circumstances could only be open to the inference that the evidence destroyed contained statements of fact contrary to the position taken by the person destroying that evidence."

The court ordered McCarthy to restore the original injunction against Quaker Dairy and to hear the case again, this time on its merits. When the retrial was held, McCarthy cut it to a one-afternoon affair, begrudgingly slapping the injunction back on his friends. But he also took time out to castigate Gilbert Lappley for "causing all this trouble." He subjected Lappley to a vituperative attack at the close of the proceedings. Rosenberry later asked Lappley why he had not walked out of court. "That was what McCarthy wanted me to do," Lappley replied, "so he could hold me in contempt of court."

For weeks afterward, McCarthy's outburst rang in Lappley's ears. He tried to get a transcript of the remarks, but he was given a brush-off. And Chief Judge Rosenberry refused to order an official search, though he promised disbarment proceedings against McCarthy if the remarks were brought in.

Lappley, one of the state's most conscientious lawyers, was further discouraged by a series of phone calls and letters condemning him for stamping his black footprint on McCarthy's lily-white record. Supersensitive, he began to brood; he even took his savings out of the bank to buy radio time to tell his side of the story, which thus far had gone virtually unreported by Wisconsin's newsmen. Political pressure was put on him to keep his mouth shut. Then Lappley's superiors, unhappy over being placed on the political hot seat, fired him. Even this was kept out of the papers, in a remarkable exhibition of journalistic silence. The case was hushed up in other ways, too; for in later years practically all records of it were to vanish. When the authors of this book went to the State Supreme Court library in Madison, where briefs of all appellate cases are filed, the Quaker Dairy briefs were missing. The attendant observed that this was the first time a search had failed to turn up such a record. Library officials gave a multiplicity of reasons to explain the absence, but the smell of cover-up was heavy on the air. Perhaps if the briefs had been allowed to lie unmolested in the Supreme Court library, it would have been too easy for some opponent to refute a paid advertisement inserted in the Milwaukee *Journal* several years later by Senatorial Candidate Joe McCarthy: "As circuit judge, built outstanding record for intelligent, impartial and speedier justice."

When the sound and fury of the Quaker Dairy case finally died down — a process hastened by the unusual silence of the press — Joe turned to his first love: political planning. In night-long huddles, he talked politics, ambitions, means, and ends with three political henchmen. One of these was Elmer Honkamp, Appleton's district attorney, who later accepted $500 from the defendant in a perversion case, and was ordered to resign by the head of the state bar investigators. The other two were Urban P. Van Susteren, an affable, wide-eyed young politician who worshiped McCarthy, and Jerry Jolin, another young lawyer with dreams of political power.

Van Susteren still speaks of Joe in awed tones. He is convinced that McCarthy will become President, and as chief executive will be able to settle the international crisis in a matter of days. "If Joe were President," Van says confidently, "the first thing he would do would be to end the cold war. He'd pick up the phone and call Joe Stalin and say, 'This is Joe McCarthy. I'm coming over tomorrow to talk about things. Meet me at the Moscow airport at one o'clock.' When he arrived in Moscow, he would sit down with Stalin in a closed room. First he'd tell a couple dirty jokes. Then he'd look Stalin right in the eye and say, 'Joe, what do you want?' And Stalin would tell him. The two men would talk man to man, not like a lot of pansy diplomats. They'd find out what each of them wanted and settle their differences. But when Joe left, he'd tell Stalin, 'The first time I catch you breaking this agreement, I'll blow you and your whole goddam country off the map.' "

Joe may not have been planning on the Presidency, but he had Washington in his sights. He told his three political apostles that the La Follette Progressives were rapidly losing ground; and he figured that the Republicans, not the Democrats, would pick up most of these changing votes. So while he was still in the middle of his first term as circuit judge, he laid plans to run on the Republican ticket for the United States Senate.

In the midst of all this furious scheming, McCarthy was
visited by an old friend from Marquette, the same young man
who had accompanied Joe to the Milwaukee City Council
chambers. "Joe," the visitor said, "you've got something most
lawyers work a lifetime for and never get. You can stay judge
all your life. If you play your cards right, maybe you can
even be Governor some day."

"No, thanks," McCarthy said. "I'm not interested in the
small jobs."

10. Call to Arms

SIX MONTHS AFTER THE STATE SUPREME COURT SLAPPED Mc-Carthy's judicial wrist, the United States was at war. One by one the north country's young men began to disappear, leaving behind the too young, the too old, and the infirm. None of these was Joe McCarthy; he fitted into a special niche of his own — exempt for the reason that he was a judge.

Now virtually alone among young political hopefuls, he redoubled his efforts to make his name a household word in every corner of the state. He tried more cases than ever before, and stepped up his schedule of speeches. But he soon learned that a young man in judicial robes wasn't half so glamorous as one in khaki. And the straw that broke the back of his resistance was a prominent Page 1 picture of a handsome young ensign — Carl Zeidler.

Zeidler cast a long shadow across Joe's projected highway to the United States Senate. He was mayor of Milwaukee, a surprise victor over the beer city's perennial mayor, Socialist Dan Hoan. All over the state, Zeidler was regarded as the No. 1 up-and-coming Republican. Young, tall, blond, and Germanic, he began his speeches by singing "God Bless America" in a clear tenor voice, and he had the voters of Milwaukee at his feet. Joe, correctly, sized up Zeidler as his most dangerous rival; and when Zeidler joined the Navy as an ensign, Joe was annoyed to see the news prominently displayed in every Wisconsin paper. Zeidler had made a politically smart move, Joe told his three political lieutenants; and he had to make an even smarter move. If a Navy uniform impressed the voters, what would impress them more? The answer was clear: Join the Marines.

The decision to sign up was no snap judgment, although McCarthy later tried to convince the voters that it came in a burst of patriotic fervor. He sat down on June 2, 1942, and penned a letter to Major Saxon Holt, recruiting officer in Milwaukee. The letter set forth his qualifications for an officer's commission, and it was written on circuit-court stationery. Two days later, McCarthy drove to the big city, Milwaukee, and rushed around to the newspapers with the story that he wanted to join up as "a private or anything else in the Marines." The result was that the Milwaukee *Journal* was duped into running a news story reporting, two days after McCarthy had requested a commission: "Judge McCarthy, who has been earning $8,000 a year, applied to Marine Headquarters here Wednesday, offering to enlist 'as a private, an officer or anything else you want me to be. I want to join for the duration.'"

The fiction that he was willing to be a buck private was played to the hilt in later years by McCarthy the campaigner. Although he was sworn in as a *first* lieutenant and never wore the uniform of an enlisted man, he authorized this release in 1944:

"Though automatically deferred from the draft, he left the bench and enlisted as a buck private in the Marine Corps. He was sent to an officers' training school, where he earned a *second* lieutenant's commission."

In the *Congressional Directory* of 1947, he inserted: "In June of 1942 applied for enlistment in Marine Corps as buck private and was later commissioned." A year later the subject was getting too hot, and he changed the entry to: "In June of 1942 enlisted in the Marine Corps and was assigned to Marine aviation," leaving out mention of being a private.

He sold the story of his going in at the bottom to dozens of Wisconsin papers, the most friendly of which, the Appleton

Post-Crescent, wrote: "Judge McCarthy is entering the Marines with no promises of a commission or special favors, but it is hopeful that he will be able to earn his way into an officers' training school. He said that right now he is 'more interested in a gun than in a commission.'"

"Although he is automatically deferred from military service because he is a judge," the article continued, "McCarthy said that he had reached the conclusion that 'we can't win the war by letting our neighbors do the fighting,' so he will take a hand in it himself."

So the myth was built up: red-blooded, patriotic Joe McCarthy was going in as a private; let the Marine Corps judge for itself whether this young man was worthy of a commission, let him earn it by sweat and ability, in open competition with his peers, the mighty Devil Dogs. As Joe modestly said later: "I thought I was in good shape, but in that first week's training at Quantico, I thought I'd die and was afraid I wouldn't. I was in a group of 18- and 19-year-old kids, most of them good athletes. We either captured or lost every hill in Virginia before we finished our training." There was one other basic difference between Judge Joe and the other men — they were struggling to win brass bars; he had already promoted a silver one.

And he got the maximum political value out of the uniform before he even reported for duty. The Milwaukee *Journal* wrote:

The judge's bench of Branch 2 of Milwaukee's municipal court was occupied briefly Wednesday by a lieutenant of the Marines in uniform. He heard one case as a farewell gesture to judicial robes until the war is over. The Marine officer is Judge Joseph McCarthy, 34, of Appleton, Wis., the youngest circuit judge in the state. Judge McCarthy obtained his commission in the Marine Corps June 4 and left at 11:30 A.M. Wednesday for the Marine base at Quantico, Va. Circuit Judge Gerald Boileau of Wausau, who had been presiding in Branch 2, invited Judge McCarthy to sit in for one case when the latter called on friends at the Safety Building.

All during his military career, "friendly" stories like this were to be sent from the South Pacific to glitter on Wisconsin's front pages.

Of course, there still remained the problem of what to do about his circuit judgeship. Most young men, when they went into service, resigned their jobs. But in McCarthy's case the bird in the hand was not to be allowed its freedom that easily. Joe made the rounds of the other circuits, convincing judges that they should take over his duties until he could return from the war front. The result was that his colleagues, begrudgingly, agreed. Campaign literature was to say later that they were happy to comply, that they wanted to do their part toward releasing a younger man for the service. But the fact was that McCarthy's unexpected decision worked a hardship on Wisconsin's circuit courts. Arnold F. Murphy, chairman of the board of circuit judges, stated his feeling when he wrote McCarthy, on July 6, 1942, saying flatly that he didn't want Joe to enlist, that his value to the nation as a judge would far exceed his value as a Marine. "It may be that time will prove the wisdom of your decision," Murphy went on, "and that Judges Hughes and Boileau will not lose their enthusiasm as time goes on in taking over your work, but I am confident that even though they give their best, and I help them, that your absence from the Bench will be a serious hindrance to orderly procedure in the courts in the three counties of your circuit."

This, McCarthy figured, was Murphy's problem, not his. He wangled a one-month preliminary leave, planted a dozen news stories about his patriotic gesture, and finally showed up for active duty on August 12. Before the war was over, McCarthy was known from one end of the state to the other as a valiant young warrior, cool under fire, stern but kind with his men, the epitome of everything America loved in its heroes. Above anything else, World War II gave Joe Mc-

Carthy more political "sex appeal" than he had ever known
before.

The war was also helpful in eliminating his political rival
Zeidler. One night Zeidler's ship was moving along in a convoy on the fog-shrouded North Atlantic. When the sun
arose, the rest of the convoy was still inching along, but
Zeidler's ship was gone, and so was Joe McCarthy's main
political headache.

11. "Tail-Gunner Joe"

JOE MCCARTHY SERVED THE U. S. MARINE CORPS FOR THIRTY months in various capacities from "rear-seat gunner" to intelligence officer. He was the average wartime American, and his record can stand on its own legs.

Had Joe been content to let matters rest right there, a biographer would find little to criticize and much to praise in this chapter of McCarthy's life. But "The Judge," as he liked to be called by his comrades, was still a poker player at heart. Holding a pair of jacks as a war record, he tried to bluff the world into thinking he held four aces.

McCarthy executed the oath of office as a first lieutenant in Appleton on August 4, 1942. He reported at Quantico, Virginia, eight days later, slogged through indoctrination training, and served at various stations until April 1943, when he embarked for Hawaii with the Fourth Marine Air Base Defense Wing. From that date until he parted company with the Marines at the height of the Pacific war, he served on islands in the Pacific — but always after the islands were well under the control of friendly forces.

He served in the New Hebrides — never in enemy hands — in July and August, 1943. From there he went on temporary duty with the First Marine Aircraft Wing, a tour that enabled him to add the heroic word "Guadalcanal" to his war record. His arrival on "The Canal" took place a year after the Americans had captured its air strip, and six months after all organized resistance had ended. Likewise his duty

58

on the island of Munda took place three months after the Allies' bludgeoning had led to the Japanese collapse.

Throughout most of this time McCarthy was serving officially as an intelligence officer, doing the paper work for a squadron of pilots. Each day he would interrogate the pilots upon their return from scouting and bombing missions: Did they get to the target area? Did they encounter any enemy planes? Did they knock out any strategic targets? His job was to evaluate the success of the missions and to correlate the information into plans for future strikes. All in all, an important assignment — but not one that satisfied McCarthy. The magic word was "missions." McCarthy knew that when an airman returned home, he would be judged largely by the number of missions he had flown — not by the number of briefing sessions he had held. So Joe cast about for an opportunity to fly.

His fellow intelligence officer, Leon Weaver, explains:

> McCarthy did go on a lot of missions. It was his own decision, since intelligence officers were not required to fly. But most felt a desire to go on a certain number of routine missions in order to understand operations better. Of course, lots of intelligence officers stayed on the ground, out of fairness to the pilot. There's just room for one extra man in a dive bomber; and if the going gets tough, that man had better be an experienced gunner, not a sightseeing officer along for the ride. But Joe went anyway; he seemed to get a kick out of shooting the machine guns.

Weaver remembers that often he was stuck with McCarthy's routine ground work while Joe was off on a flight, even as Judges Boileau and Hughes were handling McCarthy's humdrum cases back in Wisconsin's courtrooms. As for the exact number of missions flown by McCarthy, wartime facts and post-war claims all blend together into a hodgepodge of numbers. There is only one consistency about his record of missions: the number gets higher as the years go by.

In 1944, a campaign leaflet reported: "[McCarthy] participated in 14 dive-bombing missions over Japanese positions."

In the *Congressional Directory* of 1948, McCarthy wrote:
". . . Had 17 official missions in the South Pacific."

In 1951, testifying under oath in legal proceedings, Mc-
Carthy said, ". . . I was on 30 dive-bombing missions, plus
liaison missions."

His Marine Corps "jacket" fails to list a single one of the
14, 17, or 30 missions, despite the fact that it has been
validated that McCarthy went along on some convoy-cover
duty during the Empress Augusta Bay landing. But this was
extra-curricular. His official job, which never changed, was
at a desk — although almost every picture of McCarthy sent
to the Wisconsin newspapers during the war showed him
wearing a flying helmet, grinning out of the cockpit. And his
campaign literature gave him the nickname "Tail-Gunner
Joe."

There is no denying the fact that McCarthy fired a lot of
ammunition. "The Judge really loved to shoot guns," one of
his pilots reports. "He was really eager in that rear seat."
He fired so often and so wildly that one day a huge sign
appeared in the recreation area: PROTECT OUR COCONUT
TREES. SEND MCCARTHY BACK TO WISCONSIN. Nevertheless, he
was able to add another quantitative record to his growing
list. An Associated Press article in 1943 recounted how Lieutenant McCarthy fired 4,700 rounds of ammunition in a single
day, for what was believed to be a new military record. Later
Joe showed the clipping to a fellow Marine officer, Captain
Jack Canaan, now of Los Angeles. "At the time," Canaan recalls, "I was young and didn't understand the significance of
his knowing wink that this clipping and picture of himself in a
helmet would help out in the States."

Thereafter, McCarthy was the hero of a steady flow of
local-boy-makes-good stories that managed to find their way
into print in Wisconsin. For example, in a report carried by

the Wisconsin *State Journal,* Tail-Gunner Joe spoke out with becoming modesty:

I was the most involuntary volunteer you ever saw. Along with other intelligence officers, I was dissatisfied with the high-altitude photography that was done after our dive-bombing attacks, because those pictures didn't reveal enemy gun positions accurately. I squawked about them so much that one day the CO called me in and told me to get a volunteer who was rated on radio, gunnery and operation of the ZB [homing device] and who also had a rating as a photographer. That CO knew darned well we didn't have anyone with such a rating. So in about 30 minutes I had to learn how to operate a camera and when I found myself in that dive bomber plane, heading for the Jap strong points in a raid, I said to myself, "McCarthy, what in heck are you doing here?"

This gave Wisconsin's voters a clear picture of their conquering hero — modest, unassuming, yet brave and competent. But to men like Captain Canaan, the picture was more muddled. They might better have understood the confusing young lieutenant had they known that, even in the islands, he was still hell-bent for election. Only McCarthy knew that he was deadly serious when he emblazoned signs across the backs of two trucks and a jeep: MCCARTHY FOR U. S. SENATOR — and when he painted across his tent: HEADQUARTERS, MC-CARTHY FOR U. S. SENATOR.

Another report on the adventures of Tail-Gunner Joe, published in the Appleton *Post-Crescent* of November 15, 1943, disclosed that McCarthy "was wounded in one of the actions." This lent credibility to a rumor that blanketed the north country — that their hero Joe was wearing the Purple Heart. McCarthy helped the rumor along by limping conspicuously when he came home on leave in 1944. But as to what actually happened, different versions circulated around the state. One was that Joe had been wounded by exploding Jap shrapnel. Another was that he had hurt his leg when a Marine bomber, coming in for a landing, ground-looped and burned.

The suspense was more than Joe's friend, Urban Van Susteren, could stand. On his wedding day, with Joe standing by as best man, Van Susteren put the question squarely up to him. Grimly, Joe held up his foot, yanked down his sock and exposed a scar. "There," he said; "now let's hear no more about it." But when reporters pressed him for more details, McCarthy said: "I had a leg badly smashed up, burned and broken. In fact, I got a citation from [Admiral Chester] Nimitz based on that." And he added modestly: "Now, I don't claim that I'm a hero, you understand. I think there's nothing wonderful about being injured."

There was no question about it: Joe *was* injured during the war. And another fact was indisputable: the injury occurred on June 22, 1943. But the official Navy records show that McCarthy was not facing Jap shrapnel or serving on a Marine airfield at the time. On June 22, 1943, he was on board the Navy's seaplane tender *Chandeleur*, steaming toward the Pacific war area. The ship recorded him as an "officer passenger." It sailed from Pearl Harbor on June 12, but did not reach Espiritu Santo, the destination of McCarthy's squadron, until July 3. And on June 22, the *Chandeleur* was crossing the equator. The details of that day were reported later by one of Joe's shipmates:

The skipper, Commander Albert K. Morehouse, gave the enlisted men permission to have a mild "shellback" ceremony on June 22, the day we crossed the equator. That day the ocean was flat and the sky was clear. We had our "general quarters" moved up to 8 A.M. so the ceremony could be held at 10:00. And at 9:55, the uniform for "pollywog" initiates was announced as pajamas, overseas caps, and bare feet. The war was completely forgotten as we appeared before Neptunus Rex, the enlisted man enthroned on the boat deck. Rank meant nothing, of course, as we were paddled, soaked with hoses, speared by the electric trident, and generally abused. One Marine officer did an elaborate strip tease, and someone else read a long defense, typed on toilet paper. It was comic relief from the war, still hundreds of miles ahead of us.

McCarthy was nearly through his initiation when he was hurt. He was going down a ladder with a bucket fastened to his foot when he slipped. His other foot caught on a lower rung — an iron pipe a few inches from the steel bulkhead — and he fell backward, injuring his foot. . . . After my initiation was over and I had rinsed the stain from my shaved head, I went to the sick bay to see how Joe was getting along. They had decided that three bones were broken, and I watched them put a cast on his foot.

Joe was in a good humor as he hobbled around on his cast, but he admonished his buddies: "Don't ever tell that I broke my foot in this silly way." They never suspected that, before Joe's war career was over, his prank injury would grow into a "severe leg injury" and he would be cited by Admiral Chester Nimitz for bravely refusing "to be hospitalized."

How the fabulous McCarthy promoted this citation is a mystery that has never been fully solved. The Nimitz tribute reads:

For meritorious and efficient performance of duty as an observer and rear gunner of a dive bomber attached to a Marine scout bombing squadron operating in the Solomon Islands area from September 1 to December 31, 1943. He participated in a large number of combat missions, and in addition to his regular duties, acted as aerial photographer. He obtained excellent photographs of enemy gun positions, despite intense anti-aircraft fire, thereby gaining valuable information which contributed materially to the success of subsequent strikes in the area. Although suffering from a severe leg injury, he refused to be hospitalized and continued to carry out his duties as an intelligence officer in a highly efficient manner. His courageous devotion to duty was in keeping with the highest traditions of the naval service.

McCarthy's official Marine record fails to confirm some of these glowing statements. On his 14 — or 17 or 30 — missions he probably fired a great many machine-gun bullets and took some pictures, and showed a "devotion to duty." But McCarthy's record shows that he was not officially a "rear gunner"; he did not participate "in a *large* number of combat missions"; he did not suffer "a severe leg injury."

One of McCarthy's fellow officers observed: "That guy could promote anything up to and including the Congressional Medal of Honor. He's the only air intelligence officer I ever heard of who got a commendation for shooting up coconut trees. Matter of fact, he's the only intelligence officer I ever heard of who got a commendation for air work, period."

The Nimitz citation grew out of a recommendation from Joe's good friend, Major E. E. Munn, commanding officer of Marine Scout Bombing Squadron 235. But there was something peculiar about the dates: Munn signed the letter of recommendation on February 11, 1944; he finished his duty as the unit's commanding officer on February 10, 1944.

Forwarded through channels to Admiral Nimitz, the recommendation stated: "On 22 June 1943 Captain McCarthy suffered a broken and burned foot and leg. He, however, refused to be hospitalized and continued doing an excellent job as intelligence officer, working on crutches." And so, a year after Joe's bout with the bucket aboard the *Chandeleur*, he wound up with a hero's commendation for the injury — thus achieving the unique distinction of receiving what was probably the war's only citation for crossing the equator.

It is extremely doubtful that Nimitz himself ever read a line of the McCarthy commendation. As commander-in-chief of the Pacific fleet, he was accustomed to scratching his name on any citation placed before him, properly cleared, and "spoken for" through official channels. But Nimitz, as a rule, signed only the most important of the decorations. Lesser awards came from ComSoPac, headed by Admiral William Halsey, commandant in McCarthy's area. Letters of commendation, lowest-ranking in the proud hierarchy of military tributes, would customarily travel through the lower channels. Nevertheless, McCarthy's came from Admiral Nimitz himself, and Joe has made the most of it. He actually reprinted it — with all its whimsy — in his own recent pamphlet, *McCarthyism: The Fight for America*.

After the Nimitz citation, one of McCarthy's former commanding generals sent Joe a congratulatory letter. Observing that "you received a citation from Admiral Nimitz for meritorious performance of duty," Major General Field Harris told McCarthy: "The Marine Corps will not forget the fine contribution you have made." This letter was written May 14, 1945, eleven months after McCarthy had taken leave of the Pacific and two months after he had traded his uniform for civilian clothes. Still another letter, from Major General H. R. Harmon, observed that McCarthy had "unfailing good nature and ready wit," and was "well-liked and respected by his associates."

Once, on a nationwide hookup over the American Broadcasting Company, he referred to "the rough days when we lost a number of our pilots and gunners." He talked of "our first dive and torpedo bombing attack upon the Jap airfields at Rabaul." He told how "my task at night was to write home to the young wives, to the young mothers, with the hope that we might be able to make the blow fall less heavily." He said that on the night of the first Rabaul raid, "a great number of letters had to be written," and he "struggled" over them "in my dugout." The fact was that he never lived in a dugout. And the official Marine Corps history of McCarthy's outfit, VMSB-235, shows that the squadron lost five officers and two men — not in the single raid on Rabaul, but in its entire military tour in the South Pacific. Nevertheless the speech melted the heart of many a Gold Star mother.

On another occasion, after a talk in Badger Village, Wisconsin, one veteran stood up and asked: "Why do you wear built-up shoes?" At 5 feet, 10½ inches, McCarthy seemed to the veteran tall enough to stand on his own physical endowments without adding artificial height.

Joe, slightly taken aback, paused for a few seconds, then dramatically reached down and pulled the elevator shoe off. He showed the audience a special frame inside and announced: "I'll tell you why I wear this shoe. It's because I carry 10 pounds of shrapnel in this leg!"

Stunned and embarrassed, the veteran didn't question further. He was too bewildered to realize until later that no man could pack that much shrapnel in a single leg — least of all a person who had never been wounded.

12. Shooting for the Senate

In the middle of the third war year, 1944, Captain Joe McCarthy sat back and counted his blessings. He had a record of active duty in the South Pacific; he had made $42,000 on the stock market; and he had kept stories about his war career humming through the printing presses of the Wisconsin newspapers. He had come a long way from Grand Chute, spinning down the highway of back-country politics, headed for Washington by way of the Pacific. Already a Marine captain and a Wisconsin circuit judge, simultaneously, he figured that if he stretched just a little farther he could grab the brass ring — election to the Senate.

Of course, incumbent Alexander Wiley was a powerful vote-getter, and there was a military ruling that servicemen couldn't speak on political issues while in uniform. But another problem — even thornier — was buried down in Article 7, Section 10, of the Wisconsin constitution: "Each of the judges of the supreme and circuit courts shall . . . hold no offices of public trust, except a judicial office, during the term for which they are respectively elected, and all votes for either of them for any office, except a judicial office . . . shall be void."

Nothing could have been plainer. A judge could not run for office. If he did, the votes wouldn't count. Confronted with this stymie, Joe met the immovable law with the irresistible decision. He simply chose to ignore it.

With that problem pushed aside, Joe announced his candidacy in the form of a letter to one of his backers. It read:

Some time ago I received your letter in which you, in behalf of the committee, ask whether I would be willing to serve if elected to the U. S. Senate. This is the first opportunity I have had to answer, but I have been giving the matter serious consideration.

My answer is yes.

You understand, of course, that I shall take no part in the campaign. In fact, I do not even expect to be in the United States before the election, and I cannot, because of military regulations, discuss political issues. But I do have a program, and this I will submit to the people of Wisconsin as soon as the time permits.

I must, of necessity, leave this campaign to my friends and the voters of Wisconsin, because I shall continue on out here, doing to the best of my ability those tasks assigned to me.

With the release of this self-sacrificing epistle to the press, the journalistic drums began rolling. The Wisconsin *State Journal* heralded McCarthy's step as

. . . a very good sign of a public awakening to the need of vigorous intellects in high office. Captain McCarthy is the type impregnated with the mother wit and quick, penetrating ability gloved in prudence that has already redeemed the Republican party in most of the country and bids fair to rescue the nation from those who are still dizzied by subterfuge and dazzled by sophistry.

Said the Shawano *Evening Leader:*

As a Marine fighter, we, his friends, know that Joe put everything he had into the job, just as he handled every other job and assignment in his brilliant legal and judicial career. McCarthy's personal initiative and capacity for hard work were responsible for his success as a farmer, grocery store manager, lawyer, judge and as Captain in the Marines. His superior officers must have recognized these qualities of integrity and personal honesty when they assigned him to tasks upon which the lives of men and the success or failure of a mission depended.

And the Appleton *Post-Crescent* reported:

McCarthy, about 35 years of age, had the wholesome judgment to hang his robe as circuit judge in the closet, ignore the adequate income to which the law entitled him and shove off with the tough young fellows in the Marines. If a combination of the McCarthy qualities cannot make a statesman, then what can?

McCarthy's campaign literature carried on where the laudatory press left off. One piece said: "At the age of 28 he was elected circuit judge," thus knocking two years off McCarthy's age and adding a bit of extra luster to the accomplishment. "Though automatically deferred from the draft," it went on, "he left the bench and enlisted as a buck private in the Marine Corps. He was sent to an officers' training school, where he earned a second lieutenant's commission." And later: "He is ably qualified by training and experience — much of which he obtained on the battlefields of the South Pacific."

Backed up with whimsy like this, the campaign buzzed merrily along. First it was handled by Gerald Jolin, McCarthy's old crony, who later became a county judge. Jolin steered the McCarthy campaign until the two were rumored to have had words about money. Then a former Hearst editor from Milwaukee, James Colby, took over — but only after the cash had been laid on the line in the Appleton Hotel.

Another who worked in the McCarthy cause was Milton Murray, who later, as a lobbyist in Madison for natural-gas interests, was called on the carpet for failing to file complete expense reports. Joe's sister Olive checked in again, as did dozens of his poker-playing friends from the north country. By dint of heavy expenditures and long hours, the team painted a beguiling picture of "Tail-Gunner Joe" for all the voters to see. And at exactly the right psychological moment, who should turn up but the hero himself: he had wangled a thirty-day leave from the Marines.

Just two weeks away from election day, Joe tried a sneak end run around the military regulation that forbade his campaigning. Addressing the Milwaukee League of Women Voters, "I wish I could discuss the importance of oil and the importance of maintaining a strong army and navy to be used in the event any international organization breaks down, but I may not do so," Joe said — having just done so. "I am in the same position as the boy who wrote home that censorship prevented him from saying it was raining and that he was in a foxhole." He also showed up at a public meeting of the Appleton League of Women Voters. Gleaming in his captain's uniform, he arose and announced: "If I were able to speak, here's what I'd say" — and he said it.

His method of campaigning was to travel all over the state in uniform, and to take strong political stands without appearing to do so. He attended a different Catholic church almost every Sunday, bussed babies, and shook hands. And whenever two or more Wisconsin citizens got together, Joe would try to be on hand.

One night a friend turned to him and said: "I was supposed to go to a wedding party tonight, but I can't make it."

"I'll go!" Joe volunteered. He grabbed his hat, asked for the address, and crashed the party. He made a big hit, and picked up a few more votes.

McCarthy ran so fast he sometimes left his campaign manager behind. Colby once observed: "I'd get mad at him sometimes. I'd arrange a meeting in Milwaukee, and he'd turn up in Fond du Lac." Someone else "got mad" at him, too. Wisconsin's Secretary of State Zimmerman, after a casual rereading of the constitution, publicly challenged McCarthy's right to run. He waved Article 7, Section 10, under the nose of Attorney General Martin, a strong Republican, who took the matter under advisement and proclaimed: "Judge McCarthy, as we understand it, has filed the required number of signers and his papers are otherwise in order. You should certify his name on the official ballot, and any question with regard to his eligibility to hold the office of United States senator must await future determination." That disposed of the constitution and left the road clear. Now all Joe had to do was win.

But he didn't. Alexander Wiley was renominated as the Republican candidate for the Senate, later to be re-elected for another term. But standing a solid second in the primary results was "Tail-Gunner Joe," with almost 100,000 votes, ahead of two others. McCarthy licked no wounds; the publicity had made him a political name to be reckoned with. Another election was coming up in just two years, and Joe began constructing a political torpedo. On its sides he chalked out the words "Bob La Follette."

His plans were interrupted for a while by another small, but pesky, roadblock. Someone checked his financial reports on the 1944 election and put in a complaint. "Money is the easiest thing to get," Joe had told friends before the campaign, and the records bore him out. The Committee to Elect Joseph McCarthy U. S. Senator took in and spent $19,809 in 1944; and, as Joe reported it, most of the money came from his relatives. (For details, see Chapter 38.)

In October, 1944, just three months after his thirty-day leave to present himself to the voters, McCarthy applied for another sixty-day leave, explaining that he had some judicial problems in Wisconsin that needed tending. The Marine Corps turned thumbs down; and when Joe persisted, he was given his choice of fighting or resigning. And so Captain Joe turned in his resignation. It was accepted on February 20, 1945; and a month later "Tail-Gunner Joe" traded in his military career for a political band wagon.

13. "Quickie" Divorces

NOW CAPTAIN JOE HURRIED HOME TO BASK IN MILITARY GLORY for a while before the election. The voters saw him as a limping, bedraggled, war-weary veteran, returning to the circuit judgeship of Outagamie, Langlade, and Shawano counties. "Sick at heart," he said, over the terrible fate of "my boys" fighting the war, Joe trudged from meeting to meeting, lamenting the way the country was run, limping noticeably up to the microphone to cry out for "a better way of life for all of us." In one speech he reduced the assemblage to tears by a simple description of "a combat soldier's night on Bougainville," and he later told a radio audience that his prayer back in the South Pacific had always been: "O God, for one more day, spare these, *my* boys." He spoke before women's clubs and boys' clubs, church groups and bar associations; he joined the Elks and the American Legion, and made more speeches. As time went on, his love for the Marine Corps grew into an epic romance; he lived in an aura of Marine tradition, and the stirring Marine Corps hymn could bring tears to his eyes.

Of course there were those who suspected that Joe's limp was more political than medical, and that his flag-waving was largely soapbox patriotism. But on the whole the voters were grateful to Joe for giving up his draft-exempt status and enlisting in a war he could have sat out; so they returned him to the bench on an avalanche of public acclaim.

But it would take more than a war record to start a landslide that would carry McCarthy all the way to the United

States Senate. It would take help from others, who would go out and preach the gospel of red-blooded Americanism, Mc-Carthy-brand, and convince voters from Superior to Kenosha that the young judge should be sent as a replacement for Mr. La Follette. And so Joe set about looking for organizational backing. He found it in the Young Republicans of Wisconsin.

The YR's embraced Joe with open arms. He was young, like themselves; he would lead their assault on the GOP old guard, and make the Young Republicans a political force to be reckoned with in Wisconsin. Even today in the Badger State, the YR's hero-worship McCarthy; and, if necessary, they are willing to toss democratic principles out the window for Joe's sake. In 1951, for example, the state headquarters lowered the boom on a small YR chapter in Manitowoc, revoking its charter, because the chapter had committed an unpardonable, democratic sin — it had taken a vote and repudiated their leader, McCarthy.

One of the Young Republicans who were instrumental in building up this idolatry was Chester Roberts, chairman of the Young Republicans of Milwaukee. Roberts made dozens of speeches for McCarthy; reciprocally Joe told his friends that "nothing's too good for my friend Chet Roberts." And in his capacity as circuit judge, he proved that he meant every word of it. Thus began the strange saga of the "quickie divorces" which were to become a state-wide scandal.

Roberts, a $186-a-month public-utility employee, had been sued by his wife for separate maintenance in March, 1946 — a Milwaukee action in which Roberts was a willing participant. Circuit Judge Roland J. Steinle awarded Mrs. Roberts $75 a month pending outcome of the case, and set a trial date in the future. The months dragged on, and the case didn't come up. So in September, 1946, seven months after the filing of the suit in Milwaukee, Mrs. Roberts and her attorney went in search of speedier justice. "My wife and her lawyer headed for Marinette to get the divorce before Judge Harold Murphy," Roberts recalls. "It was perfectly all right with me; the sooner they got it over with, the better. On the way, they went through Appleton and happened to bump into Joe. Next thing I know, Joe had settled the whole mess."

Mrs. Roberts and her attorney appeared in Joe's court on September 5. In less than two hours the three of them had finished lunch and the divorce had been granted. As the Milwaukee *Journal* later noted: "It was quick, it was quiet, it was without publicity. And no doubt it was legal." But it also deserved a closer scrutiny. Roberts and his attorney, Max Litow, had both been active in McCarthy's campaigns, contributing time and money. "Is Wisconsin justice to be used to accommodate political supporters of a presiding judge?" the *Journal* asked. "Are Wisconsin courts the place in which to settle political debts? The *Journal* believes the answer to both questions is 'No.'" The editorial concluded by saying that "Judge McCarthy, whose burning ambition for political advancement is accompanied by an astonishing disregard for things ethical and traditional, is doing serious injury to the judiciary of this state."

Serious injury was done, too, to a progressive reform to save Wisconsin's shipwrecked marriages. That reform was the steadying hand of a county divorce counsel whose job it was to sit down and talk things over with embattled couples. The system proved sound, and hundreds of Wisconsin marriages were saved by competent arbiters. But in the Roberts case the divorce counsel performed a different function. He made no attempt to bring Roberts and his wife together; in fact, all his arrangements were aimed at getting the divorce over quickly and quietly.

The divorce counsel who performed his duties-in-reverse so skillfully was Urban Van Susteren, McCarthy's new campaign manager, joining with his boss in transplanting Reno to Appleton. For the Roberts case was not by any means the

only marital knot that they deftly untied. Another divorce
that raised Wisconsin eyebrows was granted by McCarthy
on the very same day as the Roberts decree. Once again there
were strong political odors, mixed this time with out-and-out
violation of the law.

The parties were a Mr. and Mrs. Leopold Kordas, who —
unlike the Roberts couple — had no overt political relationship with McCarthy. Lacking this qualification, Mrs. Kordas
selected as her lawyers two men who could show a political
link with the young judge — Arlo McKinnon and Charles
Kersten, of Milwaukee. Both these lawyers had contributed
more than once to McCarthy's political campaigns; and, having paid the fare, they had taken a ride on the McCarthy
band wagon. (Both were also charged with state tax viola-
tions growing out of failure to file returns during a ten-year
period; both were penalized, and McKinnon was ordered
to pay double tax for the entire time. In addition, the state
board of bar commissioners asked disciplinary action against
McKinnon for violating his oath as an attorney.)

After the Kordas vs. Kordas case had languished for a year
in the Milwaukee circuit court, Mrs. Kordas talked it over
with McKinnon, who suggested they journey to Appleton
and see Judge McCarthy. The action was filed in McCarthy's
court on September 3, 1946, and the divorce granted one day
later. But now there were complications. Mrs. Kordas' complaint, filed under oath, swore that no divorce action was
pending in any other court, even though her original action
was still pending in Milwaukee. Thus Mrs. Kordas and her
attorney, McKinnon, had violated Section 247.17 of the Wisconsin statutes, which makes duplicate filing illegal. Judge
McCarthy, by this time more sensitive to the laws of his native state, set about covering up.

Two weeks after the divorce was granted, he arranged with
Circuit Judge Walter Schinz of Milwaukee for a special order
dismissing the Kordas action in the Milwaukee court, retro-

active to September 4. This washed out the law violation
and prevented legal action against Mrs. Kordas and her
attorney. But there still remained a final problem. The
divorce judgment rendered by McCarthy bore the date September 4; obviously it would have been impossible for one
court to relinquish control and another court, a hundred miles
away, to issue a judgment on the same day. So the date of
September 4 on the Appleton judgment was scratched out,
and September 5 substituted in its place. All was well that
ended well, and one more skeleton joined the others in Judge
Joe's judicial closet.

The files of Judge McCarthy's court are loaded with a host
of similar "quickie divorces." More than once, divorce-seekers
learned that there was a leak in the dike of Wisconsin's rigid
divorce laws, and that leak was to be found in Appleton.
Joe was so anxious not only to try a host of cases, but also
to be known as a good fellow who always returns favors, that
he cut corners in other ways, too. Once he tried a case with
no clerk present — he said he just couldn't wait any longer.
Another time, he all but held a hearing as he walked up the
courthouse steps. He opened the case while he was still making a beeline for his court.

"Are you the lawyer for the plaintiff?" Judge McCarthy
asked of one of the attorneys striding alongside him.

"Yes," the lawyer answered.

"And are you the lawyer for the respondent?"

"Yes."

"Are these stipulations correct?"

"Yes."

"Is there anything anyone wants to say before we pro-
ceed?"

"No."

And within two minutes the proceedings were over. The
plaintiff looked up in surprise as she was told she could leave
the courtroom. "Am I divorced?" she asked.

"Yes," Judge McCarthy announced, "you're now a free woman."

"But is that all there is to it? I thought there would be a court trial."

"We're efficient around here," Joe said. "You wanted a divorce and now you have it."

The woman walked out of the courthouse bewildered. "I don't *feel* divorced," she said to her lawyer. "I thought it would seem more official."

14. Setting the Trap for La Follette

LATE IN 1945, AT THE HEIGHT OF JOE McCARTHY'S FEVERISH post-war activity on the bench, he traveled to Milwaukee to attend what turned out to be one of the most important meetings of his life. Together with a handful of other eager Young Republicans, he organized the state's dormant YR group and placed it under the leadership of a trusted follower, Loyal Eddy. After the organizational meeting at the Pfister Hotel, the zealous young politicians joined a tall, white-haired man in the English Room. He was Thomas Coleman, better known throughout the state as "Boss Coleman," the man who pulled the strings above the marionette stage of the Wisconsin GOP. As chairman of the Republican Voluntary Committee, he could make or break a candidate with a single word — as he had demonstrated many times. He was ready to break McCarthy, too, until their conversation that night made him reconsider.

"Joe," said Coleman sweetly, "you're a nice guy and I like you. But you're a Johnny-come-lately in Republican politics. You just don't have a part in the Senatorial picture for next year. If you work as hard as you have been working and gain more support, you may have a chance some time in the future."

Joe took a nonchalant sip at his bourbon-and-water and fired back: "Tom, you're a nice guy and I like you. But I got news for you. When that convention is over next year, Joe

McCarthy will be the Republican-endorsed candidate for
U. S. Senator."

Tom Coleman eyed the brash young man coldly. "What
you need is some self-confidence," he commented dryly and
left the table.

But Boss Coleman never forgot the incident; at first he
was angered by it — and yet the shrewd, political side of
his nature recognized that a defiant spirit like McCarthy's
was useful in the rough-and-tumble world of politics. Even
so, he never expected to form a political partnership that
would later inspire a certain editorial cartoon in the Milwaukee *Journal*. This showed McCarthy compressed into the
shape of a rubber stamp; the caption read: "BOSS COLEMAN'S
CANDIDATE."

When Joe formally announced his candidacy, the initial
reaction was laughter from one end of the state to the other.
Senator Robert ("Young Bob") La Follette, scion and name-
sake of old "Fighting Bob," had just laid his father's Progressive Party in its final resting place, and was seeking
renomination to the Senate as a Republican. There was a
strong feeling that not even a reincarnation of Abraham Lincoln could make any inroads against the powerful La Follette
name, and for an upstate judge with practically no political
experience to challenge Young Bob was the political joke
of the year. Joe, grinning with all the rest, packed his bag
and set out to make history. The first problem was to win
over the Republican Voluntary Committee, in spite of Boss
Coleman. As a starter, Joe turned again to direct-mail advertising. He sent sales letters to the several hundred
members of the Committee, and sat back waiting for the
groundswell of acclamation.

But there was nothing except a strained political silence.
Undaunted, Joe jumped into his car and took off like a low-
flying pursuit plane. He elbowed his way into seventy-one
local committee meetings in every part of Wisconsin. The

reception was almost uniformly cool, but Joe smiled his modest smile, shook all the hands, and let slip the information that he was the man of the hour.

In order to knock out as many of his potential rivals as possible, he drove to their homes and explained, with a big grin, that he just couldn't be stopped, suggesting tactfully that they drop out of the race rather than suffer humiliating defeat. "After all," he said to one candidate, "you can't expect to beat a veteran now, can you?" The candidate, who had spent World War II in Wisconsin, had to admit he couldn't.

As the pre-primary campaign progressed, Judge McCarthy began to pay less and less attention to his boring chores on the bench. He tried harder than ever to switch places with out-of-town judges in order to visit as many towns as possible; and once again some of the judicial slack had to be taken up by other judges. But little by little, McCarthy began to see daylight ahead in his political future, as the opposing Republican candidates dropped out. At the finish only one serious contender remained — ex-Governor Julius P. Heil, a wealthy manufacturer of heavy machinery. "Julius the Just," as he was called, was a roly-poly, "happy-times" politician who had never shown an excess of political talent. But he was a figure to be reckoned with because of the size of his pocketbook. He was given to throwing huge parties for people he wanted to impress; and, like Joe, he made a great show of picking up all the tabs he could lay his hands on.

The night before the Republican Voluntary Committee's nominating convention opened in Oshkosh, Heil was holding court in his headquarters, buying drinks by the bucketful for all who happened by. McCarthy hand-picked several of his delegates, not generally known as such, to visit the Heil headquarters. One by one "McCarthy's Fifth Column," as they were called later, wandered up to Heil, congratulated him on his candidacy, and then announced in gloomy tones that it was too bad the Republican powers had secretly blessed young Joe's nomination. After Heil had heard the same story about ten times, he began to fret; and before the party ended, he disappeared. The next morning, Heil refused to stand for convention endorsement, and Joe had won his toughest battle by default.

Still, there remained a few obstacles in his path. For one thing, members of the Republican "high command," formed into a special committee, were not entirely convinced that Joe was their man. They just didn't think he could win — his personal energy notwithstanding — and so they groped around for another candidate. But McCarthy was not to be denied. He spread the word that it made no difference to him whether he was nominated by the convention or not, because he would still run. And if it split the ticket — well, that would be the committee's fault, not his. Finally, as the voting time neared, Joe pulled a political rabbit out of his hat. He had noticed that the Milwaukee delegation was short a few members. Joe raced to a phone booth and called his friend Gerry Lorge in Milwaukee. "Get ten men up here as soon as you can," he barked. "I want to get those extra votes."

"But how can I get that many guys on such short notice?" Lorge asked. "How do I know they'll be for you?"

"Go down to the Marine Corps League and get names of Marines in Milwaukee. They all know me. They'll come."

"But a lot of those guys are Democrats."

"Listen. If you ask them, they'll come — and they'll vote for me."

When nomination time came around, Joe arranged for Frank Cornelisen, a Republican leader from Green Bay, to be his spokesman. Cornelisen arose and shouted: "As a result of our endorsement of McCarthy, Senator La Follette, by the grace of God and the will of the people of Wisconsin, will be retired forever August 13." Cornelisen said it was "a damned lie" that McCarthy could not legally run for the office while remaining a judge, and he angrily denied that ex-Democrat McCarthy had ever been that most hideous of all things to a Republican convention — a New Dealer. "I do not think that you will object to Judge McCarthy because he ran on the Democratic ticket for district attorney of Shawano County in 1936," he pleaded.

"We do!" a voice cried out. But Cornelisen insisted that Joe had made a speech just one week before confirming the fact that he was an ironclad member of the GOP, "a thousand per cent." So McCarthy's name was placed in nomination. Joe brazenly tapped Julius Heil on the shoulder and offered him the honor of seconding the nomination. But Heil, angry, brokenhearted, and confused at his own "repudiation" by Republican leaders, declined the privilege.

The vote on the first ballot: McCarthy, 2,328; his nearest opponent, Milwaukee Lawyer Perry Stearns, 298. Republican leaders scratched their heads, Young Republicans cheered, and Joe stepped modestly to the platform. He said he would do everything in his power "to enact into law the platform which you, the truly representative people of the Republican party, are adopting today." He pointed out that the job of Senator had become ten times as important as in the past, "because of the infiltration of foreign ideologies into the national capital." He and other returning veterans were sick unto death of "a government not of law, but of stifling bureaucracy." Then he put in plugs for farmers, laborers, white-collar workers, and businessmen, and sat down.

Ten days later, word began to leak out about some of Judge Joe's practices in bulldozing his way into the nomination. A group of Republican powers met in Milwaukee in a top-secret conference. Their aims: to attempt to convince McCarthy that he should not run because he could not win, and to seek out a dark horse to replace him.

The Madison *Capital Times* reported:

McCarthy, it is said, is exhibiting an extremely stubborn attitude and has served notice that if a candidate is entered in the race against him, he will stump the state exposing what he considers a raw deal on the part of the Republican big-wigs. Walter Kohler, Jr., son of the late Governor Walter Kohler, Sr., is said to have the inside track with the men who are determined to "do something" about the weak slate endorsed at Oshkosh.

Joe decided to do something, too. He told reporters in later years how he drove straight to Kohler's office and pointed out some salient facts. He reminded Kohler that divorced men make vulnerable candidates. Kohler, who had recently been divorced, listened closely. And when McCarthy added how distasteful such publicity would be when repeated over the radio and in the press, the ex-Governor's son dropped out. At any rate, that's the story McCarthy put out. For his part, Kohler, later Governor of Wisconsin, says he chose not to run simply because he thought the Republicans would have a better chance if they didn't split their ticket.

The plot to throw out McCarthy bubbled and boiled for a while, but when word reached the old-line Republicans that Kohler would not run, it cooled off completely. Boss Coleman threw his full weight behind McCarthy in a development headlined in the Milwaukee *Journal:* COLEMAN HURLS A FLOOD OF PAMPHLETS AT FOES. The rest of the article was a preview of coming attractions:

The State Republican voluntary organization of Thomas E. Coleman Saturday loosed a flood of literature designed to bring about the nomination and election of the slate of candidates endorsed by the Republican Voluntary Convention at Oshkosh.

The tone of the literature indicates that Coleman will put up a vigorous battle for his slate in the Aug. 13 primary, especially in behalf of Circuit Judge Joseph R. McCarthy, Appleton, candidate for United States Senator. It is Senator Robert M. La Follette, Jr., that Coleman is most anxious to beat.

Of the five pieces of literature sent out by the Coleman organization, three have to do exclusively with McCarthy's candidacy. One of these, containing press comment on McCarthy, is authorized and paid for by the Milwaukee McCarthy for Senator Club. The others are authorized and paid for by the Coleman organization.

One pamphlet slugs it out with La Follette and with editors who have suggested that McCarthy withdraw from the race because of a restriction in the State Constitution prohibiting circuit judges from running for a political office.

The pamphlet insists that the state constitution does not regulate the candidacy of a judge for Federal office, and it asks:

"Did the newspaper publishers who suggest that Joseph R. McCarthy resign his judgeship while being a candidate for office give up their $30,000 to $50,000 incomes per year? Did the Progressive senator who returns to the state only intermittently from his estate in Virginia, chiefly for campaign purposes, make any sacrifice at all?"

The pamphlet sets forth that when McCarthy entered the Marines, he took no income from his judgeship while he served, that he made sacrifices which he could ill afford to make.

The Coleman document argues that La Follette's income as a senator continues while he runs for re-election, and that, in addition, he and his wife get $25,000 a year profit from station WEMP of Milwaukee, of which they are part owners.

Boss Coleman had blown the theme on his pitch pipe. The campaign would be based on mudslinging, distortions, innuendoes, and lies.

15. Barnstorming for Senator

THE MCCARTHY-FOR-SENATOR CAMPAIGN DESCENDED LIKE A hailstorm on the people of Wisconsin. For three months the populace was blizzarded with election gimmicks dreamed up by the Judge and his backers. Direct-mail advertising, an airplane grasshoppering around the state, and speechmaking invasions of bridge parties and poker sessions — one by one McCarthy yanked forth the latest surprises from his bag of tricks.

He campaigned as a war hero, circulating 750,000 copies of a twelve-page brochure about his military record as it had been exaggerated in the north-country press. The story was spun loosely with no attempt to separate fact from fiction. A typical campaign ad, published in the Milwaukee *Journal*, shows how McCarthy cashed in his thirty-month political investment in the Marines for two hundred cents on the dollar. It reads:

JOE MCCARTHY was a TAIL GUNNER in World War II. When the war began JOE had a soft job as a Judge at EIGHT GRAND a year. He was EXEMPT from military duty. He resigned his job to enlist as a PRIVATE in the MARINES. He fought on LAND and in the AIR all through the Pacific. He and millions of other guys kept YOU from talking Japanese. TODAY JOE MCCARTHY IS HOME. He wants to SERVE America in the SENATE. Yes, folks. CONGRESS NEEDS A TAIL GUNNER. Now, when Washington is in confusion, when BUREAUCRATS are seeking to perpetuate themselves FOREVER upon the American way of life, AMERICA NEEDS FIGHTING MEN. These men who fought upon foreign soil to SAVE AMERICA have earned the right to SERVE AMERICA in times of peace.

As the campaign wore on, McCarthy turned to the favorite technique of his earlier campaigns — the handwritten note. A half million of these popped up in the mailboxes of Wisconsin, bearing the script message: "Dear ————: Your vote Tuesday will be greatly appreciated by Joe McCarthy." The last two words of the message were dropped down to the bottom of the page to simulate McCarthy's personal signature, even though it was signed in hundreds of different hands. The propaganda rain fell so heavily that the Madison *Capital Times* observed: "In commenting about the various cards, pamphlets and circulars coming through the mail, it is unnecessary to mention the 'Joe cards' because almost everybody in the state is acquainted with them."

McCarthy's backers had good reason to pour thousands of dollars into the direct-mail campaign, because they had carefully tested the system on guinea-pig voters. In Two Rivers, a poll showed Joe trailing La Follette by a 1-to-3 margin; then they blanketed the town with the postcards. Three days later a survey showed that Joe had pulled even. In De Pere, McCarthy was running 1-to-2 behind La Follette; again, the literature hit town, and the next poll showed McCarthy with a slight edge. The same happened in a small Polish town near Wisconsin Rapids, where La Follette had led 3-to-1 before the postcard deluge.

It was obvious from these costly surveys and from the quantity of McCarthy literature dumped into the mail chutes that the Republican machine was shoving all its chips into the center of the table in a frenzied attempt to defeat Bob La Follette. But the biggest asset the enemies of La Follette could count on was Joe McCarthy himself — the indefatigable warrior, the tireless campaigner for the cause of Joe McCarthy. He took a powerful yank on his bootstraps and lifted himself all the way to Washington.

As always, McCarthy's personal contribution to the campaign consisted of vast amounts of work and energy. One day he arose at 5 A.M. in Marinette, a little town on Green Bay; that evening he was scheduled to give two speeches in Superior, some 250 miles away across the top of the state. He jumped into his car and started out, shoving the speedometer past the 70 mark. En route, he stopped to make impromptu speeches in several villages. But he was moving too fast for the car — and in his first hundred miles he blew three tires. At Rhinelander, McCarthy scrapped the car and boarded a plane for Superior, figuring he could still make the speaking engagements. Over Butternut, the plane sprang an oil leak and had to put down in an oat field. Joe hired a cab for the final dash to Superior, but its motor conked out in Ashland. He jumped aboard another plane and flew the remaining distance in time to make the public meeting at 8:30 P.M.

In like manner, he stumped the state grasping for every last vote. In a four-day period he made speeches and shook hands in Owen, Thorp, Neillsville, Fairchild, Augusta, Eau Claire, Osseo, Alma Center, Black River Falls, Blair, Whitehall, Independence, Arcadia, Mondovi, Durand, Ellsworth, River Falls, Hudson, New Richmond, Menominie, Barron, Cumberland, Rice Lake, Cameron, Chetek, Bloomer, and Chippewa Falls.

A typical McCarthy visitation befell the Republican stronghold of Rock County on July 23, 1946. According to a press account, "The Appleton jurist whipped across the county from Edgerton to the Illinois line and from east to west, asking support of political and civic leaders, public officials, businessmen and plain, ordinary voters." The Rock County tour began at 10 A.M. and ended at midnight, and first on the list was the town of Evansville. There McCarthy sauntered up and down the main street, barging into the bank, the grocery store, the hotel, the barber shop, and the beauty parlor. He met and shook hands with hundreds of people, including Mayor Ben T. Green, who promised to hand out McCarthy literature after hearing a short sales talk, and a lawyer named Jones, who pleased McCarthy by saying: "Republicans around here got no time for Bob La Follette. He did all he could to wreck the Republican party; now he comes crawling back on his knees saying in one breath he wants our support and in the next that he's going to take over the party." Joe shook lawyer Jones's hand gleefully and was gone, seeking someone who needed convincing.

Next stop was Edgerton, where McCarthy dusted off his act again, ending by going down the line of elderly men seated on the shaded bench in front of the saloon, shaking each one by the hand. Once he jumped to the curb, grabbed the hand of a farmer alighting from his car, and announced: "I don't want to lose your vote, sir. My name's McCarthy; I'm running for the United States Senate — against Bob La Follette, you know." The startled farmer blurted, "Glad to know you," and retreated from this whirlwind into a store.

From Edgerton, McCarthy jumped to Janesville for a speech at the YMCA before a group of the town's lawyers. Among other things, he observed that he believed in "government by legislators and not by bureaucrats," and that labor had equal responsibilities with industry to prevent strikes. Then he went on to Footville, where a bartender observed that McCarthy seemed to be an "all right guy" who would, nevertheless, be beaten in the race. La Follette, he explained, is an "old name; everybody out here knows it. And a lot of farmers around here are German; they like the La Follettes from way back."

By mid-afternoon, McCarthy had handshaken a path all the way to Beloit, an industrial town and Rock County's largest city. There the candidate changed his approach, after two leading McCarthy-for-Senator boosters told him: "The Republican party has got too much of a name for being for the white-collar people." So Joe donned overalls and toured the Beloit Iron Works and the Gardner Machine

Company, making friends with the workers and reminiscing
about the days when "I worked as a foundry helper to pay
my college tuition." He searched out the young veterans in
the plant, discussing old acquaintances and reminding them
that he, too, had done his part. And there was a reception
at the Hilton Hotel where McCarthy heard some encouraging words from David Throne, aged 88, a lifelong Republican.
"We always vote Republican," Throne said; "and I don't
mean for the La Follettes."

Later, at a rally in the park, Judge McCarthy begged the
people to sweep out of office "the men who got us into this
sorry mess." After that, there remained speeches and drinks
at the American Legion post, the Eagles Club, and the Veterans of Foreign Wars headquarters. There were votes in
those places, and the Judge worked until midnight gathering them.

This was a typical campaign day in the life of the eager
young candidate. His enthusiasm was catching and spread to
the Young Republicans who supported him. The upshot was
"The Flying Badgers," one of the most successful political
coups ever put into operation. On a day in August, 1946,
Loyal Eddy, Young Republican chairman, handed sealed
orders to a number of select leaders. They scattered to key
Wisconsin cities, where airplanes dropped off hundreds of
thousands of campaign folders. Then 208 automobiles, each
filled with four volunteers, drove to the nearest airport in
each area and picked up packages of the campaign literature.
All over the state, the volunteers carried the message of
McCarthy, visiting all but nine of the Wisconsin cities with
populations of over five hundred. They went from door to
door, pushed their folders under the windshield wipers of
parked cars, and handed them to shoppers and moviegoers.
To squeeze the last drop of political juice out of every available second, Eddy instructed each corps of volunteers to
stay out of their own home towns, in order, as he explained,

to avoid time-consuming political arguments with friends. The entire operation involved split-second timing, skillful planning, and an abundance of energy — all drawn from the fountainhead of the leader, Joe McCarthy.

During the entire campaign period, McCarthy lived only for the fight. He had no social life; he even gave up his beloved poker. Once he took a vacation in the north woods, but it turned out to be just another political routine. The handshaking and backslapping continued in between the swimming and fishing. One night at Plum Lake, he walked into a tavern with a friend, who noticed former Assemblyman Morris Fitzsimmons of Fond du Lac standing to one side. "I think I'll go over and say hello," McCarthy's friend remarked.

"No," snapped Joe. "I'll go. What did you say his name was?"

"Morris Fitzsimmons."

McCarthy strode briskly across the floor, boomed a friendly "Hello, Morrie," and poured out all the vital statistics on his election campaign. No stratagem was too small or unimportant to McCarthy if he could see the possibility of gaining a vote. After dinner at a night club outside Eagle River, he collected from each member of his party the proper share of the heavy check, then walked over to the cashier with the money and announced: "I'm Judge McCarthy, running for the Senate, you know. This dinner's on me." He plunked the money down on the counter, shook the cashier's hand, and walked out.

Again, at a dinner meeting of the Milwaukee Society of Accountants in the Knickerbocker Hotel, McCarthy waited until Guest Speaker Phil La Follette, brother of "Young Bob," began his oration, and then went from table to table introducing himself as "the man who is running against Bob La Follette." Relations between brother Phil and Judge Joe had been strained even before that. One day the pair met in the street, and Phil inquired how McCarthy ever expected he could beat Bob La Follette for the Senate. Joe answered: "We've got thirty-five guys who are built like Bob and who have rubber masks which look exactly like him. They are going to travel the state, walking down main streets and bumping into people, asking them who they think they are, bumping into a United States Senator." Phil La Follette, former Governor of Wisconsin, walked away, scratching his head.

In his mad dash to the Senate, McCarthy also trod on an occasional personal friendship to keep from losing votes. One of his oldest friends was Marty Unmuth of Shawano, who had spent two summers with McCarthy and had been close to him from 1935 to 1940. One night during the campaign, Unmuth walked up to a table in a bar of a hotel in Green Bay, where Joe and a group of Republican politicians were whooping it up.

"Hi, Joe," Unmuth said. "Good luck in your campaign." McCarthy looked surprised. "I don't believe I've met you," he said. Unmuth, angered and embarrassed, walked out. It wasn't until later that he figured it out. He and McCarthy had been Democrats together, just after Unmuth had held the chairmanship of the Outagamie Democratic Committee. And Unmuth knew that the Democratic donkey and the Republican elephant, in McCarthy's political zoo, could no longer be cagemates.

16. "A Very Rough but Clean Fight"

THE *Capital Times* OF MADISON ONCE REPORTED:

McCarthy is very adept at working both sides of the street on almost every issue. He does so by taking only the most ambiguous stands in his public pronouncements and making private calls to the advocates of both sides of a debate. It has been learned recently that McCarthy has caused both sides of the controversial school bus referendum issue to be informed that he is with them.

This capacity to "work both sides of the street" was McCarthy's forte in the 1946 campaign. And he accomplished it, not so much by deception, as the *Capital Times* hinted, as by generalization. A close analysis of McCarthy's 1946 speeches shows that he lashed out viciously at broad, general "evils" without ever coming down to cases. He was the GOP's Don Quixote, tilting at windmills — in what seemed to be a sincere, impassioned manner.

Joe painted word pictures for his audiences, so that they could see in their mind's eye the sinister aspects of the "conspiracy" in Washington. And one of his favorite topics was "bureaucracy," a word that was just then coming into its own as a Republican rallying cry. Bureaucracy, Joe said in Eau Claire, has grown "like an octopus until its tentacles have reached into every far corner of the nation and into every conceivable phase of life, sucking the very life blood from the nation and stifling the type of initiative which had previously made this nation the greatest on earth." If his audiences couldn't visualize a bureaucracy, they could visualize an octopus; if Joe was campaigning against something like that, then they were behind him. As for correcting the "evils" he mentioned, Joe had more pictures. The way to destroy bureaucracy, he said, is to "clean out that administration from top to bottom, so that we can thereby plunge a knife into the very heart of this tentacled monster." The crowd, full of pictures of a huge octopus under savage attack by a knife-wielding McCarthy, applauded until their hands ached.

Many voters in Wisconsin are still not sure just what issues Joe used as platform planks in the 1946 election. A few can remember what he was against — war, "foreign" influences in Washington, bureaucracy, and high taxes. His stand on internationalism was nebulous and politically safe. He told the Young Republicans on April 27, 1946, that the United States should "take no part whatever" in the world unless she was playing first fiddle — that it was good to lead the world but not to follow it. Wisconsin's voters found this an easy line to swallow, since it seemed to hold out promise both to isolationists and to internationalists. As for the United Nations, McCarthy had a sop for its admirers and another for its opponents. For its admirers, he announced that the U. N. could do its job even if some other powerful nation refused to co-operate; for its detractors, he charged that the U. N. was "tragically weak." Both of these statements came in the same speech. For trade unionists, he announced that President Truman was shaping up a "vicious anti-labor policy" along with the rest of the Democrats; he let it be known that a McCarthy in the Senate would protect the rights of labor above all else. For enemies of trade unionism, he announced that he wanted to ban political contributions by unions and put teeth in the anti-strike laws. Also, he said, it's about time labor assumed its full share of the responsibility that went with the power it had attained.

But it was seldom that McCarthy ever became so specific. Most of the time he lashed out at that evil-ridden town in the faraway District of Columbia, playing on the voters' latent distrust of anything alien to Wisconsin's clean, fertile countryside. "I think the situation in Washington is foul," he proclaimed, "and that it should be changed. There are problems to be solved down there that represent a real challenge. And I think that those who actively fought the war are entitled to a chance to settle some of those problems."

One night he showed up at a meeting of the League of Women Voters in Appleton to make a campaign speech. He shied away from Wisconsin issues, evaded foreign affairs, and concentrated on Communism in Washington. He hinted strongly that the Reds were running the nation, and that the White House owed its primary allegiance to Moscow. He beat hard on his breast, cried out at the "shame of it all," and announced that he would clean up the "whole sorry mess" when he reached Capitol Hill. But when the meeting was over, the club president, Mrs. Abraham Sigman, reminded Joe that he had promised to speak on foreign affairs.

"Mrs. Sigman," McCarthy said, "I believe it is my duty to speak out on this Communist issue."

"But we wanted to know your views on foreign policy," Mrs. Sigman repeated.

"You'll hear from me when the time is right," Joe said.

McCarthy had other difficulties with the women voters of Wisconsin. He irritated several thousand Milwaukee women at the Pfister Hotel one afternoon in August, 1946. They had convened for a gala bridge party just before a pre-primary rally of the Milwaukee County Republican Women's Club, and they spilled into the corridors and the lobby of the hotel. Joe, seeing this huge gathering, set up amplifiers. He announced to the president that he would "take only four minutes of your time," and then proceeded to speak for twenty minutes above the tumult. Just barely

audible over the sounds of "Three no trump" and "Double,"
the audience could hear the doctrine of Joe McCarthy: "I
want to end that theory of government that for every ill
there must be a new federal law, for every problem a new
bureau." One of the women said afterwards that she had
rather enjoyed the speech; while it was going on, she had
made a grand slam.

Meanwhile, from his cloister on Capitol Hill in Washington, Senator Bob La Follette watched McCarthy's antics.
But as copies of Wisconsin newspapers reached his office,
bearing reports of McCarthy's glib generalities and transpar-
ent contradictions, it seemed obvious to La Follette that
this young man would eventually trip himself up. So he
stayed in Washington, working on legislation, postponing his
campaign until the last possible minute. It was the biggest
mistake of La Follette's life.

Joe's vendetta against La Follette was based on the
techniques he had learned in the ring. He bored in ag-
gressively, starting each daily round with a flurry of wild hay-
makers in a frantic endeavor to land just one solid punch.
And in the melee, it was perhaps inevitable that a few wild
blows should strike below the belt.

It was typical of La Follette that he never cried "Foul!"
In his dignified, plodding style, the ex-Progressive mistakenly figured that he could stand on his record — a
record that he had built up in unbroken Senatorial service
since 1925. And he listened too closely to the political polls
that said La Follette would defeat McCarthy by a 3-to-1 margin in the primary. To the man who had many times been
named "best Senator" by Washington's newsmen, those predictions seemed highly reliable.

Over and above his personal record, "Young Bob" could
reckon on other favorable factors. "La Follette" had been
the grand old name of Wisconsin politics for forty-five years.
Robert M. La Follette, Sr. — "Fighting Bob" — had been

elected Governor in 1901, and later had gone on to the Senate. Bob, Sr., and then Bob, Jr., served as Senators for forty years, fighting for civil liberties, labor rights, efficient government, and dozens of other important causes.

But twenty-one years in the Senate had worked a change in Bob La Follette, Jr. Sure of his state's confidence, he made a fatal mistake for anyone representing an agricultural state. He turned to broad issues of national importance and, inevitably, tended to neglect the local problems of Wisconsin's mass of voters. Automatically he affixed a "yes" vote to nearly every piece of legislation favorable to the farmers — but no longer initiated such legislation. He was too busy with the monumental La Follette-Monroney Congressional-reorganization bill; this was a vitally important measure, a milestone in governmental history, but it would bear no immediate fruit for the people who had elected him. Immersed in such high-level operations, La Follette neglected his political fence-mending, returning to Wisconsin to campaign against McCarthy only two weeks before the elections, and by then the smear campaign against him had penetrated so many voting minds that it was too late.

McCarthy kicked off his campaign against La Follette on March 18, 1946, with a speech at Milwaukee, wherein he promised a "very rough but clean fight." What followed was at least rough. First he and his followers undertook the tricky task of suggesting to the voters that La Follette was both a Fascist-sympathizer and a Communist-sympathizer. Joe hammered away at La Follette's "isolationist" stand as proof that the Senator was moving in unison with Communism. "Senator La Follette is playing into the hands of the Communists," McCarthy announced in a radio speech, "by opposing world co-operation." Two days later, the fervently pro-McCarthy Wisconsin *State Journal* traveled to the other political extreme in an editorial that described the cross-and-circle symbol of La Follette's old Progressive party as "the trappings of Fascism."

The next wild pitch was thrown on June 12 at LaCrosse; Joe accused La Follette of "making salary increases and pensions for Congressmen his chief concern." And Joe's political mentor, Boss Tom Coleman, wrote to a mailing list of GOP workers that La Follette was "more responsible for the confusion in this nation today than any other single person in the Senate."

But above all McCarthy needed to shake loose the farmers' votes, which had been electing La Follettes for forty-five years. So, ignoring Young Bob's undeviating pro-agriculture record, Joe accused him instead of neglecting the farmer and catering to labor. La Follette hadn't learned, said Joe, "that you can't cut the farmers' throat without spattering blood over labor also." The New Deal formula for prosperity was to plow up the crops, he shouted. "Then they thought that the best way to have a lot of pork was to kill off the pigs. La Follette is going to go them one better — he is going to kill off the farmer." Joe followed up this blast with a campaign folder, charging that a La Follette vote to protect organized truckers was, in fact, a vote to promote "the pocketing of the farmers' money by some unscrupulous labor czars."

McCarthy was also given to shooting questions, like arrows, in the air. They were aimed at La Follette, but they dropped aimlessly among the voters, pricking their confidence in "Young Bob." A typical volley demanded all at once: "Why have you failed to do anything to create industrial-labor peace? What, other than draw fat rations, did you do for the war effort while 15,000,000 Americans were fighting the war and 130,000,000 more were building the sinews of war? Why haven't you ever gone on record for or against any important issue until the very last moment, after you have had a chance to decide how the political

winds might blow?" Without waiting for answers, McCarthy
announced: "You call it statesmanship, but the voters of
Wisconsin have another name for it. You cannot answer
these questions, Mr. La Follette!"

And so the campaign settled down to personalities instead
of issues; but the *coup d'état* was a statement, issued by
McCarthy, that Senator La Follette was a "war profiteer"
who fixed up his business deals on the floor of the Senate.
La Follette had bought a one-fourth share of radio station
WEMP in Milwaukee. And unhappily for his political
future, the station presented him with a total profit of
$47,339.78 in 1944 and 1945, war years.

As a starting point, Joe pointed out that the Federal Com-
munications Commission licensed the station. Then he tossed
in the information that La Follette voted on appropriations
for FCC. With this slim thread of fact, McCarthy wove a
sinister picture: the FCC and Bob La Follette, conspiring
together, had milked out $47,339.78 in wartime profits, as
fine an example of government corruption as anyone had
ever invented.

"This is the type of thing that must be eradicated in Washington," McCarthy proclaimed. "An alderman in the small-
est town in Wisconsin today is forbidden to engage in business deals with his municipal government. But in Washington that 'you-scratch-my-back-and-I'll-scratch-yours' practice
is tolerated and has been tolerated for years. Connections
are considered necessary. Deals are considered common-
place. The air seems to reek with intrigue. That is why I
believe new blood should be injected into the United States
Senate and why Mr. La Follette should be retired."

McCarthy suggested that a law be passed "preventing
you [La Follette] or any other Senator from doing what you
did during the war, namely, making huge profits from dealing with a federal agency which exists by virtue of your
vote." When the newspapers refused to print Joe's farfetched

charges, he published a campaign tabloid of his own. The headlines rang out: How DID LA FOLLETTE GET THAT MONEY? GETS $47,339 EXTRA THROUGH RADIO BUSINESS. PROGRESSIVE PARTY CHAIRMAN GETS RICH IN PARTNERSHIP. NO REGULATION ON LA FOLLETTE'S PROFITS WHILE HE FIGHTS OTHERS'. LA FOLLETTE INCOME SO HIGH CITIES FIGHT FOR TAXES.

But there was still more political juice to be squeezed out of La Follette's radio venture. Joe circulated the industrial areas with handbills, adding this labor postscript: "Now that he [La Follette] is in the big money, how does he treat his own workmen? In 1941, his own business partnership paid less money to all its workmen than the profits of the partners." The circular didn't bother to explain that "Young Bob" was just one of four partners, that the other three actually ran the station, and that the wages were up to scale, despite the profits.

Of course, anyone familiar with the way the wheels turned in Washington could see through McCarthy's cellophane charges. It was simple routine for Congress to appropriate operating expenses for the FCC, as for every other federal agency. In fact, a Senator would have difficulty finding any outside business interest that didn't come under the jurisdiction of some government bureau or other. So it was a strain on the imagination to suggest that there was a connection between La Follette's single Senatorial vote and the FCC license granted to WEMP as a routine matter.

And so La Follette stood on his dignity and ignored the issue. He didn't even bother to strike back, as he could have, by pointing out that McCarthy had made wartime profits of $42,000 in a single year, by trading on the securities market. Many voters were therefore left with the impression that La Follette's silence constituted a plea of *nolo contendere* to McCarthy's charges. And Joe made the most of La Follette's refusal to fight. He challenged La Follette to a public debate, and the offer was refused; he asked hundreds of questions, and La Follette never answered. He drummed into the public mind the axiom that silence gives consent, and as the campaign drew down to the wire, McCarthy's vituperations became almost deafening.

And when the charges ran out, Joe tried to unfasten the "smear artist" badge from his own lapel and pin it on the enemy. "We have definite information," he told a Madison audience, "that this smear campaign will reach a new high, or rather I should say a new low, in the last few days of this election."

17. Winning the Communist Vote

WHEN PRIMARY-ELECTION DAY ROLLED AROUND ON AUGUST 13, 1946, Tom Coleman and his GOP machine felt a strange uneasiness. It was the same feeling that comes to a poker player who holds four aces, shoves all his money into the pot, and prays that no one has a straight flush. Boss Coleman and his hirelings knew that they had a good hand in Joe McCarthy; but they were wondering if it had been worth the gamble. The Committee to Elect Joseph R. McCarthy had spent $20,000, and another $30,000 had been shelled out in Joe's behalf by Coleman's organization. In contrast, the optimistic Mr. La Follette reported an outlay of only $3,728, and the Democratic candidate, Howard McMurray, listed $3,008. Clearly, the big money rested on McCarthy.

"Stop worrying," Joe told the Republican brass hats as they waited for the first returns on the mezzanine floor of the Wisconsin Hotel in Milwaukee. "I got it figured. No matter how you slice it, I win."

"By how much?" he was asked.

"By five per cent, maybe more."

But as the day turned into evening and then early morning, it became doubtful that McCarthy would win at all. The voting seesawed back and forth, with La Follette and McCarthy alternately taking tiny leads. And then came a bad

101

break for the young candidate. Back-country counties —
where he had counted his main support — started going for
La Follette. One by one McCarthy saw "sure things" turn
into losses; and when it finally became obvious that the election would hinge on the vote from Milwaukee County, Joe
too began to fret. In 1942 La Follette had carried Milwaukee by 55,000 votes. Now, with almost every other
county reported, La Follette led by 3,000 votes. Milwaukee
was expected to swell that lead by tens of thousands, and
sweep La Follette to another victory. That was the feeling
among Boss Coleman's boys, and heads hung low at Mc-
Carthy headquarters. Then finally the Milwaukee precincts
started to report, one by one, and the tap-tap-tap of the tele-
type sounded like a dirge to Joe's unhappy backers.

But as the figures piled up, they noticed something strange.
The heavy labor precincts were turning against La Follette;
here, in the very heart of La Follette's political empire, Joe
was picking up votes. Coleman and his boys crowded around
the machines, watching in disbelief. Soon La Follette's
3,000-vote lead had evaporated, and Joe moved into the lead
by 1,000, 2,000, 3,000 votes — coming from the last place
the Coleman machine expected. And by the time all the
last-minute returns were sifted down, corrected, checked,
and verified, Judge McCarthy was the Republican candidate
for the U. S. Senate. He had won in the primary by 5,396
votes — tantamount, in Republican Wisconsin, to election.
The final tabulation: McCarthy, 207,935; La Follette, 202,539.

Almost immediately, a cry of pain went up from La Follette's headquarters. Not only had "Young Bob" lost Milwaukee, but also he had dropped every one of the lakeside
counties from Kenosha to Sheboygan. All of them were pro-
labor, and in the past they had provided La Follette with
his thundering majorities. What had happened?

The editor of La Follette's magazine, *The Progressive*,
charged that "large segments of organized labor buried their

knife in the back of one of the best friends they ever had."
But Fred Sheasby, political expert for the non-partisan Milwaukee *Journal*, wrote:

Some Washington journalistic admirers of Senator La Follette are
shedding tears in their beer over La Follette's defeat. In blaming the
farmers, in blaming labor, such journalists overlook significant factors
of the senator's own making. For years Wisconsin has seen little of
La Follette except about campaign time. He lost his touch with the
home folks. His personal organization fell apart — the Progressive
party disbanded. He made an unimpressive campaign for the Republican nomination, avoiding the issues.

Sheasby also pointed out another La Follette boner: At
the last minute on election eve, La Follette had announced
against Governor Walter S. Goodland, popular 82-year-old
Republican who won renomination without a campaign.

Any of these Sheasby-advanced reasons would serve as an
adequate explanation for the tiny 5,400-vote margin by which
La Follette lost. But there were broader forces at work in
the campaign, too — forces which accounted not for just the
small majority, but for a tremendous portion of McCarthy's
surprising total. And one of these was the uncompromising
opposition of the Communist Party to Senator La Follette.

In almost any political setting except the Wisconsin of
1946, Communists would not have been able to exert any
substantial influence. But this was in the days before Communism had been purged from the huge Allis-Chalmers CIO
local in Milwaukee; before Harold Christoffel, local CIO
head, had been convicted of perjury for denying his Party
membership; before anyone knew that the state secretary of
the CIO, Melvin J. Heinritz, belonged to the Party; and
before it was known that the Milwaukee city garbage workers, among others, were Communist-dominated. Clearly, the
Reds were a potent force. They controlled the CIO leadership in Wisconsin and exerted a powerful influence over the
CIO's 75,000 members.

When the Reds decided to make the defeat of La Follette a major objective, it was for good reason: La Follette was hurting Communism. He had long since disavowed any possibility of reconciling Communism with democracy, as had his father before him in 1924, when Joe McCarthy was 16 years old. And while McCarthy was being quoted on such statements as "Stalin's proposal for world disarmament is a great thing and he must be given credit for being sincere about it," La Follette was preaching the gospel of complete distrust of Communism, and exposing it as a philosophy of untruth and deception. His lashing Senate attack on Soviet Russia on May 31, 1945, convinced Wisconsin's Red-complexioned CIO leaders that a McCarthy would be far the lesser of two evils. They reckoned, correctly, that the surface abuse of Communism would be much less deadly in the long run than the sincere, well-documented approach of La Follette. So they cranked out reams of hate-La Follette literature and rallied the workers behind McCarthy. When Joe was asked by reporters about this, he said: "Communists have the same right to vote as anyone else, don't they?"

But as important as this Communist knife-work was to the outcome of the election, there was another development that counted for even more. Two months before the election, the Milwaukee *Journal* had underlined the problem:

On the well-grounded assumption that thousands of Democrats will invade the GOP primary, since the Democratic party lacks spirited primary contests of its own, speculation goes this way: How would such Democrats be likely to vote on the U. S. Senatorial nomination, as between La Follette and McCarthy? Some politicians who consider themselves smart guessers are advancing the theory that many Democrats would vote for McCarthy for these reasons:

1. That McCarthy, as Democrats view it, would be a weaker candidate than La Follette for the Democratic senatorial nominee to face in the November election;

2. That Democrats, voting for McCarthy's nomination, would be getting even with La Follette — or trying to — for La Follette's failure

to join the Democratic party instead of the GOP when the struggling Progressive party folded up at its Portage meeting.

The *Journal's* prediction came true. Thousands of Democrats voted for McCarthy in the Republican primary because he promised to be a softer opponent in the general election, and because they were sore at La Follette. Only a hard core of 62,000 Democrats cast their votes for Howard McMurray, University of Wisconsin political-science professor, who campaigned on liberal principles and won the Democratic nomination.

And so, in the light of the election results, it was easy to add up all these factors and arrive at a clear picture of McCarthy's victory. The Communists and Democrats were out for La Follette's hide; and the exhaust explosion of their negativism blew Joe McCarthy right into the United States Senate.

But to Joe it made little difference how he was elected. He raced right back to Appleton, the conquering hero, to savor the proudest moment of his life. Having been up all night he arrived in Appleton in the morning. When he hit College Avenue, Appleton's "main drag," he was bleary-eyed and tired. But he pulled himself together for a march of triumph, shaking hands and slapping backs up and down College Avenue. "Hi there, Senator," the townspeople shouted, and Joe smiled modestly and said: "Not yet, not yet, we've still got a tough fight."

The next day when he had slept and recovered some of his political savvy, he delivered to a newspaper reporter a classic analysis of the campaign he had just won. "This campaign was a contest not between men," he proclaimed, "but between issues and the theories of Government."

18. Preview of Charges to Come

From the time of the primary election until the time of the general election three months later, the voters of Wisconsin were treated to a series of lectures on foreign policy, presented after the manner of Will Rogers and Aimee Semple McPherson by the people's choice, Joe McCarthy. Where had he learned about foreign policy? He had given himself another cram course — by long hours of study in the public library.

Even though Joe accused others of being "sucked in" by Communist programs, he himself said: "Russia does not want and is not ready to fight a war." His statement that "Stalin's proposal for world disarmament is a great thing and he must be given credit for being sincere about it" showed a naïveté about Soviet Russia that McCarthy today would brand as near-treason.

He reduced every issue to the simplest terms, just as he always had; and he developed a reputation among some people as a man of great wisdom. Every farmer and every schoolboy could understand the logic of statements like this: "I don't believe it is exactly correct to call the Byrnes-Vandenberg foreign policy, which I favor, a 'get-tough' policy. A Wisconsin farmer would call it a good horse-trading policy in which the rules of common sense are applied. It is sensible for us not to approve giving something away with nothing in return, and not to demand anything we have no right to demand."

This tendency to oversimplify gave McCarthy an advan-

tage over his Democratic opponent, Professor Howard Mc-
Murray (who had, incidentally, published in the Milwaukee
Journal an advertisement containing a biased and partisan
attack on La Follette and his record). To begin with, the
mass of Wisconsin voters tended to distrust a man in intellectual robes. And when the scholarly McMurray and the
earthy McCarthy climbed on the same platform to debate,
Joe always won out.

"I'm just a farm boy, not a professor," he explained in
Appleton one night, "but I'll be darned if I can figure out
this Henry Wallace view on Russia" — though McCarthy
and Wallace seemed to agree at least on Russia's "sincerity."

McMurray arose to announce that he had talked to Wallace
a few days before and "Mr. Wallace told me that when he
comes to Madison on October 31 he will discuss his view
on Russia in words that the people of Wisconsin can understand."

"He don't have to talk down to us," someone shouted. The
hue and cry became so great that McMurray had to explain
that what Wallace really intended to do was "clarify" his
views. But the incident left the Appleton audience with an
accentuated feeling of distrust in the professor and an increased respect for Joe McCarthy.

It was fortunate for McCarthy that he had this capacity to
endear himself to the average voter, because he had no real
platform to offer the electorate. In an effort to throw together some sort of "ideals," he and his campaign managers
sat down and figured out a platform. Joe was supposed to
commit it to memory, but by this time his brain was so loaded
with speech material that he couldn't remember from one
meeting to another just what his platform was. On the night
of October 16, 1946, he was telling a Milwaukee audience
about his five-point program to bring peace to labor and
industry. After he had named three points, he stopped and
began stammering. Someone in the audience prompted:

"Compulsory arbitration!" Joe took the cue and began to explain, "My fourth point, compulsory arbitration" — but the audience laughed so loud that he had to quit.

A week later in Appleton, Joe was debating McMurray, and someone asked both candidates to outline their views on labor-industry relations. Said the Madison *Capital Times:*

When the question was asked, Judge McCarthy jumped to his feet and ran to the speakers' table to get a piece of writing paper. While McMurray was outlining his program, McCarthy hastily jotted down his five points. When he rose to talk he held the notes in his hand. "Have you got them written down this time?" McMurray asked, laughing.

"Yep," McCarthy replied.

But inevitably the campaign moved on to more familiar ground, away from the intricacies and technicalities of facts and ideas, back to personal attacks on the enemy. McCarthy reverted to this approach by mentioning, quite nonchalantly, in a Milwaukee speech that McMurray was "Communistically inclined." A hush fell over the audience of 450 attending the League of Women Voters forum in Shorewood Auditorium, as McMurray jumped from his seat, ignored the moderator, and spoke in slow, measured tones: "I have never had a responsible citizen — I say a *responsible* citizen — challenge my loyalty to America before. I am sure my friends and my many students in my political science courses of past years will not challenge my loyalty." Trembling and white-faced with rage, McMurray charged: "This statement is a little below the belt. I'll leave the answer to the voters."

But McCarthy — who had accepted Communist support in the primary — hammered away. "I said that for the benefit of Howard McMurray," he stated. "But I also want to ask him: Does he then not welcome the endorsement of the *Daily Worker,* a Communist newspaper, which referred to him in a recent issue as 'a fellow traveler,' according to quotations in the Appleton *Post-Crescent* and Green Bay *Press Gazette?*"

McMurray jumped up. "I welcome that question," he said. "I have not seen the reported statement in the *Daily Worker*, nor the comments of those two most reactionary newspapers, the Appleton and Green Bay papers. But if I have the support of the *Daily Worker,* I certainly repudiate that paper and their whole tribe."

Such a clear-cut and public repudiation would have ended the matter right there had anyone but McCarthy been carrying the ball. The next week, back in Appleton, McCarthy brought it up in the same way again. "The *Daily Worker* called you a fellow traveler, meaning Communist," Joe charged. "I regret bringing this up, but you've forced me to do it."

From this McCarthy jumped into a wild attempt to wrap up McMurray and Communist Politician Edmund Bobrowicz of Milwaukee in a single package. Bobrowicz had been Democratic candidate for Congress from Milwaukee, until the Milwaukee *Journal* exposed him as a Communist. When that happened, Democratic National Committeeman Robert E. Tehan repudiated Bobrowicz and withdrew Democratic party support. McCarthy charged that McMurray sat back while all this was going on, and didn't repudiate Bobrowicz himself until "he saw how the political winds were blowing."

McMurray's answer was simple and to the point. He explained patiently that the repudiation statement by Committeeman Tehan had in fact been written by McMurray himself, "and the first reporter who got hold of me got my statement standing behind Tehan. I repudiated Bobrowicz because we had the goods on him."

As for the statements in the Appleton and Green Bay papers quoting the *Daily Worker,* the professor said: "I did not see these statements and I didn't know of their existence until Judge McCarthy brought them up in Milwaukee last

week. Had I known of their existence, I would have repudiated them immediately. If the Appleton *Post-Crescent*
is interested in getting my reactions to these things, why
didn't they call me? I can be reached by telephone." And
once again McMurray was forced to repeat his public repudiation of Communists and Communism. But even so, a
doubt had been planted in the public mind about McMurray.
The charge always held more weight than the vindication,
and Joe set about whipping up accusation after accusation.

But when the Red-baiting campaign began to crop up in
the pulpits of Wisconsin's churches, McMurray figured it
was time to put his foot down. He learned that a priest in
St. Joseph's Catholic Church in Appleton had urged his
parishioners to "vote against the Communist candidate,"
and there was no doubt in the minds of the worshipers that
the priest referred to McMurray.

"I am ashamed of the fact that men in their pulpits have
used the epithet 'Communist candidate,' " McMurray said.
"I am ashamed — because I am a Christian."

McCarthy, knowing the Catholic Church's strong hatred
for Communism, continued to slash at McMurray. The day
after the Appleton debate, he drove to Madison to charge
that McMurray was "nothing more than a megaphone, being
used by the Communist-controlled P.A.C." And by now he
had convinced a mass of voters that McMurray was indeed a
"pinko." To underline all this and to point up his own red-
white-and-blue record, Joe placed an ad in the Wausau
Record-Herald:

Some of the Democratic candidates for high offices in the government have been repudiated by the party because they have been
proven to have Communist backgrounds and Communist ways of
thinking. Others have been touched with suspicion, but the proof is
lacking. Joseph R. McCarthy is 100 per cent American in thought and
deed. No one can say that he believes in any of the foreign isms that
have plagued the Democratic party throughout their reign. This is
America. Let's have Americans in the government.

19. Manna from McCormick

Two months before the general elections in 1946, New York *Times* Reporter Felix Belair, Jr., journeyed to Chicago for a talk with arch-conservative Robert ("Bertie") Mc-Cormick. At the time (six years before he bolted to form the "American Party"), McCormick was the accepted leader of Illinois Republicans. Also, he laid some further claims to running the GOP in Wisconsin, where his Chicago *Tribune* had a wide circulation.

McCormick told Belair: "You know, I had to laugh about Willkie when he went into the Wisconsin primaries after he had been defeated by Roosevelt several years before. Poor fellow, he thought Dewey beat him in the Wisconsin primary, but it wasn't Dewey — I beat him. And the issue was Americanism. That's *Tribune* territory over there." McCormick also said: "Everybody knows that the Democratic Party is the party of the Russian-loving Communists in this country. . . . Everybody knows that Jimmy Byrnes is just a junior clerk for the British Foreign Office."

These statements led *Times*man Belair to remark: "The apparent inconsistency of a pro-British Secretary of State in a 'pro-Russian' administration was a phenomenon that Colonel McCormick seemed to think not worth explaining."

The interview was running along in this slapdash fashion when suddenly a secretary poked her head in the door and announced the arrival of "Judge Joseph R. McCarthy, Re-

publican candidate for U. S. Senator from Wisconsin, who
defeated Senator Robert M. La Follette in the recent primary." McCormick shooed Belair out of his office; and the
interview was ended.

And so it was that the voters of Wisconsin learned, by way
of the New York *Times*, that their fair-haired boy was
building some of his political plans in that citadel of reaction,
the Tribune Tower. When the news appeared, McCarthy
made a quick announcement: the Colonel had wanted to
meet him, and out of courtesy he had made the trip. "We
had a little chat, that's all," said Joe.

But it soon appeared that there might have been more to
the meeting than a social tete-a-tete. Expensive newspaper
ads for McCarthy began blossoming out over the signature
of American Action, Inc., a "new political opinion group."
A month after McCarthy's safari to Chicago, the Milwaukee
Journal wrote: "American Action, Inc., a group organized
with the avowed purpose of defeating 'radical and Communist' candidates for Congress, has begun to build itself on
the framework of the old isolationist America First committee, nationally and in Wisconsin." The Chicago *Sun*
announced that the new organization was backed financially
by General Robert E. Wood, former national chairman of
America First; Lammot DuPont, director of E. I. duPont de
Nemours Co.; and Upton Close, right-wing commentator.
Also in the list of financial contributors was the name of Joe
McCarthy's new friend: Colonel Robert R. McCormick.

American Action was reported to possess a million-dollar
war chest. Its advance man in Wisconsin, Lansing Hoyt,
former state chairman of the America First committee, announced that some of the money would be used to advance
the candidacy of Joe McCarthy, because "he has a good war
record and he's in favor of the American Constitution."

"If we gain control of the House of Representatives and
the Senate, we will have accomplished our objectives," Hoyt

said. "We will then control the purse strings. The New Deal will be busted and without money to spend. It won't take long then to put the radicals and Communists in their places." Hoyt explained that American Action had separated itself from the word "democracy," preferring instead the word "republic" to describe America. He charged that "democracy" was a Russian word used to cover up for Communism. And when he was asked if American Action would spend any money to fight Fascists or Nazis, he proclaimed: "As far as I know, there are no Fascists or Nazis in this country."

Such was the anatomy of McCarthy's political support from Chicago, and some of his own supporters didn't like the odor. One of them arose at a public meeting in Milwaukee to inquire: "What about this new America First outfit?"

"I know nothing about American *Activities*, Inc., if that's its name," said McCarthy, giving the wrong name to indicate how unfamiliar he was with the group. "If it's the old America First group, I want no part of it. If it is organized to fight Communism as they say, I welcome their help in defeating Communists and those who are Communistically inclined like McMurray."

But McCarthy must have known that the organization *was* a direct outgrowth of America First. The Milwaukee *Journal*, which he clipped daily, had headlined ten days before: FIRSTERS FORM IN NEW GROUP. This was followed by a complete exposé of American Action, Inc. And McCarthy-supporter Lansing Hoyt, Wisconsin spokesman for the group, was known far and wide as former state chairman of America First. Yet McCarthy's if-and-or-but reply was widely publicized as an adequate answer to the charges that Joe was being supported by reactionaries.

The American Action support was the first large-scale backing thrown to Joe McCarthy as a person, instead of to the Coleman political organization in Wisconsin. And it

marked the unveiling of what is today regarded as a Mc-
Carthy machine in Wisconsin. The Milwaukee *Journal* has
observed:

> It is a fact that this machine, carefully developed since the 1944
> campaign, when the young Marine made a trial run against Senator
> Alexander Wiley, was more of a factor in the chain of events leading
> to McCarthy's winning the Republican nomination than was his support
> by the "machine" of Thomas E. Coleman, state voluntary Republican
> committee chairman.

Backbone of the McCarthy machine were the Young Republicans of Wisconsin, but added to the YR's were what
the *Journal* described as "thousands of supporters throughout
Wisconsin . . . loyally devoted to him personally, rather
than to the Republican organization." They were the products of his backslapping, bourbon-buying expeditions through
the north country. And they trooped to the polls by the
thousands in November, 1946, and made Joe McCarthy the
junior Senator from Wisconsin. The vote: McCarthy, 620,-
430; McMurray, 378,772. Two other candidates split 12,000
votes. The *Journal* post-mortemed: "Political observers were
disposed to see in the Republican triumph and the Democratic debacle in Wisconsin chiefly an extension of the national revolt against the New Deal."

And the *Journal* tried with all its might and main to
swallow the bitter pill of McCarthy's victory with a smile.
Maybe, the paper hinted, there was some hope that this
young man would now shuck off the ruthlessness of his
ambition and settle down to a good job of representing Wisconsin. This Pollyanna feeling was best expressed in a report
on McCarthy shortly after his election, by Lawrence Eklund
of the *Journal* staff:

> While La Follette, over a period of years in Washington, seemed
> to grow aloof from the people down in the local precincts of the state
> he represented, McCarthy, at present, is close to the people of Wis-
> consin.

In talking with McCarthy one gets the impression that he will make a record as a liberal Republican, and that he will be closer to Republicans of the type of former Governor Harold E. Stassen of Minnesota and Senators Wayne Morse of Oregon and Joseph Ball of Minnesota than he will be to Senator Robert Taft of Ohio, the apparent conservative choice for President in 1948. Evidently he will not be satisfied with the Republican program that calls simply for "free enterprise."

McCarthy, who believes generally in the removal of "stifling government control" but who feels the necessity of some measure of government planning, will go to Washington early in December to get acquainted with some of his future colleagues, especially the younger men.

"I feel that all of the new and younger men in Congress will serve as a nucleus for a really forward-looking Republican party — one geared to 1948, 1952 and 1956 rather than to the 1920's," said McCarthy.

And hopefully, in an editorial, the *Journal* wrote:

We think that Joseph McCarthy has it in him to be a good Senator and a good representative of his state. He knows Wisconsin and its problems. He has lived on our farms, in our small towns and cities. He knows our people in all phases of their life. He is possessed of great vigor and personal charm. He is where he is today largely because of the efforts of Joe McCarthy and should be beholden to no man. If Joe McCarthy will use his talents and his experience in behalf of the people of Wisconsin and the people of the United States, he can have a bright future in the United States Senate.

All of these statements were true, if a little exaggerated. But somehow the light would fail, and the Milwaukee *Journal* would be one of the first to notice the darkness.

20. Ring Around the Constitution

TUCKED AWAY IN THE OVERFLOWING CLOSET OF SENATOR-ELECT Joe McCarthy was a lively skeleton that began rattling during the primaries and reached a crescendo after Joe was safely ensconced in the Senate Office Building. To McCarthy, it was "a small matter, entirely technical." To his enemies, it was a clear-cut violation of the law.

McCarthy, once again, had run for office without resigning his judgeship. The Wisconsin constitution made this illegal in language that was too plain to permit any other interpretation. But what annoyed McCarthy's political enemies even more than the constitutional violation was the open manner in which the young candidate used the machinery of the judgeship for political purposes. For his campaign manager, he enlisted Urban Van Susteren, divorce counsel in his circuit court. This obviated the need to pay the campaign manager a salary, since Van Susteren was already on the public payroll. Together, McCarthy and Van Susteren planned their approach to the campaign. For a starter, they sent out letters soliciting funds; these were signed by Van Susteren, and written on circuit-court stationery. To some, the letters looked official, and they forked over. To others — some lawyers, for example — it seemed the essence of good judgment to kick in a few dollars "to help the judge out."

McCarthy also used circuit-court letterheads and envelopes

116

to disseminate copies of a ten-page speech he had made before the Eau Claire convention of Wisconsin's Young Republicans. The Madison *Capital Times* took due notice of this in an editorial that observed: "The Coleman candidate has not only refused to recognize the moral issue involved but is openly and brazenly using his office as circuit judge to advance his candidacy."

McCarthy ignored the comment, continued using circuit-court stationery for campaign propaganda, and made daily reference to himself as young Judge Joe. Finally his opponent, McMurray, brought the matter up in a public debate with McCarthy in Madison. "There is an issue of basic integrity involved here," McMurray charged. He buttressed his attack on McCarthy with Section 30 of the canon of ethics of the American Bar Association: "If a judge should decide to become a candidate for any office not judicial he should resign in order that it cannot be said that he is using the prestige of judicial position to promote his own candidacy or the success of his party."

But McCarthy drew himself up, cleared his throat, and announced: "I don't belong to the American Bar Association, and I'm not bound by its code." And he attacked the A.B.A. canon as "a code of ethics written by a few lawyers . . . without the force of law."

Earlier there had been a number of attempts to force the issue of McCarthy's violation of the state constitution. George R. Morton, Milwaukee lawyer and former member of the Constitution Committee of the American Bar Association, was the first to bring the matter up, which he did in a pre-convention meeting. But he was laughed off the floor by a packed house of McCarthy adherents. Later Convention Delegate Chester Solomon, of Milwaukee, argued that "the citizens should have a moral interest in keeping the judiciary out of politics." And Perry Stearns, another Republican, wrote to the voters:

At Oshkosh, attention was called to the fact that the Wisconsin constitution prohibits a circuit judge from holding other than judicial office during the term for which he is elected, and makes every vote cast for him void. What do you suppose McCarthy's answer was and is? None other than that the Wisconsin constitution does not apply to the United States Senators from Wisconsin.

McCarthy's arguments were not sufficient for State Treasurer John Smith, who, as a member of the three-man state board of canvassers, was empowered to sign the official certificate of nomination for McCarthy after the primary election. Smith refused to validate McCarthy's victory over La Follette. "I have read the constitution and it says that a judge cannot run for office," he pointed out. "The constitution is paramount." But after Smith sat down for a brief conference with Victor Johnston, a McCarthy campaign worker, he did a sudden about-face, signing the certification with the short statement: "They tell me it is all right."

Watching all this from his insurance office in Appleton was a bespectacled elfish man, Fred Felix Wettengel. Little by little Wettengel's mild amusement at McCarthy's antics changed into scorn, and then anger. Issuing a statement that "the lawyers in this state are all a bunch of weak sisters," Wettengel marched off to Madison to "take the law into my own hands." He petitioned the state Supreme Court to knock McCarthy's name off the ballot.

"Wettengel's hot potato," as it came to be known, was juggled around for several weeks, and finally emerged as a very thin mash. To the insurance man's demand that the Secretary of State should be prevented from certifying McCarthy's name on the ballot, the Supreme Court observed that the name had *already* been certified; therefore, there was nothing it could do about that. ("Wrongs already perpetrated cannot be corrected by an injunction," the court noted.) To Wettengel's second point, that McCarthy's certification on the ballot should be canceled, the Supreme

Court held that the Secretary of State had merely exercised his statutory duty in listing McCarthy's name and "he is without authority to act further in this matter." On Wettengel's third and fourth points, that any votes for McCarthy should be voided, the Supreme Court held that it was without jurisdiction. "Obviously this court should not intrude in the disposition of a question which, under the federal constitution, has been exclusively committed to another forum," the opinion said. The Court went on to say that Wettengel's action was premature, noting: "Obviously many things may yet happen to render unnecessary any determination of the ultimate question sought to be decided here. Judge McCarthy may be defeated in November, in which case the entire matter would become moot. Moreover it might be his misfortune to die before election or he might voluntarily withdraw before the race."

Having thus bobbed and weaved with all of Wettengel's punches, the Court raced back to its corner, breathing easier now that it had passed the issues along — to higher courts and to the voters. But McCarthy saw in the opinion a wonderful opportunity to show the voters that the Supreme Court recognized and sanctioned his candidacy. Proudly he set forth his thesis in an Appleton speech. Wettengel, in the audience, bristled, and he dashed off a telegram to Chief Justice Marvin B. Rosenberry. "Permit me to request that you check the speech as rendered," he wired, "and in turn come out with a certified public announcement for the press and thereby tell the electorate that the decision made by your honorable body . . . very definitely did not recognize and sanction the candidacy of Circuit Judge Joseph R. McCarthy . . . but that your decision stated in plain English that your Court took the position that it had no jurisdiction."

Rosenberry replied: "I have your telegram of the 25th and in reply, permit me to say that the mandate in the case which you brought is just as plain and explicit as the English

language can make it. If other people misrepresent the holding of the Court, that is a matter that is not within our
jurisdiction."

And there the issue rested until long after McCarthy's election to the Senate. It wasn't until 1949 that Miles McMillin,
a lawyer and editorial writer for the Madison *Capital Times,*
revived the case by petitioning the state board of bar commissioners to study McCarthy's violation of the lawyers' code
of ethics. The board perused the evidence and announced:

It is difficult to conceive of any conduct upon the part of a presiding
judge which would bring judges and courts into greater disrepute and
contempt than the conduct of [McCarthy]. . . . He, as an officer of the
court, knowingly and wilfully placed the gratification of his personal
ambition above the interests of the public and the rights of litigants.
The defendant, by his conduct, chose to defy the rules of ethical conduct prescribed by the constitution, the laws of the state of Wisconsin,
and the members of the profession, in order to gain a selfish personal
advantage. The gratification of his ambition was in defiance of the
declared public policy and laws of the state of Wisconsin.

The bar commissioners asked the Wisconsin Supreme
Court to disbar McCarthy. Once again the Court gingerly
stuck its finger into the political wind, calculated the direction it was blowing, and sat down to write an opinion that
would make everybody happy. This time the Court admitted
that McCarthy's flouting of the Wisconsin constitution was
"a clear violation." Furthermore, said the Court, "the defendant, by accepting the office of United States Senator
. . . did so in violation of the terms of the constitution and
laws of Wisconsin, and doing so violated his oath as a circuit
judge and as an attorney-at-law."

Having thus satisfied McCarthy's enemies, the Court ro-
tated a little in its judicial chair and set about pleasing
McCarthy's supporters. "[The violation] is one in a class by
itself which is not likely to be repeated," the Court said,
thus making the understatement of the year, since it was

unlikely that McCarthy would ever return to the circuit judgeship and run through the same dance-step again. Furthermore, said the Court, the voters had had a chance to rule on this same matter, and had chosen to elect McCarthy. And for one final clinching argument, the Court said that the defendant had "practiced law for many years" and "has never been derelict in the discharge of his duties and obligations as a lawyer." He could go and sin no more.

For McCarthy, it was a close call. But instead of letting the sleeping dog lie, he tried once again to turn it against his attackers. Despite the fact that the Supreme Court of Wisconsin had held that McCarthy "violated the terms of the constitution," "violated the laws of the State," "violated his oath as an attorney" and was "guilty of an infraction of the moral code," Joe announced: "In view of the unanimous decision of the court in dismissing the case as having no merit, it must be assumed that the bar commissioners knew their case had no merit and were playing politics or that they were completely incompetent as lawyers. In either event their actions are a disgrace to every honest, decent lawyer in the State of Wisconsin and they should resign."

21. Meeting the Press

THE DAY AFTER HIS ELECTION AS SENATOR FROM WISCONSIN, Joe McCarthy took off for Land o' Lakes on the northern border, checked into the plush King's Gateway Hotel, a former gambling casino, and flopped into bed at 7:30 P.M. After eighteen hours of sleep, he awoke, ate two steaks for breakfast, and climbed back under the covers. The following noon he was awakened by the jangling of his telephone. It was a reporter who wanted to know McCarthy's formula for success. Joe growled about being awakened "in the middle of the night," yawned and announced sleepily: "I don't claim to be any smarter than the next fellow, but I do claim that I work twice as hard and that's what I intend to do in Washington the next six years."

Having thus summed up his credo, McCarthy caught some more sleep, arose for a short session of duck hunting, and then launched his assault on Washington. *Life* magazine singled him out for special publicity and assigned a girl photographer to take pictures of his first day in the Senate. She dutifully tagged after him, clicking her camera. Then she told McCarthy that her assignment was finished except for one thing: the editors wanted to know what his first words had been on his arrival in the nation's capital. McCarthy replied gravely: "When we pulled into Washington, I stepped down from the train, took a look around and said, 'Hell, it's raining!'"

It was the time of the crippling coal strike which was occupying the attention of nearly every government official. On his second day in Washington, before he had been sworn in, Joe called a press conference. He felt that capital newsmen would be happy to learn the views of a two-fisted Midwesterner on a subject as important as the strike. The reporters were so amazed at his audacity that they showed up mainly out of curiosity. One of the first questions was: "Mr. McCarthy, what makes you think a new Senator is important enough to call a press conference?" Joe shrugged the question off, but it was obvious that Washington reporters would not be as soft a touch as the press in Wisconsin's north country.

"Now, then," Joe announced, after a silence in which it appeared that the newsmen's curiosity was turning to boredom, "let's get down to business. About this coal strike, I've got a solution. The Army should draft the striking coal miners. That would solve the problem."

The reporters didn't know whether to be amused or amazed. "What about John L. Lewis?" one of them asked.

"Draft him too," said Joe. He explained that once the miners and their "dictatorial" leader were in the Army, they would be forced to mine coal.

"And what if they refused?"

"Then they could be court-martialed for insubordination, and you know what that means."

The newsmen could hardly believe their ears. One of them, searching for a headline, asked: "You mean you would line up men like John L. Lewis and have them shot?"

Joe shrugged his shoulders as if to say, "What else?" And one by one the reporters backed out of the conference, convinced that here was a brash young man who would provide many a headline for the yellow segments of the press. But several days later the New York *Times* gave publicity to McCarthy's direct approach to the coal strike by quoting him:

. . . I believe the President should use his powers to immediately draft John L. Lewis into the armed services. Lewis should be directed to order his miners to mine coal. If he does not do that, he should be court-martialed. We should go straight down the line. If subordinates of Lewis fail to order the miners back, they should be court-martialed. All this talk about you can't put 400,000 miners in jail is a lot of stuff. They won't go to jail. They will mine coal first.

The *Army and Navy Bulletin,* unofficial service publication, protested: "The idea that the Army should be turned into a vast prison camp is ridiculous"; the profession of arms "is a noble calling"; proposals under which "the army would be considered a vast penal institution and compulsory enrollment in the ranks a punitive measure, reflect discredit upon their authors." The New York *Times* ran that story, too, and Joe gleefully tweaked his rabbit's foot. He had been in Washington only a few days and already he had been mentioned twice in the nation's Number One newspaper. This was to be his first inkling of how to make a name in the newspapers: throw out a wild statement and watch it grow. Clarifications, denials, rebuttals — day by day the story would pyramid, and soon all the readers would know that magic name: Joe McCarthy.

Even before taking his oath on January 3, 1947, Joe had set about buttering up the press. "When you want me, don't hesitate to call me, night or day," he told the correspondents. He sent to Wisconsin for huge wheels of cheese to donate to the National Press Club bar. And to get on the good side of the feminine correspondents, he invited eight of them to a fried-chicken dinner at the home of a Republican friend. The aproned, chef-hatted McCarthy greeted the women one by one as they arrived, then ducked into the kitchen to continue baking the biscuits and basting the chicken. The result was a rash of friendly stories about the personable young Senator.

Pleased by his first success, McCarthy jumped into the

social whirlpool with both feet, picked up a tuxedo, and
made himself available five and six nights a week. His name
cropped up in the society columns as an "eligible bachelor."
Over the cocktail glasses, Joe would hold forth on "a sensible
foreign policy, based on good old-fashioned horse trading."
He impressed many a young Washington belle with his
roundhouse condemnations of foreign-policy "experts," fellow legislators, State Department officials, and newspaper
"thinkers." He called them "timid, confused intellectuals,"
"cookie pushers," and "teacup strategists."

But in his first contacts with fellow Senators and government officials, a pronounced inferiority complex seemed to
show through his brave, boisterous front. At one of his first
lunches in the Senate cafeteria, he was ready to walk out
when Senator Claude Pepper of Florida walked in. Joe had
read about Pepper in the newspapers, had even attacked him
once or twice in political speeches, but had never seen him
in the flesh. So the freshman Senator from Wisconsin forgot
all about leaving, ignored his luncheon guest, Gerry Lorge,
and stared for several minutes in open-mouthed awe at the
veteran Senator from Florida.

Joe moved into a single room in the small Anacostia apartment of his office manager, Ray Kiermas, and spent night
after night cramming parliamentary procedure, foreign relations, and economics into his head. He began to study
Russian against the day when he hoped to be a major figure
on the Foreign Relations Committee and meet in dramatic
rendezvous with Marshal Stalin, there to thrash out face to
face the rugged business of power politics. But no textbooks
on any subject could ever teach him restraint; in discussions
with his fellow lawmakers, he was likely to come out with
scathing charges against persons and groups or to advocate
wild schemes for the conduct of foreign affairs, on the grounds
that "the old approach failed." Statements like these, made
in the presence of men who had spent their lives studying

such problems, brought only silence and condescending smiles. But early in the game, his colleagues learned not to argue with him: the inevitable result was a tirade.

In his first sessions on the floor of the Senate, McCarthy tended to be quiet. In an effort to appear dignified and respectable among his colleagues, he also junked dozens of loud ties he had brought from Wisconsin and replaced them with somber colors. He bought dark-blue suits, black shoes, and conservative hats. He painted himself as the rough, tough young war hero who could instantly throw off the mantle of battle for the mantle of statesmanship, and he spoke in public only when he was sure of himself. One night he drove to a veterans' hospital and boned up for a dramatic speech he wanted to make the next day. He talked to a few Marines, then returned to the Anacostia apartment and began to write. The next day he announced to his Senate colleagues:

Five minutes will be more than sufficient. I shall speak briefly as one of the 15 million men who took part in the fighting of World War II. I do not speak for them, but I speak as one of them. I had not planned to speak today, but yesterday afternoon and last evening I spent approximately three hours at one of the veterans' hospitals. I spent that time talking to some of my friends who are permanently crippled and disabled. Rather than speak for myself today in the Senate, I should like to repeat a few of the words that some of those men spoke to me.

One young man, a Marine with both legs amputated, said — I shall try to quote him as nearly verbatim as I can: "When we were in the Islands and the days were especially rough and the number of dead and injured mounted, and you would lie there at night and listen to the moan of the jungle on the one side and the music of the sea on the other, then the veil between life and death became very, very thin, and very often your good friends who had died that day were much nearer to you than those who still lived, and we knew then and know now that many of those men died because of graft and corruption which the Senate proposes to investigate."

The speech was a real tear-jerker. Sitting up late the night before, McCarthy had incorporated every saccharine line he could remember. The result was that Senators on both sides of the aisle applauded the earnest young man and hailed the speech as a rare example of brevity. During these early months in 1947, Joe McCarthy was at his peak in Washington. He was best-liked and most respected when he was still a befuddled and confused newcomer, when by day he sat quietly at his desk on the Senate floor, and by night mingled with the high society of the nation's capital. It was at one of these parties — an especially fashionable one — that he bared an innermost fear to a friend. Standing in the corner, watching the blue-blooded women and the tuxedoed men pass by, Joe tilted his head and whispered: "I wonder what these people would think if they knew I once raised chickens."

22. "Pepsi-Cola Kid"

SENATOR MCCARTHY PLAYED THE PART OF THE NEWCOMER TO Congress for a few months, obeying the Senate tradition that freshmen lawmakers should be seen and not heard. But soon he began to squirm and fidget in his seat on the majority side of the Eightieth Congress. He watched some of the senior Senators hold forth regally for hours on end, and he noticed that their remarks often showed up in the press next day. And when it came to a choice between tradition and publicity, Joe chose publicity.

One of his first efforts to this end came in conjunction with Senator Alexander Wiley, McCarthy's senior colleague from Wisconsin. Wiley took McCarthy by the hand, and together they introduced various bills and amendments to modify the tax laws on furs. Some of the measures passed, and some did not. But the fur farmers of Wisconsin — a powerful group — learned that they had another voice in the Senate. As McCarthy told a reporter, after pushing a law favorable to the fur interests: "Now the fur farmers think I'm God."

Meanwhile Joe was building up a close friendship with the ill-fated John Maragon, the ex-bootblack who had free run of the White House until his five-percenter activities were found out and his headquarters transferred to Petersburg Penitentiary. This friendship began, like many of McCarthy's liaisons, with a party. The affair was promoted by Maragon, who had an ax to grind. Together with Milton R. Polland, lobbyist for the Allied Molasses Company, Mara-

128

gon was trying to straighten out some of the company's difficulties with the Agriculture Department. Polland suggested a little "blowout" in honor of McCarthy on February 2, 1947, figuring that it would never hurt to curry the favor of even the newest Senators. And over a sumptuous meal in Washington's Old New Orleans restaurant, Maragon and McCarthy sealed their new friendship in wine.

It was a time in the life of John Maragon when he needed all the Senatorial good will he could promote. His "client," Allied Molasses Company, was on the Agriculture Department's black list for finagling a million and a half gallons of high-grade sugar-cane syrup at a time when sugar was scarce and closely rationed. Allied Molasses refined the syrup and sold it to the Pepsi-Cola Company. The Agriculture Department promptly clamped a restraint on Allied Molasses, preventing the company from receiving its quota of molasses until the million and a half gallons for Pepsi-Cola were made up. It was this order that Maragon and Polland were trying to crack.

When the government lifted controls on molasses, all the company's troubles were over. But Pepsi-Cola still champed at the bit over sugar controls, which had not yet been removed. So from Maragon and molasses, Joe shifted his attention to Pepsi-Cola and another colorful friend — handsome, cavalier Russell M. Arundel, wealthy sportsman, gentleman farmer, gilt-edged lobbyist, and self-styled Prince of Outer Baldonia. This mysterious province consisted of an island off the coast of Nova Scotia, where the Prince was in the habit of taking guests for week-end fishing trips. In fact, Arundel seemed to have a weakness for islands and once threw a lavish stag party for three hundred prominent Democrats, including President Harry Truman, on Jefferson Island in Chesapeake Bay. This outing was described by the Boston *Herald* as a "two-day frolic which made the Biblical feast of Belshazzar look like a White Tower feed."

The free-spending Arundel was the Washington spokes-man for a long list of sugar interests, including Puerto Rican firms whose Spanish names he himself had difficulty in remembering. He owned the Pepsi-Cola bottling plant on Long Island and, for a while, the Pepsi-Cola plant supplying northern Virginia.

Along with Arundel, McCarthy included Pepsi-Cola Presi-dent Walter Mack in his widening circle of friends. Joe shared breakfasts, lunches, and suppers with Mack, and turned up at Pepsi-Cola lobbying parties. So it was a natural sequence that Arundel (who has since denied that his con-nection with McCarthy had anything to do with sugar) and Mack should take up their sugar problems with Senator Joe. He carried the ball so openly that he became known in Washington newspaper circles as the "Pepsi-Cola Kid." He started off by introducing a bill "to prevent sugar hoarding and to continue export controls, as a gradual way out of rationing." This was the first blow in a successful fight to defeat sugar rationing at a time when sugar was still ex-tremely scarce.

Step by step, McCarthy set about "proving" that there was ample sugar on hand. "Either we have sufficient sugar to do away with rationing," he said in the Senate, "or we have not. It is a matter of tons." Then he began a long disserta-tion on sugar supplies, with thirteen quotations of figures, carefully calculated to leave his Senatorial auditors in con-fusion. He mentioned harvesting time in Cuba, international agreements on Cuban sugar, and surpluses of sugar in Ar-gentina, Peru, and Brazil. His conclusion, delivered with a positive air: "That will give us 791,000 tons of sugar upon which we had not counted."

Senator Ralph Flanders of Vermont, noticing that Mc-Carthy had been flagrantly violating the arithmetical precept that oranges and apples cannot be added in the same column, remarked: "The Senator from Wisconsin has raised questions

so fast that I am having difficulty in keeping up with him.
. . . On the various points on which I am at issue with the
Senator from Wisconsin, I wish to say that we cannot deal
cavalierly with the question of sugar stocks, figures regarding
the Cuban crop, the receipts, the amounts — "

"Mr. President," McCarthy interrupted, "I sat here for
four hours yesterday while [Flanders] held the floor on this
subject. I do not object to being asked questions, but I do
not think the Senator should make a speech at this time. . . ."

Another Senator, a Bible-quoting veteran of many a hard-
fought debate, sat back and watched this maneuvering
through narrowing eyes. Senator Charles Tobey hailed from
New Hampshire, where many of his constituents devoted
long months to canning, a process that requires a lot of sugar.
And he noticed that the McCarthy bill was aimed at providing more sugar for industrial users, to the detriment of housewives. But Joe claimed to be on the housewives' side and
announced: "Within the past ten minutes I have received
word from the Department of Agriculture that they . . .
wish to discuss with us the possibility of agreeing to make
available to the housewife during the third quarter — that
is, during the canning season — a total allotment of 20
pounds of sugar. . . ."

Suspicious of McCarthy, Senator Tobey walked to a telephone and called Agriculture Secretary Clinton Anderson.
When he had his answer, Tobey took the floor. "The Department of Agriculture's announced position was misrepresented
by the Senator from Wisconsin today," he said. "Here is
the answer which came from Secretary Anderson just three
minutes ago, over the telephone, to me: 'I authorize you to
state that I have not at any time made a statement that we
can give more sugar for home consumption now . . . there
is no more sugar available for home consumption. But if any
more does come across the horizon, we will allocate it to the
housewives.' That is Secretary Anderson's statement, and it

refutes the statement which has been made by the Senator from Wisconsin."

McCarthy bristled at Tobey's tactics in doublechecking a McCarthy statement. He jumped to the floor and shouted: "Then, Mr. President, let me say that in view of the unquestioned figures, I do not give a tinker's dam what Secretary Anderson says about the matter. The sugar is here."

"But [Anderson] has said the sugar is not available," Tobey persisted. "That is his own statement. Yet the Senator from Wisconsin, putting himself in a higher orbit above the Secretary of Agriculture, says the sugar is available. On the question of veracity, I would not choose between the two gentlemen, but on a question of fact, I take the Secretary of Agriculture any time."

McCarthy's anger knew no bounds. He rose to the floor and announced that he was quoting a statement made by Tobey to him a few days before. Tobey had told him, McCarthy said, that he, Tobey, was "going to introduce some type of fictitious amendment which in effect will do nothing more nor less than deceive the housewife."

Tobey, red-faced and angry, cried: "Mr. President, that is a personal challenge, and I demand an opportunity to answer it." There was a squabble over who had the floor, and Tobey won out. "I heard the statement by the Senator from Wisconsin," Tobey said. "My hearing is fairly good. . . . He charged that my amendment is deceptive and fictitious. I take exception to his derogatory remarks. The Senator's statement, I submit, far contravenes the truth, to put it plainly. I want to go a little further and say that this amendment was not authored as a fictitious statement, but as an honest-to-God amendment — as sincerely as anything the Senator from Wisconsin ever wanted to do."

McCarthy interrupted: "Mr. President — "

"I am not quite through yet, sir," Tobey snapped. "I point out that the Senator is confusing the Senate of the United

States by a heterogeneous mass of figures which will not stand the test of accuracy. . . ." And after a vote, the Tobey amendment passed.

But McCarthy continued his attack on the over-all bill. The Senate had fixed March 31, 1948, as the tentative date for lifting sugar controls. McCarthy, seeing that it would be impossible to kill sugar rationing on the spot, set about shortening its life. His amendment to lift controls five months earlier — by October 31, 1947 — passed, despite a ringing oration by Tobey: "There is a certain clique in this country which is going to capitalize on the action we take today in changing the date to the 31st of October. The speculators are singing a Te Deum in their hearts tonight throughout the country. They are singing 'Hail, hail, the gang's all here. We are ready for the kill.' By the removing of controls on October 31, the speculators are being put on notice that the doors are ajar. The flood-gates of speculative profit are open to greedy hearts. . . . I want the country to know where the blame lies. It lies," he said, looking straight at McCarthy, "with a group in my own party, in the Republican party, who have been trying to sabotage this measure at every possible opportunity."

Ironically, Senator McCarthy voted against the final version of the bill, even though it incorporated many of his own scuttling amendments. Joe was angry because the Senators had turned down the amendment closest to his heart — to give the industrial users an equal share with the consuming public of any extra allocation of sugar.

After the tumult and uproar of the sugar debate, an interesting sequel took place in quiet and confidence. Joe's roller-coaster ride on the stock market had taken a sudden dive, and he desperately needed more security to keep from being derailed. So he found a friend who would make good his note for $20,000. The friend's name: Russell M. Arundel, the Prince of Outer Baldonia.

Joe telephoned the news to his banker, Matt Schuh, of Appleton, Wisconsin, president of the Appleton State Bank. And in a letter dated December 4, 1947, Schuh replied:

DEAR JOE:

In accordance with our telephone conversation of today, I am enclosing herein a note for $20,000, for a period of six months which you are going to sign and have endorsed by Russell M. Arundel. Have Mr. Arundel endorse the note on the back so in the event it isn't taken care of on the day it is due, we won't have to protest it. Kindly date the note the day it is signed and also when returning the note, give us Mr. Arundel's complete address.

I will be looking forward to seeing you soon.

> Yours very truly,
> MATT
> *President*

P.S. Try to get this note back to us by return mail.

And so before the year was ended, Joe's Senate battle for his Pepsi-Cola friends had paid off. He rushed a letter back to Banker Schuh on December 9, 1947:

DEAR MATT:

Enclosed you will find my note in the amount of $20,000.00, endorsed by Russell M. Arundel. His residence is Warrenton, Virginia, and that is the address he would prefer your using. He does, however, have a Washington office at 1200 18th Street, N.W.

He tells me that if at any time the bank finds it inconvenient to hold his $20,000.00 note, Matt, that he can have it transferred to Washington. However, I assume that you have looked up his credit and find that he is good for an amount far in excess of this. If this is true I, naturally, prefer having one of your banks hold it.

I wish you would not use this $20,000.00, Matt, to reduce the old note but hold it until I see or call you.

> Sincerely yours,
> JOE

Joe had good reason for his faith in Arundel's credit standing, for the Prince of Outer Baldonia lived high, wide, and handsome. Called on the Congressional carpet in 1944 to explain his lobbying activities, he had testified that his farm

alone brought in $60,000 a year. The Congressmen had
recited figures showing that Arundel's deposits at the Munsey
Trust Company in Washington, D. C., totaled $524,416.16
from January 1, 1940, to August 10, 1944 — a cool half-million
dollars. "Is that about right?" the Congressmen asked. "I
don't know," the Prince replied with a shrug. "It probably is."

So Joe was taken aback when another letter arrived from
Matt Schuh four months later. Wrote the banker:

> As to the note which we are carrying for $20,000.00 endorsed by
> Russell M. Arundel, the directors haven't looked too favorably on this
> note for the reason that Mr. Arundel hasn't any liquid assets shown on
> his statement, as his statement shows mostly some local companies
> which he controls and real estate which is encumbered. Therefore, I
> think you should advise Mr. Arundel to be prepared to pay this note
> when it is due on June 8, 1948.

But McCarthy stalled and wangled an extension. Finally,
on September 29, 1948, Schuh wrote again:

> Last week we were finished with an examination by the state [bank-
> ing] department and they placed your note endorsed by Russell
> Arundel on the objectionable list, meaning that we either must get the
> note paid within the next ten days or charge it off. Of course, when it
> comes to charging it off, it would mean immediately handing it out
> for collection.

But Joe ignored the ten-day deadline for payment and received another letter from Banker Schuh fourteen days later:

> I received your letter of October 9th, but in that letter you made no
> mention of our letter to you of September 29th with reference to the
> Arundel note. Lawrence tells me that he heard through Bill Lawlor
> that it is your intention to sell the preferred stock of Chicago, Mil-
> waukee, St. Paul & Pacific and pay the Arundel note. This, of course,
> will lower your collateral by $20,000.00 and surely it would put both
> you and me in the doghouse.

But Joe managed to hold off the crisis until January 4,
1949, when the state banking department ordered the Apple-

ton bank to charge the Arundel note off its books. (See Chapter 39 for further details.)

Meanwhile, Joe's friendship with John Maragon slowly dissolved, and he even seemed to forget the existence of Milton R. Polland, who had thrown the big party at the Old New Orleans. Two years later, when Polland was being questioned by the Senate Committee on Expenditures, Committee Counsel William P. Rogers asked Polland how he was connected with the Allied Molasses Company.

McCarthy interrupted: "I didn't get the name of this company." Polland repeated it for the third time.

"That was run by your nephew, did you say?" McCarthy asked.

"Yes."

"And his name was what?"

"Harold Ross."

"Harold Ross?"

"R-o-s-s."

"What is the name of the town in which they do business?" McCarthy asked, although the name of the town had been mentioned several times.

"Perth Amboy, New Jersey," Polland said.

"Perth Amboy, New Jersey?"

"Yes."

Reporters covering the session watched this dialogue closely, impressed by the Wisconsin Senator's obvious desire to keep all facts straight. Only a few knew that names like Harold Ross, Allied Molasses Company, and Perth Amboy were old hat to McCarthy.

Of course, McCarthy still had the problem of dissociating himself from Maragon, who was by now in disrepute around Washington as a five-percenter. Joe severed this cord with one deft clip of his Senatorial scissors. Maragon had testified that he "received no money because of any negotiation with the government" on behalf of Allied Molasses Company.

When Polland testified later that he had indeed paid Maragon for the maneuver involving Allied Molasses and Pepsi-Cola, McCarthy displayed all the signs of shock. White-faced and indignant, he demanded that Maragon be indicted for perjury. Chairman Hoey pointed out that it would be unfair to indict anyone until all the evidence was in.

But McCarthy insisted again on a perjury prosecution, throwing in a demand that Maragon be prosecuted on an old perfume-smuggling charge. And when Maragon returned for another appearance before the Committee, Senator Joe took charge. He asked Maragon — whom he called "John" — if he had made any threatening phone calls to members of the Committee. Maragon refused to answer, whereupon McCarthy quipped: "You talk less today than I have ever heard you."

Spectators watching the interrogation would never have guessed that angler McCarthy and the hooked-and-wriggling Maragon were old poker-playing, party-going comrades.

23. Housing Expert

ALL THROUGH THE FIRST SESSION OF THE EIGHTIETH CONGRESS
in 1947, Senator Joe McCarthy thrashed about looking for
issues. He watched other Senators bask in the glitter of the
spotlight day after day, while he struggled along unspectacu-
larly in the syrupy interests of Pepsi-Cola.

Briefly he considered the issue of Communism as a vehicle
for lifting his name into the headlines. He introduced a bill
aimed at encouraging labor unions to inform on any Communists in their midst and forcing management to fire them.
But Senator Robert Taft of Ohio was on his feet in a minute.
"In the first place, is it necessary to compel employers to fire
Communists?" he asked. "Can we not trust the employers to
do it without writing into the bill a specific clause requiring
them to do it?" McCarthy thought not. But objections were
so violent that he let the bill drop.

A month later he read into the *Congressional Record* a long
resolution adopted by the Green Bay Diocesan Union of Holy
Name Societies, meeting in Shawano, Wisconsin. It said, in
part:

> The Communistic powers are insidiously carrying on their avowed
> determination to dominate the earth. . . . A woeful and dangerous
> tendency is to be seen on the part of many in high places to evade,
> hedge and compromise in these tragic circumstances, but we rejoice in
> what seems to be the *determination of the new Secretary of State*
> [George Marshall] to set a pattern for American diplomacy which
> seems to be taking the initiative in China, Korea, Japan, the Middle

East and virtually throughout the world, thus putting Communism on the defensive.

But neither the labor bill nor the Shawano resolution resulted in more than tiny squibs in the newspapers. It would be another four years before Joe would hit the journalistic jackpot with Marshall's name. Then the headlines he had failed to get by praising Marshall for "putting Communism on the defensive" Joe would finally stir up by accusing Marshall of participating in the Communist conspiracy — "a conspiracy so immense and an infamy so black," Joe would say, "as to dwarf any previous such venture in the history of man."

In the meantime, Joe turned to veterans' issues for publicity. He dropped a handful of bills into the hopper — some practical, some impractical, but all newsworthy in the proveteran atmosphere of the post-war period. He joined with fifteen other Senators to introduce a bill incorporating AMVETs; fought to continue certain wartime tax exemptions for servicemen two years after the war had ended; offered a bill to provide new homes for paraplegic veterans, and another for continued research in development of prosthetic appliances; and announced that if Congress unified the Armed Forces, the nation would "live to regret it more than any other piece of legislation of the last century."

Mindful of his ties to the Marine Corps, McCarthy fought tooth and nail to make sure that the Leathernecks lost none of their sovereignty in the Armed Forces unification bill. One of his proposed amendments — later rejected — asked that none of the Marine Corps's "existing functions or missions be transferred to other services."

"I feel that if, for example, it is to be decided at some future time that naval planes should not protect shipping, if it be decided that the Marine amphibious units should be disposed of, it should be done by the Congress, and not be left to the whim and caprice of some supersecretary who at that particular moment might happen to hold the position of authority," McCarthy explained.

Senator Henry Cabot Lodge of Massachusetts took immediate objection to the use of the word "supersecretary." "I think that it's a sort of smear word," he said, "and I do not think it is accurate."

Senator Raymond Baldwin of Connecticut also took the floor to protest McCarthy's amendment. He said he could envision a situation in wartime when there might be an Army convoy needing protection, and nothing but Marine planes on hand. Under McCarthy's amendment, Baldwin pointed out, the convoy would have to sail unprotected, unless Congress jumped in and passed a quick law granting a special dispensation.

Later Senator Lister Hill of Alabama announced that General Alexander Vandegrift, Marine Corps Commandant, had approved of the unification bill unimproved by McCarthy's amendment. "The mere fact that the committee may have sold General Vandegrift a bill of goods," McCarthy stormed, "does not make this [bill] right." But the Senate, by a vote of 52 to 19, left the bill intact — minus the amendment — despite a McCarthy warning that the bill "can and will in the next twenty years give to the military complete and absolute dictatorial control over civilian life."

Another McCarthy bill, possibly aimed at Bob La Follette, made headlines, but only in the Wisconsin papers. The measure asked that members of Congress and their wives be prohibited from holding radio-station licenses. Fellow Senators felt that the bill was motivated by personal animosity, and the measure — S.1309 — was pigeonholed.

After jabbing at a dozen different issues, Joe finally came into full stature with a two-fisted, roughhouse attack on public housing. This was just the first round in the post-war housing fight, which found Joe not on the side of his fellow veterans but in the corner of the real-estate lobby. The result was another nickname for the man already known as "Tail-Gunner Joe" and the "Pepsi-Cola Kid"; now he was dubbed "the water boy of the real estate lobby" — a name bestowed on him by Mayor Wendt of Racine, Wisconsin. "The homeless people of Wisconsin can thank Senator McCarthy for keeping them homeless," the Mayor observed. Spokesmen for other states said the same, and then sat back and tried to figure how it all came to pass.

The real explanation probably began with Walter Harnischfeger, a Milwaukee industrialist, who was quick to see that the man who could mass-build inexpensive houses in the post-war era would make a fortune. But standing between Harnischfeger and his dream of assembly-line houses stood the specter of public housing, which promised to solve the housing shortage on a national basis. Harnischfeger needed someone to fight public housing in the Senate, and so he threw his financial weight behind McCarthy.

"I'm for public housing," Joe had said publicly, "but that is only a part of the answer." The rest of the answer took several months to unfold, beginning with a sleeper play that ultimately enabled him as a freshman Senator to quarterback all housing legislation. McCarthy and Senator Chappie Revercomb of West Virginia asked Congress to set up a committee to investigate housing conditions all over the nation. The resolution got the approval of both houses of Congress, and a special fourteen-man committee was formed. But to Joe's dismay he discovered that the committee had a conscience — the same straight-laced Senator Tobey who had mixed with McCarthy before. To make matters worse, Tobey was the senior Republican and was entitled to the chairmanship under the unwritten rules of Senate seniority.

On August 19, the Housing Committee met on short notice to go through the motions of picking its chairman and vice-chairman. Five members of the Committee were absent, but they had entrusted their votes to others. McCarthy held one such proxy, and Tobey held four. This would have assured Tobey the chairmanship. But with the press and the public shut out of the meeting, Freshman McCarthy slyly moved that no proxies be accepted. Representative Wright Patman of Texas was flabbergasted. The wishes of absentees, he said, had been observed for twenty years, and he saw no reason why that long-standing tradition should be changed at the whim of a rooky Senator. Senator John Sparkman of Alabama pointed out that many members of the Committee had not received notice of the meeting until it was too late, and that the only way they could vote would be by proxy. He asked McCarthy to withdraw the motion to keep the absent members from feeling "that they've had something put over on them." And Senator Tobey exclaimed: "McCarthy whispered around and found out what proxies we had before he made the motion. I can't take it, frankly. Let's play our cards out on the table here!"

This was all right with Joe, since he knew the deck was stacked. For days before, he had made frantic phone calls to make sure that all Committee members who opposed public housing would be present. With the majority in the room on his side, Joe's motion to ignore proxies passed. This put McCarthy in the driver's seat; he made Representative Ralph Gamble, of New York, chairman and modestly took the vice-chairmanship for himself. Senator Tobey — who later gained fame as God's angry man of the Senate crime committee — was furious. And he responded with a torrent of Biblical language and clichés, all mixed up in a hash of angry rhetoric. "This child [the Committee] is born as a result of malpractice," he said. "I hope the forceps didn't hurt it. Behold, I am a good soldier in the ranks with malice toward none. But I do like straight shooting."

As for McCarthy, he emerged from the meeting grinning from ear to ear. "I frankly didn't want Tobey to be chairman," he told reporters. "He thinks the sole answer to the problem is public housing. . . . It doesn't make much difference who the chairman is. We shouldn't be sidetracked by personal animosity between two Senators."

But the most surprised man to emerge from the committee room was the new chairman, Representative Gamble. As an ardent spokesman for the real-estate interests, Gamble was desirous of winning the chairmanship, but he had thought that his obvious prejudice in favor of the realtors would disqualify him in the eyes of the other Committee members. As he told reporters later: "I didn't have the remotest thought of being chairman. I certainly didn't seek it. It was thrust upon me, you might say."

But Gamble, having received the lateral from quarterback McCarthy, proceeded to carry the ball. He suggested that a hefty cut of the Committee's $100,000 budget be used "for a good staff."

"Do you have any ideas, Joe?" he asked.

"Yeah," Joe said, "I've got a couple of good people in mind."

He referred to the New York public-relations firm of Bell, Jones and Taylor, which had turned out real-estate propaganda for the National Association of Home Builders, the U. S. Savings and Loan League, and the National Association of Real Estate Boards. Bell, Jones and Taylor was the real-estate lobby's No. 1 press agent.

But with this and similar maneuvers, McCarthy was able to take command of the housing probe and subvert it to the interests of the real-estate lobby. Gamble, chairman of the Committee, soon became nothing more than a figurehead. When the Committee went on the road to hold its hearings, it was McCarthy who presided. His every move was calculated to show public housing in its worst light and private building in its best. The answer, he said — glancing in the general direction of his friend Harnischfeger in Milwaukee — lay in mass-produced houses, not in public housing. And instead of gleaning information on housing problems, the McCarthy-led Committee served only to spread the gospel of the pre-fab house from Maine to California.

A typical performance of the Committee's roadshow took place in Milwaukee on November 10, 1947. McCarthy made a great show of seating Mayor Bohn next to him. By the rules of protocol, the Mayor also should have been the first witness to tell the story of Milwaukee's critical housing problem. But Joe allowed Bohn to twiddle his thumbs until finally the Mayor had to file his statement and return to official city business. Another who sat in the wings but was never called on stage was the chairman of the Milwaukee Common Council's housing committee, who had held city-wide hearings of his own and who could have summed up the Milwaukee housing problem in a short, succinct statement. Joe, meanwhile, was taking up time with contractors and building-suppliers who spoke the language of the real-estate lobby.

The few witnesses who indicated support for the public-housing provisions of the Taft-Ellender-Wagner bill were harassed by Acting Chairman McCarthy. "If you want to endorse one bill out of the 255 pending before Congress," he announced, "you'd better know every detail of that bill before you testify here." Anyone who flew in the face of this directive and mentioned the T-E-W bill was asked technical questions about this-or-that obscure section of the bill. One member of the Madison housing authority, who had traveled to Milwaukee to testify, saw red over McCarthy's antics: he observed aloud that Joe seemed to be "enjoying himself" asking detailed questions about an involved and complicated bill that was not even understood in all its details by experts. And Mrs. W. A. Hambley, who represented the Joint Action Committee for Better Housing, pointed out scathingly that McCarthy himself had shown ignorance of the T-E-W bill in at least two cases.

By this time, spokesmen for public-interest groups were beginning to make themselves heard, and Joe announced that he had to catch a 4:30 plane. But bad weather closed in on the Milwaukee airport, grounded all traffic, and forced McCarthy to continue the hearing until almost all the witnesses had been heard. The transcript of the hearing, however, eliminated much of the effectiveness of the public-interest speakers. Someone had deftly edited their remarks, cutting out their most telling arguments, and polishing the Senator's questioning into glittering prose.

In this trip across the country, McCarthy left no brick unturned to defame any public-housing development he visited. After a trip to the 1,424-unit Rego Park Veterans' Housing Project in New York City, he pronounced the place a "breeding ground for Communism."

"This is the first time I've seen a deliberately created slum area, at federal expense," Senator McCarthy said. "This housing was built over a garbage disposal area. Wives of veterans were wading in mud up to their ankles to hang out the washing. I, myself, saw four dead rats. Gas from the garbage was seeping up from the mud and slime. Baby carriages were up to their hubs in mud."

Obviously the first to complain about conditions like these should have been the tenants. But instead of rallying around Senator McCarthy's banner and demanding that Rego Park be cleaned up, the tenants announced that, although they knew the development had its shortcomings, the place was not nearly as bad as McCarthy had painted it. The tenants' association observed that Joe was "interested not so much in seeing to it that the veterans are provided with a place to live, but with arousing sentiment against continuing the very vital program of public housing."

Joe McCarthy was so eager to please private housing interests that one night he forgot all about being impartial and wielded the gavel at a session of the Building Officials

Conference of America in Columbus, Ohio. While two hundred construction experts looked on, Joe congratulated the conference for developing a model building code for all cities throughout the country. He did not mention the fact that the building code which pleased him so much would also make life easier for the pre-fab manufacturers, who were closest to his heart.

Later he lowered his mask of impartiality another notch to congratulate the American Legion on its criticism of the Taft-Ellender-Wagner housing bill. But he overlooked the fact that the Legion's housing committee had been dominated by recognized real-estate men. And Bill Todd, of Atlanta, Georgia, had shouted over the microphone at the Legion convention: "Go home and tell your folks you voted *no* on housing for veterans."

As a result of the ripening smell of the "impartial" housing probe, at least some members of the populace became convinced that McCarthy was not exactly a white knight pursuing the Holy Grail of housing for the unhoused. In 1947, Joe had been able to talk the AMVETs into ignoring the T-E-W bill; but at the 1948 AMVET convention, his ringing personal appeal was not enough to keep the veterans from voting approval of the bill. Almost simultaneously, Mayor Wendt issued his famous statement calling McCarthy "the water boy of the real estate lobby." Joe was also booed at a meeting of the National Veterans' Housing Conference, where Senator Tobey announced: "Don't be misled by men in public life down here with substitute legislation. . . . The little people can't be helped by lobbies." Representative Franklin D. Roosevelt, Jr., said: "It is a shock to see the representatives of the people turn away from the needs of the many to bow and scrape before the real estate lobby." And Leo Goodman, chairman of the CIO housing committee, reminded McCarthy that he had promised to solve the hous-

ing problem or resign; Goodman observed it was time Mc-
Carthy did one or the other.

Clearly, the heat was on. Joe raced back to Washington
and looked about for a scapegoat to distract public attention
from his labors on behalf of the real-estate lobby. Conveniently, a 300-pound grey-marketeer named Isador Ginsberg trotted onstage. Inquisitor McCarthy tore Ginsberg
limb from limb on the witness stand. Ginsberg's appearance
did nothing to solve the national housing problem, but it
served as a timely attention-getter after McCarthy's cross-
country hearings.

24. Ginsberg and Gypsum

THE GINSBERG INQUISITION WAS RIGHT DOWN SENATOR McCarthy's alley. To begin with, grey-marketeers were bleeding Joe's friends, the pre-fab manufacturers. Sometimes a long production line of mass-produced houses would sit idle for weeks because a single hard-to-get material was not available. This would force the manufacturers to hunt up a grey-marketeer, who would obtain the material and sell it to them at an exorbitant price. One such material was gypsum, and the biggest dealer — physically if not financially — was Isador Ginsberg. After two pre-fab manufacturers, Andrew Higgins of New Orleans and William Levitt of Manhasset, New York, had testified that grey-marketeers were adding 50 per cent to the cost of housing, Joe unleashed a broadside attack on Ginsberg, calling him "the most vicious of the grey-marketeers." He condemned what "men like Ginsberg are doing," whereupon the balloon-shaped witness drew himself up and announced: "Sir, men like Ginsberg are as proud as men like McCarthy."

McCarthy threatened to hold Ginsberg in contempt unless he handed over a list of dealers from whom he had purchased gypsum. The witness tried to reply by reading a statement into the record, but McCarthy interrupted to read what he described as "information on Ginsberg's background." The "information" included the claim that Ginsberg had been charged with grand larceny three times. The portly witness issued an angry denial. He shouted that the Committee was not "sitting as a grand jury," and had no right to make such statements."

Ordinarily Ginsberg's remarks would have been glossed over as self-serving and excusatory. But in this case, the witness had the backing of Representative Wright Patman of Texas and several other members of the Committee. Patman protested that McCarthy "had violated every law of procedure." And the Texas Congressman put his finger squarely on the real issue when he announced that the hearing was doing "absolutely nothing" to solve the housing problem, which was its assignment.

After Ginsberg testified that he handled only "three-fortieths of 1 per cent" of the gypsum business, Patman said to McCarthy: "I'm not interested in three-fortieths of 1 per cent. Let's get the gypsum companies up here and get at the 100 per cent."

"Pat," McCarthy said, "if you'll just give me time, that's what we'll do. We've even got the man in the room." And when Ginsberg tried to talk again, McCarthy shouted: "Let's not get excited, Mr. Ginsberg."

"Excited?" Ginsberg roared. "I'm not excited. I'm very calm. You haven't heard me when I get excited."

The whole Ginsberg hearing was a madhouse, and it made fascinating stories for the newspapers. There was so much tumult and shouting, so much "color" and human interest, that the names "McCarthy" and "Ginsberg" became known from coast to coast. And by the time the grey-marketeer was led away to face criminal charges, Senator Joe had accomplished his objective. The tweedledum and tweedledee housing hearings conducted by Vice-Chairman McCarthy were forgotten in the publicity fanfare about grey-marketeers. Joe became a reaccredited authority on housing, and he set about producing a Committee report that would kick the last gasp of breath from the inert form of public housing.

For literary assistance, he turned again to the real-estate lobby's press agents — Bell, Jones and Taylor. Together, they produced the first draft of a scathing attack on all forms of public housing. One Senator who read the version announced: "Why, you'd think only Rabbis, Priests and Communists had any use for public housing!" McCarthy, Gamble, and the advertising agency pulled the report back and rewrote it, softening some of the harsher phrases. But still the full Housing Committee refused to give its approval. Finally, Senators Tobey of New Hampshire, Flanders of Vermont, and Wagner of New York despaired of getting any sort of fair report from the McCarthy-Gamble real-estate gang controlling the Committee. So they assigned their own staff employees to the task, and a twenty-page report was approved on March 12, 1948. Chairman Gamble sat down and wept. He said the report repudiated his leadership. But Joe announced to the press that he had in fact won. "It makes no difference who gets the credit," he said, "so long as the objectives are obtained."

But McCarthy's objectives had not been obtained, and he knew it. On March 22, the *Congressional Record* noted that "Mr. McCarthy . . . submitted his individual views relative to the report . . . which were ordered to be printed." Joe was dissenting, and he had arranged to have his personal views printed under the guise of an official Committee publication. He had been ordered to print only "a limited number" of this report, and to include on its cover the phrase that it did "not reflect the views of the committee." But the McCarthy booklet appeared in great quantity and without the qualifying phrase on its cover. There were charges that McCarthy and Gamble sent large numbers of Joint Housing Committee envelopes to the National Association of Home Builders and the National Association of Real Estate Boards, so that these groups could distribute the McCarthy report in "official" envelopes. And persons who wrote in for copies of the Committee report mysteriously obtained the McCarthy booklet instead.

Later in 1948, when the Taft-Ellender-Wagner bill came up for Senate debate, McCarthy introduced substitutes to lift all of its public-housing sections. His tactics moved Senator Wayne Morse, of Oregon, to announce that he was voting against the McCarthy substitute bill "not only because of its demerits but also because of the parliamentary procedure which is being used in connection with it." Morse referred to McCarthy's assaults on his fellow Senators, described by the New York *Post* as "terrier tactics":

> With a senator like Flanders who spoke in broad philosophical terms, McCarthy would interrupt repeatedly to ask his impression of the meaning of some words on the fifth line of page 27, offering revisions, modifications, and corrections of his own until Flanders was dizzy. Then he would purringly sympathize with Flanders for not knowing what the measure was all about. With a senator like Sparkman who understood the technicalities of the bill as well as he did or better, McCarthy would resort to rhetorical broadsides about "socialism."

In this manner, Joe overplayed his hand, and the Senate held firm on the T-E-W bill. But the House, led by the Gamble faction, threw the bill out, and Congress adjourned without passing any major housing legislation. When President Truman called a special session the following summer, Senator Taft withdrew from the battle for his own public-housing bill long enough to allow passage of the McCarthy measure. Thus were the people deprived of public housing at a time when thousands of veterans and non-veterans alike were living in garages and attics from coast to coast.

25. Lustron: Bankruptcy and Profits

THE LUSTRON AFFAIR IS A CASE HISTORY OF HOW TO MAKE money by going bankrupt. The company was engaged in manufacturing pastel-tinted porcelain-and-aluminum houses; a little fast talking and influence-buying in Washington enabled the firm to snag $37,500,000 in taxpayers' money to finance its noble experiment. Merl Young, erstwhile messenger boy who traveled in White House company, first helped to arrange the deal with the Reconstruction Finance Corporation, then popped up as Lustron's $18,000-a-year vice-president. Carl Strandlund, the president, dragged down a $50,000-a-year salary. Both men made money; and when Lustron went broke in three short years, it was the taxpayer who was left holding the empty purse.

When the scandal finally exploded in Washington, there was so much talk about mink coats, influence-peddling, and perjured testimony that no one paid much attention to a peculiar-smelling portion of the Lustron stew. The company, two years before its assets went down the drain, had peeled $10,000 off the bankroll it had borrowed from the taxpayers, and had gratefully handed the money to Senator Joe McCarthy.

Seldom in American political history had a cash pay-off been so fully earned. McCarthy, in his role as self-appointed medicine man for American housing, had used his high position to further the cause of pre-fabricated houses. He journeyed from town to town booming pre-fabs as the cure-all

for the housing ailment; and in Columbus he went straight to
the Lustron plant to learn firsthand about the advantages
of aluminum housing.

A fast friendship developed between McCarthy and
Strandlund, a friendship that flourished in spite of some unfriendly testimony about Lustron at a Joint Housing Committee hearing in Washington. The witness was Robert
Byers, another Columbus builder, who had earlier engaged
in a business flirtation with McCarthy that profited the
Senator by at least $1,000 plus "whiskey and entertainment."
But by this time Joe was tiring of Byers, preferring instead
the attentions of the fat-and-wealthy Lustron company. And
it embarrassed Joe that Byers insisted upon dragging Lustron
into his testimony. Among other things, Byers charged that
Lustron was using its "government capital" to corral labor,
thus making it impossible for the Byers firm to hire construction crews at reasonable wages. "I recommend this
Committee make a thorough investigation into a government
loan to Lustron," Byers said. "One of these aluminum houses
was built for their president the other day and the fire department is now investigating why it burned clear down to
the foundation, and yet it was made of metal."

Here was the stuff for a rewarding investigation, as later
events proved; but Joe wanted no part of it. As acting
chairman, he quickly shifted the hearings into other avenues.
But if the Joint Housing Committee wasn't interested in
Lustron, the Senate Investigating Committee was. On November 5, 1948, Chief Counsel William P. Rogers opened an
investigation of Lustron. He wrote to the Reconstruction
Finance Corporation:

As you know, the Reconstruction Finance Corporation has advanced
to the Lustron Corporation of Columbus, Ohio, considerable sums in
connection with the construction of a plant wherein prefabricated
houses will be produced. . . . It would be appreciated if you will
furnish us with the status of the production activities of Lustron and

also to what extent these so-called purchase orders are being used as evidence of financial progress as well as the status of the existing loan account and the basis for loans rendered.

By coincidence, Joe was also a member of the Senate Investigating Committee in addition to his position as acting chairman of the Joint Housing Committee. This made Strandlund and his new vice-president, Lorenzo Semple, so aware of McCarthy's importance that they decided it was time they did something tangible for him. So on November 12, 1948, Semple scratched his signature on a check for $10,000. The payee: Senator Joe McCarthy.

Thus, exactly one week after the Senate Investigating Committee began investigating Lustron, a member of the Committee pocketed $10,000 from the company being investigated. This may explain why RFC Director Walter L. Dunham, in reply to the Committee's request for information, wrote:

Mr. Strandlund, during the meeting [on Lustron's indebtedness], intimated that he had powerful friends within the administration and in Congress. He said he thought that the RFC, Congress and the administration had a moral commitment to him to carry on this obligation regardless of expense until its complete success had been established. I regard this attitude as distinctly dangerous to a promotional type of man, which I believe Mr. Strandlund to be.

Technically, the $10,000 check from Lustron was a down payment on the first literary opus of Joe McCarthy, author. What Lustron got in return was a 7,000-word portion of a pamphlet inappropriately labeled *A Dollar's Worth of Housing for Every Dollar Spent.* It bore Joe's by-line. The payment represented something of a new world's record in the literary field —$1.43 a word, 43 cents more than the previous record set by Winston Churchill when he sold his war memoirs.

The public heard the first installment of the affair when McCarthy called a press conference three months after signing the hush-hush contract with Lustron. Beaming with pride, McCarthy announced the arrival of his first-born effort in the literary field. The reporters were anxious to know how much Lustron had paid him, and Joe said: "It's embarrassingly small. Besides, I have to split it with ten people who helped me."

It turned out to be true that something like ten people helped McCarthy — but untrue that he was splitting the money. His income-tax return a year later listed the entire $10,000 as income for 1948. Joe tried to save $3,975 on his federal taxes by listing the $10,000 as 1949 income, but the Internal Revenue Bureau refused to go along with this scheme.

By 1950, Lustron had gone into bankruptcy, and the details of McCarthy's literary coup spilled forth. One of the first to complain about the deal was Clyde Foraker of Cleveland, receiver in bankruptcy for Lustron. "I'll bet he couldn't have gotten [the $10,000] if he weren't a Senator," Foraker said. "It's unethical."

As for Lustron President Strandlund, he simply said he had "purchased the name" of Senator McCarthy. "McCarthy named the price," Strandlund said, "but the price was worth it."

All along, Joe sought to create the impression that he had written the pamphlet himself; but the press and the RFC investigating sub-committee began to smoke out a host of ghost writers and researchers. The trail was picked up at the Federal Housing and Home Finance Agency, where a private office memo reported on August 10, 1948:

Senator McCarthy talked with Mr. Foley [Federal Housing Chief Raymond Foley] this afternoon. Senator said a Miss Jean Kerr is working with some of the other members of his office on a handbook for housing — a booklet intended to educate the veteran on use of cooperatives, loans, etc. McCarthy said she did not have good legal background and he wondered if she might talk with some of our legal staff.

Foley assigned one of his staff members, Walter M. Royal, Jr., to assist in preparing the material. Royal testified later that "nearly a dozen others" contributed research to the manuscript or suggested changes in it. Lustron also took the precaution of hiring a professional writer, Maron Simon, of New York City, to assist with the booklet; but Simon later claimed that he had devoted his talent chiefly to the promotional material. One of the authors of the present book also had a hand in reviewing the manuscript and offering professional criticism at Joe's request. The first draft was written in the rambling, florid style of McCarthy's familiar speeches and reports. But three weeks later, Joe handed this author a "revised manuscript," which had no similarity to the first draft at all, being written in a rigid technical style.

After all this came out in the wash, Joe figured the worst was over. But one day Merl Young climbed to the witness stand and remarked under cross-examination: "McCarthy is a funny man when it comes to betting. . . . He will go and bet on a tip anyone gives him." Young said that was exactly what happened at the 1949 Pimlico Preakness. McCarthy "lost his wad" on the first race, Young testified, and then gave a check for more money to Carl Strandlund, and later Strandlund tore it up. He quoted Strandlund as explaining: "I do that quite often for McCarthy."

But Strandlund, a portly, nervous man, gave a different version. He admitted he had cashed two checks for McCarthy at race tracks, one at Laurel in October, 1948, the other at Pimlico in May, 1949; but he denied that he was in the habit of tearing up checks for the Senator. Strandlund said he did tear up a $50 McCarthy check once, but only because a larger check was substituted. No one brought up the question of just how ethical it was for a member of the Senate Investigating Committee to get cash at a race track from a man who was under investigation by the Committee.

Just as the RFC investigation died down and McCarthy

appeared to be out of the woods, the scandal suddenly shifted from cash at a race track to a crap game at a Columbus, Ohio, hotel. Joe's castoff house-building friend, Robert Byers, complained at a bankruptcy proceeding that Mc-Carthy had "welshed" on a $5,500 gambling debt to his son. The debt was incurred during a crap game in McCarthy's hotel room, Byers said. But McCarthy let out a howl of righteous indignation, denying he had ever played dice with the junior Byers.

And there the story rested until Joe's staunch friend and outspoken defender, Clark Wideman, took the witness stand at a Senate hearing a year later. The Columbus, Ohio, real-estate broker was asked about the disputed dice game. He pooh-poohed the incident as "horseplay with dice and ficti-tious sums of money." But he admitted that a crap game had been going on in McCarthy's room, and even that "small amounts" of money had exchanged hands. Then, Wideman said, a man named Robert Byers, Jr., got hold of the dice, and he asked if anybody wanted to fade him. And, just for the fun of it, McCarthy said he'd fade him; and young Byers rolled and made his point. This kept up for several rolls of the dice; the Senator kept fading him, and Byers kept making point after point. Byers hit "quite a streak of luck" and began to double his bets with McCarthy, said Wideman. They finally reached $2,400, which would have been unlucky for Joe if they had been playing for greenbacks. But, Wide-man explained, it was just "conversation money." Anyway, Wideman quoted the Senator as saying: "Well, we might as well shoot the whole $2,400." And on the last toss, "Byers lost and that was the end of the incident," Wideman said.

As episodes like this began to pile up, Joe took a whiff of the aroma that was beginning to circulate nationally, and announced that it was being stirred up by "the elements of the press which have been rather vigorously opposed to my fight against Communism."

26. The Malmedy Massacre

AT CHRISTMASTIME, 1944, WHEN CAPTAIN JOE MCCARTHY WAS busy signing papers to get out of the Marine Corps, a grisly drama was being enacted at Malmedy crossroads in Belgium. German SS men lined up captured American soldiers in wheat fields, then mowed them down with machine guns. Out of their screams was to come another *cause célèbre* for Senator McCarthy. His "clients": the murderers.

The case has since become known as the "Malmedy Massacre"; it involved atrocities committed by the first SS Panzer Regiment under command of a swaggering, Himmler-trained killer — Colonel Joachim Peiper. Peiper ordered his men to take no prisoners; Nazi Germany's back was to the wall, and the niceties of international law, he said, would have to be discarded. His most elite battalion earned the nickname of "Blowtorch Battalion" after it burned two villages in Belgium and killed all the inhabitants. It was this same group which laughingly murdered 150 captured American soldiers and 100 Belgian civilians.

After the war, seventy-four members of Peiper's Blowtorch Battalion were brought to trial by shocked American prosecutors. Forty-three were sentenced to die, and then began a long series of legal maneuvers aimed at putting off the execution date. Little by little, the Malmedy case dropped out of the public memory, and soon the convicted Nazis and their lawyers decided the time was ripe to beat the rap. Sixteen months had already passed since the trials when,

158

mysteriously, dozens of affidavits began pouring out of the death blocks where the Nazi war criminals were held. Each affidavit said the same — that American prosecutors had tortured the confessions from the prisoners. They alleged that matches were forced under their fingernails and lighted, that they were clubbed around their abdomens and sex organs, and left in pools of their own blood until they signed confessions.

Such allegations appeared only skimpily in the American press; their origin and their purpose were too obvious. But in Germany the charges were circulated via headlines all over the country. The result was a new wave of anti-American feeling, a wave that cost the United States dearly in the vital campaign to win German hearts and minds to American ideals. The noise reached such a volume that the prisoners were granted a U. S. Supreme Court review; this gave the German Communist press another excuse to rehash the charges. When the Supreme Court upheld the sentences, the Red news organs called this positive proof that the United States was anti-German and anti-justice.

The Senate became so concerned with the propagandistic guerrilla warfare that it appointed a three-man investigating sub-committee in April, 1949. Senators Baldwin of Connecticut, Kefauver of Tennessee, and Hunt of Wyoming announced before they began their study that they would make no report until every last witness had been interrogated, until every shred of evidence had been studied and fitted into the picture. And with a Congressional Medal winner, Marine Colonel Joseph Chambers, as counsel, the committee went to work.

Baldwin, the mild-mannered Senator from Connecticut, opened the hearings with Senator McCarthy at his side. Joe had demanded the right to "sit in," although he was not a committee member. And Baldwin consented, rather than risk a long imbroglio with the brass-knuckled young man from Wisconsin. McCarthy drew up a list of witnesses, and Colonel Chambers accepted it, again in an effort to keep McCarthy happy. Joe's next major victory was committee permission to cross-examine witnesses. And from that point on, Joe dominated the hearings.

When Colonel Burton F. Ellis, chief prosecutor in the Malmedy trial, took the witness stand, Joe interrupted him after one minute, accused him of making "phenomenal" statements, and issued a scathing denunciation. Senator Hunt, a calm, quiet ex-dentist, intervened.

"This is not a prosecution," he said. "What we are trying to do is just to get the witnesses' statements, and then we will be the judge of whether they did things in the right manner."

"I entirely disagree," Joe shouted. "If that is the purpose, I am wasting my time!" McCarthy also hinted darkly that the American prosecutors made up a "vengeance team," composed of Jews with a violent hatred for Nazis. Later, this made interesting reading in the German press.

The committee called Kenneth Ahrens, one of twelve survivors of Malmedy who had escaped the Nazis by falling to the ground and feigning death.

Senator Hunt asked him: "As I understood your statement, during the killing, the SS troops seemed to be in a hilarious mood and seemed to be enjoying their work?"

"Very much so," said Eyewitness Ahrens.

Joe was on his feet. He accused Ahrens of trying to "inflame the public" and instigating "a Roman holiday" by his testimony. McCarthy seemed to grow angrier and angrier. Red-faced and perspiring, he screamed that the judges who had convicted the Nazis were "morons." As for the U. S. officers who obtained the confessions, McCarthy demanded that they be given a lie-detector test. Evidently, the thought that the convicted men could be lying never entered his mind; he asked for no such test on them. He reserved all of his wrath for American officers, and once he shouted at a witness: "I think you are lying! You may be able to fool us. I have been told you are very, very smart. I am convinced you cannot fool the lie-detector!"

McCarthy, a former circuit judge, knew that evidence obtained from the lie-detector is admissible in almost no U.S. courts. But he continued to insist on lie-detector tests, threatening to accuse the committee publicly of whitewashing the evidence. Finally, patient Chairman Baldwin took the proposal before the full Senate Armed Services Committee, where it was voted down as ridiculous. At that point, Joe walked out and denounced the hearings as "a shameful farce" and a "deliberate and clever attempt to whitewash the American military." Baldwin, he charged, was "criminally responsible."

McCarthy's denunciations kept up for several weeks, both on and off the floor of the Senate. The Communist press in Germany was echoing every word; mass meetings were held, and an inflamed Germany threatened riots if the convicted murderers were executed. There was nothing left to do but commute the sentences. The committee had proved beyond a question of a doubt that the verdicts were just; but the United States was in no position to cope with German mass riots incited by what seemed to the Germans as true statements made by an accredited American lawmaker. The defeat went to Baldwin's committee, the victory to German Communism and German Naziism — and Joe McCarthy was the man who had turned the tide.

But there remained more sinister aspects of the case to be investigated. Where had McCarthy turned up his "evidence" against the American prosecutors? Where did Joe get the information that enabled him to say: "I have seen documentary evidence that [the German war criminals] were subject to beatings and physical violence in such forms as could only be devised by warped minds. They were subjected to sham trials, to mock hangings; and families were deprived of rations. . . ."?

The answer came out one day when McCarthy carelessly mislaid a brown manila envelope in a Congressional hearing room. It bore the return address of Rudolf Aschenauer, of Frankfurt, Germany. A check was made with Army intelligence officers, who reported that Aschenauer was a member of a Communist spy ring. He funneled the trumped-up charges to McCarthy, then planted the charges in the German press between Senator McCarthy's quotation marks. Joe gave Aschenauer's Communist fictions the ring of truth, and the German people were convinced. The finesse worked to perfection.

One of the present authors has examined the brown manila envelope in the files of the Armed Services Committee. But McCarthy denied that he was getting material from Aschenauer. Under oath in legal proceedings in 1951, he testified as follows:

> Q — Do you know Mr. Rudolf Aschenauer yourself?
> A — *I don't think so.* . . .
> Q — Senator, you did actually receive and send communications to Rudolf Aschenauer, did you not?
> A — *Not that I recall.* . . .
> Q — [Was Aschenauer] one of the principal informants who sent you communications?
> A — The answer is *no.*
> Q — He was one of the informants, but not a principal one?
> A — I have had *no contact* with Aschenauer of any kind.

But two years previously Aschenauer himself told the Committee a different story, before it was learned that he was a Communist charged with fomenting anti-American hatred in Germany. At Committee hearings in Germany, there was this testimony:

> Q — Where are you submitting the affidavits? . . .
> A — For example, to McCarthy. . . .

And later:

Q — Why did Diefenthal send this letter to you, Dr. Aschenauer, to be transmitted to Senator McCarthy?

A — So that Senator McCarthy is informed about the various statements that had been made.

The Malmedy investigation, like similar affairs in the life of Joe McCarthy, was the beginning of the end of someone else's political career. Calm, docile Raymond Baldwin was overmatched in a knife fight. He issued a statement pointing out some of McCarthy's contradictions, then threw up his hands in despair as Joe shot back that Baldwin would "bitterly regret this deliberate and very clever attempt to whitewash" the Americans who had convicted the Malmedy murderers. And despite the complete vindication of Baldwin by the full fourteen-man, bi-partisan Committee, the Connecticut Republican decided to retire from the Senate in the middle of his term. He admitted at the time to one of the authors that the brawl with McCarthy was the last straw that persuaded him to pull out of politics.

Meanwhile, the sub-committee summed up:

Through competent testimony submitted to the subcommittee, it appeared that there are strong reasons to believe that groups within Germany are endeavoring . . . to discredit the American occupation forces in general. The subcommittee is convinced that there is an organized effort being made to revive the nationalistic spirit in Germany through every possible means. There is evidence that at least part of this effort is attempting to establish a close liaison with Communist Russia. Due to the manner in which the allegations in this case were being handled [by McCarthy, Aschenauer, et al.], it was also clear that no matter what the facts were in the case, in the minds of practically all Germans, the allegations were accepted as fact. This was certain to damage the American position in Germany.

And why had McCarthy taken his stand on behalf of the Nazi war criminals? Part of the answer might be traced to the strong pro-German groups in Wisconsin's voting populace, with whom McCarthy has always sought to endear himself. Then, too, McCarthy's old friend Walter Harnisch-feger, the Milwaukee pre-fab manufacturer, was ordered in 1942, by the President's Fair Employment Practices Commission, to stop discriminating against workers because of race and religion. The FEPC charged that Harnischfeger refused to employ either Negro or Jewish Americans and advertised for "gentile, white and protestant" help. In the post-war period, Harnischfeger made frequent trips to Germany, returning to criticize the war-crime trials, to urge that Germany's pre-war colonies be restored, and to protest against the dismantling of German factories. The old man's views were widely reprinted by the fellow traveler of the Axis, Upton Close — and by Senator Joe McCarthy, in the *Congressional Record*.

Ten days after the Malmedy investigation was begun, a young man named Tom Korb arrived to act as McCarthy's brains on the case. Korb worked for six weeks, carried on the books as McCarthy's "administrative assistant." He stayed long enough to help Joe write a Senate speech on the Malmedy Massacre, delivered on July 26, 1949, and then he went back to his job as a lawyer and corporation official in Milwaukee. His employer: the Harnischfeger Corporation.

27. Scuttling the Secretary of the Navy

JOE MCCARTHY FLITTED FROM CAUSE TO CAUSE DURING HIS Senate career, alighting successively on such variegated issues as fur tariffs, sugar rationing, public housing, and dozens of others.

But underneath his resounding chords played on the nation's publicity pipes, there was a recurrent theme — a good, safe, and stirring cause for which Joe always maintained a returning affection. And that was, in his own words, "My buddies, the Marines." Joe acted as a self-appointed spokesman, a sort of Congressional father-protector, for the Leathernecks. Let anyone try to tarnish the bright shield of the Marines, and he had Joe to reckon with.

So it was inevitable that in 1949 McCarthy should throw himself headlong into the battle over Navy carrier planes vs. Air Force long-range bombers, a fight which found the Marine Corps solidly on the side of the Navy. Joe reached the high point in this battle when he stood on the floor of the Senate and loudly proclaimed: "Mr. President, if the Senate had the right to impeach, I would suggest that impeachment proceedings against Mr. Matthews be instituted."

"Mr. Matthews" was Francis Matthews, Secretary of the Navy and one of the nation's most distinguished Catholic laymen, whom Pope Pius XII had named Secret Papal Chamberlain with Cape and Sword. But as the civilian boss of the Navy, he had dared to defy the Navy admirals and Marine Corps generals.

Joe's talk about impeachment had one gratifying effect: it made headlines all over the country. That having been accomplished, Joe quietly let the matter drop, and a few weeks later, at a party given by Mrs. Perle Mesta, he sidled up to Matthews and grinned amiably. "Hello," he said, "I'm Joe McCarthy."

The controversy sprang up over what seemed to be conflicting statements made by Matthews on the one hand, and by Admiral Louis E. Denfeld, Chief of Naval Operations, on the other. The whole feud between the Navy and the Air Force had been thrashed out before the House Armed Services Committee, which had finally called in the Navy's top-line officer, Admiral Denfeld.

Denfeld had told the Committee that he believed President Truman, Defense Secretary Johnson, and Navy Secretary Matthews were plotting to scuttle the Navy and to wipe out the Marine Corps as a fighting force. The Admiral said that he, as the Navy's representative on the Joint Chiefs of Staff, had found "a pattern of resistance" to naval aviation and the Marine Corps; he said it came principally from "lack of study, or lack of experience, or both." Then, in a thinly veiled reference, Denfeld criticized Secretary Matthews as an incompetent man, inexperienced in naval problems, who was not working for the Navy and Marine Corps but against them.

Matthews, sitting only a short distance away, hurriedly got up and left the room. He had good reason. Several days before, Matthews and Denfeld had gone over the whole issue in the privacy of the Secretary's office. And they had reached agreement; Denfeld had promised that he would go along with Matthews in his battle with the rebellious admirals. Hence Matthews' dismay when Denfeld did an embarrassing about-face in front of the Committee.

The situation was untenable for both Matthews and Denfeld; and a few days later, Denfeld was removed by the

President. The request came from Matthews. With that, the fur began to fly. Cries of "persecution," "censorship," and "brass curtain" were hurled by Navy and Marine partisans, both in and out of Congress; and the hue and cry raged fiercely on the front pages of the nation's newspapers.

On January 12, 1950, after Congress had taken a two-month recess, Senator Millard Tydings of Maryland arose on the Senate floor to ask that the nomination of Admiral Forrest P. Sherman as Chief of Naval Operations be confirmed. "I make the request," Tydings said, "for the reason that there has been no confirmed chief of naval operations since last August. The armed services committee has had full and extensive hearings . . . and the report was unanimous."

At once Senator "Wild Bill" Langer of North Dakota — a close friend of McCarthy — jumped to his feet and asked for a quorum call, a common Senatorial delaying practice. A few minutes later Joe McCarthy rushed full tilt into the chamber, starting his speech as he strode down the aisle of the Senate. Looking at Tydings, he declared:

I might say that it will take infinitely more than this [Sherman's confirmation] to convince me that it will put the Navy back in the defense picture. I have just looked over the President's budget, and I see that we are now in the unusual position of having a Marine Corps with practically no Marines, and we shall very shortly have a Navy without any ships.

When McCarthy simmered down, the presiding officer offered the confirmation of Sherman for unanimous approval. But Joe said he would "reluctantly . . . be forced to object, not because I have anything against Admiral Sherman." His reason for objecting, he said, was to give himself time to prepare a speech about "the unusual circumstances under which Admiral Denfeld's nomination was withdrawn" and also about "a situation which I think is viciously dangerous to the security of the nation, namely, the current usurpation of congressional prerogatives by the brass in the Pentagon, and the complete iron curtain which has been established around the Pentagon."

There the subject rested for six days, while Joe prepared his speech. And on January 18, he arose on the floor of the Senate, characteristically waving a document over his head, and said:

I have here today a photostat of an official document which I intend to read to the Senate, which raises questions of a vastly more important nature than the mere confirmation of the nomination of any man to any post. It brings up the very important question of whether the office of chief of naval operations is now actually vacant. It brings up also the more important question of whether the Secretary of the Navy is a man who is completely incompetent or whether the other day before the Armed Services committee he was just plain untruthful. . . .

I specifically call the attention of the chairman and the members of the Armed Services committee to the question whether there actually is a vacancy in the post of chief of naval operations to which Admiral Sherman can be appointed, or whether the job is already filled by Admiral Denfeld. . . . Mr. President, we must decide whether or not Admiral Denfeld has been legally removed before we can put another man in his place. . . . Last week, Secretary of Navy Francis P. Matthews appeared before the Senate Armed Services committee to support the nomination of Admiral Sherman as chief of naval operations. He testified, in effect, that a vacancy existed in the post . . . because this document did not exist. . . .

I hold in my hand . . . a photostatic copy of the commission which was issued to Admiral Denfeld. The original is in his possession. This is the commission which Secretary Matthews told the Armed Services committee did not exist. It is Admiral Denfeld's commission as chief of naval operations. . . . It is signed, Mr. President, by Francis P. Matthews and Harry S. Truman. . . . This is the commission which Secretary Matthews told the committee did not exist. I assure the Senate that it does exist.

Gradually McCarthy's talk changed into a harangue against Matthews. "I think it is a great mistake to call a witness before any committee without his first being sworn," McCarthy said, referring to Matthews' testimony before the Armed Services Committee. He continued:

Only last week the grand jury indicted a man for testifying falsely before our committee on a much less important matter, a matter which certainly did not affect the security of the United States. That man will be tried, and, if convicted, will, of course, serve time. . . . It is hard to understand how [Matthews] could so unequivocally say to the committee that the document was never signed, even though he himself had signed it. . . . It may be that the man is so incompetent that he did not know what he was signing.

Then Senator William Knowland of California rushed into the chamber with the transcript of the Senate Armed Services Committee hearing at which Matthews was questioned on the removal of Denfeld. The pertinent testimony read:

SECRETARY MATTHEWS: Well, at the present time the vacancy occurs by the fact that Admiral Denfeld's first term has expired and he never has been appointed for a second term. His name was suggested, he was confirmed, but the commission was never issued to him.

Said McCarthy:

I thank the Senator very much. Mr. President, who is this man Matthews who says that anyone who disagrees with him on how to run the Navy will be transferred to Siberia or an inferior post? . . . Mr. President, upon checking we find that this man Matthews is a fine family man and apparently a likeable lawyer from Omaha. Aside from practising law and having a short tour of duty in the USO, he has no background which could even remotely entitle him to the claim of being a great naval strategist. In fact, Mr. President, when he was first appointed by President Truman, he told newsmen in Omaha that he had never sailed in anything larger than a rowboat. . . . I wonder why the President . . . appoints such a man to such a critically important job in our defense set-up.

Certainly not because of his ability. . . . It appears that Mr. Matthews is not a man who has any conceivable knowledge of the Navy or any conceivable interest in it. . . . He came to the post of Secretary of Navy, but apparently he has no loyalty either to the Navy or to the President. Apparently he did not know what he was doing. I do not think he was actually lying. . . . The reason I say that I do not think he was lying is that the use of the word "lie" presupposes that the person concerned knew what he was talking about. However, I do not think

Mr. Matthews even knew that he had signed the document appointing Admiral Denfeld. . . . I am not concerned with making out a case. I come before the Senate and state the facts which I have discovered. . . . We want to find out why Matthews lied before the committee.

When McCarthy's last thunderous words had been spoken, reporters in the Senate press gallery rushed to the telephones. They called the White House and the Pentagon to find out the facts behind the sensational charges made by McCarthy. The next day all Washington knew that Joe's accusation that Matthews was a "liar" was improbable and unprovable, and his claim that Denfeld still held the post of Chief of Naval Operations was false.

The fact was that Matthews had been completely truthful when he told the Senate Armed Services Committee that he had not "issued" the commission to Denfeld. The document had not gone through the usual channels but had been delivered to Denfeld unofficially by a White House naval aide; Denfeld had not taken the oath of office, and therefore the commission that had been short-circuited into his possession was not in force.

But far beyond this fact, McCarthy's arguments were faulty — because the President, as Commander in Chief of the nation's armed forces, had the power to relieve or transfer any officer as he saw fit. As Senator Tydings pointed out: "It looks to me like a sham battle. What difference would it make? The President could have removed him if he had taken 10 oaths, signed 75 commissions, put 415 seals on it and if he had held office for 15 years and 6 months."

In other words, if McCarthy had been 100-per-cent correct in every one of his charges, the situation would nonetheless have remained the same. Truman could have removed Denfeld, and Matthews could have asked the Senate to confirm Sherman. Whether a commission had been signed, sealed, and delivered to Denfeld would not have mattered the slightest. And all this McCarthy knew even as he lit the fires of innuendo under Secretary Matthews. For he told Tydings and the Senate: "I may say I personally think the President could have removed him."

But Joe's tirades against Matthews were good for dozens of pages of torrid reading in the *Congressional Record*. The argument was academic and abstract; the publicity was real and valuable.

CHAPTER 28

205, 81—or 57?

IT WAS A STRANGE GATHERING.

There were scholarly Father Edmund Walsh, dean of Georgetown University's staid foreign-service school; big, garrulous Washington Attorney William A. Roberts, a tough-talking liberal; modest Professor Charles Kraus, a political-science instructor at Georgetown; and Senator Joe McCarthy. It was January 7, 1950, and Joe's political fortunes were ebbing. He confessed this fact to his three fellow Catholics, as they relaxed after dinner at Washington's swank Colony Restaurant. He said he desperately needed an issue on which to base his 1952 campaign for re-election; but so far he had found none that suited him.

Eager to help their personable friend, Father Walsh and Lawyer Roberts threw out suggestions. "How about pushing harder for the St. Lawrence seaway?" Roberts proposed.

Joe shook his head. "That hasn't enough sex," he said. "No one gets excited about it."

He then outlined a Townsend-type pension plan for all elderly Americans; he would pay $100 a month to everybody over sixty-five years of age. But his three friends called the idea economically unsound. Finally, the priest had an idea. "How about Communism as an issue?" he offered.

Joe thought this sounded like a good idea. "The government is full of Communists," he stated flatly. "The thing to do is hammer at them." But Roberts warned that such a campaign must be pegged on facts; he said that the public was weary of "Wolf! Wolf!" cries about "pinkos" and "Reds" hurled indiscriminately from political platforms. Joe said he would get the facts. And his three fellow Catholics went away with the feeling that the sincere McCarthy would do his country a service by speaking out against the Communist fifth column. They little realized that a day would come when they would all have to repudiate the young man who started his Big Show with their basic idea.

Joe put his staff to digging; but real, live Communists in government were hard to find. To begin with, the Republican Eightieth Congress had already dragged the river bottom of the Democratic administration for Communists, and had hauled submerged facts and stray pieces of evidence to the surface. The FBI had also maintained a constant vigilance against Communists infiltrating into the government; and every federal department and bureau had sifted its employees through a loyalty screen.

But of all the government departments, probably the most security-conscious had been the State Department. GOP Congressman Bartel Jonkman of Michigan had been led to say in behalf of the House Foreign Affairs Committee: "Before the Eightieth Congress adjourns, I want the members to know that there is one department in which the known or reasonably suspected subversives, Communists, fellow travelers, sympathizers, and persons whose services are not for the best interests of the United States have been swept out. This is the Department of State."

The machinery of government security had been grinding slow; but it had been grinding exceeding fine, removing one by one the Hisses, Coplons, and Wadleighs as they were found out. Some three hundred employees of the government had been fired for one reason or another under the loyalty program, and there was not a single "doubtful" government employee who had not been investigated at least

once. And the big names had already put on their performance under the klieg lights of the House Un-American Activities Committee.

But Joe McCarthy was armed for a shooting match, and
though he hadn't found any targets, he nevertheless opened
fire. At Wheeling, West Virginia, on February 9, 1950, he
let go his first deadly volley in a direction where rumor had
told him some of the enemy might be hiding. "I have here
in my hand" — he squeezed the trigger — "a list of 205 . . . a
list of names that were made known to the Secretary of
State as being members of the Communist Party and who
nevertheless are still working and shaping policy in the State
Department."

The news, to the ladies of the Ohio County Women's Republican Club, served as a glorious substantiation of all the
wild rumors hopefully circulated since the war's end by a
small group of "out" politicians who wanted to become "ins."
They clasped Joe to their bosom, while the nation read the
wire services' reports about his charges.

The next day, the fast-moving McCarthy popped up in
Denver, where the 205 "Communists" became 205 "bad security risks." And on the following day, in a speech at Salt
Lake City, the 205 of Wheeling and Denver had changed to
"57 card-carrying Communists."

Whatever else had happened, Joe had hit publicity pay-
dirt. His charges made Page 1 headlines in almost every
newspaper in the nation, and the name of Joe McCarthy
was heard again in the land. When he was called for an
accounting on the Senate floor eleven days after the original
speech, Joe shifted and feinted and weaved and dodged. But
he didn't let go of the dangerous grizzly bear he held by the
tail. Instead, he juggled numbers for several days, and finally
shook his case down to "three big Communists involved . . .
case No. 1, case No. 2 and case No. 81."

"If we can get rid of these big three," he said, "we will

have done something to break the back of the espionage ring within the State Department." He labeled Case No. 81 as an "extremely dangerous and active Communist, completely disloyal to the United States and loyal to Soviet Russia." And by way of showing his sincerity, Joe made two promises:

"I urge," he said, "that the proper Senate committee convene, and *I shall be glad to give the committee the names.*" *
And he told Majority Leader Scott Lucas: "I should like to assure him that I will not say anything on the Senate floor which I will not say off the floor. *On the day when I take advantage of the security we have on the Senate floor, on that day I will resign from the Senate.*"

Both these promises were to be broken. But the Senate, anxious to substitute fact for demagoguery, created a five-man investigating sub-committee, led by Maryland Democrat Millard Tydings. The intent was to make McCarthy put up or shut up. He did neither.

By this time, Joe had made it plain by his shadings of phrases and his oratorical jaywalking that he had no list of 205 Communists in the State Department, as he had claimed in Wheeling. But he did insist that there were "vast numbers of . . . Communists with whom we must be concerned." The Tydings committee went to work, and the first witness was Senator Joe himself.

On the witness stand, McCarthy let it be known that he was tired of "playing this silly numbers game"; so he ignored the numbers, turning instead to one individual — Judge Dorothy Kenyon of New York. He outlined the "case" against Mrs. Kenyon, neglecting to mention that she was not a State Department employee at all. Joe continued throughout one day and part of the next, lambasting Judge Kenyon with a long string of charges. He also demanded the State Department files.

But Chairman Tydings' fingers were growing itchy on the

---

* Italics added here and elsewhere.

gavel; he was impatient with McCarthy, who had been so free to fire broadsides but was now pecking away with a BB gun. So Tydings asked Joe if he would please repeat, for the record, some of the charges he had been scattering around the country. This was a significant request, since McCarthy was now under oath. If he repeated his statements and could not back them up, he could be caught in perjury. Joe began to sweat and begged for more time. He would be ready on March 13, he said, to present the name of a man occupying "an important post" in the State Department. But when that date arrived, Joe announced that he had to go to the Senate floor for the debate on housing. He had almost reached the door when someone observed that the debate had been postponed. Joe said he would have to go anyway to take care of several of his constituents. But the committee would not accept his excuse.

Cornered on the witness stand, Joe had to name names. He alleged that four persons were "pro-Communists": Haldore Hanson, working on the government's Point Four program to aid underdeveloped countries; Mrs. Esther Caukin Brunauer, attached to the State Department's UNESCO Relations Staff; her husband, Stephen Brunauer, a civilian Navy scientist; and Owen Lattimore, professor of international relations at Johns Hopkins University, and director of its Page School of International Relations.

Now gone too far to turn back, Joe rushed recklessly on. Protected by Senatorial immunity from libel suits, he chose to bluff his way through and take a chance on perjury. He even began warming up to the task. So the next day he named four more "pro-Communists": John Stewart Service, State Department consular officer in Calcutta; Gustavo Duran, ex-State Department employee, who had resigned four years previously to go to the United Nations; Professor Harlow Shapley of Harvard, never a State Department employee; and Dr. Frederick L. Schuman of Williams College, whose only affiliation with State consisted of a free lecture he had once given to a group of employees. McCarthy also handed Chairman Tydings the name of another former State Department employee who, Joe said, had a "police record" for homosexuality.

At this point Tydings began to get the willies over all the name-calling. One by one, American citizens were being held up to the world as traitors, and still the proof was lacking. Tydings became convinced that McCarthy was bluffing, that he had no list of 205, 81, or 57 names; and once again Tydings asked McCarthy to turn the list over to the committee. Joe said he would comply on March 20. In the meantime he got an opportunity to make good on his promise to quit the Senate if he didn't repeat his charges off the Senate floor. Joe appeared on an NBC television program — and refused to repeat any of his charges against individuals.

When deadline time arrived, Tydings reminded McCarthy that they were still waiting for the list of Communists in the State Department. For reply, Joe showed Tydings a registered-mail slip, and explained that the list had been mailed to the committee; but a search of the incoming mail failed to locate the registered letter from McCarthy.

Next Joe announced to the press that he had telescoped his charges into a single case. The man in question, he said, was the "boss" of Alger Hiss "in the espionage ring in the State Department."

The name turned out to be that of Owen Lattimore, already fingered by McCarthy in a previous session. Reporters went to work digging up Lattimore's State Department record. They couldn't find one. Lattimore had never been a regular employee of the State Department; he was on the staff of Johns Hopkins. Joe also confided to one of the authors that four Russian spies had been landed on the American coast by submarine and had gone straight to Lattimore for their orders.

Meanwhile Lattimore, in Afghanistan on a United Nations mission, sped toward Washington to fight back. As for the McCarthy charges, he termed them "pure moonshine," "unmitigated lies." "McCarthy," Lattimore said, "will fall flat on his face." But the professor, like many another who tangled with McCarthy, underestimated his opponent (see Chapter 34). Joe sent up such a smoke screen that the public was never able to distinguish clearly the facts from the haze.

29. Witch-Finder General

Three hundred years ago, England was swept by a wave of hysteria against witches. Fear and suspicion haunted the people, until neighbor suspected neighbor and child denounced parent for being "in league with the devil." No one was safe from accusation. *Government business slowed to a stop as top officials of the realm, themselves afraid of being named, took a leading part in the hunt.*

Then a man named Matthew Hopkins appeared on the scene with a new and "infallible" method of detecting witches; it consisted of some original techniques in torture. Within a short time he became one of the most powerful men in England, feared even by the King himself, who conferred upon Hopkins the title of "His Majesty's Witch-Finder General."

With two assistants, Hopkins traveled through the eastern counties, hurrying from place to place, often at the urgent request of mayors and town corporations. No one dared oppose him, for he had power of life and death over all "suspects" brought before him to be "tested." Those who failed his tests were put to death; and for each such victim Hopkins was paid a sum of money. In Essex and Suffolk alone, he tested more than three hundred persons; and the money flowed in. Over a two-year period he collected more than £2,000 — a magnificent sum in those days.

But his fees grew more exorbitant, and the atmosphere more chaotic, until a group of officials took matters into their own hands and arrested the Witch-Finder General himself — as a witch. He was subjected to a series of tests so severe

*that his health was completely broken, and soon afterward
he died and was buried at Mistley, August 12, 1647.*

Within days after McCarthy's first Communist-in-government
speech at Wheeling, he found himself a powerful
national figure. He was besieged by reporters wherever he
went, and his name stayed in the headlines. But even more
gratifying, money began pouring into his office — currency
and checks — sent to him by persons all over the country
who wanted him to "keep up the fight." McCarthy couldn't
back out; he had struck pay dirt again.

The country was disturbed about Communism, and it had
good reason to be. Abroad, Communist power was threatening
the peace of the world. At home, Alger Hiss had just
been convicted, William Remington had been named and
temporarily cleared under a cloud of doubt, and rumors of
Communist plans and Communist spy rings were heard on
every hand. The time was ripe for a clever politician to
seize upon this feeling and put it to work for him.

But even so, Joe had a tough fight on his hands; for one
thing, he had to make a formal accounting to the Senate.
This was finally scheduled for February 20, 1950 — eleven
days after his Wheeling bombshell. Late in the afternoon,
the Senate sounded a three-bell quorum call, and the Senators
shuffled into the chamber to hear McCarthy's firsthand
report. Joe was in a genial mood when he made his entrance,
carrying his now-famous tan briefcase, bulging with documents.
The Senate sat fascinated as he took out his voluminous
"proof" and spread it in little piles over the top of his
desk.

A silence fell across the chamber as he arose.

"Mr. President," he began, "I wish to discuss a subject
tonight which concerns me more than does any other subject
I have ever discussed before this body, and perhaps more
than any other subject I shall ever have the *good fortune* to

discuss in the future." Already, in his first sentence, he had let it slip that he was pleased at having stumbled across the Communist-in-government issue. He was still smiling as he continued: "It not only concerns me, but it disturbs and frightens me."

Then for six hours the members of the highest legislative body of the greatest nation on earth sat back and listened. It was a scene from *Alice in Wonderland*. Senators leaned forward, trying to follow Joe's hop-skip-and-jump account. Even before he began on his "81 cases," he set the stage for what followed: "I think a group of twisted-thinking intellectuals have taken over *both* the Democratic and Republican parties to try to wrest control from them." He never bothered to clear up the interesting little mystery of why these sinister "intellectuals" were still trying to "wrest control" if they had already "taken over."

Midway in the proceedings, Senator Brien McMahon of Connecticut rushed into the chamber in white tie and tails, having been recalled from a formal party, and walked about the floor asking Senators what was going on. "I left the Senate chamber at 7:30 P.M.," he said. "What number of case is the Senator now on?" He was told No. 34. "I merely say that when the Senator reaches Case No. 81," he remarked, settling wearily into his seat, "I hope to be home in bed."

Later, while trying to get McCarthy to admit that he had taken out only the derogatory material from the files of his victims and omitted other material which would have cleared them, McMahon said: "I have examined many government files and many investigation records, and I have seen in the files statements that 'This man McCarthy' or 'This man —' "

"Make it Jones," McCarthy suggested. McMahon thought a moment and decided on Smith.

In a way, McCarthy's performance was masterful. Although his cases were digests of investigations long concluded by the Eightieth Congress, no one was able to make him admit that fact — or even acknowledge statements attributed to him by leading newspapers across the country.

The discussion eventually narrowed down to the number 205. It was to be proved later, without possibility of doubt, that McCarthy had used this figure at Wheeling, West Virginia, on February 9, when he said: "And ladies and gentlemen, I have here in my hand a *list of 205* . . . a list of names that were made known to the Secretary of State as being members of the Communist Party and who nevertheless are still working and shaping policy in the State Department" (see Chapter 28).

This 205 figure had been read by millions in their hometown papers. That McCarthy actually used this figure is attested by:

(1) The advance copy of the speech which McCarthy handed out.

(2) James K. Whitaker, news editor of WWVA, which broadcast the speech; Whitaker signed a sworn statement that McCarthy said 205.

(3) Paul A. Myers, program director of WWVA, who signed a similar sworn statement.

(4) Fran Desmond of the Wheeling *Intelligencer*, who covered the speech and wrote a story from his notes that quoted McCarthy as saying 205.

(5) Numerous persons who heard the broadcast speech.

These were the facts when McCarthy addressed the Senate on February 20 to explain the furore he had created. But he blandly ignored the facts, and gave the Senate a new version of what he had said at Wheeling. Quoting from himself, McCarthy carefully omitted any mention of 205; instead he substituted the following sentence: "I have in my hand 57 *cases* of individuals who would appear to be either card-carrying members or certainly loyal to the Communist Party, but who nevertheless are still helping to shape our foreign policy."

West Virginia's Senator Matt Neely snorted: "It is obvious that someone . . . is lying as deliberately and outrageously as Ananias." Several other Senators plunged into the fray, concentrating on the misstatement; if that was proved false, they could go on to others. But for all their effort, they could not pin McCarthy down. The questioning grew tighter and angrier: Did you or did you not say 205?

McCarthy replied: "The speech in Reno, Nevada, and that in Wheeling, West Virginia, were recorded, so there is no question about what I said. I *do not believe* I mentioned the figure 205." For a fleeting moment it seemed that McCarthy was weakening, but a little later he categorically denied using the 205 figure. As the smoke screen of figures, dates, and places grew thick, McCarthy himself began to lose his bearings. He went so far once as to explain where he got the figure 205 — which he claimed he had not used. Then Illinois' Senator Scott Lucas, the majority leader, decided to end the game once and for all:

LUCAS: I now repeat the question I asked the able Senator in the beginning: Did the Senator from Wisconsin . . . declare that he had a list of 205 persons working for the State Department, who were known by the Secretary of State to be members of the Communist party?

McCARTHY: I may say, if the Senator is going to make a farce of this, I will not yield to him. I shall not answer any more silly questions of the Senator. This is too important, too serious a matter for that.

LUCAS: The Senator keeps talking about 57; the newspaper says the Senator said there were 205 . . . it is of importance whether the Senator from Wisconsin made the statement or did not make it. He can answer yes or no to that.

McCARTHY: May I answer the Senator's question.

LUCAS: It is serious to me.

McCARTHY: Let me answer the Senator's question, for the third time. I will tell the Senator, and I am now repeating it — if the Senator will sit down and give me the time to do it — that there are at least 57 Communists in the State Department. . . . I will not answer the Senator a fourth time. I *have said* there were 57 Communists in the State Department. . . .

LUCAS: Mr. President, will the Senator yield?

MCCARTHY: I am not yielding to the Senator now. . . . Let me tell him now, so there may be no question in his mind, I said 57.

This was crystal clear; McCarthy denied that he had said 205, and repeated his assertion that 57 was the number he had used. Yet in his very next sentence, Joe declared flatly: "I said there were 205 in the State Department whom the Secretary of State refused to discharge. . . ." The Senate was now completely confused. Did McCarthy mean that he had used both numbers? Wearily, Lucas resumed his questioning:

LUCAS: I am trying to find out . . . whether the newspapers have deliberately distorted what the able Senator said in his speech.

MCCARTHY: I refuse to yield further to the Senator.

LUCAS: I want to find out.

But McCarthy had much more important subjects to talk about. He replied sharply: "I will ask the Senator please not to interrupt me."

Gradually the Alice-in-Wonderland atmosphere gave way to one of dead seriousness. As Lucas pressed harder and harder for facts, McCarthy's face grew redder, his answers became shorter, and his voice edged higher. Once he gained a few moments' rest by asking for a quorum call. This gambit launched a long series of parliamentary interruptions, climaxed by Lucas' successful motion to have the sergeant-at-arms "compel" Senators to come on the floor to hear the proceedings. It was the first time in five years that this rule had been invoked.

Senators Owen Brewster of Maine and Karl Mundt of South Dakota added to the confusion by breaking in with critical observations about the federal loyalty program and their feeling that innumerable Reds had infiltrated the government. Only one vote was taken during McCarthy's six-hour presentation, and it followed a disgusted motion by Lucas that they quit for the night and go home.

New York's Senator Herbert Lehman, sometimes called the "conscience of the Senate," found it impossible to believe what was going on before his eyes. When he pleaded with McCarthy to tell the whole story in straightforward language, he was given this reply: "I am afraid that if it is not clear to the Senator now, I shall never be able to make it clear to him, no matter how much further explanation I make."

Then McMahon re-entered the battle, trying a new tack: "Does not the Senator think it is the American system that when a man is accused, he shall be given a hearing, that all witnesses for him and against him shall be heard and adjudged? Star chambers are not for the United States of America, nor are trials *ex parte*, on the basis of the files of the persons concerned, on the floor of the United States Senate, the way to handle this matter."

McCarthy's answer was to continue reading the list of "Communists" he had "uncovered" in the State Department. It developed that his "81 cases" added up to only 77, since Cases 15, 27, 37, and 59 were missing. And Cases 21 through 26 were lumped together as Voice of America employees who, he said, had been recommended for their jobs by Communists.

McCarthy did not seem concerned whether his "State Department Reds" were in the State Department or not. For, as early as Case No. 12, he had to admit that "where he is as of today, I frankly do not know"; but he hastened to add that the last place he was known to be was in a section of the Commerce Department, "with which the State Department works."

Nor did McCarthy seem to care whether his "Reds" were really Reds. He had stated clearly that he was "only giving the Senate cases in which it appears that there is a definite Communistic connection." But it developed that this was not quite true. Case No. 14, he admitted, was primarily a morals case. The same was true in Case No. 62:

This file is not important insofar as Communistic activities are concerned, but rather is important because it sheds light on some rather unusual mental aberrations of certain individuals in the department. . . . This file I recommend to the attention of any committee that cares to investigate it. It goes into some detail in regard to the peculiar — how can I put it — the peculiar mental twists. I was trying to handle this matter delicately [Joe grinned broadly at this point]. I think this will be of interest to the committee.

And Case No. 76, he said, "does not involve Communistic activities."

Apparently McCarthy wanted people to believe that he could throw a stone anywhere in the State Department and hit a Communist. At one point, he even suggested that an employee must be guilty if there was no information to prove him innocent. Commenting on Case No. 40, in which he had mentioned no Communist affiliations, McCarthy said: "I do not have too much information of this, except the general statement by the agency that there is nothing in the files to disprove his Communistic connections."

But the strangest Communist that McCarthy had found in the State Department was Case No. 72, which he described as that of a man never employed by the Department, but an interesting case nevertheless, "in that it is the direct opposite from the cases I have been reading. . . . I do not confuse this man as being a Communist. This individual was very highly recommended by several witnesses as a high type of man, a democratic American who . . . opposed Communism."

It was almost midnight when McCarthy reached his Case No. 81, gathered up the scattered documents which covered his own and another desk, and hurried out. He had fought his toughest round and escaped with hardly a bruise. And tomorrow there would be stacks of new clippings for his scrapbook.

30. The Men Behind
the Charges

"Tail-Gunner" Joe McCarthy, who shot up the coconut trees in the South Pacific — once breaking the record for firing the most rounds in a single day — was shooting wildly again. From his foxhole of Senatorial immunity, he blazed away at the Communist menace, shooting first and asking "Who goes there?" afterwards. Many public servants, standing like coconut trees in Joe's way, were hit; and he broke the record for firing the most charges from the Senate floor in a day.

But the press and the public were so blinded by the fireworks of Joe's broadsides that no one seemed to notice where he was getting his ammunition. His own cryptic explanation was that he had penetrated "the iron curtain, Truman's iron curtain, of secrecy," and had gained access to secret files never before available to Congress. "If it were not for some good, loyal Americans in the State Department," he said, "I should not have been able to present this picture to the Senate." But he warned that the jobs of his informants "would not be worth a tinker's dam" if he revealed their names.

And yet to anyone who bothered to run down McCarthy's charges, his sources were no mystery. The records at the Library of Congress show that he requested a special room for his assistants, so that they could wade through old inves-

tigative reports and back copies of the *Daily Worker*. And
among the old documents, his staff came across a letter written by former Secretary of State James Byrnes to Congressman Adolph Sabath of Illinois on July 26, 1946. It revealed
that a screening committee of the State Department "had
recommended against permanent employment" of 285 individuals, some already on the payroll, others merely appli-
cants. Of these, the letter went on, 80 had resigned or been
fired, leaving 205 still under question. The charges against
them were various, ranging from incompetence and drunken-
ness to suspicion of disloyalty. But the charges were by no
means final; the screening committee had acknowledged that
those on the list might be "subsequently approved if the
further investigation resolves the investigation in favor of
the employees."

But for McCarthy's purposes, the 205 undergoing job-
screening in 1946 became "205 members of the Communist
Party . . . still working and shaping policy in the State
Department" in 1950. There was no question that Joe was
talking about the same 205 people; he even quoted Byrnes's
figures during his hectic, six-hour Senate speech of February
20. "Former Secretary Byrnes said," blurted Joe, "that 285
of those men are unsafe risks. He goes on to say, of this
number only 80 have been removed." Of course, if McCarthy
had explored beyond the Byrnes letter, he would have discovered that only 46 of the original 205 were still on the
State Department's rolls as late as 1950. And in all 46 cases,
the skeletons from their past had been exhumed and aired
by squads of investigators.

The second number in Joe's bingo game was 57; he backed
down from the 205 figure and advertised instead that there
were 57 varieties of traitors in the State Department. "Despite the State Department blackout," he said, "we have been
able to compile a list of 57 Communists." But this figure
also came from the dusty records of the past. In mid-1947,

a House appropriations sub-committee under Congressman John Taber, New York Republican, had set out to investigate the State Department. For six weeks, committee agents raked through the State Department's personnel files; and they found prejudicial information against 108 persons. The hostile GOP committee bloodhounded all 108 cases, searching for tracks of Communism that might embarrass the Democratic administration. But only 57 of the original 108 persons were still employed in the Department; and most of those had been pronounced loyal after FBI investigations. In fact, Republican Congressman Jonkman of Michigan was so impressed that he announced to the House that the State Department was one place that had been swept clean of subversives (see Chapter 28).

But Senator McCarthy, searching for crumbs in the discard pile of the 1948 investigation, stuffed his pockets with the old case histories. And on February 20, 1950, he spread out the old leftovers and served them up anew. Joe also added an extra helping from the worthless portion of the original list of 108; so instead of the 57 chewed and digested cases of the Eightieth Congress, he expanded the number to 81 and served them sizzling hot-off-the-griddle.

But the 81 cases, after passing through McCarthy's meat grinder, still came out a rehash. For example, the Eightieth Congress report had given the following description of Case No. 100 on pages 173-174:

He is an applicant for a P-8 position with the State Department. He has been employed by the Treasury Department from April, 1940, to the present time, except for military leave from July, 1942, to December, 1942.

McCarthy's Case No. 78 sounded remarkably similar. Joe reported to the Senate:

This individual has made application for a P-8 position in the State Department. He has been employed by the Treasury Department from April, 1940, up to the present time, except for military release from July, 1942, to December, 1942.

The most curious coincidence was the reference to a "P-8 position" since the government had abolished the "P-8" classification several months before McCarthy's speech. But the similarities continued, case for case, line for line; and a striking resemblance took shape between the 1948 report and McCarthy's 1950 speech. In fact, the differences were so poorly disguised as to appear ludicrous. Reporting on Case No. 3, the 1948 document had stated on page 177:

The applicant came to the United States from Hungary in 1938 and was naturalized in New York City in August, 1944. She has been employed since October, 1944, as a translator and script writer with OWI and the Office of International Information and Cultural Affairs. . . . A report of April 24, 1947, contains the statement made by the subject's supervisor with the State Department: "I feel sure she is a fellow traveler." This supervisor later, on re-interview, changed his mind, saying she is loyal but liberal.

Except for a few startling differences, McCarthy's Case No. 4 sounded like the same individual. Joe's version:

The individual came to the United States from Hungary in 1944. He was employed as a translator and script writer for OWI, and later by the Office of International Information and Cultural Affairs. . . . Another reference, of April 24, 1947, showed that this employee's supervisor in the State Department felt he was a fellow traveler.

Joe had reversed the employee's sex and confused the date of her entry into the United States; he also had neglected to mention that her supervisor changed his mind about her being a "fellow traveler" and decided she was really "loyal but liberal." This was a common failing throughout Joe's cases: he had the habit of leaving out favorable material and exaggerating the unfavorable.

For example, Joe said of another case: "He was recommended for the position by an individual who is listed by the

FBI as a *principal* in a Soviet espionage case," though the 1948 report had identified the person who made the recommendation as a "suspect" in an espionage case.

Another employee was described in the 1948 report as a "very ardent New Dealer" and a "live liberal," to which a fellow boarder in the International House added: "He was one of those accused of being a Red here." Joe, with a sudden regard for brevity, reported on the same case: "He was described in reports by various witnesses as interested in Communism and by his roommate at the International House as a Communist."

In McCarthy's Case No. 5, he switched the place of birth from New York to North Carolina; and in his Case No. 13, he promoted "an applicant for a position as a foreign service officer" to a full-fledged "foreign service officer." But in spite of such discrepancies, the parallel between the Eightieth Congress' dead cases and McCarthy's live ones was unmistakable.

Doggedly, Joe pursued the elusive "proof" he needed to back up his charges. He chased pink shadows through the maze of government bureaus and agencies; he set up his own private spy system; and he pestered newspapermen and petty officials for leads. He also telephoned Congressman Richard Nixon of California, who was later to graduate into the Senate but who was then a big gun on the House Un-American Activities Committee. One of the authors sat opposite Joe in his private office while he pleaded with Nixon over the phone for a peek at the Un-American Activities Committee's secret files.

What help Joe got from the press came from notoriously biased elements: Chicago *Tribune*, Washington *Times-Herald*, and the Hearst chain. These papers had been riding the Red issue for years, and they welcomed Joe aboard and made him chief conductor. Douglass Cater, writing in the *Reporter* magazine on June 6, 1950, said nine-tenths of the

Washington press corps knew that "the Chicago *Tribune* Washington man, Willard Edwards, supplied McCarthy's speech writer with the material for the Lincoln Day address at Wheeling." Later *Times-Herald* Reporter George Waters turned up on McCarthy's payroll; and Hearst's political trouble-shooter, Ken Hunter, became a familiar fixture in Joe's office, pecking at a typewriter.

McCarthy also managed to tap the Loyalty Review Board, a reservoir of rumors, where the waters of fact were processed and the impurities removed; and, for a while, a trickle of confidential information leaked into his office. Invariably, Joe made public only the excerpts that put his victims in a bad light, and kept the rest as it was marked — confidential. It took the Board's parent agency, the Civil Service Commission, a year to plug up the leak; McCarthy's informant appeared to be a 52-year-old spinster, Miriam M. DeHaas, who had held the job of a $7,000-a-year legal examiner.

But there were more sinister forces lurking in the shadows. With startling regularity, the key targets of Joe's attacks turned out to be State Department officials who had opposed the Open Pocketbook policy toward Nationalist China. Certain men had questioned the ability of Chiang's demoralized armies to defend the Chinese mainland; they had reported that American aid money was being diverted into the pockets of corrupt Nationalist officials. And they ended up on McCarthy's Red list.

As scraps of information bubbled to the surface, it became clear that the campaign against Chiang's critics had originated with the "China Lobby." This was the appellation bestowed on a hard core of hired lobbyists, influential friends, and outspoken advocates of Chiang Kai-shek; and few other lobbies exerted such relentless pressure on American foreign and domestic policy. Two of its chief spokesmen were William J. Goodwin, an old Christian Fronter, and Alfred Kohlberg, an importer of Chinese lace.

Goodwin collected a $25,000-a-year salary from the Chinese News Service, the propaganda arm of the Nationalist government. For the benefit of thirsty Congressmen, he threw fancy parties at the Mayflower Hotel and the Metropolitan Club in Washington and at the Wee Tappee Tavern in New York. In an interview with Edward R. Harris of the St. Louis *Post-Dispatch*, Goodwin estimated that he had entertained about one hundred Congressmen a year and had converted half of them to support more aid for Nationalist China. And Goodwin added boastfully that he had "helped materially" to lay the groundwork for Senator McCarthy's attacks on the State Department.

Even more than Goodwin, Lace Dealer Kohlberg ranted and rumbled against the "Communists" in the State Department who were denying American aid to the Chinese Nationalists. But nobody paid much attention to the dapper little man until bigger and louder voices started echoing his charges. In the August 1949 issue of the *China Monthly*, Kohlberg lashed out:

Professor Jessup must therefore be honored by our State Department as the initiator of the smear campaign against Nationalist China and Chiang Kai-shek, and the originator of the myth of the democratic Chinese Communists.

Speaking to the Senate a year later, on March 30, 1950, McCarthy said:

Professor Jessup must therefore be credited by the American people with having pioneered the smear campaign against Nationalist China and Chiang Kai-shek, and with being the originator of the myth of the democratic Chinese Communists.

There could be no doubt that Joe was drawing ammunition from the China Lobby; but the ramifications were far more insidious. The China Lobby was manipulated by five shrewd Chinese emissaries — Chen Chih-mai, Peter T. K.

Pee, W. K. Lee, K. H. Yu, and P. T. Mow — who formed a
sort of "politburo" inside the Chinese embassy. They reported directly to Chiang Kai-shek, using the code signature
"Kung," meaning "group."

The hidden aims of this group were revealed in a collection
of secret cables that fell into American hands through a
Chinese code clerk. The cables were turned over to Senator
Wayne Morse of Oregon, who had them carefully translated
by the Library of Congress. One cable, dated December 5,
1949, reported the likelihood that Soviet-American relations
would not deteriorate; then an ominous sentence appeared
in the message: "Our hope of a world war so as to rehabili-
tate our country is unpalatable to the [American] people."
The implication was that the Nationalists hoped to embroil
the United States in a third World War so that they could
ride back to power in the rumble seat of an American victory.

Another hint was dropped in a cable dated July 14, 1950,
just three weeks after the Korean invasion. "Whether the
Chinese Communists send troops to Korea or not is of sec-
ondary importance, but the war in South Korea will be
extended in any case," cabled the Chinese embassy group.
"We must be patient at this time. Whether or not the war
will extend to other places in Europe and Asia, we should
make little comment and wait for the development of the
situation."

The secret cables also made it clear who was blocking
Nationalist aid and aims in Washington. "In the past years
we have been very patient with General Marshall, but he
has never changed his attitude towards us," reported another
cable, dated August 24, 1949. "But in order to avoid a direct
break with the American administration, it is better for us
not to attack him personally." It was left for McCarthy to
carry the attack to Marshall personally, which he did in a 60,-
000-word Senate speech on June 14, 1951 (see Chapter 36).

Joe was finicky about being seen in public with anyone Chinese. He tried to avoid the slightest appearance of a connection with the China Lobby; and once he returned a $500 check mailed to him by Alfred Kohlberg. But the liaison existed nonetheless.

Joe's was a one-man performance, but many prompters stood in the wings.

31. Spies for Hire

AMERICANS HAVE BEEN BROUGHT UP ON TALL TALES OF FOREIGN
spies; secret-agent dramas can be heard almost nightly on
the radio; and spy-thriller movies enjoy a high box-office
appeal. This public enthusiasm for cloak-and-dagger adventure was never more pronounced than in 1950, when there
appeared on the American scene Joe McCarthy, counter-spy.

The "Joe McCarthy Counter-Spy Agency (with Branches
in All States and Many Capitals of the World)" operated out
of room 5-A of the Senate Office Building. In this basement
room there were telephones, dictaphones, tape-recording
devices, and other scientific marvels useful to a spy-catcher
in the modern age.

A first-person account of what went on in room 5-A has
been given, under oath, by Emmanuel S. Larsen, an old
China hand who spied for the Chinese Nationalists but who
was caught on the other side of the Chinese fence in the
Amerasia case. Larsen had been told that Joe would attack
him personally on the Senate floor; so he asked for an interview with McCarthy in April 1950 to explain how he got
mixed up in the *Amerasia* matter. Joe said he was too busy
to listen, but suggested that Larsen and Investigator Don
Surine adjourn to room 5-A and talk it over.

"So we went downstairs to room 5-A," Larsen recalled.
"That is their chamber of horrors, bristling with dictaphones
and recording machines. There must be eight or ten of them
there. We sat down at a desk, he on one side and I opposite."

Larsen said Surine told him: "If you give the evidence we want . . . if you string along with us, then it will go easier with you." When Larsen started to interject a comment, Surine

. . . stood up and roared at me: "Are you defending *Amerasia?*" and I said, "No, Mr. Surine, I am defending myself." He kept standing up. The phone rang. . . . Surine . . . said, "Uh, uh, uh, all right, all right," and put the phone down.

But for all its implications, Joe's counter-spy show was more of a comedy than a tragedy. For sheer, raucous humor, nothing could beat a visit to Senator Joe's office while he was "making" a case. McCarthy did not carry a magnifying glass or smoke a curved-neck pipe, but he utilized all the other standard props of the fictional detective. The writing brothers, Joseph and Stewart Alsop, summed up such a madcap scene for the *Saturday Evening Post:*

A visit to the McCarthy lair on Capitol Hill is rather like being transported to the set of one of Hollywood's minor thrillers. The anteroom is generally full of furtive-looking characters who look as though they might be suborned State Department men. McCarthy, himself, despite a creeping baldness and a continual tremor which makes his head shake in a disconcerting fashion, is reasonably well cast as the Hollywood version of a strong-jawed private eye. A visitor is likely to find him with his heavy shoulders hunched forward, a telephone in his huge hands, shouting cryptic instructions to some mysterious ally.

"Yeah, yeah, I can listen, but I can't talk. Get me? You really got the goods on the guy?" The Senator glances up to note the effect of this drama on his visitor. "Yeah? Well, I tell you. Just mention this sort of casual to Number One, and get his reaction. Okay? Okay. I'll contact you later."

The drama is heightened by a significant bit of stage business. For as Senator McCarthy talks he sometimes strikes the mouthpiece of his telephone with a pencil. As Washington folklore has it, this is supposed to jar the needle of any concealed listening device.

Joe's agents have been scattered from Washington to Formosa, from Paris to Calcutta, from Los Angeles to

Geneva. The size of his private Gestapo has numbered as high as sixteen. Their assignment: to dig up "evidence" enabling Joe to shout "Communist" at a few more Americans.

Heading up this far-flung organization was Don Surine, a former FBI investigator. Surine was fired from the FBI in 1950, after it was learned that he was consorting with a buxom Baltimore beauty, whom he was supposed to be investigating on a white-slavery charge. It was only a dispute, Surine testified, "over the question of the development of an informant which involved my taking a practical means to a desired end." A few weeks later, he turned up as Joe McCarthy's chief operative.

Joe often boasted about his investigation system and delighted in telling visitors that his agents covered the entire globe. According to McCarthy, his spy network was necessary to continue the fight against Reds in government. "I began to be swamped with tips," he explained. "Most of them could be run down in this country, but some of them required investigation abroad. When I need a man in some particular part of the world — and I've needed help in quite a few places — I just check around and get in touch with someone I can depend upon. Much of the stuff I get is worthless, but on the other hand some of it has proved very valuable."

Once he hired a man who secured for him five photostatted pages of Chinese records. This was no mean feat, since the records came from old Chinese Nationalist secret-police files, and China was then under Communist control. How Joe's agent was able to smuggle secret Nationalist files from under the nose of Communist Mao Tse-tung, McCarthy has never made clear. "You just can't operate unless you protect your sources," Joe explained.

On another occasion, Joe sent an investigator to India to track down rumors that the Army had dumped ammunition into the Indian Ocean rather than deliver it to the Chinese

Nationalists. It turned out that the baptized ammunition was deteriorated and dangerous, and that the Chinese were allowed to pick out what they wanted before it was jettisoned. But Joe stuck to the original version of the story, which made for more indignant speeches.

In an interview with Associated Press Writer Marvin Arrowsmith, McCarthy disclosed additional information about his spy system that enabled the reporter to write: "So he [McCarthy] hired a man in Paris, for example, a trained investigator. That produced material, McCarthy said, which figured in some of the charges he later made." This statement, made early in 1950, seemed totally insignificant at the time, but it turned up in an entirely different light some months later.

McCarthy's "trained investigator" in Paris was John Farrand, who, on McCarthy's behalf, hired an American Negro with Communistic leanings to dig up some evidence against John Carter Vincent, then American Minister to Switzerland. The American Negro, Charles Davis, attempted to frame Vincent with a faked telegram. He affixed the name of a known Communist, Emile Stampfli, to the spurious message in an attempt to make it appear that Vincent was in communication with Communists. Although the trick had been carefully worked out by Davis and Farrand, the Swiss police discovered the source of the telegram and arrested Davis; Farrand was safe in Paris.

At the trial before a five-man Swiss court, Davis confessed receiving money "from certain persons in the U. S. of rightwing tendency in return for information."

Justice Albert Rais demanded to know their identity.

"I can only state," said Davis, "that one with whom I had contact was Senator Joseph R. McCarthy."

Davis testified that he had been in close touch with McCarthy's European chief, Farrand, and had talked to McCarthy himself by transatlantic telephone.

"You tried to compromise the American Minister," Justice Rais accused, "by implying he was a Communist, as you sent a telegram demanding information on a Communist."

Prosecutor René Dubois asked Davis if he alone drew up the telegram.

"There was another person involved in sending it," Davis replied. "The other person was Farrand."

The Swiss court added up the score against Davis in a blistering *acte d'accusation,* which is comparable to an indictment in a U. S. court. It charged:

Davis was called to Paris by an emissary of McCarthy, John E. Farrand, who charged him with watching the relationships and contacts of the American diplomatic and consular personnel in Switzerland, particularly Mr. John Carter Vincent, Minister at Berne. Davis was paid for this by Farrand. McCarthy transmitted a part of the information to the United States Federal Bureau of Investigation.

In observing the actions and movements of persons in Switzerland, and informing foreign agents of findings and deductions made, Davis maintained a political intelligence service punishable by law. With this service, he was acting in the interest of a foreign power.

In supplying information to Senator McCarthy, he was acting in the interests of a foreign intelligence service. McCarthy, a spokesman or representative of the opposition in the American Senate, seeks to collect information to confound the Truman administration and establish, if possible, a connivance between the diplomatic and consular corps of his country and the Communist world.

To this end, he has surrounded himself with assistants and investigators. In view of the aims pursued by the Senator, one is confronted by a foreign political organization whose activity on our territory is incompatible with the independence of Switzerland and constitutes, in the final analysis, a violation of our sovereignty. Davis is accused of political espionage.

The final verdict: guilty. The sentence: eight months in jail, followed by deportation to the United States. When Joe learned what had happened to his operative in Geneva, he ducked, then shrugged. In the tradition that a captured spy is on his own, Joe at first denied all knowledge of the

hapless Mr. Davis. But the Swiss court produced letters to
Davis from McCarthy, who then refreshed his recollection
and admitted that a letter or two had passed between them.
Joe even remembered talking to Davis on the transatlantic
phone, but he explained that Davis just wanted $25.

"Davis was just one of the many thousands of people who
write to me offering to sell information," Joe said. And, as an
afterthought, he added: "I've had some experience right
along with the State Department trying to plant phonies on
my staff, although I don't claim that Davis was one."

Thus disowned by his chief, Charlie Davis was a disillu-
sioned and hurt young man. "I never dreamed the Senator
would turn his back on me," Davis said. And after he was
deported from Switzerland, he made a beeline for Washington and marched up to Capitol Hill to see if McCarthy had
really betrayed him. "I won't believe it until I hear it from
the Senator's own lips," he said. But he learned it was true —
whereupon he filed a $100,000 suit for libel and back wages
against McCarthy. Later it developed that Davis had been
discharged from the Navy after admitting he was a homo-
sexual. He also signed an affidavit, confessing past membership in the Communist Party.

And thus Joe, who had been searching high and low for
someone with a Communist record in the State Department,
discovered one had been on his own staff.

This was not the only time McCarthy had been tripped up
in his own international net. One day Joe and his assistants
were sitting in his office, reveling in newspaper accounts of
Louis Budenz' testimony against Owen Lattimore. The
phone rang, and Joe answered. "I can furnish you documentary evidence to support your charges against Lattimore," the caller said in a low tone. Joe took the man's name
and address and said: "I'll have one of my investigators come
around and talk to you."

The mysterious caller turned out to be a Washington cab

driver, who described himself as a one-time member of the NKVD, Russia's powerful secret police. Joe's investigator was impressed by the man's recitation of names and dates, and he asked for the "documentary proof" against Lattimore. "The evidence is buried in the sand down in Cuba, behind an old seamen's union building near Havana," the cabbie said.

Thus began a strange international adventure. Joe deputized a close friend as an investigator and dispatched him to Cuba with the cabbie. After three days of disappointing searches, the cabbie said he had finally located the spot where the evidence was buried. But a terrible thing had happened; someone had built a concrete floor over the top of it. Now if Joe's friend would just put up a little money to remove the floor . . .

McCarthy's friend flew back to Washington and told Joe he had been hoaxed. A few days later a woman visited Joe, told him she had heard about the deal, and informed McCarthy that the cabbie had never been a member of the NKVD. What he had wanted was a few days of expense-paid vacation in Cuba to get over a cold. "But where did he get all the information about ex-Communists and fellow travelers?" asked one of Joe's assistants. "Oh," the woman said, "he was once an investigator for a fraternal organization." Thus the case ended. And McCarthy tried to get back on the good side of his friend, an ex-naval officer, who had put up the money.

Joe's agents worked hard chasing leads around the world. But for all their hocus-pocus, secret messages, and carefully drawn affidavits, at this writing they have produced no proof of a single Communist in the State Department.

32. Rabbit Hunter

SENATOR McCARTHY'S STATE DEPARTMENT "COMMUNISTS" had a troublesome habit of turning up in other places; only one of the first four he named was even in the government. But to Joe, this was an unimportant detail; he lumped them all together in the State Department anyway.

Of the four who led his list, Gustavo Duran and Mrs. Mary Jane Keeney were employed by the United Nations and had no direct connection with the United States government. Joe was right about the third, Julian Wadleigh, who had indeed indulged in subversive activities in the State Department. The only trouble was that he had been a prosecution witness in the Alger Hiss trials and had admitted passing documents to Whittaker Chambers — all this some time before Joe got around to naming him. Only John Stewart Service was still employed by the State Department when McCarthy first mentioned his name.

Nor did Joe's accuracy improve. When he discovered he was behind the times on Wadleigh, he hastily dropped Wadleigh's name and substituted Harlow Shapley. But this one was even further off the mark: Shapley was a Harvard astronomer who had never had any connection with the State Department (see Chapter 28).

And so it went with McCarthy's "list." Dorothy Kenyon was a New York lawyer who had never worked for the State Department; the closest she came was as U. S. representative (and thus paid out of State Department funds) to the United Nations Commission on the Status of Women. Dr. Frederick L. Schuman was a Williams College professor, whose connection was limited to a one-hour lecture delivered without pay in 1946 to the Foreign Service Institute. George Wheeler, who McCarthy claimed had been cleared by the State Department's loyalty board, was never considered by that board, although under a technicality he drew his salary through the State Department for three months in 1946.

Of McCarthy's controversial list of 205, only 46 were on the State Department payroll in February 1950, when he addressed the worried ladies of Wheeling. All 46 had survived full field investigations by the FBI and had been cleared by State's own loyalty and security board. It was the same with Joe's list of 57 "Communists"; many had taken jobs in other departments and in private employment. Even after Joe expanded the list to 81, only half were actually connected with the Department; and they also had gone through the investigative mill.

Joe's carelessness with details also extended to the "proof" he dished up. His recipe for a "case" was to mix up an assortment of Communist-front organizations, add a helping of hearsay testimony from professional ex-Communists, and splatter the mixture over the most convenient victim. Then it would turn out that the unsuspecting victim had never been connected with the Communist fronts in the first place, or else had joined innocently and under honorable circumstances. And as for the mischievous testimony of the repentant Communists, those perennial witnesses demonstrated a remarkable facility for remembering more details as the years went on and the publicity rewards increased.

From time to time, Joe was embarrassed to find his "evidence" pointing in the wrong direction — at members of his own crowd. Such Rock-of-Gibraltar Republicans as Senator Robert Taft of Ohio and Senator Homer Ferguson of Michigan turned up on Joe's suspect lists; for few prominent people got through the wartime period of Russo-American co-operation without sponsoring some dinner or joining some organization or issuing some statement friendly to Russia. So Joe's slapdash methods might just as easily have incriminated Taft, who once posed chummily with Communist Earl Browder; or Ferguson, who joined the Institute of Pacific Relations, which later became a target for investigations of Communist infiltration; or Columnist George Sokolsky, who wrote glowingly about Frederick Vanderbilt Field until he turned out to be a sugar-daddy for Communist causes — or even Joe McCarthy himself, whose skirts were covered with the Red fingerprints of Rudolf Aschenauer and Charles Davis.

So from the very start Joe tended to shift his charges downward. Victims who started out as "card-carrying Communists," in McCarthy's book, usually ended up simply as "bad policy risks." Those who had been called "traitors" on the Senate floor became "stupid," "suspicious," or "degenerate" in public speeches — "bad for America and good for Soviet Russia" was a favorite McCarthy phrase.

And Joe was noticeably braver when he stood on the solid, libel-proof floor of the Senate. Away from his Senate shooting gallery, his cannon balls often disintegrated into powder puffs; or at such times as he let go full blast at specific individuals, he slyly read from his own Senate speeches, which gave him immunity. During a speech in Reno, he was carried away by his own oratory and used epithets stronger than he had intended. He anxiously explained to reporters afterwards that he had not meant to imply that the persons he named were disloyal. But the reporters insisted he had actually called them traitors. Angrily, McCarthy shouted: "I did not! And I didn't call them Communist either!"

Even on the Senate floor he came close to backing down on some of his charges. On March 30, 1950, the Senate was surprised to hear him say: "Perhaps some of those individuals would be able to produce facts to offset the effect of the material in the files and show that they were actually loyal employees." He went on to explain that making the names public would be "unfair to some of the individuals who might be able to produce evidence giving them a clean bill of health." But there was another reason for Joe's touching regard for the feelings of the innocent: He was referring to his 81 cases, whose names he had previously offered to give to the Senate. It later developed that he never possessed the names at all; he had only the case histories without the names; so — in a great show of fairness — he refused to mention names that he didn't have in the first place.

But as other items bubbled up in Joe's Red mudpot, he changed his policy about holding back names in order to spare the innocent. And he vigorously defended this new policy at the Fifth Marine Division's 1951 convention in New York City. Shouted Joe:

Let me assure you that those who shed crocodile tears for the families of traitors whom I expose, with no tears left over for the families of American boys who were betrayed by those traitors, are scaring no one. Let me assure you that regardless of how high-pitched becomes the squealing and screaming of those left-wing, bleeding-heart, phony liberals, this battle is going to go on.

As McCarthy's fame spread, audiences across the country flocked to see his traveling medicine show. He accepted more and more outside speaking engagements; and his lecture fees climbed from an average of $300 a night up into the four-figure bracket.

Joe's speeches followed pretty much the same pattern. Usually he would be preceded by a color guard, followed by a mass recitation of the Pledge of Allegiance to the Flag. Then Joe would walk on stage to the thunderous roar of the crowd. He would wave tolerantly or clasp his hands above his head in a gesture of bravado; then he would hold up his hands for quiet. Invariably, his first sentence would be:

"Well, it's good to get away from Washington and back here in the United States." And with the attitude of a martyr, he would begin by telling the same story to each new audience, illustrating why he "had to do this dirty job":

Take my word for it, I don't enjoy this task. It is a dirty, disagreeable job, but a job which must be done. When I was a boy on the farm, my mother used to raise chickens. The greatest enemy the chickens had were skunks. In order to protect mother's chickens, my three brothers and I had to dig out and destroy those skunks. It was a dirty, foul, unpleasant, smelly job. And sometimes after it was done, people did not like to have us sit next to them in church.

But the high spot of Joe's speech would come when he waved a sheaf of papers wildly in the air and shouted: "I hold in my hand the proof." Then he would shuffle through the papers and read excerpts from affidavits and testimony. (It was the same old mixture of hearsay and innuendo, the kind of "evidence" that would not stand up in court.) To many it sounded convincing. For it had the ring of documentation; and Joe spoke with a trace of awkwardness that audiences took for sincerity.

But there were others who saw through the affable grin and the homey speaking style, the table-pounding and the arm-waving. One such listener reported that McCarthy's proof reminded him of the story about the rabbit-hunter who claimed that his quarry had run up a tree. When other hunters doubted the story, he replied indignantly: "Yessir, that rabbit certainly did climb a tree. What's more, my dog had to run up the tree to catch him. And if you don't believe me, I'll show you the tree."

33. Smoking Out the Facts

MANY AMERICANS, AFTER A FEW WHIFFS OF THE SMOKE pouring from Senator Joe McCarthy's office, came to the conclusion that "where there is so much smoke, there must be some fire."

When the authors hunted for McCarthy's fire, they discovered, of course, the ashes where the fires of treason had burned — the Alger Hiss, Judith Coplon, and Julian Wadleigh cases; but these fires had already been discovered without any help from Joe. Here and there, they glimpsed a flicker of suspicion; but the McCarthy smoke blotted out any real fire that might have been underneath. Was all of Joe's siren-blowing just one big false alarm?

The authors, of course, could not look into the hearts of Joe's victims; the cases could be judged only by the facts on the record at the time. McCarthy, probably, had fingered some fellow travelers and even Party members by the simple accident of pointing in all directions at once. But so far the record was plain — two and a half years after making his first charges, Joe had failed to come up with solid evidence that could convict a single Communist, spy, or traitor. To dramatize this, Maryland's ex-Senator Millard Tydings called Joe's bluff with a $25,000 offer if he could prove his charges in court; and more than two years later, after frequent repetitions of the offer, Joe still had not made a single move to claim this fat prize.

Some years ago, it was an intellectual fad in certain quarters to view Communism as a new tide rolling in, and to regard the Soviet Union as the lunar force governing that tide. Men of this mind thought they saw the approach of a Communist flood that would engulf the world; they did not notice that their "wave of the future" — like the Nazi "wave of the future" that swamped certain other Americans — had already washed out the rights and liberties of once-free men.

In the authors' opinion, the camp followers of both Moscow-centered and Berlin-centered tyrannies have been equally dangerous.

This didn't mean that all men whose names turned up on somebody's letterhead were fellow travelers, though some were fooled by the counterfeit coin that the Communists flashed, for the Reds pretended to champion many humanitarian causes; but these were only tactical maneuvers in the battle for men's minds.

Joe, however, wasn't one to make fine distinctions; he lumped all his victims under the same label: "Red." Many were innocent even of the taint of Communism; some had bathed in the pink waters of Marxist ideology; and if a few were actual card-carriers, Joe with all his bluster had not managed to prove it. Yet the fact that Joe couldn't prove his case against a single victim didn't deter him. He simply moved on to the next.

Once Joe thought he had found a real Communist, and he announced that his whole campaign against the State Department would "stand or fall" on that case. But when the evidence failed to measure up to his expectations, he manufactured new evidence more to his liking. The case was that of a mysterious Mr. X, whom Joe described as "a Moscow-born Communist high in the State Department." Then Senator Brien McMahon of Connecticut introduced twenty-one affidavits supporting the loyalty of Mr. X, and Senator Wayne Morse of Oregon revealed his name as Edward G.

Posniak. He was not "high in the State Department," as Joe had said, but only an economist in the East European division. And he had been driven out of Russia with his family by the Communists.

After Senators McMahon and Morse took sides with Posniak, Joe came up with a document which he said was a secret FBI report showing Posniak to be a Red agent. This was news to the FBI, which investigated and found the document to be an out-and-out forgery. Disturbed over this, G-man J. Edgar Hoover sent two agents around to talk it over with McCarthy; but the Senator declined to discuss the matter and ordered his staff not to answer the FBI's questions. It struck the authors of this book that forging an FBI document ought to be against the law; so one of them asked J. Howard McGrath, then the Attorney General, why the Justice Department did not prosecute the case. "We don't want to make a martyr out of McCarthy," was the answer.

But Joe showed no such restraint when it came to going after his victims. He dribbled out new names every few weeks; and every time he rolled one off his tongue, another reputation was damaged. The victims' statements couldn't begin to compete with the sensational charges made against them; the stain on their reputations couldn't be wiped clean. You can't unscramble eggs.

And Joe must have known what he was doing. More than once in Joe's early youth, the fierce patriotism of the Wisconsin north-country folk flamed up and got out of control. When he was eight years old, the United States entered World War I, and the region was fired with a hot hatred against the Germans. John Durel, a German farmer who lived a few fields away from the McCarthys, was dragged from his home in the early morning and ordered to purchase Liberty Bonds, then and there, or be hanged. The farmer had already bought bonds; and not liking intimidation, he said: "I will not sign up at this time of night." A rope was already around his neck when cooler heads prevailed and his life was spared.

In 1936, Joe's home town of Appleton echoed with the assault-and-battery of a riot between the students of Lawrence College and the advocates of the Gold Star Mothers. The cause was a suspicion that Red subversives had sponsored a student parade. It developed that the parade had been authorized by the college president, Dr. H. M. Wriston; but many students had already been clubbed and injured.

So Joe was familiar with the explosive force of such words as "disloyal," "Communist," and "traitor." But even as he hurled these words with reckless abandon, he denied that he was hurting any innocent people. At the height of his clamor against "Communists," Joe appeared on the slicked-up, streamlined television show "Keeping Posted." His adversary was the affable, homey, but ineffectual Phil La Follette — the former Governor of Wisconsin and brother of "Young Bob" La Follette, Jr. La Follette roamed from one generality to another, but always returned to his basic theme: a sweeping charge that McCarthy's unsubstantiated charges were "hurting innocent people." Joe, however, with an air of injured innocence, demanded: "What people?" La Follette rambled on, and never gave a specific answer. But dozens of Joe's victims, blacklisted at work and blackballed by their neighbors, could have answered. They had learned that a man can be ruined regardless of how false the charges against him, because no amount of back-page truth can offset a front-page lie.

34. *L'affaire* Lattimore

Senator Joe McCarthy put on his act under the white-domed Capitol, a Big Top in marble and pillars.

The crowd, subdued by the stately environment, would surge into the hearing room; Joe, arriving at the last minute, would walk into an electrical storm of exploding flashbulbs; reporters would scramble for seats at long picnic tables spread with yellow scratch paper; the newsreel and television crews would focus their photographic field artillery on the target area; klieg lights would produce sudden sunrises and sunsets in the room, plunging the proceedings into alternate glare and gloom. And Joe, in the role of the accuser, would be ready to deliver another dramatic, finger-pointing harangue on the subject of Communist spies and international intrigue.

In the first year of his campaign, Joe played the same scene over a dozen times. The script varied; he injected new names into each performance; but it was always the same old act. Some names he hit once in passing and never mentioned again; others he came back to; but there was one case he never let rest. This was the case of Owen J. Lattimore.

L'affaire Lattimore began in March 1950, with the cryptic McCarthy announcement that he would reveal the name of the "top Russian espionage agent in the United States" (see Chapter 28). If true, this would have been the sensation of the year; reporters dogged Joe's trail, trying to learn the identity of this sinister figure. Joe, wearing a conspiratorial air, whispered the name "off the record" until it got around town; finally he told one of the authors of this book to go ahead and publish it. Then Joe sat back and waited for the explosion. The result was a front-page story in every newspaper in the land; the name of the "top Russian spy" was Owen Lattimore.

But Lattimore was a strange man for such an awesome role — a prissy, mild-mannered professor of political science at Johns Hopkins University. It soon developed, however, that the gentle manner concealed a tart tongue. Lattimore lashed out at McCarthy with derisive invective, stinging him with such epithets as "the Wisconsin whimperer" and "a graduate witch-burner." As for the professor's role in the Communist scheme of things, he claimed to be a babe in the woods. "I was not an expert on Communism," he said. And he complained: "I'm probably the least listened-to Far Eastern expert in the country."

The professor was much too modest. He had been personal political adviser to Chiang Kai-shek, on the nomination of President Roosevelt, 1941-42; chief of Pacific operations for the Office of War Information, 1942-44; traveling companion with Vice President Henry Wallace in Soviet Siberia and China, 1944; an economic adviser on the President's Reparation Mission to Japan, 1946; and a participant in a State Department conference on China policy, 1949. One of the authors, as a wartime correspondent in China, also recalls that Lattimore's views were widely quoted among diplomats in Chungking.

McCarthy, for his part, announced: "I am willing to stand or fall on this one. If I am shown to be wrong on this, I think the sub-committee would be justified in not taking my other cases too seriously." As for the proof, Joe said it could all be found in the FBI files. Ordinarily, this would have been a safe gambit, because the FBI files had always been shut tight to outsiders. It had been the announced policy of President Harry Truman and FBI Director J. Edgar Hoover not to open the files, even to snooping, subpoena-armed Senators.

But there was nothing in the rules to prevent G-man Hoover from examining his own files and reporting back to Congress. On the witness stand, he repeated the warning that opening his dossiers would result in "complete collapse" of FBI procedures and would dry up its sources; besides, he said, the files contained unchecked rumors and idle gossip. But he testified that he had gone over the Lattimore file himself and could state that it contained no evidence to back up McCarthy's charges. And he made available to members of the Tydings sub-committee a summary of all the information the FBI possessed on Lattimore.

Badly shaken, Joe recovered in time to issue a statement saying that Hoover's testimony meant only that he, McCarthy, knew things even the FBI didn't know. But with all his heavy artillery, he couldn't drown out the effect of Hoover's bomb burst; so Joe made a strategic retreat. "In the case of Lattimore," he acknowledged to the Senate, "I may have placed too much stress on whether or not he had been an espionage agent." What was really important, he now said, was Lattimore's position as "chief architect of our Far Eastern policy . . . forgetting for the time being any question of membership in the Communist Party or participation in espionage." Even the Marine Corps League, when it bestowed its 1950 Americanism award on Joe at Passaic, New Jersey, could not goad him into repeating his charges that Lattimore was an espionage agent. "I think that Owen Lattimore is extremely dangerous," McCarthy said — thus putting the professor in the same general classification with TNT and acute hyperacidity.

Then began the parade of witnesses before the Tydings

sub-committee. Louis Budenz said that, as former editor of the Communist *Daily Worker,* he had been "officially informed" by the highest American Communists that Owen Lattimore was a member of their underground. Yet in all his years of informing the FBI, Budenz was forced to admit, he had never happened to mention the name of Owen Lattimore. Following Budenz on the stand came Dr. Bella Dodd, another former high-ranking American Communist who had turned Catholic. She told the sub-committee: "In all my association with the Communist Party, I never heard his [Lattimore's] name mentioned either as a Party member or as a fellow traveler, or even as a friend."

The next person scheduled was John J. Huber, a New York "private eye" and a McCarthy "mystery witness," who turned out to be even more mysterious than his billing. This much was known: he reached Washington and got as far as Senator McCarthy's office, because he covered this distance with the Senator himself. But when it came Huber's turn on the witness stand, he was nowhere to be found. The next day, he telephoned the Associated Press from a Manhattan pay station. He said that he had "blacked out" just before the hearing and, when he came to, found himself back in New York. Later Huber improved on his story by claiming he had also been mysteriously assaulted by unidentified men. And so Huber was forgotten until he turned up a year later, his amnesia cured, on McCarthy's private payroll.

The next witness was Earl Browder, the Kansas-born ex-boss of the U. S. Communist Party, who said that he had never met Lattimore, did not know him as a Communist and had never heard him mentioned in Communist circles. Then came Frederick Vanderbilt Field, who had been a financial angel to the Reds. He testified that he had known Lattimore since 1934; but, said Field, "to the best of my knowledge and belief," Lattimore was not a Communist. Next, Mrs. Freda Utley, an ex-Communist writer, said she had no proof that Owen Lattimore had joined the Communist Party, although she suspected he had followed the "line."

Finally, Brigadier General Elliot Thorpe, chief of counterespionage and civil intelligence for General Douglas MacArthur during World War II, was sworn in. He told about three investigations he had made of Lattimore. The evidence in support of Lattimore's loyalty was so conclusive, General Thorpe testified, that the professor had been given access to top secrets. Furthermore, said Thorpe, he would unhesitatingly commit his own personal safety and that of his command to Lattimore. It was also brought out that Lattimore had helped raise funds for Finland when that tiny nation was attacked by Russia, and had supported the Marshall Plan — which Russia opposed.

The Lattimore case was laid to rest in 1950 by the Tydings sub-committee, only to be resurrected a year later by a new sub-committee, led by Senator Pat McCarran of Nevada. This group had raided the E. C. Carter farm in Lee, Massachusetts, during a snowstorm, and had come up with some old files of the Institute of Pacific Relations. (See Chapter 50.) Among the papers were articles, letters, and memoranda written by Lattimore, giving a new insight into his activities. These documents still fell far short of proving McCarthy's first charge — that Lattimore was Russia's "top espionage agent" in this country. But evidence was brought to light that the professor had used his influence to deflect American policy toward Moscow.

Probably the most embarrassing document was a letter Owen Lattimore wrote to E. C. Carter on July 10, 1938. Here are the two most pertinent paragraphs:

I think that you are pretty cagey in turning over so much of the China section of the inquiry to Asiaticus, Han-seng, and Chi. They will bring out the absolutely essential radical aspects, but can be depended on to do it with the right touch.

For the general purposes of this inquiry it seems to me that the good scoring position, for the IPR, differs with different countries. For China, my hunch is that it will pay to keep behind the official Chinese Communist position — far enough not to be covered by the same label — but enough ahead of the active Chinese liberals to be noticeable. For Japan, on the other hand, hang back so as not to be inconveniently ahead of the Japanese liberals, who cannot keep up, whereas the Chinese liberals can. So the chief thing is to oppose the military wing of Japanese aggression in China, counting on a check there to take care of both the military and civilian components of aggression in Japan. For the British — scare the hell out of them, always in a polite way, but usually in a way that looks as if it might turn impolite. The British liberal groups are badly flustered; but being British, the way to encourage them to pull themselves together is to fluster the Tories. For the USSR — back their international policy in general, but without giving them or anybody else the impression of subservience.

Confronted with this letter, Lattimore insisted that "I used the word 'radical,' of course, in its dictionary sense of 'fundamental.'" But few, even among those inclined to be favorable toward him, were convinced by this novel argument.

This letter alone didn't prove that Lattimore was tuned to a Moscow wave length, for many sincere Americans were thinking along the same line in 1938. But it was a strange line for an IPR official who was supposed, above all, to be academic and objective. The little professor, while editor of the IPR magazine *Pacific Affairs*, also got into four disputes in print; on all four occasions, he defended the Communists. The first was a quarrel with a Britisher over the two great Asiatic powers, Japan and Russia; Lattimore argued that Japanese policy was aggressive, while Russian policy was strictly defensive. The second was a dispute with Dr. Hsu Shuhsi, which finally led the learned Chinese to tell Lattimore: "I have no quarrel with you over your sympathy with the Mongols and the Communists." In the third dispute with W. E. Wheeler, the professor came to the defense of Edgar

Snow and the Chinese Communists. But the fourth disagreement, with William Henry Chamberlin, was the most revealing; Lattimore in 1938 defended the infamous Russian purge trials.

Testimony before the committee showed that Lattimore contradicted himself on several issues related to the Soviet Union. In the case of Outer Mongolia, Lattimore told Ambassador William C. Bullitt that Mongolia was a completely independent republic, with no Moscow control, and should therefore be accorded diplomatic recognition as such by the United States. On the other hand, when he wanted to *enter* Outer Mongolia, he sent his application for the necessary papers not to Mongolia but to Moscow.

In the case of Korea, Lattimore wrote in 1949: "The thing to do, therefore, is to let South Korea fall — but not to let it look as though we pushed it."

He wandered so far toward the Soviets that he was asked to join the editorial board of *China Today*, an out-and-out Communist magazine. The chief editors were listed as Frederick Spencer, J. W. Phillips, and Hansu Chan — pseudonyms for Frederick Vanderbilt Field, Philip Jaffe, and Chi Ch'ao-ting, all Communist spokesmen. Lattimore turned down the invitation with the comment: "There has already been considerable kick about my being on the board of *Amerasia*," he wrote. "It is probably better for me not to invite extra kicks by going on the board of *China Today*, which is more partisan, and more obviously partisan, than *Amerasia*."

Meanwhile, Presidential-hopeful Harold Stassen, Ex-diplomat Eugene Dooman, Professors William McGovern, Kenneth Colegrove, Karl Wittfogel, and David Rowe variously testified before the McCarran sub-committee that Lattimore followed a line favorable to the Communists. Another witness, former Red Army Intelligence Officer Alexander Barmine, said that his Russian superiors referred to the

Johns Hopkins professor as one of "our men."

The angry professor answered with a blistering, fifty-page statement, flailing away at the McCarran inquiry as "a reign of terror." But he was interrupted at every sentence by the cantankerous McCarran; and it took three days for him to finish reading his statement. Under cross-examination by Chief Counsel Robert Morris, who had left McCarthy's payroll to go to work for McCarran, Lattimore began to retreat a little. Morris' procedure was to ask Lattimore to recall events, conversations, and correspondence a decade or more in the past; and when he suffered a lapse of memory over that long stretch, Morris would pounce on him with something from the files.

Previously, Lattimore had said he didn't realize Frederick Vanderbilt Field was a Communist until 1940-41 — after Lattimore's term as *Pacific Affairs* editor had ended. But a letter from the IPR file persuaded him that the date was wrong. "My memory was in error by about two years," he admitted. And one IPR memo from Field to Lattimore produced at the hearing warned Editor Lattimore, concerning a certain article, that "the analysis is a straight Marxist one and . . . should not be altered."

In the McCarran report of the hearings held from July 25, 1951, to June 20, 1952, by the Senate sub-committee on internal security, Lattimore was charged specifically with having been "from some time, beginning in the 1930's, a conscious articulate instrument of the Soviet conspiracy." The report went into detail about what it considered the non-objective, pro-Communist policy of *Pacific Affairs*, which Lattimore had edited up until 1941, and declared that Lattimore had "testified falsely before the sub-committee with reference to at least five separate matters that were relevant to the inquiry and substantial in import." It was on the basis of these alleged false statements — including Lattimore's claims of ignorance of the Communist connections of several writers for the magazine — that the sub-committee asked for a Justice Department investigation for possible perjury.

In the report, close association between various IPR officials and Russian leaders, including several in the intelligence service, was indicated, and a number of witnesses testified to the high repute in which the IPR was held by the Soviet Union, ostensibly for propaganda purposes. Questioning also emphasized the close relationship between Lattimore and other IPR leaders — including Frederick Vanderbilt Field — who had an important role in influencing the organization's policies.

Lattimore himself was shown to have been usually commendatory toward the Soviet Union, which had set up an affiliate organization with the IPR, although on several occasions he was critical of Russian policy. He seemed to be walking a tightrope between his desire to publish articles by leading Marxists that would put over the Soviet line in the strongest possible language, and his desire to avoid being tripped up by non-Communist nations that were also members of the IPR.

Stated Lattimore: "I have already denied under oath any sympathy for or participation in Soviet activities. . . . I am convinced that when this long record is read and studied, no reasonable man can place credence in any of the charges against me."

An old American trait is sympathy for the underdog. One consequence of McCarthy's tactics of machine-gunning everything in sight — as he treated the coconut trees of his Marine days — was this: many decent citizens automatically sympathized with virtually every McCarthy target. And this complicated, rather than helped, the nation's effort to find the truth.

In the case of Lattimore, the truth was elusive. It seemed to be clear, however, that as the controversy dragged on,

Lattimore was winning few new supporters, even though many had been repelled by the undocumented, shoot-from-the-hip accusations of McCarthy months before.

The *New Leader* magazine, in its issue of March 31, 1952, published a sixteen-page indictment of Lattimore and the IPR, written by Professor Richard L. Walker of the Far Eastern History Department at Yale. Lattimore replied to it and charged that the article was a "slanderous attack." Professor Walker wrote a rebuttal, in which he stated that Lattimore had juggled dates and shifted ground on his opinions for the purposes of testimony. Walker also re-emphasized his documentation of an apparent pro-Communist slant in Lattimore's editing of *Pacific Affairs*.

Meanwhile, Joe McCarthy again began making industrious use of the Lattimore case. By the middle of June 1952, the rumor leaked out of McCarthy's office that Lattimore might try to skip the country; it was spread by Joe's henchman, Don Surine. The whisper took on substance a few days later, when the State Department confirmed a Baltimore news story that Lattimore had been barred from leaving the country. The Department had acted on a "reliable tip" that Lattimore was planning to slip behind the Iron Curtain.

Interestingly, the Lattimore travel ban was invoked on June 6, but it wasn't until June 20 that the story broke in the Baltimore *Sun*. This just happened to be two days before the publication date of Joe's book, *McCarthyism: The Fight for America*. Thus Joe conveniently managed to get in the headlines at the same time his book was released. It may have been significant that Surine, who apparently knew about the Lattimore ban in advance, was once stationed in Baltimore and was acquainted in Baltimore newspaper circles.

In any case, the story stood up exactly seven days. It turned out that the "reliable tip" had been passed on to the State Department by the Central Intelligence Agency, which in turn had picked it up from a Finnish-born travel agent, Harry A. Jarvinen. The only trouble was that the tip was a sheer fabrication. Jarvinen admitted this to FBI agents; and by the end of the week, he was indicted by a Seattle grand jury for knowingly giving the government false information.

Meanwhile Lattimore and the nation waited for the results of the Justice Department investigation.

35. The Harassed Professor

RUSSIA'S ANDREI VISHINSKY, HIS WHITE HAIR FLOWING AND his arms windmilling, had the United Nations buffaloed in 1948. He out-roared, out-argued, and out-bluffed everyone the West put up against him, until neutral delegates described him as "a matador fighting with cows." Then a lanky, rumpled American college professor slipped into the vacant United States seat in the General Assembly.

From that day on, the mild professor quelled the Russian windstorm with quiet logic, cold facts, and needle-pointed wit. The professor flung Vishinsky's own words back in his face, tripped him up in international law, and made the Soviet spellbinder look ridiculous. The victory went to the professor. His name: Philip Caryl Jessup.

Overnight, Jessup landed on the Soviet list of "capitalistic warmongers." And when he was moved up to be ambassador-at-large, the Soviet denunciations grew shriller. Jessup, as the State Department's new trouble-shooter, continued to score diplomatic victories, including partial responsibility for breaking the Berlin blockade. And the Kremlin heaped nastier sobriquets on the troublesome professor.

"Jessup brought into action slanderous fabrications against the USSR," screamed the official Soviet newspaper *Izvestia* on March 3, 1950. "In general, Jessup tried with all his might, but he had little success. The imperialistic aggressive character of the policy of the United States . . . is so evident that no hypocritical speeches and anti-Communist philippics could hide it."

Five days later, Jessup came under attack from another source. Senator Joe McCarthy, rising on the floor of the United States Senate, accused Jessup of belonging to "five organizations which had been officially declared as fronts for and doing the work of the Communist Party."

Henceforth, Jessup was under steady fire from two directions, Moscow and McCarthy. Remarking on this twin opposition, Jessup said later: "Anyone who believes in the concept of guilt by association, might draw some startling conclusions from this fact. . . . I have no evidence that Senator McCarthy was motivated by a desire to assist the international Communist movement, even though his words and actions have had that effect."

What about this man whom the Communists called a warmonger and McCarthy called a Communist tool? Jessup's ancestors came to this country in the seventeenth century; one of his great-grandfathers was chairman of the platform committee that drafted Abraham Lincoln's platform in 1860. During World War I, Jessup quit Hamilton College, enlisted as a private, and served at the front as a machine gunner. Back at Hamilton after the war, he collected honors as a Phi Beta Kappa member, drama-club actor, leading debater, track-team captain, and Rhodes scholar-elect. A classmate, Senator Irving Ives of New York, described Jessup as "the outstanding man in the college at that time," adding: "Whatever he did, he did well."

Jessup was too poor to accept the Rhodes scholarship, which paid only part of the expenses. Instead, he went to work at the First National Bank of Utica, New York. He became superintendent of the First Presbyterian Sunday school and commander of the local American Legion post within the next two years. In 1921, he married Lois Kellogg and enrolled in Columbia University's law school. The going was tough; he had to work at night, and his wife taught school. But he waded through two difficult years at Columbia, then transferred to Yale for the final polish.

After graduation in 1924, Jessup climbed fast. He joined the Columbia University faculty and gained recognition as an expert on international law. From time to time, he took leave from Columbia to serve the government. He was sent to Europe by President Herbert Hoover in 1929 to see what could be done for the World Court. During World War II, Jessup taught military government to Navy officers and lectured at both the Army and Navy war colleges. After the war, he helped organize the Bretton Woods monetary conference, which is contributing to a healthy world economy. His next assignment was as legal adviser to the United States delegation at the San Francisco conference, which created the United Nations. *Collier's* magazine had this to say about Jessup's work in San Francisco:

To the amazement of the State Department, he [Jessup] got Koretsky [Russia's noted lawyer, Vladimir Koretsky] to accept Harvard University's international law research as the basis for the new code — a victory tantamount to getting Russia to permit a portrait of J. P. Morgan to be carried at the head of a May Day Parade.

It was on October 4, 1948, that Jessup made his debut before the United Nations General Assembly. Vishinsky was going through his usual histrionics; he screamed, pleaded, threatened, cajoled, and finally sat down. Then the new American delegate arose to speak. He contradicted Vishinsky with his own words; and the Russian's face turned pink. As Jessup spoke on, Vishinsky furiously scribbled notes. But he never again regained the diplomatic offensive; Jessup had tamed the old bear, Vishinsky.

The lean professor was just as effective in dealing with Vishinsky's successor, Jacob Malik, a broad-shouldered, back-slapping giant. He once chided Jessup for the spectacular failure of Dr. George Gallup, the poll-taker, to predict the outcome of the 1948 Presidential election. "Perhaps Dr. Gallup should transfer his activities to your country," retorted Jessup. "It would be much easier to predict the results there."

When the Berlin blockade cast its ominous shadow across Germany, Jessup exposed it as a naked use of force that threatened world peace. He used scathing language that, according to Major George Fielding Eliot, made the Russians writhe. Jessup kept up his verbal hammering to the accompaniment of the steady drone of the airlift until the Soviets were willing to talk terms. And it was Jessup who handled the delicate discussions with Malik.

But the end of the Berlin blockade didn't end the verbal shellackings that the Russians took from Philip Jessup. During the December 1949 debate on China, he told the United Nations:

I hope, Mr. Chairman, it will be crystal clear that the United States policy is against imperialism everywhere. We flatly reject it for ourselves, and we condemn it when practiced by any other state. We condemn it specifically as revealed in the Soviet-Russian continuation of the Tsarist-Russian imperialism in the Far East.

And in reply to the Russian charge that the United States had "bought off" neutral nations to win their support, Jessup said:

The Soviets find themselves without support not because anyone else controls a majority of the votes, but because the Soviet proposals are absolutely unacceptable to free nations. . . . It is too much to expect that they [the Russians] have yet learned that a state based upon the murder of every local dissident cannot indefinitely survive.

Meanwhile, Joe McCarthy was making speeches of a different nature. At Milwaukee on June 9, 1950, he accused Jessup of "hitting Communists at the front door with silk handkerchiefs while they beat the brains out of your friends at the back door." Joe charged that Jessup was "preaching the Communist Party line" and linked him with a "three-horse team." The other two horses, Joe said, were "the Communist *Daily Worker* in this country and the Soviet publication *Izvestia* in Russia."

As evidence, McCarthy submitted "documents" which he said "proved" that Jessup belonged to five Communist fronts. The first of the five (later it became six) was the Institute of Pacific Relations. There was no question that Jessup had been active in this organization — but so had Gerard Swope, president of General Electric; Dr. Ray Lyman Wilbur, president of Stanford University; Republican Senator Homer Ferguson of Michigan; Robert Sproul, president of the University of California; and Dr. Hu Shih, former Chinese Nationalist Ambassador to Washington.

Joe was able to show that Frederick Vanderbilt Field, a contributor to Communist causes, had also contributed funds to the IPR. But his donations were penny-ante compared to the money poured in by such respectable organizations as the Rockefeller Foundation and the Carnegie Foundation. And heading IPR's finance committee had been such solid Americans as Henry Luce, publisher of *Time, Life,* and *Fortune* magazines; Juan Trippe, boss of Pan American Airways; and William Herod, who later became president of the International General Electric Company. Using McCarthy's logic, all these men should have been considered Communists.

The second Communist front that McCarthy tried to tie like a tin can to Jessup's tail was the National Emergency Conference for Democratic Rights. Joe's proof consisted of a letterhead, dated 1940, containing Jessup's name along with sixty others. Jessup stated, under oath, that his name had been used without his permission. "I have no recollection whatsoever of the organization," he said. Anyway, the outfit was not branded as a Communist front by the House

Un-American Activities Committee until 1944 — four years after Jessup's supposed affiliation.

The third organization cited by Joe was the American Russian Institute. McCarthy produced "photo-copies" of two lists of sponsors, in all 384 names; and, sure enough, on both lists was Jessup's name. But it turned out that those listed were not sponsors of the American Russian Institute at all, but sponsors of two dinners given by the Institute. The first dinner was held in 1944 at the height of wartime co-operation with Russia; the second, in 1946, was for the purpose of presenting a posthumous award to the late President Franklin D. Roosevelt. The sponsors included persons of all political shades; among them were Radio Commentator H. V. Kaltenborn, Major George Fielding Eliot, and Holyoke College President Mary Emma Woolley. Jessup didn't even bother to go to the dinners, but permitted his name to be used because of their stated objectives. In any case, the American Russian Institute wasn't cited as subversive until 1949.

As Jessup's fourth "Communist" tie, McCarthy came up with the American Law Students Association. Jessup agreed that he had acted as faculty adviser to the organization for two years. But no one had ever suggested that the group was subversive until Joe mentioned it; the organization did not appear on any of the official listings of Communist fronts. However, Joe discovered the customary union-shop printers' label on one letterhead, and cried: "It is union label No. 209 . . . the Communist print-shop label." He never backed up this statement; but he gave newsmen a mimeographed sheet claiming that, if the American Law Students Association wasn't a Communist front itself, at least it was "affiliated" with three other Communist fronts. Jessup's last connection with the law students' group was dated 1940. "If this particular charge is boiled down," said Jessup, "it shows that I was associated with an organization which was connected with another organization that a number of years after I had terminated my connection with the first organization was cited as subversive."

The fifth Communist front in which McCarthy tried to enroll Jessup was the Co-ordinating Committee to Lift the Embargo Against Republican Spain. This might have looked bad for Jessup — except that he had never had anything to do with the organization. But Joe, already experimenting with composite photographs, distributed a tricky composite document. This made it appear that a piece by Charles C. Burlingame and Philip C. Jessup had been written for the pinko Co-ordinating Committee. Actually, it was written as a letter to the New York *Times*, later clipped by the Co-ordinating Committee, and still later misrepresented by McCarthy.

But the strangest of all Jessup's alleged Communist affiliations was the sixth and final organization on Joe's list — the China Aid Society. It soon became apparent that it was not Philip Jessup, but his wife, who had belonged to the group. And she had been drawn in by none other than Madame Chiang Kai-shek. Their work was humanitarian, helping Chinese orphans.

As Joe bounced from audience to audience, he ignored the evidence Jessup had brought in and kept shouting across the country: "Why does Jessup always join Communist fronts? Why not anti-Communist organizations?" The answer: Jessup belonged to the American Bar Association, the Foreign Policy Association, the American Philosophical Society, the American Legion, and half a dozen other 100-per-cent patriotic groups. In fact, his American Legion post at Utica, New York, passed a resolution defending Jessup in vigorous terms and mailed a copy to Senator McCarthy, declaring that his "reckless and despicable conduct in this instance cannot be condoned by any right-thinking American."

But Joe never let up. In his revival-meeting style, he continued to denounce Jessup up and down the country, even hinting that the professor-turned-diplomat was effeminate. The way Joe pictured it, the State Department was a nest of elegant perverts and wild-eyed Bolsheviks. "For nearly twenty years we have allowed dilettante diplomats to do the 'fighting' for us with kid gloves in perfumed drawing rooms," McCarthy said, referring to Jessup.

But the man McCarthy called a "dilettante diplomat" had anchored the relay team in college. And twenty years later, in 1941, when a plane he was traveling in crashed in a thick South American jungle, Jessup — though severely injured — crawled out of the wreckage and made his way in great pain down the side of a mountain. He stumbled into a village below, organized a rescue party, and led it back up the mountain to bring out one remaining survivor and ten bodies. For this heroic action, Brazil's Foreign Minister Oswaldo Aranha presented him with the Ordem Nacional do Cruzerio do Sul.

But the public was getting its information on Jessup from McCarthy, not from the recorded facts. Finally, in August 1951, Senator Herbert Lehman of New York spoke out: "The time has long passed when we should have rebuked [McCarthy]. . . . Jessup has served his country well [and] . . . does not deserve the shabby and dastardly treatment accorded him on the Senate floor under the cloak of Senatorial immunity." Senate Republican Leader Kenneth Wherry of Nebraska jumped to his feet, demanding that Lehman be silenced for "impugning the motives" of a fellow Senator. "I withdraw the word 'dastardly,'" said Lehman, "and substitute 'cowardly.'"

Then, in October 1951, came the showdown; the President renominated Jessup to sit in the United Nations and sent his name up to the Senate for confirmation. Five times he had been okayed for diplomatic posts without objection;

but this time McCarthy announced his opposition at once. Joe put on a ten-hour marathon performance before a Senate Foreign Relations sub-committee, rehashing his old charges and speeches. It was comic, but it was terrible.

At last Senator William Fulbright of Arkansas could stand it no longer. He said to his fellow Senators: "This is perfectly ridiculous. Are all his cases just as flimsy?" McCarthy, sweat rolling down his face, turned angrily on his colleagues, making repeated references to the fate of other Senators who had opposed him, such as Millard Tydings, by this time defeated for re-election. "Men of little minds," Joe shouted hoarsely, "are trying to make this [Communism] a political issue."

"You wouldn't try to do anything like that, would you?" Fulbright asked. The audience tittered; and McCarthy, like an enraged bull, pawed the floor and stretched his neck. But he spoke more warily. "I can't keep all the details in my head," he said. "I'm dealing with too many of these slimy creatures to do that." The remark was aimed at Jessup; it brought a stunned silence. As the silence lengthened, Joe's face flushed and he sputtered: "I am referring to the Communist-front organizations, not to individuals." But as McCarthy left the witness stand, Fulbright declared: "I want to say for the record that in all my experience in the Senate, never have I seen a more arrogant or rude witness before any committee."

It was obvious that McCarthy's testimony had helped, not harmed, the Ambassador. So Joe sent out a hurried SOS; and into the hearing room walked Harold Stassen, the ex-Governor of Minnesota and quadrennial candidate for President. Joe had been a key figure in Stassen's 1948 triumph over General Douglas MacArthur in the Wisconsin primary; and later Joe showed up at the Republican convention in Philadelphia as Stassen's chief lieutenant. Now Stassen happily arrived to verify Joe's charge that Jessup had followed the "Communist line." As evidence, the Presidential hopeful reported that the late Senator Arthur Vandenberg, father of the bi-partisan foreign policy, had told him about a White House conference on February 5, 1949. The story, as passed from Vandenberg to Stassen to the sub-committee, was that Jessup had proposed stopping aid to China. But the United Nations produced official records proving that Jessup was in New York City at the precise time of the White House meeting. Stassen then recalled attending a State Department panel at which it seemed to him Jessup had sounded pro-Communist. But the State Department came up with a verbatim transcript of the panel; and newsmen could find nothing subversive in it. When Stassen's own aide hurried to New York and verified the United Nations' records, Stassen dropped the question. But he never apologized to Jessup for the attack on his integrity and patriotism.

Warren Austin, distinguished former Republican Senator from Vermont and now chief American delegate to the United Nations, told the sub-committee that Jessup was a "powerful protagonist" of American interests, "with no trace of Communist sympathies." And a letter from General Lucius Clay, former occupation commander in Germany, said that Jessup was "firm" and took "a realistic approach toward the Russian problem," especially during the Berlin blockade. Jessup also produced a letter from General George Marshall, who wrote that he was "shocked and distressed by the attack on your integrity," and another letter from General Dwight Eisenhower saying that "no one who has known you can for a moment question the depth or sincerity of your devotion to the principles of Americanism."

As the hearings drew to a close, a Republican Senator, H. Alexander Smith of New Jersey, told Jessup: "I have known you too long to have any doubts about your loyalty and integrity. I know darn well that you are not a Communist." But the letters poured in from McCarthy's followers, threat-

ening political consequences if the sub-committee approved
Jessup. When the roll was called, three of the five Senators
opposed Jessup; and one of the three was H. Alexander
Smith.

After Congress adjourned, President Truman made an
interim appointment of Jessup as a member of the United
States delegation to the sixth session of the United Nations
General Assembly.

36. Tarnishing the Brass

Ex-Captain Joe McCarthy, as he gained political rank, began chipping away at the military brass. And he left his chisel marks on the shields of the nation's top generals: Douglas MacArthur, George Marshall, and Dwight Eisenhower.

But Joe's post-war policy toward five-star generals had a convenient, 180-degree leeway. In 1948, for example, he suggested that 68-year-old General MacArthur was too old to be President and ought to be retired. But three years later Joe announced that the general (now in his seventies) was "definitely young enough" to run for the Presidency.

Joe had similar difficulty keeping his views straight on General Marshall. In 1951 McCarthy accused the wartime Chief of Staff of conspiring with those who wished to see the Communists inherit the earth — although four years earlier Joe had inserted a resolution in the *Congressional Record*, praising Marshall's anti-Communist stand (see Chapter 23). McCarthy also implicated General Eisenhower in the Marshall "conspiracy" — then turned around and supported Eisenhower for President.

In the spring of the 1948 Presidential contest, MacArthur's five stars, glittering from far-off Tokyo, cast a shadow across the political path of Joe's friend, Harold Stassen. The Wisconsin primary was the first big road test on the highway to the Republican convention, causing a traffic jam of Presidential band wagons in the state. Joe beat the big bass drum

234

for Stassen; the Hearst press clanged the cymbals for Mac-
Arthur; and Herbert Brownell passed through the state, blar-
ing the trumpets for New York's Governor Tom Dewey. But
the major threat was the glamorous though absentee "favorite son," Douglas MacArthur.

The situation clearly called for a hatchet job, and Joe
began hacking away at MacArthur's political weak points —
his age and his divorce. By March 15, 1948, thousands of
letters had deluged the mailboxes of Wisconsin, bearing a
message to the voters from their Senator, Joe McCarthy.
To those who remembered Joe's campaign against elderly
Judge Werner, the letter was familiar. It read:

DEAR FOLKS:

Governor Stassen is in the prime of life. He will be the same age
as Teddy Roosevelt was when as President he handled the Panama
Canal and the Alaskan situation without getting our country into
trouble.

General MacArthur has been a great General. But he is now ready
for retirement. He would be 72 years old before a term as President
ended. Twice before we have had Presidents who became physically
weakened during their term of office and both times it had very sad
results for our country. . . .

General MacArthur would be much older than either of these two
men [Franklin Roosevelt and Woodrow Wilson] were. It has been
50 years since he commenced his Army career, and he has been
out of touch with civilian problems of government and has not been
in the United States for 10 years. That is why I believe that we
should give the General his well deserved hero's acclaim and retirement when his job is done and not try to have him undergo the
strain of years as President of our country in this difficult time.

On returning to Wisconsin, I notice that hundreds of big campaign
billboards tell the people to support the General because he is a
native son of Wisconsin. The Hearst papers, which are booming the
General's candidacy, refer to him as the "Wisconsin-born General."
This is not true.

The General was born in Little Rock, Arkansas, on January 26, 1880,
and not in Wisconsin. He is not listed on any poll list as a voter of
Wisconsin. Neither his first nor his second marriage, nor his divorce,

took place in Wisconsin. He was first married in Florida to Mrs. Walter Brooks of Baltimore, who now lives in Washington, D. C. After she divorced him in Reno, Nevada, he was remarried in New York City. Neither wife ever resided or voted in Wisconsin. In a sworn marriage application for his second marriage he did not claim Wisconsin as his residence, but gave Manila as his residence and Baltimore, Maryland, as the domicile of his former marriage. . . .

May I also extend to you my personal greetings and best wishes.

Sincerely,

JOE MCCARTHY

Beneath the more-or-less charitable tone of Joe's letter, the knife marks were plainly visible. And the people of Wisconsin got the idea that MacArthur might be too old, too divorced, and too peripatetic to qualify as a "favorite son." When the ballots were counted, MacArthur trailed far behind Stassen.

But the political winds have a habit of shifting; and in 1951 MacArthur returned to the United States on a hurricane of popular acclaim. Joe promptly hitched his wagon to MacArthur's five stars, and told the Senate in an earnest voice: "The Communists have been leading the smear attack on General Douglas MacArthur." Presumably, McCarthy was not referring to his own political hatchet work of 1948.

But as Joe was thus taking MacArthur off the shelf, he sought to retire another five-star personality, General George Marshall, who happened to be a year younger than MacArthur. Joe suggested in a mimeographed handout that Marshall should not continue "his heavy responsibilities at his advanced age," but "would be much more valuable to the nation as the elder statesman at Leesburg." The same handout, dated December 6, 1950, added cautiously that Marshall had been "heavily involved in the erroneous China policy." This was the first hint of McCarthy's forthcoming Jack-the-Giant-Killer attack on the respected Marshall.

When President Truman had called Marshall back to duty as Secretary of Defense in September 1950, *Time* magazine had commented: "Twice before, in deep predicament, Harry Truman had gone looking for a man of honesty, dignity and prestige. . . . Both times the rays of Mr. Truman's lamp fell . . . on the homely, sorrowful, willing face of General George Catlett Marshall." This was the man whom McCarthy was shortly to accuse of participating in a traitorous, Moscow-directed conspiracy.

At three o'clock on the afternoon of June 15, 1951, a hush fell over the packed Senate galleries as Senator Joe McCarthy rose to speak. Jean Kerr, his girl Friday, and Don Surine, his ace investigator, sat on a couch at the rear of the chamber. A pair of crutches — belonging to Miss Kerr, who had broken her hip in a fall — lay between them. They leaned forward as McCarthy cleared his throat, shuffled some papers on his desk and began to speak:

Mr. President, in closely following the testimony before the Joint Committee on Foreign Relations and Armed Services, which is conducting an investigation of the dismissal of Douglas MacArthur, I have become more and more impressed by two inescapable facts:

First. That it is impossible to develop the facts in the MacArthur inquiry without at the same time bringing to light some of the facts which bear on the question of why we fell from our position as the most powerful nation on earth at the end of World War II to a position of declared weakness by our leadership.

Second. That it will be equally impossible to obtain the answers to the above without uncovering a conspiracy so immense and an infamy so black as to dwarf any such previous venture in the history of man. . . .

I found to my surprise that Marshall, who, by the alchemy of propaganda, became the "greatest living American," and the recently proclaimed "master of global strategy" for the party in power, has never had his record subjected to the searching light of any historian. . . .

Unless we carefully study the records of Marshall and Acheson, who have worked together so closely, it will be impossible to foretell the next move on the timetable of the great conspiracy.

For two hours, McCarthy droned on, weaving a fantastic tale of complicity between the Secretary of Defense and the Communist enemy. The spectators were the first to tire and began to drift out; then Joe asked unanimous permission to suspend the Senate rules so that he could eat a sandwich and drink a glass of milk. After the short recess, Joe returned to his speech.

"The President is not master in his own house," he said. "Those who are master there . . . belong to a larger conspiracy, the world-wide web of which has been spun from Moscow." General Marshall, Joe said, was a man "whose every important act for years has contributed to the prosperity of the enemy." He described the General as being "steeped in blood," and cried: "How can we believe General Marshall, under oath or otherwise?"

By this time, even Miss Kerr and Surine had wandered out of the chamber; and their place was taken by George Greeley, another McCarthy employee. But Greeley's attention wavered, too; and at one point he seemed about to fall asleep. Joe continued the byplay with his own echo until 5:50 P.M.; then he gave up in the middle of his discourse and inserted the rest of the speech unread into the *Congressional Record*.

From McCarthy's point of view, the 60,000-word bombshell was a dud. It stirred up more disgust than excitement, and Marshall didn't even take the trouble to comment. But, undaunted, Joe put the speech between cardboard covers and announced it as his second literary effort. He called the book *America's Retreat From Victory* and showed up to defend it on the television show "Author Meets the Critics." He said:

The book is what the name implies. It covers the retreat of America from victory, the story of George Catlett Marshall — a story, I should say a picture, not drawn from the pen of McCarthy but a picture drawn from the pen of Winston Churchill, Admiral Leahy,

Cordell Hull, Henry Stimson, Jimmy Byrnes, Sumner Wells, Edward Stettinius, and about thirty others. We're trying to restrict ourselves to using, as source material, only the sources friendly to Marshall or at least neutral towards him. I felt that in view of the fact that we've been losing, losing this war to international Communism at the rate of 100 million people a year in a general war and losing in the Korean war, a disgraceful planned disaster, that perhaps we should examine the background of the men who have done the planning and let the American people decide whether these individuals are stupid, whether we've lost because of stumbling, fumbling idiocy, or because they planned it that way. I very carefully refrain from drawing the conclusion. I merely present the facts, the facts from the pens of MacArthur's friends — MacArthur, I'm sorry, Marshall — Marshall's friends, and let the reader decide whether these individuals have been dupes or whether they are traitors.

McCarthy's chief critic on the program was Leo Cherne, executive secretary of the Research Institute of America, who replied:

According to Senator McCarthy, General Marshall led a vast conspiracy to subvert American interests and advance the power of the Soviet Union. Neither General Marshall nor General Eisenhower, who in the book is called General Marshall's chief collaborator in this plan, needs any defense against these thinly veiled charges of treason, but the American people need to know whether the charges made by the junior Senator from Wisconsin are true or false.

For instance, Senator McCarthy says General Marshall lied about his whereabouts the morning of Pearl Harbor. He charges that Marshall was actually meeting Maxim Litvinov at the National Airport in Washington. I have a letter from Mr. McCarthy's informant admitting that Marshall was not at the airport.

Senator McCarthy says that the Inspector General of the Army issued an unfavorable report about Marshall's handling of the Eighth Infantry in 1933. I received a telegram this morning from General Adams, adjutant of that regiment, saying this charge is wholly and outrageously false.

The Senator says General MacArthur told General Pershing that because of this unfavorable report he couldn't promote Marshall. The truth is Lieutenant Colonel Marshall was promoted to a full colonelcy with the approval of Chief of Staff General Douglas MacArthur.

Senator McCarthy, in praising the Truman Doctrine, says that General Marshall had nothing to do with it. I have photostats with me of Senator Vandenberg's private papers proving conclusively that General Marshall personally convinced the great Senator Vandenberg of the urgent importance of that doctrine.

Senator McCarthy accuses General Marshall of sabotaging Generalissimo Chiang Kai-shek and aiding the Chinese Reds. The truth is Generalissimo Chiang sent a message to General Marshall within the last year to express his eternal gratitude for the help he gave the Chinese Nationalist government.

Senator McCarthy says that General Marshall was made Chief of Staff because Harry Hopkins recommended him to President Roosevelt. The truth is that President Roosevelt asked General Pershing to nominate the Chief of Staff. He nominated General Marshall, and after doing so told his friend, Bernard Baruch: "I did a great thing for my country this morning."

Senator McCarthy charges that General Marshall kept from President Roosevelt an intelligence report of fifty Army officers advising against the Yalta Agreement. I have absolute proof with me tonight that the report was not completed until three months after the Yalta conference took place and couldn't have been kept from President Roosevelt because it was completed on the very day that President Roosevelt died, April 12, 1945.

Once the opening statements were out of the way, the debate quickly deteriorated into a shouting match. "I'd like to call your attention to a number of misstatements made, Mr. Cherne," blurted McCarthy. "I would assume as director of the Research Institute of America you should have read this book or have had someone else read it for you."

"Senator McCarthy, I'm going to make a wager with you right now," said Cherne.

"No, no, no, no, no, no," said McCarthy, shaking his head vigorously. "No, no, no, no, no."

"If you find one misstatement," continued Cherne, "if you find one misstatement that I made, I will offer $1,000 to your favorite charity."

"Please let me finish, please let me finish," said Joe.

"And I want a similar response if you fail to find it," added Cherne.

"All right, let's . . . let's . . . let's take up Leo's offer, and please don't interrupt me, please, please," said Joe.

"I'll be glad to hold the money, gentlemen," volunteered glamorous Faye Emerson, the moderator.

"Now let's . . . now let's get down to the book," said Joe. "Now let's . . ."

But Miss Emerson, on second thought, interrupted: "Gentlemen, in the first place, I believe it's illegal to gamble and we have a Senator with us. And I don't wish to get into any trouble. I think we're crossing interstate lines with television." And that was about the last intelligible word heard on the program until Miss Emerson signed off fifteen minutes later, and Joe shouted a parting word to the audience: "Read the book."

Meanwhile, bits of verbal shrapnel from McCarthy's 60,000-word blast at Marshall struck still another five-star general, Dwight Eisenhower. Joe accused Eisenhower of joining, part and parcel, in Marshall's "traitorous" schemes. Specifically McCarthy said that Ike favored a trans-Channel invasion of France as early as 1942 to ease German pressure on the Russians — despite the fact that the invading Allied soldiers might be wiped out for lack of equipment and training. "The planning section [for the alleged premature invasion] was under the command of Colonel Dwight D. Eisenhower," McCarthy charged. And as Joe went on to condemn Marshall for serving Russian rather than American interests, he added: "In all these attitudes, Eisenhower, who had become commander in chief in North Africa, was Marshall's firm supporter." And again in the same speech: "Churchill brought to bear upon Marshall and Eisenhower, who invariably sided with Marshall, the whole battery of persuasion."

McCarthy's attack was taken up by a whole cabal of

political obsessionists and demagogues. The Chicago *Tribune* charged that Ike's political support came from foreigners, leftists, and chorus girls. Joseph Kamp, the neo-fascist propagandist, said that "Ike coddled Communists while president of Columbia University." Gerald L. K. Smith, the anti-Semitic rabble-rouser, called Eisenhower "the terrible Swedish Jew." And Robert H. Williams of Santa Ana, California, published a pamphlet with a trick photo of Eisenhower talking with Russia's Marshal Zhukov.

At the opposite political pole, the Communists matched the McCarthyites, slur for slur and slam for slam. But Ike's popularity continued to soar. And McCarthy, after a few more flourishes of the Red cape, left the ring — and, in time, endorsed Eisenhower for President of the United States.

37. Aiding the Communists

"I'LL TELL YOU NOW. IT DON'T TAKE NO COLLEGE DEGREE TO know that Joe is doin' good. Joe fights bare knuckles. He don't pull no punches. I know he tells a lot of tall stories. But when you add it all up, Joe is getting the Communists out of the State Department. He is the worst thing ever happened to them Communists. They hate him like thunder!"

So said a Shawano County (Wisconsin) farmer, as he leaned against his barn and discussed Senator Joe McCarthy with one of the authors. Dress up the language a bit, and you have the same argument the way a traveling salesman put it to the authors in a Washington hotel lobby. Add some glowing phrases about "internal security" and "Communist infiltration," and you have the argument all over again, this time as set forth by a Republican national committeeman.

These people represent millions of Americans who maintain that Joe is "doing a job," "cleaning out the skunks," using harsh means but toward a good end. They admit that McCarthy is often off base; but they insist that the good cancels out the harm, leaving the balance sheet in his favor.

But the real experts, the men who have made a lifework of exposing Communists, have a different opinion of Joe's crusade against Red will-o'-the-wisps. FBI Chief J. Edgar Hoover, the nation's top authority on ferreting out Reds, wrote in the June 9, 1947, issue of *Newsweek:*

We can successfully defeat the Communist attempt to capture the United States by fighting it with truth and justice, implemented with a few Don'ts:

243

Don't label anyone as a Communist unless you have the facts.

Don't confuse liberals and progressives with Communists.

Don't take the law into your own hands.

If Communists violate the law, report such facts to your law-enforcement agency.

Don't be a party to a violation of the civil rights of anyone. When this is done, you are playing right into the hands of the Communists.

Don't let up on the fight against Fascists, the KKK, and other dangerous groups.

McCarthy has made a career of violating these precepts. He has been the Communists' Exhibit A, supporting their case that the United States is entering its final stage of "capitalistic decadence." The more Joe has attacked them in his noisy but harmless way, the more they have secretly smiled and rubbed their hands.

This was confirmed in January 1952 by Herbert Philbrick, who had spent nine years in the Communist Party as a volunteer counter-spy for the FBI. He came out of hiding, after rising higher in the Communist hierarchy than any other revealed FBI agent, to appear as the government's ace witness against the eleven top Communists. Discussing the attitude of Red leaders toward McCarthy, Philbrick said:

According to leaders of the Communist Party, McCarthy has helped them a great deal. The kind of attacks he has made do three things that the comrades like: They add greatly to the confusion, putting up a smokescreen for the party and making it more difficult than ever for people to discern just who is a Communist and who is not; they make the Party appear a lot stronger than it is; and they do considerable damage to some of the "stupid liberals" whom the party hates.

Philbrick added that the hard-bitten Communist elite hope to

. . . force all non-Communists to the extreme right, toward fascism and state control. The Communist seeks by every means to create a split in our society, to provoke class hatreds and intense conflict. All capitalist governments, the Communist is taught, inevitably become states of fascist oppression, thus creating the demand for violent revolution as the only possible cure. . . . Time after time I learned in my party experiences that the Communist movement is not genuinely anti-fascist, any more than it is genuinely in favor of civil liberties, better housing, peace or any of the other causes its leaders so ardently espouse. . . . Any suggestion that the country is moving to fascism is always greeted in the Communist press and party pronouncements with rejoicing, however much it may be disguised by indignation.

Philbrick also warned that McCarthy's habit of baring his breast and denouncing Communists from the housetops jeopardized the secret under-cover work of FBI informants. J. Edgar Hoover himself had said as much on March 27, 1950, when he refused to open the loyalty files for McCarthy's benefit — when he warned that if the "raw" files were made public, it might wreck the entire loyalty program, cut off sources of information, smear innocent persons, and cast adrift dangerous "half-truths" about Communism. But at Janesville, Wisconsin, on May 7, 1950, Joe demanded that he be turned loose in the secret files not only of the FBI, but also of the Central Intelligence Agency, Civil Service Commission, Naval Intelligence, and Secret Service.

McCarthy's shout-and-run tactics — his slam-banging from charge to charge without slowing down for the proof or stopping to see who was injured — have alienated sincere anti-Communists. For example, Joe has claimed strong Catholic support; but this has come from the over-zealous and the uninformed, not from the church's experts on Communism. The Rev. John F. Cronin, who spent twelve years compiling a vast file on Communism for the Catholic Church, reported that his investigation showed not one known Communist Party member in the State Department at the time McCarthy charged there were 205. It was "unfortunate that Senator McCarthy went to such extremes," Father Cronin said.

Joe was also fond of planting his American Legion cap at

a jaunty angle on his head, rolling up his sleeves, and roistering before veterans' groups, thus giving the impression that the American Legion too was behind him. But the Legion's committee on un-American activities had its doubts about Legionnaire Joe. Chairman Walter E. Alessandroni wrote to McCarthy on January 6, 1951:

> Too often charges of Communist affiliations are brought against individuals without regard for the facts. . . . The country badly needs to have the muddy waters in all phases of our national thinking filtered of extraneous matter. Having done this, we can then hasten to the business at hand — national security within the framework of the American Constitution.

Even the House Un-American Activities Committee displayed a strong hostility toward Joe. Committee investigators claimed that McCarthy's work was bombastic, irresponsible, inaccurate, and detrimental to the cause of anti-Communism. This attitude of the responsible Communist-hunters was perhaps best summed up by J. Edgar Hoover, who declared: "We shall contribute to our internal security by protecting the innocent as well as by identifying the enemies within our midst. Witch-hunting weakens internal security."

Ironically, few would be more vulnerable to an attack by McCarthy than McCarthy himself:

He was elected to the Senate with the help of the Communist propaganda machine, which ground out smear attacks against his opponent, Senator Robert La Follette, Jr. (see Chapter 17).

Later McCarthy was caught red-handed in possession of a manila envelope with the return address of a German Communist, Dr. Rudolf Aschenauer, in the upper left corner. The envelope had borne across the Atlantic tall tales of American torture, allegedly practiced on Nazi war criminals. Joe gave the charges respectability by repeating them on the Senate floor; and the Communists circulated his speeches throughout Germany to stir up anti-American feeling (see Chapter 26).

The Swiss police also caught a confessed Communist working for McCarthy, and convicted him of spying — the embarrassing Charles Davis episode (see Chapter 31).

But the most ironical note was buried in a set of routine FBI statistics, made public on April 11, 1952. These figures showed the decline of the American Communist Party during the preceding year. Communist membership had dropped off in all but three of the forty-eight states. In Missouri, the Communists had gained four new members, boosting the total from 358 to 362. A slight gain was also registered in Ohio, where the Communists increased from 1,060 to 1,290. But the greatest proportional boost occurred in McCarthy's home state, Wisconsin, where the number of card-carrying Communists leaped from 270 to 420.

Joe's favorite device for tagging a victim with the Red label was to line up his views side by side with similar quotes from the Communist press and radio. But even this trick could be turned against McCarthy:

The *Daily Worker* has called President Harry Truman a vicious and irresponsible man. So has McCarthy.

The *Daily Worker* has attacked Secretary of State Dean Acheson at every opportunity. So has McCarthy.

The *Daily Worker* has opposed the Marshall Plan. So has McCarthy.

The *Daily Worker* has called the United Nations' effort in Korea "Truman's War." So has McCarthy.

Of course it would be ridiculous to suggest that McCarthy was actually a Communist — though he has made the charge against others with less to go on. But the evidence is overwhelming that Joe has helped the cause of Communism. Senator Estes Kefauver of Tennessee said in a speech in

Milwaukee, on June 24, 1951: "We can't build up America by tearing down American leaders." He was referring to the long list of prominent Americans whom McCarthy has sought to discredit; the list includes President Harry Truman, General George Marshall, General Dwight Eisenhower, Secretary of State Dean Acheson, Secretary of the Navy Francis Matthews, Ambassador Philip Jessup, Senator Millard Tydings, Publisher Henry Luce, and countless others. His attempt to destroy these leaders has had a direct and discernible ill effect on the nation's welfare.

To put it bluntly, Joe was doing the work of the Communists in effect, by creating fear, distrust, disunity, and loss of faith in the government. The New York *Times* expressed it plainly in an editorial:

> If a major objective of Russian foreign policy is to undermine the faith of democratic peoples in their own governments, then the Kremlin must rejoice every time Joseph R. McCarthy opens his mouth in the Senate of the United States. For what McCarthy has been doing with tireless reiteration in the past year and a half is to attempt to destroy the confidence of the American people in the honor, integrity, and loyalty of some of their most highly placed servants from the Secretary of State and Secretary of Defense on down.

McCarthy has also aided and abetted Russia's war of nerves against the United States. The Soviet stratagem, according to a Joint Chiefs of Staff analysis, has been to strain American nerves to the breaking point — by sowing seeds of doubt and confusion, by holding out the hope of peace one day, dashing it with the threat of war the next. When it comes to spreading confusion and adding to the tension, Joe has been the best psychological secret weapon the Communists ever had. And Russia has made the most of it in her propaganda outpourings. One Soviet broadcast, monitored during the summer of 1951, lied happily that hundreds of thousands of Americans were under suspicion and suspended from their jobs because of the McCarthy hysteria.

Nor could our disturbed allies help but notice the Red frothing at the mouth on our side of the Atlantic. As early as May 1950, the London *Economist* referred to "the national hysteria and Red witch-hunts that mark the national life of America today." A weekly Swiss humor magazine, *Nebelspalter,* carried a cartoon of a grinning man with both hands deep in a garbage pail; the caption read: "The Senator prepares for the hearings." The daily *O Jornal* of Rio de Janeiro, Brazil, said: "Tomorrow it would not surprise anybody if President Truman is accused of being a Communist." In Sweden, the Gotheborg *Posten* said: "The [McCarthy] campaign reflects on the United States' foreign-policy position at a time when firmness, clarity, and strength are needed most of all."

McCarthyism has helped to create an atmosphere of timidity in dealing with foreign problems. For fear of criticism, the State Department has often taken the safe course rather than the daring approach. The vigorously anti-Communist magazine, the *New Republic,* in March 1950 had this to say about the formation of policy in a climate of intimidation:

There is no automatic calculating machine in government which eats up undigested intelligence and grinds out new and decisive ideas like the Marshall Plan and the Point Four program. These ideas are born in human minds unfettered by fear of persecution. They take shape in the clash of many different approaches and points of view. The Western world is suffocating now from lack of new ideas. If we destroy in government the power to generate new ideas by reducing it to one flat level of unimaginative conformity, then we destroy the hope of peace and our own chance of survival.

A democracy is only as strong as the moral fiber of its people; creating hysteria on the basis of trumped-up charges is one way to break down that moral fiber. Senator William Fulbright of Arkansas said in a Senate speech on March 27, 1951:

A democracy can recover quickly from physical or economic disaster, but when its moral convictions weaken, it becomes easy prey for the demagogue and the charlatan. Tyranny and oppression then become the order of the day. . . . Democracy is, I believe, more likely to be destroyed by the perversion of, or abandonment of, its true moral principles than by armed attack from Russia.

Many of these moral principles are embodied in the legal code — the right to trial by jury, the right of the accused to confront and cross-examine his accusers, the right to "due process of law," and the right to be secure in the possession of one's good name. The president of the Wisconsin State Federation of Labor, George Haberman, had the preservation of these rights in mind in October 1951, when he said that McCarthy was "an individual who would sell his country down the river for thirty headlines a month." There seems little doubt that McCarthy has violated the long-established moral principles upon which the United States was founded, and upon which it must rely to convince other nations that the democratic system is better than the Communist system. Or, as *Time* magazine said:

Some have argued that McCarthy's end justifies his methods. This argument seems to assume that lies are required to fight Communist lies. Experience proves, however, that what the anti-Communist fight needs is truth, carefully arrived at and presented with all the scrupulous regard for decency and the rights of man of which the democratic world is capable. This is the Western world's greatest asset in the struggle against Communism, and those who condone McCarthy are throwing that asset away.

38. Financial Tangles

To Joe McCarthy's fellow Senators, one question has always been paramount: Who has financed him? Certainly he has not always been capable of paying his own way, to judge by his income-tax returns. In fact, he listed no taxable income at all during his first three Senate years.

Yet Joe somehow has managed to stay at the best hotels, eat expensive steaks, bet heavily on the horses, finance investigations all over the globe, and generally present a front similar to that of a business tycoon. Where was the money coming from?

Although this question had been asked most frequently after he was elected Senator, it could just as easily have been asked when Joe was a struggling circuit judge whose salary had just shot up from $2,500 to $8,000 a year. Somehow or other, the Judge accumulated enough cash to buy about $50,000 worth of railroad stocks, and a year later he cashed in with a $42,353.92 profit.

In 1944, when he ran against Alexander Wiley for the Senate, Joe dredged up an extra $18,000 to help with the campaign expenses. He explained that the money came from his relatives (see Chapter 12). The breakdown showed a contribution of $10,600 from brother Howard, a farm auctioneer who had never made more than $4,000 a year in his life, and who had never reported any income to the state before 1944. Sister Olive's husband, Roman Kornely, was put down for $3,000 in a year in which his income, as a grocery clerk, was less than $2,000. Joe's father, Tim, contributed $4,000, although the old man had never reported any income to the state. The total was $17,600, all from the McCarthy clan, which had had no wide reputation for affluence before that time.

Down through the years, Joe had shown a similar dependence on his family, even though he was making more total income than all the other McCarthys combined. As late as 1950, he was listing heavy interest payments to his relatives, some of it running back as far as twenty years. In 1949, for example, he said he paid brother Howard $2,557.70 in interest, explaining to the press later that some of the indebtedness dated back to 1929. Figured at 4 per cent, this would be the annual interest on $63,942.50. In that same year, Joe deducted another $2,258 for an interest payment to brother William, a Chicago truck driver — which, at 4 per cent, would be the amount of interest on $56,450. Joe said the debt "went back to my chicken-raising and college days."

Why did Senator Joe McCarthy, earning $12,500 a year as a Senator and picking up little tidbits like $42,000 on the stock market and $10,000 from Lustron, have to turn to his relatives for money — which he did as late as 1950?

Joe said the answer lay in the high cost of his "crusade against Communism." But no matter what the reason, it is significant to note that interest payments on loans are deductible when computing income taxes, and they enabled Joe McCarthy to pay low taxes on a high income. In 1949, for example, Joe listed the very substantial income of $17,000; but at first he paid no Wisconsin state tax because, in that same year, he deducted the staggering total of $15,172 in interest payments. The Wisconsin Department of Taxation took exception, shifted some of the interest to earlier years, and added $6,000 to Joe's taxable income. There was nothing new about this. The department had found seven of Joe's

previous eight returns in error. In a nutshell, here is
McCarthy's financial history as recorded in his state income-
tax returns from his first year as a lawyer — 1935 — up to
the latest available information at this writing:

Year	Income	State tax paid
1935 (lawyer)	$ 777.81	None
1936	2,059.24	$ 6.32
1937	2,500.00	14.01
1938	2,475.00	10.28
1939	1,055.00	None
1940 (circuit judge)	8,000.00	267.54
1941	8,000.00	196.41
1942 (Marine)	5,336.36	86.84
1943	42,353.92	2,677.86
1944	5,527.14	27.50
1945 (circuit judge)	9,231.55	135.05
1946	7,334.00	None
1947 (Senator)	13,537.51	None
1948	28,947.08	None
1949	17,120.00	None (later paid $134.23 on orders of state tax commission)
1950	22,025.00	1,175.78

Joe first stubbed his financial toe over his 1943 return. In
a carefree manner he filled in a state tax blank, listing his
occupation as "U. S. Marine (temporarily I hope!)" and
posted it from the Marine Air Station at El Toro, California.
But he slipped a businesslike note into the envelope. It read:

During the entire year of 1943, I was serving in the Armed Forces
of the United States, during which I spent no time in Wisconsin. I
had no property in the state and received no income from within
the state, having waived my salary as circuit judge. Therefore, I
assume it is unnecessary under the present laws to file a return. If
you do not so understand the law, I shall be glad to file a return.

Joe neglected to mention that he had netted $42,353.92
from stock-market speculation and dividends in 1943. Joe
also failed to explain why he did not claim non-residence

in 1942, when he was similarly on duty with the armed services outside of Wisconsin. In a later memorandum, McCarthy claimed he was not a resident of Wisconsin in 1943 and therefore not obliged to pay income taxes — though he had been born, raised, and educated in Wisconsin, still held a judgeship in a Wisconsin circuit court, and was planning to run for the U. S. Senate from Wisconsin. The reply McCarthy received from J. L. Tibbetts, Assessor of Incomes, at Appleton, read:

I am advised by the legal division that it is of the opinion that you were a resident of Wisconsin in the year 1943 and therefore required to file a return of your income for that year with the Wisconsin Department of Taxation.

Joe was given a thirty-day deadline to pay up; he grumbled that the deadline was "arbitrary in the extreme," but finally forked over $2,459.54 in tax, plus $218.32 in interest. At the same time, the federal Bureau of Internal Revenue was levying an additional assessment of $3,500 on McCarthy for 1943.

During Joe's first three years in the Senate, he reported a total gross income of $59,604.59; but he didn't pay a penny of state income tax until the authorities finally forced him to hand over $134.23 for his 1949 tax. He was able to get away with this by claiming stock losses of $43,217.87 and interest payments of $18,262.96. A little arithmetic shows that his total loss for the three years was $61,480.83, as against a total income of $59,604.59. In other words, he went in the hole $1,876.24; yet he managed to keep his pockets jingling with cash. By 1950, these remarkable figures had brought such a storm of bad publicity down on Joe's head that with his 1950 state tax return he mailed a check for $1,175.78 — the largest state tax he ever paid without prompting from the authorities. This was the tax on his $12,500 Senate salary, $6,675 in dividends, and $2,850 from speaking fees — a total of $22,025.

But meanwhile, McCarthy was weaving a tangled financial web; and he got so twisted up in it that it took his rich friends to extricate him. Joe had borrowed over $300,000 to underwrite his stock speculations, judging from the "interest payments" listed in his income-tax return. Of this, his home-town banker, Matt Schuh, dug into the coffers of the Appleton State Bank for $75,000 (see Chapter 22), and then sweated out the repayments while the state bank examiners watched over his shoulder.

Joe was skating on thin financial ice; and the nervous Schuh kept dunning him for more margin. When the bank directors threatened to sell Joe's collateral out from under him, he sent out an SOS. The rescue party included Mc-Carthy's hired office man, Ray Kiermas; the industrialist, Walter Harnischfeger; a millionaire manufacturer, Frank Sensenbrenner; an Appleton liquor dealer, Abe Polisky; and the Prince of Outer Baldonia, Russell Arundel.

Joe may have plunged too deep into the stock-and-bond market; it was sink or swim. But before he went down for the third time, thousands of $1 and $5 bills began to come in from patriotic Americans, anxious to help finance the fight against Communism.

39. Tangles and Ulcers

LIKE MOST OTHER PLUNGES IN JOE MCCARTHY'S CAREER, HIS joy ride on Wall Street was hectic; he cut some capers that almost made a nervous wreck of his banker friend, Matt Schuh.

The small-town bank president kept sending up distress signals (see Chapter 22): "Something must be done immediately . . ." "I am really on the spot . . ." "It would put both you and me in the doghouse . . ." "I thought probably with your contacts . . ."

These brought such responses from Joe as: "Hold up everything . . ." "I have been so badly tied up . . ." "My ulcers are getting worse . . ."

From the day Joe blew into Washington, the mail became heavy between his Senate office and the Appleton State Bank; and the letters grew more urgent as Joe sank deeper in the quagmire of extra-curricular, marginal speculation. McCarthy had interested himself in Wall Street as far back as 1943, when he played the stock market in between his Marine duties and made a killing of $42,353.92. Where Joe got the money for this provident venture was a question that took the authors from Chicago to Milwaukee to Appleton. But except for a few dim traces, the trail was obscure. The track was picked up again after McCarthy turned in his Marine uniform for his old judicial robes. On the letterhead of the circuit court chambers, Judge Joe wrote to Banker Schuh on June 18, 1945:

DEAR MATT:

In making my request for a loan of approximately $75,000.00 in which I will put up as security certain stocks, I am fully aware of the fact that you may find it necessary or may be called upon to dispose of the stocks to protect this loan. If and when that situation should arise, obviously there can be no objection on my part.

In other words, Matt, I am requesting this loan, being fully aware of all hazards.

Yours sincerely,

JOE MCCARTHY

By April 9, 1947, Joe had fallen behind on his payments; and Schuh wrote anxiously:

DEAR JOE:

I was very much surprised that you did not call here at the bank when you were in Appleton last weekend, as it is very necessary that your notes have your attention. . . .

I am very much concerned about these notes, because in the event the examiners call on us while the notes are past due, they will immediately ask us to sell the collateral and pay the notes in full. Therefore, I would like to hear from you . . . what you intend to do regarding these past due notes.

Yours very truly,

MATT SCHUH

Joe touched his hired man, Ray Kiermas, for a stop-gap loan, and dashed off another "Dear Matt" letter six days later. It proposed:

DEAR MATT:

Instead of having Ray give you a check for the interest on these two notes, Matt, I wonder if you would apply it on the principal instead, in that I would like to wait until near the end of the year to decide whether the interest should be paid this year or next year for income tax purposes.

I note that I am short $1,800.00 in collateral. I will get this to you within a few days.

Sincerely yours,

JOE MCCARTHY

The banker replied on April 18 that "Ray made a payment of $574.73 principal on the large note." And he added wistfully: "Trusting that you will mail us an additional check so we can again get your margin up to 20 per cent without much further delay so the loans won't be criticized by the department, I am, Yours very truly . . ." Before the month was up, Joe thought he had found a solution. He wrote to Banker Schuh on May 9:

DEAR MATT:

I have made complete arrangements with Walter Harnischfeger, of Harnischfeger Corporation, to put up sufficient collateral to cure both of our ulcers, but as bad luck would have it, I was completely laid up in the Naval Hospital under a "No Visitors" rule when Harnischfeger came through Washington. He left for Europe and won't be back for about a month, so if I can only keep this up to 20 per cent until he gets back, I am sure I can then take care of it so as to relieve you of this permanent headache.

Yours very truly,
JOE McCARTHY

But Joe's promise had little cash value; and the worried banker wrote back cryptically about "our friend in Chicago" and suggested: "It would be a good idea if you wired him and told him you had just received a wire from me advising you that something must be done immediately." When this failed to bring any money, Schuh wrote McCarthy:

DEAR JOE:

I am again compelled to write you with reference to your $53,000.00 loan which is held by the bank, secured by collateral. You no doubt are familiar with the quotations on this collateral and that the margin is under 20 per cent, which you will recall, was the margin agreed upon when we made the loan. . . .

I thought possibly, with your contacts, it might be possible for you to make such arrangements. In the event that the parties you might be in a position to discuss this matter with haven't the ready cash, they might have collateral. . . .

I am really on the spot. . . .

Yours very truly,
MATT SCHUH

On July 12, Joe came through with a polite letter and a tip on the stock market: "Today's tip on the market — buy."

But the bank needed something more tangible; so Joe went back to his office manager, Ray Kiermas, and got him to put up his $10,000 savings account. Joe also arranged for Liquor Dealer Abe Polisky to sign a $2,500 note. And by December, McCarthy was able to take his banker friend off the spot, at least temporarily, by submitting the $20,000 promissory note, vouched for by the self-styled Prince of Outer Baldonia, Russell Arundel. This $20,000 note looked big enough to Kiermas to loosen the strings on his $10,000 savings; and so at the urging of his employee, Joe wrote another letter on April 1, 1948:

DEAR MATT:

Ray has been after me . . . to write you in regard to the $10,000.00 which he put up as collateral. His position is that while he has no objection to helping me out when I actually need additional collateral, that in view of the $20,000.00 item covered by Arundel, his $10,000.00 is unnecessary at this time. . . . Obviously if the market drops, I shall be in a position to somehow supply you with more collateral.

Sincerely yours,

JOE McCARTHY

But McCarthy's finances stayed about as steady as an earthquake; and in another five months the state bank examiners not only placed the Arundel note "on the objectionable list," according to Schuh, but "were very much insistent that we take the $10,000.00 savings account of Ray Kiermas on payment of the note." Joe made hasty plans to sell some of his Chicago, Milwaukee, St. Paul and Pacific stock; but the harassed banker warned that this would "lower your collateral by $20,000.00 and surely it would put both you and me in the doghouse." He suggested sticking Arundel for the $20,000.00, adding: "I hope that you can arrange this within the next few days, so I won't have to dip into Ray Kiermas' savings account in order to adjust your loan." Joe sent a frantic letter to Schuh to "hold up everything until I return to Appleton"; and the financial crisis was put off until the new year, 1949.

On January 4, 1949, Banker Schuh totaled up Joe's collateral, which came to $56,869.93. Of this $23,452.50 belonged to Employee Kiermas, including his handy $10,000.00 savings account. But all this still wasn't enough to hold up McCarthy's financial house of cards. Schuh warned wearily: "With both your collateral and that of Ray Kiermas, the margin is only 7 per cent, so you can see that something will have to be done immediately with reference to bolstering this collateral or paying the loans." Eight days later, McCarthy replied:

DEAR MATT:

I am extremely sorry I didn't get to answer your letter earlier. The reason is I have been so badly tied up, what with the reorganization of committees, etc. . . .

Ray tells me he has additional stock, valued at approximately $14,000, which could be put up. I wonder if this would take care of the situation temporarily. I say "temporarily" for the reason that the book which I sold will be published very shortly, and I have high hopes that the sales will be sufficient to substantially reduce the loan. . . .

I would naturally be glad to assign the benefits on that contract to the bank. . . . I assure you any monies received on that contract will be immediately applied in full to improve the picture at the bank.

If you can spare any, I wonder if you could send me some of those ulcer pills.

                                        Sincerely yours,
                                        JOE MCCARTHY

But it was too late. "Dear Matt" had already passed the last stages of the nervous skitters; and he replied resignedly on January 19:

DEAR JOE:

The bank examiners were very insistent when they discussed the loan with the directors. . . .

It would seem to me that you should go to some friend of yours and try to convince him that if you ever needed help financially, this would be the time that it would be appreciated. This loan is out of my control now, and from here in I can only take orders.

Yours very truly,
MATT SCHUH

Joe poured more verbal oil on the roily financial waters, promising on January 25 that he would "either get cash or additional collateral. . . . However, I am leaving today to go to Kansas City to speak to the Lumber Dealers' Association, and on my way back have to speak at Toledo, Ohio. . . . I wonder, therefore . . ."

But wonderment had worn out for the state bank examiners, who put pressure upon Banker Schuh to collect past-due loans from Senator McCarthy. Finally, on November 25, 1949, Schuh wrote:

DEAR JOE:

The directors have now given me an outright order to the effect that unless your loans are paid in full, I am to immediately contact Wayne Hummer and Co. [McCarthy's broker] and sell out your collateral. . . .

I am sorry this has come about, but it is now definitely out of my hands, and I have no alternative but to do as I am directed.

I might add that no telephone calls, telegrams or letters will bring about any extension of these loans.

Yours very truly,
MATT SCHUH

It was only three months later that McCarthy made his big splash against Communists-in-government. And with the front-page clippings came paper of a more substantial nature: greenbacks to help finance his crusade. By September 1951, Joe was able to pay off his bank loan and a balance of $14,016.63 that he still owed his millionaire friend, Frank J. Sensenbrenner. "This should help your ulcers," Joe wrote to Matt Schuh on September 11, as he wiped out the debt.

But McCarthy's costs had also increased. When he lamented after 1950 that "it costs money to fight Com-

munism," he was telling the truth. He had shelled out
salaries and expenses for as many as five investigators working on the single subject of Communism. One of the investigators, Don Surine, boasted to an acquaintance that he
averaged $700 to $800 a week in salary and expenses. Only
a small portion of this money could come from the general
hiring fund allowed for each Senator; the rest had to come
out of Joe's pocket.

As Joe told a reporter: "It's sort of breaking me, but I've
had a lot of help from friends. Investigators don't work for
peanuts. Right now, I've got four and a half investigators;
that is, four working full time, one half time. I got a man
over in Europe full time, a temporary employee. I guess you
would call it five and a half. They average $25 and $30 a day
plus their expenses. The expenses depend upon where you
send them. Take transportation to Berlin — $666, I believe."

To find out how McCarthy accumulated such high sums,
the authors studied confidential reports from a member of
McCarthy's own office staff. One such report, written early
in 1951, said:

> Mail is still pouring into McCarthy's office at a heavy rate. Many
> of the letters contain contributions. I gathered from an offhand remark
> . . . that the money from the mail on one day amounted to over
> $1,000, but was unable to determine whether this was just the usual
> daily amount from the mail, or whether this was an exceptional day.
>
> I was also told that Mr......... of .... Corporation had
> made a financial contribution toward McCarthy's work. I was unable
> to find out whether the contribution was by currency or by check
> and whether it represented Mr. ....'s individual funds or
> corporate funds.

Later the McCarthy employee reported:

> While in Senator McCarthy's office, Surine showed me the large
> volume of mail that McCarthy receives and claimed that this mail
> now averages about 1,000 letters per day. Surine also boasted that
> many of these letters contained contributions varying from $1 to as
> high as $50 toward McCarthy's work.

It should be made clear that McCarthy, in accepting this money and paying no tax on it, violated no law. Gifts, as such, need not be declared as taxable income; so when a Nebraska farmer tucked a $5 bill in the mail and sent it to Joe for his fight against Communism, the money was legally a gift.

Of course, Joe did nothing to discourage such assistance. On the contrary, he was not averse to priming the pump by continual references to "the tremendous expense of my undertaking." He had publicly lamented his "heavy borrowings." And once he wrote in a form letter: "I have really been scraping the bottom of the barrel in order to hire the necessary investigators to develop the facts." As a guest on the radio program of professional Anti-Semite Upton Close, Joe spoke earnestly about the heavy expenses of his anti-Communist campaign, most of which, he said, came out of his own pocket. The sympathetic Close picked up the cue and urged that a million Americans send their contributions to McCarthy for his "crusade."

There were other occasions when the McCarthy money-raising effort appeared to skirt the bounds of propriety. For example, employees of the Schweiger Manufacturing Company — a Jefferson, Wisconsin, furniture plant — received letters from their foremen asking contributions to the McCarthy crusade. There were loud protests, but most of the workers kicked in. The money was forwarded by L. P. Schweiger, president of the company. And Joe gratefully dashed off a form letter to each of the helpful employees "thanking you for the help you have given me."

Thus the nature of McCarthy's financial backing became clear. Much of it came from the furniture employee, the farmer, the butcher, the baker — anyone who was sufficiently impressed by Senator Joe's campaign to drop a dollar bill in the mail. McCarthy has received thousands of such contributions; the fact that he never mentions them is his own business. He is not required to account for gifts, and he knows it.

Joe's talent for cards has also come in handy; and he has supplemented his income at the poker table. Once he made a date to play gin rummy with Senator Bob Kerr of Oklahoma, the millionaire oilman. But first, Joe sent to the Library of Congress for a copy of Oswald Jacoby's *On Gin Rummy*, and he studied it intensely before his match with Kerr. The rich Oklahoman wouldn't say how much he lost to Joe; but another Senator, close to Kerr, told the authors it ran into thousands.

McCarthy also managed to scrape up some extra money by making speeches for hire. On February 15, 1951, a McCarthy aide told the Associated Press: "The Senator receives substantial fees — in addition to his expenses — for special talks outside of Wisconsin." It went without saying this his price varied directly with the amount of furor Joe was currently creating in the Senate. Before his Communist splash, he showed one of the authors a $500 check that he had received for an evening's lecture. It was understood, however, that his fee went up after his front-page publicity on the Red issue.

Joe also made money by appearing at parties where, for one reason or another, his presence was desired. Robert Byers, the Columbus house-builder, testified that he twice paid McCarthy $500 plus expenses for attending his company's parties. This took place while McCarthy wielded tremendous prestige as vice-chairman of the Joint Housing Committee.

Joe swore that all such outside income was dutifully reported on his state income-tax returns, although he sometimes had trouble pointing out just where he listed a particular item. In 1948, for example, he admitted receiving $100 for a piece on housing in *Collier's*. His tax return listed a number of specific income items, including the $10,000 from

Lustron; but the *Collier's* payment was not listed. Joe explained: "I think that is included under the general item of 'speeches.' There is an item of $1,000 or something . . . that I received from speeches, and I think that is included."

McCarthy's finances led the St. Louis *Post-Dispatch* to inquire editorially:

> How can a Senator lose money year after year, lose more than he makes from his government salary, his lecture fees, his literary efforts, and other sources of revenue — and still manage to eat as well and entertain as lavishly as Senator Joseph R. McCarthy does?

This question could not be answered yet.

40. The Publicity Turns "Red"

Say you're an editor of a big afternoon paper.

It's fifteen minutes before the deadline for the final home edition — the edition that goes into people's homes and makes up 95 per cent of your circulation. And you've got no hot stories.

Sure, there's an automobile wreck, and a mayor's announcement, and maybe a riot in faraway Iran — but these aren't exactly banner-headline stories in a big city. So what do you use for an eight-column black "line" in the Night Final?

By this time you're scratching around, desperate. And then the wire editor pushes across a piece of yellow paper, marked Washington (AP). And you read: "Sen. Joseph R. McCarthy (R., Wis.) charged today that Ambassador-at-Large Philip Jessup had an unusual affinity for Communist causes. In a speech on the Senate floor, the Wisconsin Senator said he has the proof for his sensational charge . . ."

Quickly you scribble a headline across the copy and mark it "P.1." Then you stuff it in the capsule and send it up the airtube to the composing room. And you've got your Night Final banner headline!

There, in a nutshell, you have 99 per cent of the reason for Joe McCarthy's success. You can discount his personal ambition: that may have started the McCarthy flywheel, but it was the press that kept the wheel turning. You can discount his native cunning: had it not been for the fourth estate, he'd have used this talent in a vacuum. Any way you slice it, it adds up to the same thing: if Joe McCarthy is a political monster, then the press has been his Dr. Frankenstein.

Joe's publicity build-up started back in the north country, where reporters wrote glowingly about the hustling young circuit judge. As a Marine, he circulated his own version of *South Pacific* and watched it pop out like the measles in one back-country paper after another, until the myth had become accepted that "Tail-Gunner" Joe was a wounded hero. Later, his first campaign for Senator was masterminded by an ex-Hearst managing editor, James Colby.

After Joe had taken the oath of office, the news stories began to flow in a steady stream:

MCCARTHY DENOUNCES SUGAR RATIONING

MCCARTHY PROMISES VETERANS' HOUSING

MCCARTHY HITS TAFT ON HOUSING BILL

MCCARTHY DEMANDS ARMORED TRAIN RUN BERLIN BLOCKADE

MCCARTHY CHARGES ARMY TORTURED NAZIS

MCCARTHY DEMANDS LIE DETECTOR TESTS FOR OFFICERS

MCCARTHY SAYS NAVY SECRETARY LIED

Capitol Hill reporters learned to like the smiling, accommodating Senator from Wisconsin, who always had something to say. Even if his pronouncements were far-fetched, they were always good for a Night Final line. And Joe would do anything to oblige. He would even call high government officials on his own phone while reporters listened in on an extension, enabling them to get confidential information which the officials would not have released knowingly.

But the headline that capped all other McCarthy headlines exploded on the morning of February 10, 1950, across the nation's front pages — after his Wheeling, West Virginia, speech. It was just the kind of sensational charge that reporters had come to expect from the Wisconsin

Senator; and they gave it full play. For the rest of the year, the magic name "McCarthy" appeared more often in the teletyped stories that moved out of Washington than the name of any other Senator.

How did Joe do it?

Part of the answer lies in the newspaper fraternity's devotion to the principle of objectivity. It is a violation of the unwritten creed for newsmen to mix opinion with fact; and so they gave Joe's wild accusations complete and factual coverage. They were telling the truth when they wrote: MCCARTHY CHARGES 205 REDS IN STATE DEPARTMENT. Joe had indeed made that charge. As to the truth or falsehood of his statement, the reporters felt that was out of their line; appraisals of Joe's accuracy were left for the columnists and editorial writers.

For a long time, the editor of the Littleton (Colorado) *Independent* had observed — with rising blood pressure — this unwitting build-up of McCarthy by the American press. One day in March 1951 he angrily watched his tickers pounding out "take" after "take" about McCarthy. Thoroughly fed up, he pushed a sheet of paper into his typewriter and began:

For decades the American press had worshiped the God of objectivity. This seemed to keep the voters informed on all sides of a question until the invention of the technique of the big lie.

Under this technique, a public official can use totalitarian methods — knowing his utterances will be reported "straight" and that truth will never catch up with his falsehoods.

This practice, particularly since the rise of Senator Joe McCarthy of Wisconsin, has been subjected to re-examination by the press in recent months. Editors have been searching for a way to present something more than the naked facts, as the whole truth is often not embodied in a news report. Editorial comment the next day never quite seems to correct the wrong impression made on the front page.

Senator McCarthy has callously exploited this advantage to the limit. He has used his immunity on the Senate floor to break reputations of noble public servants. With the customary parliamentary

tricks which his committee assignments permit, he has further blocked
the functioning of government in time of peril.

William T. Evjue, editor of the Madison *Capital Times*,
took up the cry. He declared editorially:

A picture of Senator McCarthy, posed with a large broom in front
of the Capitol in Washington, D. C., was sent to every newspaper
in Wisconsin subscribing to the mat service of the AP.

Along with the picture was sent the following blurb: "Senator Joseph
McCarthy (R., Wis.), advocate of cleaning Communist influence from
government, shows off a big new broom sent to him by constituents at
Little Chute and Appleton, Wis."

Note in this cutline the easy pro-McCarthy assumption on the
part of the AP that there is "Communist influence" in government.
The cutline did not say the "Communist influence which McCarthy
alleges to be in government."

We will venture the guess that if a Democratic candidate against
McCarthy showed up in an AP office with a gag as corny as this he
would be laughed out of the place. . . .

On one occasion it [the Associated Press] turned over its wire to
a lengthy story describing how the Senator from Wisconsin fried
chicken. But the AP did not have the men nor the time to cover a
story as significant as the one showing that a poll of distinguished
political scientists voted McCarthy the "worst" Senator in the United
States.

Evjue followed up with a series of editorials, pointing out
prima-facie examples of news-slanting by the wire services.
For example, in September of 1951, a *Capital Times* editorial
said:

Last week Secretary of Labor Maurice J. Tobin spoke before the
Veterans of Foreign Wars convention in New York City. In his speech,
Secretary Tobin attacked the "slanderers" in the U. S. Senate who
use the Senate as a "citadel" to hide from the libel laws.

The New York *Times* covered Secretary Tobin's speech. It records
the fact that his attack on the "slanderers" in the Senate was interrupted by applause. The AP and UP stories do not mention that he
was applauded.

Reporting the reaction of the VFW to . . . a demand that McCarthy
be invited to address the convention, the New York *Times* said:

"A chorus of boos welled up from all quarters of the great assembly hall, fairly drowning out the scattered cheers." The AP and UP did not report that . . . the demand was booed by VFW members.

But two days later, when McCarthy made his reply, the AP covered the story in much greater detail. Up near the top of the story, it made this observation:

"McCarthy, himself a Marine veteran and VFW member, was loudly cheered. . . . Once during his speech, a delegate shouted loudly, 'McCarthy for President.' "

The AP story refers to McCarthy as "the fiery Wisconsin Republican." No such descriptive adjectives were used on Secretary Tobin.

A few other editorial voices, such as that of the Toledo (Ohio) *Blade,* agreed with Evjue. But at least one person thought the wire services weren't giving McCarthy enough publicity; this person was Joe McCarthy. On August 5, 1950, he sent a letter to every daily-newspaper editor in the country, criticizing the Associated Press for giving his charges "inadequate" coverage. Up to the time the American Society of Newspaper Editors had met in Washington the previous April, Joe wrote, "the press coverage of our fight to rid the State Department of Communists left much to be desired. Fortunately, many of the editors, during the days they were in Washington, personally saw the news being made in this case, and also witnessed the press coverage out of Washington."

Joe's idea of "adequate" coverage was plenty of publicity, flavored to suit his tastes. And if an editor didn't like the McCarthy version of the news and raised his head above the supine mob to voice his disapproval, he was quite likely to have it cracked by McCarthy's waiting shillelagh.

For Joe took the position that the enemies of McCarthy were the enemies of America; and anyone who dared criticize McCarthy was automatically branded a Communist. So it was that McCarthy, like the Frankenstein monster, began to turn on his creator — the press. On March 14, 1951, on the Senate floor he lashed out violently against "those

camp followers in press, radio, and motion pictures. . . .
[They] have done deadly damage to this nation in aiding
the conspiracy of the three active Communist divisions at
work in America." And on September 7, 1951, Joe told
Newsweek magazine:

I think the people are with me despite the camp-following elements
of press and radio . . . those who follow the party line. Budenz has
named 400 Communists in press and radio. He has given this information to the government. Now if the names of these 400 people
were known to the public, they could never put their propaganda
across. If also the well-meaning, deluded, intellectual radicals, who
consider themselves as great liberals, did not contribute to the cause,
this propaganda would not be poisoning our channels of information.
. . . Louis Budenz gives the names of 400 people who are depended
upon by the Communist Party. The task of these individuals is to
try and locate themselves on the so-called respectable newspapers
and magazines — that's their job — because if they are working for
known Communist publications they can do no damage. . . . The prime
aim of the Communist Party, as you know, is to get control of the
medium of communication. That they are having some success is
obvious.

By May 18, 1952, Joe's critics had grown so numerous
that he felt constrained to speak of a "vast number of Communists in press and radio." In the McCarthy jargon, a
Communist was now any person who opposed the junior
Senator from Wisconsin — which would include the editors
of such magazines as the *Saturday Evening Post* and *Collier's,* and of such newspapers as the Washington *Post*, the
Milwaukee *Journal,* and the St. Louis *Post-Dispatch.* All
were the butts of Joe's accusations; and all, in the strange
new lexicon of Senator Joe, were dupes of Moscow.

41. Answering the Critics

SENATOR JOE MCCARTHY HAD AN ANSWER FOR HIS CRITICS, and the answer was always the same: he called them Communists. Whatever the criticism, he never argued over the substance but simply Red-washed the source.

Joe regarded some critics as more subversive than others, depending on how severely they criticized him. But probably the most persistent thorn in his side, and dean of the McCarthy critics, was elderly Editor William Evjue of the Madison *Capital Times*. He was the first to poke his thumb in McCarthy's financial pie and pull out the juicy plums Joe had hidden there. Evjue was noted for the caustic tone of his typewriter; and he threw the dictionary at McCarthy.

Joe's reaction was inevitable; he announced that "the Madison *Capital Times* is closer to the [Communist] *Daily Worker* than any other newspaper in the country." But Evjue didn't let up in his attacks; he fastened new editorial burrs to McCarthy's sore spots. Finally, Joe let go a real McCarthy blockbuster at Evjue's paper. It came in the form of a large manila envelope, mailed without postage under Senatorial frank. The envelope contained eleven mimeographed sheets stapled together into a booklet, and a note which said: "Enclosed is a document which I thought you might be interested in. I intend to discuss this matter in some detail while back in Wisconsin. Copies have been sent to all newspapers and radio stations in the state." The note was signed: "Joe McCarthy."

The booklet turned up in the mailboxes of *Capital Times* subscribers. It raised four questions:

1. Has the Communist Party with the co-operation of the Capital Times Corporation won a major victory in Wisconsin?
2. Is Cedric Parker, city editor of the *Capital Times*, a Communist?
3. Is the Capital Times Corporation the Red mouthpiece for the Communist Party in Wisconsin?
4. What can be done about this situation?

Question No. 4 was an artful way of implying that there *was* a situation which needed attention without making the libelous statement outright. The accompanying mimeographed "evidence" consisted mainly of a warmed-over charge that Evjue in a fit of pique had called Cedric Parker a Communist ten years before. At the time, Parker was a reporter and the pair were on the outs.

Evjue quickly explained that he had used the McCarthy bogey-word against Parker at a time when the label "Communist" was used in the same broad sense as "reactionary," "conservative," and other general terms "referring more to a general philosophy than the connotation now given it." Evjue had long since repented of his impulsive attack on Parker, and had hired him as his city editor. The grizzled Evjue considered the issue closed once and for all when Parker, in 1948, signed a non-Communist affidavit as president of the Madison Newspaper Guild. "Senator McCarthy isn't so much concerned over any Communism in connection with the *Capital Times* as he is over the fact that it was this newspaper that exposed his tax difficulties," Evjue cracked back.

Meanwhile, the Milwaukee *Journal* — which had hoped editorially in 1946 that Joe would turn in a creditable job as Senator (see Chapter 19) — had become fed up with him in less than a year. And because the paper blankets the state, its public disgust at McCarthy finally got under his skin.

But the *Journal* was the last paper in the state that could be suspected of Communist leanings. It had led the fight to purge Milwaukee's labor unions of Communist influence, and had pointed the accusing finger at two Communists who worked up to key positions in the Milwaukee CIO, Harold Christoffel and Melvin Heinritz. (This was the Communist faction, incidentally, which had helped McCarthy pull La Follette's Senate seat out from under him.)

But none of this deterred Joe, who promptly labeled the *Journal* "the Milwaukee edition of the *Daily Worker*." And on August 6, 1950, he urged the Milwaukee Retail Food Dealers to withdraw their advertising. Joe told the grocers: "Keep in mind when you send your checks over to the *Journal* . . . you are contributing to bringing the Communist Party line into the homes of Wisconsin." In another speech to the Wauwautoa Republican Club in Milwaukee, Joe asked housewives to boycott advertisers who bought space in the *Journal*.

It was not easy to find "evidence" that Communists were controlling the conservative *Journal*. But the enterprising McCarthy claimed that the paper had been strongly influenced by a New York lawyer, conveniently dead. This dead man's influence over the *Journal's* editorial policies could be assumed, Joe said, because the lawyer had been married to the younger sister of the wife of a *Journal* executive. Joe also charged, from the safety zone of the Senate floor, that two of the *Journal's* editorial writers had contributed to the defense fund for Alger Hiss.

All this the *Journal* categorically denied.

But of all Joe's journalistic feuds, his attacks on Columnist Drew Pearson had been the bitterest and most sustained. The two squared off early in McCarthy's Senatorial career, when Pearson showed up Joe's connections with the real-estate lobby. It was Pearson who first exposed Joe's $10,000 payment from the bankrupt Lustron Corporation. Later, the columnist burst McCarthy's war-hero bubble by revealing that Joe had quit the Marines in the middle of the Pacific war; that he had been promoted only one rank instead of working up from private to captain, as he boasted; and that his much-publicized "wound" was a phony.

But Joe preferred to keep his powder dry. He held his fire until the end of 1950, although he confided to reporters that he was preparing a blast at the much-cussed columnist that would make all previous criticism of him look like praise. The day before the scheduled speech, Joe staged what appeared to be a publicity stunt to attract attention to the speech; he provoked a public brawl with Pearson at a dinner party loaded with celebrities. But if Joe figured someone would tip off the press, he was wrong. The Sulgrave Club was too respectable a locale for this roughhouse scene; not one of the well-mannered guests breathed a word.

The next day, Joe put off his speech. A couple of days later, several million radio listeners heard Joe's friend, Fulton Lewis, Jr., broadcast an "exclusive" item on the incident, implying that Pearson had provoked McCarthy.

The Lewis report turned out to be a distortion; the witnesses, including Senator Richard Nixon of California, said that Joe had been spoiling for a fight all evening.

The day after Lewis' play-by-play description of Joe's assault, McCarthy made a two-hour Senate speech against Pearson. And the advance publicity had packed the press gallery. Joe launched into his philippic:

It appears that Pearson never actually signed up as a member of the Communist Party and never paid dues. . . . [But] if the loyal American newspaper editors and publishers and radio-station owners refuse to buy this disguised, sugar-coated voice of Russia, the mockingbirds who have followed the Pearson line will disappear from the scene like chaff before the wind. The American people can do much to accomplish this result. They can notify their newspapers that they do not want this Moscow-directed character assassin being brought into their homes to poison the well of information at which their children drink. They can notify the Adam Hat Company by actions what they think of their sponsoring this man. It should be remembered that anyone who buys an Adam hat, any store that stocks an Adam hat, is unknowingly and innocently contributing at least something to the cause of international Communism by keeping this Communist spokesman on the air.

When Joe had concluded his speech and walked buoyantly out into the night, he absently planted a gray fedora on his head — an Adam hat (size 7⅞) that Drew Pearson had once presented him with.

Joe followed up with two more Senate speeches against Pearson, and then bound the three together in a booklet. Once again, he used his free mailing privileges to send the booklet to all newspapers that published Pearson's column.

As for Pearson's radio sponsor, the Adam Hat Company nervously announced that it would not renew his contract. But others with more courage came to Pearson's defense. After all, the record was plain: Pearson had been the first to publish the facts about the Russian spy ring in Canada; and a year before Elizabeth Bentley put the finger on a Washington spy ring, Pearson had told how the ring had photographed blueprints of the B-29 and smuggled the secret photographs off to Russia. James Dunn, then Ambassador to Italy, had credited Pearson's Friendship Train and letter crusade with helping to defeat the Communists in the crucial Italian election of 1948.

One of the many who spoke up for Pearson was Chairman Walter Alessandroni of the American Legion's committee on un-American activities (see Chapter 37), who wrote McCarthy:

I have taken cognizance of your charge that Mr. Drew Pearson, author of the "Washington Merry-Go-Round" column, is the spokesman for international Communism. If your charge is factually correct — if Mr. Pearson, who, by virtue of his vast audience, has helped to shape contemporary history; who has conceived and executed such projects as the Friendship Train, Democracy for Italy Letters, and substantially aided the Tide of Toys; and who has smoked out corrupt government officials — if he is a Communist affiliate, then we must conclude that he is a genius at subterfuge.

Time magazine, for its part, had been inclined to sit on a lofty perch and observe these goings-on, meanwhile expressing itself neither one way nor the other on the tempestuous Senator. Back in March 1950, *Time* was running reports like this:

Across the committee table in the Senate's marble-columned caucus room, Wisconsin's pugnacious Senator Joe McCarthy glared defiantly at his tormentors. On the witness table in front of him lay the case histories with which he promised to prove his charge that the State Department was infested with card-carrying Communists and their friends. But for two days he had been too busy fending off the heckling questions of Democratic committeemen to spread out his evidence.

Republicans sat back out of the line of fire as the Democrats bored in. Ex-Marine McCarthy might turn out to have something, after all; the State Department's reputation for security was none too savory.

On June 5, 1950, *Time* was still non-committal:

Could Republican Senator Joseph R. McCarthy be stopped? After three tries, administration strategists were beginning to despair. Neither anguished denials of Communism in the State Department nor vitriolic attacks on McCarthy and his witnesses could quiet the uproar the Wisconsin Senator had caused.

During this period, Joe had nothing but warm praise for Henry Luce, editor of *Time* and *Life;* and he found no sinister evidence of Communism in Luce's magazines. McCarthy's "research" turned up such "evidence" only when *Time,* and its sister magazine *Life,* grew increasingly critical of the junior Senator from Wisconsin. Finally the day arrived when Joe felt he should inform Editor Luce about the "Communist" slant of his magazines. The letter, on November 6, 1951, began:

Dear Mr. Luce:

As you know, ever since I commenced the public phase of my fight against Communists high in our government, the Communist *Daily Worker* has led a vicious personal smear attack against me, which has been gleefully joined in by a vast number of the camp-following elements of the press and radio.

The "evidence" which changed McCarthy's mind on the loyalty and veracity of *Time* and *Life* consisted of such material as the *Life* editorial of September 27, 1951, which called upon Senator Robert A. Taft of Ohio to "renounce and repudiate all political connections" with McCarthy "before it is too late." The editorial continued:

The cumulative debasement of U. S. politics has gone far enough. Somebody must forego the pleasure of further groin-and-eyeball fighting. . . . The nation owes no debt to Joe McCarthy.

But the straw that broke the back of Joe's patience was printed in *Time* on October 22, 1951. McCarthy's picture appeared on the cover of that issue, and four inside pages were devoted to him. The article said:

In a nation that had finally learned (without any help from McCarthy) that it was locked in a life-or-death struggle with world Communism, these [McCarthy's] charges were as grave as any that could be made. The underlying accusation was that its State Department was harboring Communists, knew they were Communists, and was doing so deliberately. . . . McCarthy, who said that he "held in his hand" the names of 205 Communists then in the State Department, did not give the Tydings committee the names of the 205. He did not give it the names of 57. He did not produce the name of even one Communist in the State Department. . . . He set up a barrage of new accusations which caught the headlines, drawing attention away from the fact that he had not made good on his original charge. . . .

His most sensational charge was that he knew the name of "the top Soviet espionage agent" in the U. S. [but] to this day McCarthy has not produced a scrap of evidence indicating that Lattimore was a spy or in any way disloyal. The question of whether Lattimore's analysis of the Far East was correct or incorrect — which is still a highly relevant and important question — does not interest Joe. Such questions have no interest to demagogues. . . .

The Reds in government, if any, were safe. After nearly two years of tramping the nation, shouting that he was "rooting out the skunks," just how many Communists has Joe rooted out? The answer is none. . . .

No regard for fair play, no scruple for exact truth hampers Joe's political course. If his accusations destroy reputations, if they subvert the principle that a man is innocent until proved guilty, he is oblivious. Joe, immersed in the joy of battle, does not even seem to realize the gravity of his own charges.

This report apparently convinced Joe that *Time* had gone Communist; and he warned his disciples about "the depth to which this magazine will sink in using deliberate falsehoods to destroy anyone who is hurting the Communist cause." Joe's attacks on *Time* and *Life* ran the full course, ending in an attempt to put the magazines out of business. He wrote Luce: "As you already know, I am preparing material on *Time* magazine to furnish all of your advertisers, so they may be aware of the type of publication they are supporting."

This smacked of intimidation and suppression; and the sentinels of the free press sat up and took notice. But Joe stuck to his guns:

I feel that I have a duty to let those advertisers know that *Time* magazine publishes falsehoods for a purpose. Those advertisers . . . are entitled to have it called to their attention if unknowingly they are flooding American homes with Communist Party line material. . . . If they continue to advertise in *Time* magazine after they know what *Time* is doing, in my opinion no one who is for America and against Communism should buy their product.

Finally the press had made its ultimate discovery: McCarthy was a threat to their individual security unless they wrote what *he* wanted.

42. The "Communist" Press

By JOE McCARTHY'S COUNT, THE COMMUNISTS APPEARED TO control more newspapers in the United States than in Russia. And Joe was ever discovering new Communist mouthpieces, just as fast as they joined in the editorial clamor against him.

In his anti-newspaper campaign, he started with the Madison *Capital Times* and the Milwaukee *Journal*. Then he added the Washington *Post*, the New York *Post*, the St. Louis *Post-Dispatch*, the Portland *Oregonian*, and even the *Christian Science Monitor*. "They, of course, criticize Communism generally to obtain a false reputation of being anti-Communist," Joe explained in a booklet of questions and answers. "They then go all out to assassinate the character and destroy the reputation of anyone who tries to dig out the really dangerous under-cover Communists."

But when Joe suggested that the staid *Saturday Evening Post* had fallen for the Communist line, it must have brought an amused twitch to Stalin's mustache. In the July 9, 1950, issue of the magazine, McCarthy discovered a "subversive" article. It was authored by the column-writing Alsop brothers, Joseph and Stewart, and described their firsthand observation of McCarthy's counter-spy activities. Joe saw Red, and wrote editor Ben Hibbs on August 15, 1950: "It is disturbing to find that this article is almost 100 per cent in line with the official instructions issued Communists and fellow-traveling members of the press and radio by Gus Hall, national secretary of the Communist Party."

To those who knew the Alsops, it was patently ridiculous to think of their taking orders from Gus Hall; their column had consistently tolled the warning against Communism. At first, the brothers thought about suing; but McCarthy had taken the precaution of inserting the letter in the *Congressional Record*, where its contents automatically received immunity.

After reading Joe's letter, Hibbs called in his secretary and dictated an answer:

The Alsops and the *Saturday Evening Post* are against the employment of "traitors and perverts" in government, just as you are. But we are also against wild, unsupported charges such as you have been making. We feel very strongly that the tactics you have employed succeed only in muddying the waters and playing into the hands of the enemy.

So it went with newsman after newsman who had the temerity to criticize McCarthy; in public statements Joe revoked their American citizenship and bestowed Russian citizenship upon them. Among the first to discover this was Martin Agronsky, commentator for the American Broadcasting Company. Agronsky was a competent and serious-minded reporter with a reputation for digging out stories behind the news. After McCarthy's Red charges broke in February 1950, Agronsky spent many long hours interviewing, investigating, and poring over official documents, trying to sort out the separate strands of the whole tangled web. After all, if McCarthy was right, this was one of the biggest news stories of the decade.

But Agronsky learned, as did many others, that Joe's charges wouldn't stand up. And he reached additional conclusions which were not complimentary to the Senator from Wisconsin. Agronsky — with years of experience as an overseas and Washington correspondent — went on the air and called the shots as he saw them.

The first hint he had that his name had been added to

Joe's purge list came when McCarthy refused to answer his questions at a mass press conference. Shortly afterward, in September 1950, Joe popped up in Houston, Texas; and he dropped dark hints about Agronsky in private talks with members of the Houston American Legion post. Incited by Joe's remarks against this man with the suspiciously Russian-sounding name (he was born in Atlantic City, New Jersey), Post No. 52 passed a resolution voicing disapproval of Agronsky's "left-wing philosophy" and asking his sponsors to drop him. And a few days later — with appropriate fanfare — McCarthy inserted the resolution in the *Congressional Record.* But Agronsky's sponsors refused to be intimidated and instead praised him for his objectivity.

Sometime later, the United Press filed an "overnight" story which wrapped up the latest developments in the case. It mentioned in passing that McCarthy had once promised that he would repeat without benefit of immunity any charge that he made on the Senate floor.

The story was written by John Steele, a top-notch UP reporter assigned to the Senate press gallery. The next afternoon Steele dropped in at one of the frequent press conferences called by McCarthy. At first Joe ignored the reporter; then he angrily lashed out at him for "following the Communist line."

Steele snapped back: "That's absurd!"

McCarthy said: "You want me to repeat what I said without Congressional immunity so they can sue me. That's the Communist technique, to bring suits of libel."

Steele headed for the door, but McCarthy called after him: "Come, come. I didn't mean you were actually following the Communist line. It wasn't willful, anyway."

A similar experience happened to Marvin Arrowsmith, who covered McCarthy's antics for the other major wire service, the Associated Press. No reporter on Capitol Hill had a better reputation for impartiality; but Joe thought Arrowsmith's dispatches ought to be more pro-McCarthy. First, Joe took the AP man aside and warned him good-naturedly: "I don't like the way you're playing it, Marvin."

Then he went over Arrowsmith's head to the AP editors. Joe resorted to his tried-and-true technique of direct mail; he sent out a two-page letter and a large dossier of illustrative material to editors in every part of the country, charging the AP with "inadequate coverage" of his activities. The wire service dutifully investigated the charges, and returned a verdict of innocent. McCarthy had not been slighted, the report said; on the contrary, it went on, many editors were incensed by the large amount of wire copy that was "wasted" on the Wisconsin Senator and his unproved charges.

Later, Joe concluded that it was the rewrite men who were the real villains. He said:

There was impressed upon me the painful truth that the stories written by the competent, honest AP, UP, or INS men assigned to cover the Senate . . . might not even be recognized by them when those stories went on the news ticker to the thousands of newspapers throughout the country. Before being sent out to America's newspapers, the stories pass across what is known as a rewrite desk.

Here, Joe complained, the "cards were stacked" against him.

Meanwhile, Joe's roll call of "Communist" newspapermen grew ever longer. After Columnist Marquis Childs came out with an unfriendly column, Joe promptly made him a charter member of the "Communist camp-following" set. As for proof, Joe reported darkly that Childs "had bitterly attacked General MacArthur's headquarters for exposing Communist agent Agnes Smedley."

Another whose dry, grating commentaries went against the McCarthy grain was Radiocaster Elmer Davis; Joe's comeback was that "Stanislaw Mikolajczyk, one of the anti-Communist leaders of Poland, had warned the State Department, while Davis was head of the Office of War Information, that OWI broadcasts were 'following the Communist line consistently,' and that the broadcasts 'might well have emanated from Moscow itself.'"

Political Cartoonist Herbert Block also qualified for a place on Joe's list by lampooning McCarthy with the same brush that he used in caricaturing the Communists. Joe, oblivious to Herblock's frequent and biting anti-Communist cartoons, announced indignantly: "He has cartooned violently against every attempt to dig out unexposed Communists, including my anti-Communist fight."

Even the *Christian Science Monitor*'s distinguished writer, Richard Strout, couldn't criticize McCarthy and get away with it. Joe scratched around for some basis of suspicion and finally came up with the ominous report:

> I saw Richard L. Strout of the *Christian Science Monitor* shaking the hand of Rob Hall of the Communist *Daily Worker*. . . . As I witnessed that comradely handshake between an American newspaperman and the reporter for the official Communist newspaper, there flashed across my mind the story of Gunther Stein, who had been the *Christian Science Monitor*'s correspondent in China. General MacArthur's intelligence headquarters had exposed the fact that Gunther Stein was a Communist and an "indispensable and important member" of the famous Sorge Communist spy ring. . . . I thought that Stein had cleverly deceived the *Christian Science Monitor* when they made him their China correspondent.* But now I began to wonder as I watched Strout of the *Christian Science Monitor* and Rob Hall of the *Daily Worker* cheek by jowl . . . and then read the venomous, distorted, parallel stories which they both wrote.

---

* Editor Erwin D. Canham of the *Monitor* replied: "Gunther Stein was never on the staff of the *Christian Science Monitor*. However, in 1937 on the recommendation of William Henry Chamberlin, a distinguished anti-Communist writer, we began to accept special correspondence from Mr. Stein. We ceased this relationship, and published no further dispatches from Mr. Stein in China, at a date long before publication of the spy charges against him. During all the period of his writing for us, Mr. Stein was highly regarded in the profession and enjoyed the confidence of the National Government of China."

Just to keep the record straight, it should be said that none of these prominent journalists was even light pink in his articles about Communism. And as for the alleged handshake (Strout has emphatically denied ever meeting Hall), Joe had even more reason to indict his journalistic pals of the Chicago *Tribune* and the Washington *Times-Herald*, who had the subversive habit of playing gin rummy in the Senate press gallery with the Soviet news agency's correspondent, Jean Montgomery.

It was in September 1951 that the New York *Post* leveled a blast at McCarthy, so blistering that Joe's temperature rose in direct proportion to the increase in the *Post's* circulation. The series, by Oliver Pilat and William Shannon, was called "Smear, Inc.," and it won the New York Newspaper Guild's 1951 award for the best job of reporting and writing.

As soon as Joe saw the first article in the series, he jumped under his favorite umbrella, Congressional immunity, and started replying. He said that the editor of the *Post*, James A. Wechsler, was a Communist. McCarthy, who embraces many ex-Communists, must have known that Wechsler had long admitted to being a member of the Young Communist League for three years while in college in the mid-thirties — and that he had since become such a vigorous anti-Red that he was a whipping boy for the *Daily Worker*.

Later, Joe added the Sheboygan (Wisconsin) *Press* to his list. He pulled himself up in a hot temper before thirty-five schoolchildren and charged that the *Press* was pro-Communist. The newspaper responded: "Having played himself out with grownups, he is now trying to sell his stock in trade to students, those who have yet to determine how they will vote when they reach 21 years of age."

But McCarthy only stepped up his campaign against the press; if accusations of Communism didn't discourage press criticism, he would try financial injury. And so he slapped a $500,000 libel suit against the Syracuse *Post-Standard* for printing an allegedly untruthful editorial about his relationship with the convicted spy, Charles Davis. "I decided that sooner or later one of these left-wing smear articles would go so far we'd have to teach [the editor] a lesson," Joe told the *Post-Standard* lawyers. "Your paper went even farther than the *Daily Worker*."

At the pre-trial examination, Joe took the occasion to scatter his shot all over the journalistic lot. Speaking of the Milwaukee *Journal*, he remarked that he wouldn't read it "unless ordered to by the court," because "I would know the line they would follow — the *Daily Worker* line."

He added: "I read substantially the same editorial either in the *Daily Worker* or the Washington *Post*."

This led New York Supreme Court Justice Jesse Kingsley to ask in bewilderment: "Are you confused between these two papers?"

Joe replied: "They parallel each other pretty close." He went on to denounce the *Christian Science Monitor*, the *Saturday Evening Post*, and *Time* magazine.

Afterwards Mrs. Eleanor Roosevelt felt constrained to comment in her daily column: "This is too much, Senator. You must leave us a few conservative Republican and independent publications!"

Joe's popping-off finally stirred up the magazine *Editor and Publisher*, chief trade journal of American newspapers. In February 1952 this non-partisan but strongly conservative magazine took cognizance of McCarthy's attempts to intimidate the press. It concluded: "It is one thing to answer or attack critics — it is another thing to attempt to intimidate and silence them. And in this case the dignity and influence of the United States Senate is being perverted to this end. The whole thing reeks with totalitarianism."

Meanwhile, the specter of McCarthy hung over the nation's newspapers (which were preponderantly pro-Republican).

43. Sokolsky, Pegler, McCormick & Co.

OF THE NINETY-SIX SENATORS, JOE McCARTHY STOOD NINETY-sixth with the press. This was determined by a formal vote of Washington correspondents taken by *Pageant* magazine; and Joe won the title of "worst Senator" hands down, polling three out of every four votes.

But to a small fraction of the press, Joe was a lone, hair-shirted prophet crying in the political wilderness, waiting to lead the people back into the promised land of milk and honey, low taxes and world peace.

A comparison of journalistic opinion of McCarthy proved to be enlightening. With rare exception, he was condemned by the country's leading newspapers and praised by those with records of irresponsible and partisan handling of news.

Probably the best judges of the nation's "leading" news-papers were the publishers themselves, who each year named the "ten best." Year in and year out the choice was virtually the same, and 1952 was no exception: the publish-ers had again selected almost the same ten for the papers most nearly approaching the high ideals of journalism. And here is what these ten have said about Joe McCarthy:

(1) The New York *Times*:

In making a political career out of mud-slinging and Red-baiting, Senator McCarthy has launched irresponsible, unprovable, and ridicu-lous charges against so many respected citizens that his attacks have become almost an accolade.

287

(2)   The St. Louis *Post-Dispatch*:

McCarthyism . . . comes from the name of Senator McCarthy of Wisconsin, who has used the device of unproved but frequently repeated assertion, as has no one else before him in American politics.

(3)   The *Christian Science Monitor*:

If Congress does not itself curb McCarthyism and official character assassins cannot be shamed into facing the libel laws, then the people must apply at the polls an effective penalty for unjust accusation.

(4)   The Louisville *Courier-Journal*:

Senator McCarthy . . . is campaigning . . . on an issue calculated to offend no Wisconsin voter. . . . That campaign, based upon the current popular and headline-producing issue of Communists in high places, rests upon a shifting fabric of misstatements, innuendo, and just plain lies.

(5)   The Kansas City *Star*:

The feud between Senator McCarthy of Wisconsin and Benton of Connecticut is aired once more. . . . The whole business reflects no great credit on either of the two Senators. McCarthy, however, is chiefly responsible for the current stage of it, because the hearings now in progress might never have been held had it not been for his entirely gratuitous action denouncing the sub-committee.

(6)   The New York *Herald Tribune*:

Senator McCarthy's tactics have been hard to evaluate accurately as they unfolded from day to day in the headlines he knows so well how to capture. In launching the suit [against Senator Benton], Senator McCarthy announced that Senator Benton would not have attacked him except for the fact that he [Senator McCarthy] attacked "Communists in government." This is the kind of argument by innuendo which the Senator from Wisconsin uses to make his points; it has too frequently been efficacious in the political hurly-burly.

(7)   The Chicago *Daily News*:

Senator McCarthy has donned the shoe thrown by President Truman, who denounced "hatemongers" in a speech at Philadelphia.

. . . Senator McCarthy has alienated a great many people with his reckless and unsupported charges of Communist affiliation against persons in and out of government.

(8) The Washington *Post*:

When a Senator is caught in a bare-faced falsification, as Senator McCarthy was caught in connection with his Wheeling, West Virginia, speech, should the facts be glossed over? When a Senator uses his Senatorial immunity from suits for slander to call loyal, conscientious employees of the government spies and Soviet agents — and then fails to back up the vilification — should the Senate minority let the injustice go unchallenged? When a Senator wantonly plays on popular anxiety in a time of crisis to create doubt and dismay in the minds of his countrymen, should the matter be ignored? . . . A motion to censure Senator McCarthy is clearly in order.

(9) The Baltimore *Sun*:

In the defense which Mr. McCarthy put up on the floor of the Senate for the conduct of the Maryland Senatorial campaign of last November [1950] . . . there was one glaring lack. The Senator ignored the record of the law and of the courts. . . . The trial proved that money was spent wildly in this campaign far beyond the legal limits. The man on trial, one Jon M. Jonkel, was convicted on six counts. . . . The only reference to this part of the campaign which Senator McCarthy made in his speech was to describe it as a "technical violation." By Senator McCarthy's code, such conduct may be merely a technical violation. By the code to which reputable Marylanders subscribe, a law is a law and a crime is a crime.

(10) The Milwaukee *Journal*:

Recent addresses of McCarthy in Wisconsin . . . display his reckless irresponsibility and inconsistencies. . . . He has recently repeatedly attacked the Milwaukee *Journal,* charging it with a Communistic complexion. . . . The *Journal* is in its sixty-ninth year. It has before been accused by mountebanks of bending to outside interests, once to a big bank, once to a local utility. McCarthy's irresponsible accusations now are just as false as were all the others.

As for the published praise of McCarthy, it emanated from two main springs — the press empires of William Randolph

Hearst and of Colonel Robert R. McCormick. The Hearst public-opinion-forming system consisted of eighteen newspapers, nine magazines, three radio stations, and such widely distributed services as International News Service, the *American Weekly*, King Features syndicate, and assorted subsidiaries. This formidable editorial rooting section adopted McCarthy's crusade along with such other "causes" as antivivisection and boosting MacArthur for President.

The Hearst newspapers whooped up McCarthy's charges; and the Hearst magazine *Cosmopolitan* featured a rambling, self-serving article by McCarthy in the May 1952 issue.

But McCarthy's most constant echo came from three top Hearst columnists — George Sokolsky, Westbrook Pegler, and Fulton Lewis, Jr. — all given to extreme opinions.

Oddly, George Sokolsky had held many of the views for which he so often denounced others. As a self-styled China "expert," Sokolsky once wrote:

The morally best elements of the nationalist movement in China are now in the Communist ranks. . . . And Chiang may fail, and the Soviet China may yet come into existence. But will it matter much? Will China be altogether altered? Will China take on a Russian facade? It is doubtful.

Later, Sokolsky joined McCarthy in attributing near-treason to everyone (except himself) who had once held those same wrong views. Sokolsky was also out in front in heaping the verbal tar-and-feathers on the Institute of Pacific Relations. In a column published on August 21, 1951, Sokolsky said: "Thus far, it has been shown that the principal personalities during the development of the Institute were Edward C. Carter, Frederick Vanderbilt Field, and Owen Lattimore."

He might have added the name of George Sokolsky — for he, himself, had been close to the organization. And the three men he named — Carter, Field, and Lattimore — had been his friends. In the dedication of his book *The Tinder Box of Asia*, Sokolsky wrote:

> To John Van Antwerp MacMurry of the Walter Hines Page School, Johns Hopkins University [the same school Lattimore headed], and to Frederick V. Field of the American Council of the Institute of Pacific Relations, I must express my deepest gratitude for their friendship and devotion in reading my manuscript, chapter by chapter, as it was written, and for their kindly advice.

After McCarthy denounced the IPR as a Communist nest and Frederick Vanderbilt Field turned out to have been an easy touch for the Communists, Sokolsky denied his former associates. The only skeleton that Sokolsky seemed to recognize from his past was Red Spy Agnes Smedley. He wrote on September 1, 1951: "I knew Agnes Smedley in Shanghai in the years between 1926 and 1931. . . . I knew that Agnes Smedley was a Communist, because at one stage she tried to recruit me and became antagonistic to me when I acted dumb and seemed not to understand what she was talking about." Yet, if Sokolsky knew that Agnes Smedley was an American Communist, he "acted dumb" for a long time and did nothing to expose her.

Joe would have a field day if he ever found an enemy with such a record. But in Sokolsky's case, McCarthy highly recommended him as a speaker to the University of Wisconsin's Republican club. Joe told the president, Ben Rosenthal, that Sokolsky was "a fighting liberal of the right kind." For Sokolsky's part, the McCarthy charges became an obsession with him; he could talk and write of little else. Typical was his column on November 12, 1951, which might easily have come from Joe's own mimeograph machine. It said: "McCarthyism is an issue in the 1952 campaign, and no candidate will be able to avoid it. He will have to say whether he favors or opposes the employment of Communists in public positions. That is all McCarthyism means."

Another McCarthy cheerleader, Hearst Columnist Westbrook Pegler, was a strong contender for the title of America's No. 1 Hater. Pegler hated *people,* whom he called "faceless boobs."

Hating people, Pegler logically hated democracy. He once suggested that the state of Arizona would be better off if it abandoned popular elections and let a local industry run its affairs. On February 8, 1950, he wrote: "Instead of saying, 'Democracy is no good, so to hell with it,' this Republican organization goes wheedling for votes with promises of modified democracy." And in 1949 he told a Congressional committee: "I am not interested in democracy, except to oppose it."

Like Sokolsky, Pegler had once been chummy with the comrades. In the 1930's, he took a raincheck on an invitation to write an article for the Communist magazine *New Masses,* expressing his regrets in a pleasant note which ended: "Hope there'll be a return date." In 1935, he gave an interview to the *Daily Worker* in which he supported the Communists' plans for a farmer-labor movement. For many years he was a close friend of Heywood Broun, whom he later denounced as a Communist. He wrote two columns condemning his old friend in the vilest terms while Broun, just converted to Catholicism, lay dying. Pegler even described his boss-to-be, William Randolph Hearst, in 1940, as a "never to be adequately damned demagogue and historic scoundrel." Soon afterward, Pegler became a Hearst columnist.

Pegler had pleasant words for only a few causes, and most of these were based on hate. He had praised Gerald L. K. Smith, the anti-Catholic, anti-Negro, anti-Semitic rabblerouser; Pegler had advocated the revival of the night-riding, cross-burning, Negro-lynching Ku Klux Klan; and he had backed McCarthy to the hilt. In a column published May 22, 1952, he wrote: "Joe McCarthy is so right it hurts." Pegler recommended the *Cosmopolitan* article by McCarthy as "must" reading for all Americans, claiming that it answered

> . . . the whole pack of lies about his [McCarthy's] anti-Communist
> crusade that have been circulated by the Communists in our govern-
> ment and our journalism and by their allies, the anti-anti-Communists.
> . . . My only criticism of his opening statement is that he concedes
> that some of the friends of the enemy have been innocent dupes.
> They are not.

The third Hearst columnist who had been egging McCarthy on was Fulton Lewis, Jr.; he was also a five-days-a-week news commentator over the Mutual radio network. Lewis, known as the "golden voice of radio," had been criticized for slanting the news he put into his columns and broadcasts. In 1950, for example, the Providence *Bulletin* published an analysis of his output, and found it wanting. The paper stated: "The 15-week study revealed that more than 70 per cent of Lewis' broadcasts could be judged misleading." In 1949, the commentator was singled out as an example in the study of "irresponsibility on the air" by Giraud Chester in the *Public Opinion Quarterly*. And in 1947 the Rev. Wilfrid Parsons, then editor of the Catholic magazine *America*, said Lewis' handling of the news "could only proceed from some obscure ill will."

Lewis' view of current events was as distorted as the reflection in a Fun House mirror. Lewis regularly hit into McCarthy's enemies as savagely as Joe himself. "To many Americans, McCarthyism is Americanism," reported Lewis.

Colonel Robert R. McCormick's Chicago *Tribune* and its Washington echo, the *Times-Herald*, contributed their editorial brass to the McCarthy fanfare from the beginning. But there was one slight alteration: the Colonel gave McCarthy's charges a peculiar anti-British twist of his own.

The Colonel's hatred of "aliens" was significant in view of McCarthy's similar xenophobic views. He cried out that more "Americans" were needed in top government positions.

He described Acheson as "the alien, elegant Acheson, English as to manner, Russian as to intent."

The Colonel was another Johnny-come-lately among the "sell-out in Asia" spielers. When he was interviewed by the Associated Press after a McCormick inspection of the Far East in November 1947, he warned that Nationalist China was not competent to end its internal difficulties, which were ". . . falsely called a Communist insurrection. Although Communist-backed, it is still a bona-fide insurrection against a government which is little more than an agency of the Soong family." Two years later, McCormick's *Tribune* would have branded as Communist anyone who thus interpreted the fall of the Chiang Kai-shek government.

But Joe McCarthy overlooked the sour notes of his supporters' past record as long as their present tune was played according to his score.

44. The Purge of
Senator Tydings

STREWN ALONG THE POLITICAL HIGHWAY THAT JOE MCCARTHY traveled to the nation's capital lay several bruised-and-bandaged bodies. There was Mike Eberlein, the north-country lawyer who had a political dream — and then saw his hired hand fulfill it. There was Edgar Werner, the old judge — who wasn't nearly as old as McCarthy made him out to be in order to pass him by. There was Gilbert Lappley, the agriculture lawyer who tried to uphold the laws of Wisconsin — and lost his job. There was Robert La Follette, Jr., the second generation Senator who thought his record would assure his re-election — but discovered too late that Joe had obscured the record with mud. And there was Senator Raymond Baldwin, the mild Republican from Connecticut — who was driven into political retirement by a torrent of McCarthy abuse.

There were others who tangled with McCarthy. All except a few were kayoed in early rounds; all were pelted and pummeled. The lesson that you couldn't beat McCarthy was one that was assiduously spread by Joe himself. McCarthy fought Dogpatch style, and anything went — gouging, biting, scratching, kicking, and head butting. He threw himself into a match with every ounce of his strength, as he proudly attested.

So it was that when Senator Millard Tydings, a gentleman of refinement, took off his coat with Joe, the outcome was foreordained: Tydings was whipped so soundly that he probably could never run for political office again. Tydings was an ultra-conservative Democrat who voted consistently against the New Deal — incurring thereby the enmity of Franklin D. Roosevelt, who was the first to try to purge Tydings from the Senate. FDR failed; some years later McCarthy succeeded.

Tydings' troubles with the Wisconsin whirlwind started when he became chairman of the sub-committee that was assigned in March 1950 to investigate McCarthy's charges of Communists in the State Department. Almost before the probe had begun, McCarthy was yelling "whitewash of State" — just as in the Malmedy investigation. But despite the ominous fate of Baldwin, who had headed the massacre probe, Tydings stood his ground.

It was said by some who were close to McCarthy that when the Tydings report came out, Joe could hardly sleep. "He was so preoccupied with Tydings," one reported, "that he'd sit by the hour figuring out ways to get revenge." It was no wonder that Joe was fighting mad, for the report lambasted his charges as "a fraud and a hoax." It accused Joe of "hit-and-run" tactics, of a "cavalier disregard for facts," of "twisting, coloring, perverting, and distorting" the truth. The 313-page report described the genesis of Joe's charges in these terms:

Starting with nothing, Senator McCarthy plunged headlong forward, desperately seeking to develop some information which, colored with distortion and fanned by a blaze of bias, would forestall the day of reckoning.

After the report was made public in July 1950, McCarthy began making plans for the Maryland campaign in the fall, when Tydings would be up for another term. Joe went to see Tydings' opponent, a Baltimore lawyer with an impressive name, who had never before run for office: Mr. John Marshall Butler. The two went to dinner, accompanied by Butler's campaign treasurer, Cornelius Mundy. Also present were McCarthy's sharp-tongued secretary, Jean Kerr, and a New York lawyer who had served as Republican counsel during the Tydings investigation, Robert Morris. That night, over wine and *filet mignon,* the five worked out a plan for the defeat of Tydings.

A few days later, McCarthy hurried over to the downtown office of the powerful young newspaper editor, Mrs. Ruth McCormick ("Bazy") Miller, chief of the Washington *Times-Herald* and niece of the publisher of the Chicago *Tribune,* Colonel Robert McCormick. Mrs. Miller agreed to help out in Maryland, and as a starter recommended hiring a high-priced Chicago press agent by the name of Jon Jonkel for the job of Butler's campaign manager. This was done in the face of a Maryland law prohibiting the use of out-of-state campaign managers.

As the campaign progressed, it became apparent that the only thing being furnished by Butler was his euphonious, stately, and magnificent name.

Joe and "Bazy" were the brains of the team that turned the trick. When Joe asked for *Times-Herald* assistance in compiling and printing half a million copies of a tabloid newspaper attacking Tydings, "Bazy" agreed at once and, for the record, quoted a price that was far below that which regular job printers were able to charge. "Bazy" turned the job over to her chief editorial writer, Frank M. Smith, who became Butler's assistant after the election. Smith testified before the special sub-committee later investigating the Maryland campaign that McCarthy's office had supplied much of the written material for the pamphlet, but that the *Times-Herald* had provided the pictures.

These pictures included the now-famous fake photograph, which showed ex-Communist Chief Earl Browder and Senator Tydings in friendly conversation. To accomplish this photographic magic, the *Times-Herald* art department had taken an old picture of Browder and another of Tydings, put them together, and rephotographed the composite. Beneath the picture was the caption:

Communist leader Earl Browder, shown at left in this composite picture, was a star witness at the Tydings committee hearings, and was cajoled into saying Owen Lattimore and others accused of disloyalty were not Communists. Tydings (right) answered, "Oh, thank you, sir." Browder testified in the best interests of those accused, naturally.

Many voters who read the tabloid did not catch the significance of the word "composite"; many who did understand the word did not read the complete caption and thereby learn that the picture was a phony. Despite the fact that the picture was intended to misrepresent the fact, *Times-Herald*man Smith in his testimony termed it "not a fake . . . not a fraud," and the paper's assistant managing editor (who later graduated to be "Bazy's" husband), Garvin E. Tankersley, said he didn't see anything wrong in the picture. But Campaign Treasurer Mundy said the picture was "stupid, puerile, and in bad taste," and claimed that he had had nothing to do with putting it out.

On the tabloid's front page was a story asserting that Tydings, as head of the Senate Armed Services Committee, had failed to prevent war in Korea, and that he had spent only $200 (for baling wire) out of millions appropriated for arms for South Korea. The truth was that $495,700,000 worth of material had been sent to South Korea before the Red invasion. And what was more, a detailed list of the equipment was released by the Defense Department and published in the *Congressional Record* on August 16, 1950 — two months before the anti-Tydings tabloid went to press. Nevertheless, the baling-wire story remained a valued part of McCarthy's repertoire. He still liked to quote what he called "concrete" figures to make this charge sound authentic. And a year later, on August 8, 1951, he repeated in a speech that the $200 had been spent merely "to load some baling wire on a ship." Again on September 9, 1951, he was back on the subject of baling wire; and the audience — this time it happened to be the Hager Family Reunion Association in Ramage, West Virginia — applauded the baling-wire charge longer and louder than any other.

The anti-Tydings tabloid, according to its masthead, was authorized and distributed by the "Young Democrats for Butler." This formidable-sounding organization consisted of six persons who held only one meeting after the "club" was organized and knew nothing about the tabloid until it had been printed. In short, it was a "front" organization; and it didn't put up a cent. Who, then proposed the tabloid? This question was answered at the Senate hearings by "Bazy" Miller, who testified:

> The first time I heard of the contemplated production of the tabloid was when Senator McCarthy called me and told me that a group of persons interested in Senator Butler's campaign were considering producing a tabloid, and Senator McCarthy asked me if they reached a decision to produce such a thing, could the *Times-Herald* do the job.

The three Democratic and two Republican Senators who investigated the Maryland election reported that the tabloid contained

> . . . misleading half-truths, misrepresentations, and false innuendoes that maliciously and without foundation attacked the loyalty and patriotism not only of former Senator Millard Tydings, who won the Distinguished Service Cross for battlefield heroism in World War I, but also the entire membership of the Senate Armed Services Committee in 1950.

One of the witnesses before this sub-committee was William Christopher, a volunteer worker in the Butler campaign headquarters. Christopher testified that the tabloid was "an insult to the people's intelligence" and that on his own initiative he had burned or sold for scrap paper about 150,000 copies. On the other hand, Jean Kerr, McCarthy's secretary, told the sub-committee defiantly that the tabloid was "the type of literature that should go out in campaigns. The voters should be told about what is going on, and certainly this did it." Her only criticism of the tabloid, she said, was that it didn't go far enough.

This led Senator Tom Hennings of Missouri to inquire as to who in the Butler campaign crew was responsible for toning it down. "Who," he asked, "was the sissy in the crowd?"

45. Masterminding the Maryland Campaign

THE PATTERN OF JOE MCCARTHY'S CAREER SHOWED A DOGGED dependence upon tried-and-true techniques — the methods which had paid off for Joe in the past. He always returned to them; and he returned to them in the Maryland election.

This became evident after the campaign got under way. All over Maryland, mailmen were struggling under the added load of tens of thousands of postcards — handwritten, "signed" by the candidate, John Marshall Butler. Half a million postcards went out to a carefully selected list of doubtful voters. This would have been enough to give Butler acute writer's cramp; but the cards were written and "signed" by crews of women working almost around the clock — the same technique Joe had used so successfully in Wisconsin.

The contract for this huge project went to William Fedder, a Baltimore printer. His job was to farm out the work, and also to handle the folding, addressing, and distribution of the tabloid. Fedder was snowed under with work; and his penwomen starting losing interest at the pay rate of $15 a thousand cards. When it looked as if Fedder and his crew of women were going to miss the deadline, Candidate Butler jumped in with a helpful spirit and wrote a note to Fedder, designed to buoy up the printer's efforts. It read:

At this time I want to give you my personal assurance that I do guarantee payment for any of your services that have not been paid for at the time the campaign is completed. This assurance applies to materials that have been delivered and to materials that were not shipped in time for use in the campaign.

Sincerely,

JOHN MARSHALL BUTLER

Butler didn't know it, but he had written what might have turned into a political suicide note. For by personally guaranteeing to pay Fedder all that he owed him — more than $11,000 — Butler was laying himself wide open to charges that he violated Maryland's corrupt-practices law, which limited campaign spending to $5,000 per candidate. It wasn't long before McCarthy's men heard about the note. When they patiently explained to Butler what he had done, the Senatorial candidate wrung his hands in dismay. But McCarthy told him not to worry; his boys would get the letter back.

Two days later the hapless Fedder, according to his sworn testimony, was taken on a midnight ride through Maryland by McCarthy's henchmen, who kept trying to make him hand over the letter. The printer said the fateful night began when he was summoned to the Emerson Hotel in Baltimore to confer with Don Surine. He was met instead by Ewell Moore and George Nilles, also of McCarthy's office. Fedder's story continued:

I asked for Don Surine, and they said he would be here soon. We left the hotel, took the finished cards from my car, and went into the post office. We took a rough count, and it was about 5,000 cards. They mailed those cards. They continued to bother me about a group of cards I had said I mailed earlier. I told them that I would explain it to Don Surine when he arrived. Surine arrived about 1 A.M. . . .

I told [Surine] that we had only three stops to make, which should be completed in an hour, and when he picked up the finished work and the leftover stamps, that he would see for himself that they would check out. Then Surine became abusive, too. His eyes looked like they were going to pop out of his head. I said that he was working himself up for nothing, that three more girls were waiting for us to pick up their work. "Let's get this done and over with. I'm tired and I want to go home." As I made this statement I started walking toward the door, intending to have them follow me, so we could pick up the rest of the work. Surine reached out and jerked me back by the coat. He said: "Listen, I want that letter back."

I said: "What letter?" He said: "The guarantee letter that you got from Butler." I told him that he wasn't going to get the letter. He told me that if I didn't give him the letter, they would fix me up and put me through a McCarthy investigation. He bragged about being good at that sort of thing. I told him that I couldn't give him the letter even if I wanted to — that this letter was in my attorney's office.

He then asked if I knew Kriss. I said I didn't. He said he meant Captain Kriss of the police department, who was a friend of his and could make it tough for me. I said the police don't worry me because I haven't done anything wrong. I asked him to please let me finish and go home. He said that where they came from, my kind would be lucky to get home at all.

I sat in the back seat but was too frightened to think about anything, because I didn't know what was going to happen next. There was absolutely no conversation. We were riding around for no purpose, going no place, and I was getting sicker by the minute.

Fedder said he was allowed to go home at 4 A.M., but only to pick up a $500 check which Surine said the printer owed them for not finishing the postcards. By now trembling with fear, Fedder obeyed the order and came back to the car with the check. "Surine said: 'We're not through with you yet — get back in the car.' And with the three men crowding me, I ended up in the back seat again," Fedder testified.

After more aimless driving around, the group stopped at an all-night restaurant where, Fedder said, he signed two statements put before him by Surine. The first concerned work that Fedder was doing for them, and the second, designed to undo the harm of the letter from Butler, stated that Butler owed the printer nothing.

That, at any rate, is the whole story as Fedder told it to the Senate elections sub-committee. Later the three McCarthy assistants, one by one, denied the charges, insisting that they had spent the pre-dawn hours with Fedder picking up postcards from the homes of women who had been addressing and signing them. Here is how the Senate group evaluated the conflicting testimony:

> The explanation given by Surine, Nilles, and Moore for their activities on this occasion is not convincing; and it is the opinion of this committee that the "picking up and mailing of the addressed cards" was not the only purpose of their mission.

The sub-committee had good reason to question the word of Surine, leader of the three-man squad, against that of Fedder. In an effort to test truthfulness, the sub-committee questioned Surine further, especially about his previous employment with the FBI (see Chapter 31). The McCarthy lieutenant testified that he quit the FBI on his own volition; but this didn't agree with J. Edgar Hoover's records. The FBI chief set forth the facts in a letter to the sub-committee chairman, Senator Mike Monroney of Oklahoma, on April 3, 1951. Hoover wrote:

> With reference to the inquiry directed to this Bureau regarding the service record of former Special Agent Donald A. Surine, I wish to advise that he entered on duty as a clerk on June 12, 1939, and was appointed a special agent on January 13, 1941. On February 9, 1950, Mr. Surine was advised by a communication emanating from the Bureau's headquarters that he was being dropped from the rolls of the FBI effective at the close of business on February 8, 1950.
>
> In this connection, Mr. Surine did submit his resignation dated February 7, 1950, which was not accepted. Under date of March 6, 1950, Mr. Surine was advised by communication that it would not be possible to change the manner in which he was separated from the Bureau's rolls.
>
> In this communication Mr. Surine was advised that the Bureau's action was based upon his disregard of Bureau rules and regulations, and no facts had been submitted by him to warrant altering the original action in this case.

The sub-committee concluded that Surine's testimony contained "an apparent willful and knowing misstatement of a material fact relating to the circumstances of the termination of his services with the Federal Bureau of Investigation prior to his employment by Senator McCarthy." As a result, the sub-committee recommended that Surine's apparent perjury "should be transmitted to the Department of Justice for such action as it deems appropriate." As Surine thus tripped over his own testimony and landed in a puddle of trouble, his boss, Joe McCarthy, stood by in the hearing room, walked up to him as he left the witness stand, wrapped a husky arm around his shoulder — and the two strolled out together arm in arm.

Another aspect of the Maryland campaign that came under the sub-committee's microscope was its financing. This phase of the probe caused frantic scurrying around by the McCarthy-Butler forces. When the sub-committee turned up evidence that a lot of campaign expenditures had not been listed as required by law, Jonkel raced to Baltimore and blandly filed what he called a "supplementary" statement listing $27,100 in out-of-state contributions. Of course, the tardy filing was still in violation of Maryland law, since the legal deadline had passed. But the penalty would be reduced; it was a case of better-late-than-never.

Jonkel, on the witness stand, said the extra funds had been short-circuited around Campaign Treasurer Cornelius Mundy, "to save time." Included in the out-of-state contributions that Jonkel accounted for at the last minute were $5,000 from "Bazy" Miller Tankersley, $1,000 from Senator Owen Brewster, and $1,000 from Alfred Kohlberg, the free-lance China Lobbyist.

Eventually, Jonkel was charged with violating the Maryland election laws and brought before the Baltimore criminal court, where he pleaded guilty to six charges and was fined $5,000. Jonkel's lawyer contended that the violations were "technical," but the judge didn't agree. He said: "These violations are more — much more — than technical violations." Then he dressed Jonkel down for "debasing a campaign for one of the highest elective offices." But Jonkel, in the opinion of many an astute Washington observer, was only the "fall guy." The consensus was that he took the rap for the real behind-the-scenes operators who had run the campaign. In this respect, the Senate sub-committee, looking in the general direction of Senator McCarthy, recommended:

The question of unseating a Senator for acts committed in a Senatorial election should not be limited to the candidates in such elections. Any sitting Senator, regardless of whether he is a candidate in the election himself, should be subject to expulsion by action of the Senate, if it finds such Senator in practices and behavior that make him, in the opinion of the Senate, unfit to hold the position of United States Senator.

The sub-committee noted that there were actually two campaigns in Maryland, explaining:

One was the dignified "front street" campaign conducted by candidate Butler in his speaking coverage of the state and in which that group of responsible citizens of Maryland who differed with candidate Tydings on traditional, historic, and basic beliefs operated on a reasonable, efficient, and decent plane. The other was the despicable "back street" type of campaign, which usually, if exposed in time, backfires.

In this particular case, the "back street" campaign was not exposed until Butler was elected. By then it was too late.

Anyone who knew Joe McCarthy could have anticipated his reaction to the sub-committee report and the scandal that grew out of the campaign. Anyone who knew Joe could sit back and wait for the inevitable — a McCarthy denial and counter-attack from his favorite sounding board, the Senate floor.

It came. Joe said that Butler's campaign was "intelligent and courageous," and that Communists in government had been the "one big issue." "No loyal American is an outsider when it comes to getting rid of Communists," Joe said, apparently by way of explaining his feet-first intrusion into Maryland's affairs. He also bored into his Senatorial accusers: "As long as puny politicians try to encourage other puny politicians to ignore or whitewash Communist influences in our government, America will remain in grave danger."

He went on to single out the two Republican members of the sub-committee, Senators Robert Hendrickson of New Jersey and Margaret Chase Smith of Maine; both of them, he said, lacked a "background of legal training." Joe suggested that the two were prejudiced against him because they had signed a "Declaration of Conscience" against rabble-rousers a year earlier (see Appendix, p. 407). Although the Declaration did not specifically mention McCarthy by name, he apparently realized that the shoe fit — and he put it on.

But the Baltimore *Sun* got a different impression from the fact that both Democrats and Republicans had signed the scathing report. The newspaper commented:

This means that Republicans as well as Democrats were ashamed of the tactics which were employed in the campaign. Marylanders, above all others, should share this shame.

But one of the most stunning blows came from within Joe's own church. The distinguished Catholic magazine *The Commonweal* said in a leading editorial on August 17, 1951:

The Congressional sub-committee gave this warning: "Such campaign methods and tactics are destroying our system of free elections and undermining the very foundations of our government."

This, certainly, is a serious charge. It raises some serious questions: If the West Point cadets are to be tried for cheating, why not McCarthy? Has he done less than these cadets to debase the integrity and honesty of our national life?

The issue here is not whether or not Communism must be fought at home: it must. The issue is whether or not we must have the intelligence and the courage to do it in the American way, or whether we will leave the job — and our liberties — to a man who runs along the back streets to do his cheating when he hasn't the stuff it takes to do things the straight and open way.

But Joe remained happily oblivious to such growing criticism. He told the *U. S. News and World Report* in an interview: "I think [the Maryland election] was one of the cleanest campaigns in the country." And with his friends, he took full credit for finishing off the veteran Millard Tydings.

And, logically enough, by 1952 the message was apparent to almost every man in Congress: Buck McCarthy and you're in for trouble. A chill had gone down the back of the legislators. Certainly few had seemed more securely ensconced in their Senate seats than Millard Tydings. Joe got him; *ergo,* Joe could get you, too. To jittery politicians, the logic followed inevitably. And although some doubted it, few were willing to put it to the test.

46. The Plot Against
Anna Rosenberg

FASCISM HAD BEEN DEMOCRACY'S PUBLIC ENEMY DURING
World War II; and, when it was put down, Communism
emerged as the main danger. In that simple transference of
national hostility, Fascism got a new lease on life under the
guise of anti-Communism.

Native hate-mongers crept out of the shadows and set
up shop at the same old corners — such men as Gerald L. K.
Smith, Upton Close, Joseph Kamp, Benjamin Freedman, Leo
DeAryan, the Rev. Wesley Swift of Los Angeles.

In Senator Joe McCarthy, these hate-peddlers found a
rallying point, a common hero. There was nothing strange
about this political liaison, nothing contradictory when
viewed against the ragged tapestry of Joe's career. Didn't
McCarthy defend the Nazi storm troopers who had been
found guilty of the Malmedy massacre of American troops?
Didn't he insert into the *Congressional Record* the wild sentiments of such Axis-apologists as Opinioncaster Upton Close
and Industrialist Walter Harnischfeger?

McCarthy had frequently used his office to further the
aims of the gutter-crowd, but seldom so glaringly as in the
1950 squabble over the appointment of Mrs. Anna Rosenberg
as Assistant Secretary of Defense. "Evidence" was brought
to Joe's office that Mrs. Rosenberg had been a Communist;

309

the informant was the Rev. Wesley Swift — an anti-Semite
who had refused to believe that Christ was a Jew. Later,
Swift got in to see Colonel Mark Galusha, member of the
staff of the Senate Armed Services Committee; the Rev. Mr.
Swift confided that he had already given his "evidence" to
Senator McCarthy. Galusha reported the incident to the two
ranking Democrats on the Committee, Senators Richard Russell of Georgia and Harry Byrd of Virginia. They held a hasty
huddle and decided that, in view of McCarthy's interest,
the Committee had better investigate the charges — no matter how preposterous.

Meanwhile, Joe dispatched his No. 1 agent, Don Surine, to
New York to seek further evidence. Accompanying Surine
was Edward Nellor, Surine's counterpart in Commentator
Fulton Lewis' office. They carried with them a letter of
introduction to another figure in the case, Benjamin Freedman. The letter read:

DEAR MR. FREEDMAN:

Congratulations on the terrific job you are doing in helping to keep
the Zionist Jew Anna M. Rosenberg from becoming the director of the
Pentagon. This is to introduce two gentlemen who are helping in this
fight. One is the bearer of this note. I understand that he is
Mr. Nellor, the chief aide to Mr. Fulton Lewis. Mr. Lewis and
Mr. Nellor should be treated very kindly. You should give any information that will help them, because Mr. Lewis is doing a magnificent job in the Rosenberg matter.

Please destroy this upon reading it.

Sincerely yours,

GERALD L. K.

Senate investigators later identified the signature as that
of Gerald L. K. Smith, the professional rabble-rouser who
had set up secret headquarters in room 405 of Washington's
Congressional Hotel, where he masterminded the strategy
against Mrs. Rosenberg. Nellor, called to the witness stand,
swore it was Surine who picked up the letter at the Con-

gressional Hotel; but he claimed that Surine didn't know that Gerald L. K. Smith had written it.

In any case, Surine and Nellor flew to New York City and presented the letter to Benjamin Freedman at midnight on December 5, 1950. Through Freedman, the two legmen were put in touch with Ralph DeSola, an ex-Communist. The details of this contact were brought out later at the Senate hearings. When DeSola was asked if he had ever discussed the Rosenberg case with anyone except Freedman, he testified as follows:

DeSola: I discussed this with two members of your committee, who visited my home. . . .

Senator Russell: Who were the members of this committee that you discussed [the Rosenberg case] with?

DeSola: The gentleman was introduced to me as one of the investigators of your committee. . . .

Russell: Was he a member of the committee or an investigator?

DeSola: He was an investigator.

Russell: Did he tell you he was an investigator for this committee?

DeSola: Yes, sir, he said he was an investigator for the Armed Services Committee of the Senate of the United States.

Russell: They told you they were investigators for the Senate Committee on Armed Services?

DeSola: Yes, sir.

The two "committee investigators" were, of course, Surine and Nellor. When it was Freedman's turn at bat, he was asked what he knew about them. He recalled that they had dropped around to his home and inquired about Anna Rosenberg. "It was around twelve o'clock at night, and one of them said he represents a Senator or something," explained Freedman. He had been expecting them, he said, because he had been advised of their coming by long-distance telephone from Washington. Freedman, the picture of dignity in pince-nez and pin-striped suit, seemed embarrassed to identify the telephone caller. He said the name was "Smith," and beat about the bush when asked for details. After a dozen questions about Smith, Freedman apparently decided to make a clean breast of it, took a deep breath, and announced: "He is — it is this Gerald Smith."

Freedman was asked whether he had ever seen the two mysterious investigators again. "When Mr. DeSola and I came over on the train together," he said, "we went to Senator McCarthy's office, where he was told to go, I think."

Later, Nellor took the stand to clarify the situation; he denied indignantly that he or Surine had misrepresented themselves to the New Yorkers. As proof, Nellor pointed out that when DeSola came to Washington to testify, "he came direct to Senator McCarthy's office and asked for Surine." How did Gerald L. K. Smith get mixed into it? All Nellor knew was that Surine had told him on the way to New York that "Gerald L. K. Smith had been running around the Senate Office Building with a copy of Freedman's statement regarding DeSola."

For a while, it looked as if McCarthy had struck pay dirt in DeSola. When the ex-Communist stood up in the committee room and "positively" identified Mrs. Rosenberg as a former Communist, Joe rubbed his hands together, and Fulton Lewis, Jr., went on the air to say that it reminded him of another time "when Alger Hiss was confronted across a table with Whittaker Chambers." But Mrs. Rosenberg hit back:

He is a liar. I would like to lay my hands on that man. It is inhuman what he has done to me in the past few days. . . . Now if this man is crazy or a Communist, I want to face him, Senator. I have never been a member of the John Reed Club; I have never been a Communist; I have never sympathized with Communists; I have spent my life trying to do something to help my country.

I tried to think — where do I know this man? How do I know him from some place? How can a human being do this to someone? What can he have against me? I don't know him. . . . I plead with you, finish this. If you don't think I am fit to take this office, say so.

I don't care what you charge me with, but not disloyalty, Senator. It is an awful thing to carry around with you.

Then, gradually, the case began to fall apart. DeSola was proved a liar. A parade of witnesses, who he had promised would confirm his story, instead denied it. James Mc-Graw, identified by DeSola as the ex-Communist who had introduced him to Mrs. Rosenberg, stormed into the committee room and angrily denied it all. William Harris, an "ex-FBI agent" who was supposed to have told Ted Kirkpatrick, publisher of *Counterattack*, of Mrs. Rosenberg's alleged Communist affiliations, swore he had never said any such thing, and — what was more — had never been an FBI man. Kirkpatrick also contradicted DeSola's story and confirmed Harris' testimony. George Starr, a retired FBI agent, to whom DeSola said he had told everything about Anna Rosenberg, denied that DeSola had done anything of the sort.

Benjamin Freedman admitted he had no evidence against Mrs. Rosenberg. J. B. Matthews, a Hearst super-sleuth and McCarthy informant, was forced to acknowledge that he, too, had been barking up the wrong tree. Fulton Lewis began to simmer down and make excuses; and Senator Joe conveniently forgot that he had ever had anything to do with digging up the "evidence."

The crusher came when the FBI discovered that the "Anna Rosenberg" who had indeed been a member of the Communist John Reed Club was another Anna Rosenberg living on the West Coast. The loyal Mrs. Rosenberg, by now nearly a nervous wreck over the false accusation, was confirmed as Assistant Secretary of Defense. And one of those who conspicuously voted for her was Joe McCarthy — the same man who had sent his agent to New York with a letter of introduction from Gerald L. K. Smith "to get the proof" against "the Zionist Jew, Anna M. Rosenberg."

47. Senator Benton Speaks Up

WHEN JOE MCCARTHY CAME TO THE SENATE IN 1947, THE first order of business proved to be prophetic. The question before the Senate was whether to seat Theodore ("The Man") Bilbo, the Mississippi demagogue. (Bilbo died before the Senate got around to taking any action.)

Less than five years later, it was Joe McCarthy's seat that was being challenged.

The resolution to impeach McCarthy was introduced on August 6, 1951, by an angry freshman Senator — Connecticut's William Benton. He explained: "The only thing to do with a fellow like McCarthy is to go after him hammer and tongs." Overnight, the McCarthy-Benton feud became the talk of the Senate cloakrooms; and the comment usually took the form of a memorial for Benton.

From the first, the Benton resolution was handled like a hot ingot. It was tossed gingerly from hand to hand, and was finally passed to a group of low-seniority Senators. This sub-committee, headed by white-maned Senator Guy Gillette of Iowa, reluctantly took a look at a ten-point bill of particulars, drawn up by the persistent Benton.

As a starter, this document charged that McCarthy had committed perjury under oath before the Tydings committee; that he had accepted $10,000 "influence money" from the Lustron Corporation; that he had tried "to hoax the Senate with an incredible charge" that General George Marshall was part of the Communist conspiracy; that Mc-

Carthy had falsely tried to pin the blame on Senator Millard Tydings for dragging the names of the McCarthy victims into the open; that McCarthy was guilty of "fraud and deceit" for his part in the 1950 Maryland Senatorial election; that he had offered to repeat without Congressional immunity "libelous statements which he later refused to repeat off the [Senate] floor"; that he had practiced "deliberate deception" in claiming to possess an FBI chart which J. Edgar Hoover later disclaimed; that McCarthy had been "forced to renege" on his promise to reveal the names of eighty-one Communists in the State Department; that he had "falsely accused Americans and excused convicted Germans involved in the infamous Malmedy disaster"; and that he was keeping on his payroll a man "who, while still in his employ, is charged with committing perjury as well as other serious misdeeds."

Joe at first assumed an air of nonchalant disinterest in the investigation; he said the whole affair was beneath his notice; but he reacted typically toward the instigator, William Benton. Joe announced to reporters: "I'm too busy to even bother reading or answering the tripe put out by Connecticut's odd little mental midget." Joe was so delighted with this phrase that he used it from then on to describe his adversary.

But Benton's career seemed to belie the "mental midget" description. He had graduated from Yale University, had built a very successful New York advertising business with Chester Bowles, and had served successively as vice-president of the University of Chicago, Assistant Secretary of State in charge of public affairs, a delegate to six international conferences, and chairman of the board of the *Encyclopaedia Britannica*.

As for Joe, he counter-attacked with unusual violence for a man who was taking no notice of Benton. Joe said that "all the Alger Hisses and William Remingtons still in government" would cheer the investigation and that Benton had "established himself as the hero of every Communist and crook in and out of government." Then, with a subtle reminder of what had happened to Senator Tydings in Maryland, Joe declared:

I call the attention of all honest, loyal Democrats to how men of little minds are destroying a once great party. While Benton was Assistant Secretary of State, he worked hand in glove with the crimson clique who have been so bad for America and so good for Communist Russia. The exact number that he personally brought into government is not fully known at this time. No wonder he squeals and screams in panic as the McCarran committee starts to uncover some of them.

But the Connecticut Senator invited Joe to invade his state, promising that the people "have very strong stomachs" — and the battle was on. Benton came out of his corner swinging; but few Washington fight experts expected him to last until the final round. Joseph Harsch, of the *Christian Science Monitor's* Washington news bureau, gave this pre-fight size-up:

Something like a shudder of horror ran through political and journalistic Washington when the news broke that the friendly, pink-faced ex-advertising man from Connecticut personally had challenged the dark-jowled man from Wisconsin who has come to be feared by his colleagues more than Huey Long ever was. For it is possible that Benton went into this thing as an innocent, walking blithely to his doom, and that is what most Washingtonians assumed. . . .

Benton did what many another Senator would like but never would dare to do. The fact is that the Senate is afraid of Joseph McCarthy. He is something its members don't understand. He doesn't really belong to their club. He doesn't join the groups in the lobbies where party differences are laid aside and good fellowship prevails. He has no personal friends, even on his own side of the aisle. Mostly he sits alone, keeps his own counsel, goes his own way. When Senator Taft offered help in the campaign against the State Department, Senator McCarthy replied that he would do it himself.

Huey wasn't like this. . . . Huey was feared. But Huey had friends in the Senate, even among his political opponents. . . . He used humor in his speeches. . . . Joseph McCarthy is a totally different quantity. His power is intangible. He wields tremendous influence, had a major part in the defeat of Millard Tydings in Maryland and Frank Graham in North Carolina and Claude Pepper in Florida. . . . He is impervious to criticism. He seems to thrive on abuse. Anyone who has tangled with him has regretted it in the end. . . . Perhaps the key secret of his power is that he really doesn't care what others say about him, while others do care what he says about them.

William Benton has no such power, no such protective coating. . . . This might look like David and Goliath, except that this David doesn't have a slingshot, or any other visible weapon. If there is a secret weapon, and if it works, William Benton will be applauded and thanked by every member of the Senate. But scarcely a one dares show himself openly in the Benton corner during the battle. The odds are 99 to 1 on the slugger from Wisconsin.

Benton's opening flurry caught Joe with his guard down, and the Connecticut Kid landed a few hard body blows. The ten-point bill of particulars sent McCarthy reeling; and on August 26, 1951, Benton followed up: "I regard Senator McCarthy as a menace to our American way of life." He added that "two courageous Republicans," Senators Robert Hendrickson of New Jersey and Margaret Chase Smith of Maine, had joined in denouncing McCarthy's methods.

Joe perhaps sensed that his colleagues, who had crowded around the ring to watch the fight, might gang up on him when they saw he was not invincible; so from time to time, he waved a threatening fist in their direction. At Savannah, Georgia, for example, he charged that "several United States Representatives and Senators have known Communists on their staffs." Benton struck back in the name of his fellow Senators:

McCarthy should hand over to a United States district attorney any evidence he has to support his charge that several members of Congress have known Communists on their staffs. . . . If he doesn't turn over the evidence, he is derelict in his duty as a citizen and as a United States Senator. It is time we put a stop to these reckless charges. He has never proved one of them.

It was the last time Joe ever suggested publicly that Reds might be working in Congress, although he continued to make menacing gestures toward his colleagues. He taunted that they didn't "have the guts" to press for a showdown vote on his ouster. "This Benton resolution," he said, "is just an excuse to give some of the pin-heads a chance to smear." But Benton kept wading in with more rights and lefts. On September 28, 1951, he presented his case before the Gillette sub-committee. The next step after the Senate hearings, he suggested, would be to refer the charges to the Justice Department for prosecution. "I concede cheerfully," he said, "that if this is done, my resolution asking for McCarthy's expulsion from this body becomes somewhat academic. After all, a Senator in jail, for all practical purposes, has been expelled."

The sub-committee invited McCarthy to put up his dukes and defend himself in the same ring. But he refused with a condescending snort and instead wrote a series of sizzling letters to the sub-committee. In one he said:

I am not in the slightest concerned with what this sub-committee does insofar as my fight to expose Communism and corruption in Washington is concerned. This sub-committee cannot in the slightest influence my activities. . . . I think the committee should require Mr. Benton to be placed under oath if he is to act as the megaphone for the Communist Party line type of smear attack on me.

Another letter, addressed to "Dear Guy," as Joe was wont to call Chairman Gillette, continued in the same tone.

The Benton type material can be found in the *Daily Worker* almost any day of the week and will continue to flow from the mouths and pens of camp followers as long as I continue to fight against Communists in government. Frankly, Guy, I have not and do not intend to read, much less answer, Benton's smear attack.

By this time, McCarthy was troubled with a continual tremor of the hands and head, and he caught the next plane to Phoenix, Arizona, for a rest cure. But he took time out from lolling in the sun to reassure Phoenix reporters: "If Benton had any intelligence he'd be a very dangerous man, and I'd have to do something about him. As it is, I'll probably have him yapping at my heels for a long time, but I promise you it won't affect my actions in the least."

But the louder Joe proclaimed his lack of interest in the investigation, the more desperately he worked to discredit it. On November 6, 1951, he loosed a bitter letter, accusing the Gillette sub-committee of hiring a "horde of investigators . . . at a cost of tens of thousands of dollars of taxpayers' money" to dig up dirt on McCarthy. "The sub-committee is guilty of stealing," wrote McCarthy, "just as clearly as though the members were engaged in picking the pockets of the taxpayers and turning the loot over to the Democratic National Committee."

This caught Gillette midway between his dignity and his temper; he replied coldly that the charge "as to the use of a large staff and the expenditure of a large sum of money in investigation relative to the [Benton] resolution is, of course, erroneous." But Joe came back with his Sunday punch, a haymaker in the form of a statement from one of Gillette's temporary agents. The investigator, Daniel G. Buckley, charged that his job had been to smear Joe, not to find the truth. He had been expected to "substantiate" Benton's charges against McCarthy, he contended, and the sub-committee was engaged in an effort to "discredit and destroy any man who fights Communist subversion — in this case, Senator McCarthy."

The startled sub-committee sat up and took another look at its ex-employee. The record confirmed that Buckley had, indeed, been assigned to a minor phase of the McCarthy investigation. He had been dropped from the payroll, then had tried to get his job back. Counter-investigation also revealed that Buckley, before releasing his pro-McCarthy

statement, had made five long-distance calls from New York
City to McCarthy's office. Finally, after the furor over
Buckley had died down, he turned up as an employee of the
Republican National Committee, working closely with Sen-
ator McCarthy's office.

But Joe made the most of Buckley's statement, citing it as
proof that the sub-committee was prejudiced against him.
Finally, Senator Monroney, a sub-committee member, decided to call McCarthy's bluff; he put the question squarely
up to the Senate.

48. The Senate Takes a Stand

SENATOR JOE McCARTHY HAD A HABIT OF CALLING THE PLAY before the ball was pitched. By Joe's signals, both the Baldwin committee investigating the Malmedy massacre and the Tydings committee probing Communists in government struck out before they ever came up to bat. He didn't bother to wait for their findings; he yelled in advance that he would be smeared and that his victims would be whitewashed. And the Gillette committee was no exception; the familiar cries rose from McCarthy's office.

Joe's first pitch was a low inside curve to Chairman Guy Gillette. The statuesque Iowan looked like an easy out; after all, he had voted against the confirmation of Ambassador Philip Jessup on the grounds that McCarthy's attacks had weakened the country's confidence in Jessup. So, to Joe, it seemed that Gillette might be open to persuasion. Joe began by mailing a steady stream of *billets-doux* to "Dear Guy." And when the soft soap failed, he added acid to the letters. Finally McCarthy wrote impatiently: "If one of the Administration lackies were chairman of this committee, I would not waste the time or energy to write, but from you, Guy, the Senate and the country expect honest adherence to the rules of the Senate."

Failing to persuade Gillette, Joe turned his attention to the other committee members. He set his pack of investigators loose on the trail of Senator Hennings of Missouri, with their noses to the ground for Communists. They reported that they had picked up the scent in Hennings' office, and Joe raced in with his shotgun for the kill. But before Joe could trigger the first barrel, FBI Chief Hoover took a look around and assured Hennings his office was free of Reds.

Joe showed no more chivalry toward the Senate's only lady, Margaret Chase Smith of Maine. Ever since she had affixed her name to the "Declaration of Conscience," denouncing McCarthy's methods, Joe had scarcely behaved like a gentleman toward her. He had pulled his seniority on her, unceremoniously dumping her off the Senate Investigating Committee; now he challenged her right to sit on the Gillette committee. Disgusted, Mrs. Smith resigned, and her seat was taken by Senator Herman Welker of Idaho. Welker was perhaps Joe's closest friend in the Senate. His contribution to the investigation was to request a thirty-day delay while he left town to make speeches praising McCarthy.

The only other Republican on the committee, Senator Robert Hendrickson of New Jersey, was accused of prejudice by Joe because he also had signed the "Declaration of Conscience" as well as the Senate report on McCarthy's "despicable, back-street" Maryland campaign. Like Mrs. Smith, he decided the best way out was to resign from the subcommittee. But he changed his mind one day in the Senate cloakroom when Joe sidled up to him, wrapped a friendly arm around his shoulder, and said in a patronizing tone: "You are doing the right thing by resigning, Bob. It's the only thing to do with your prejudice." Hendrickson, who didn't exactly regard himself as prejudiced, called Chairman Gillette and withdrew his resignation. ,

Joe's sniping at the individual committee members was followed by a heavy bombardment of missives, aimed at the committee but exploded in the press. On December 5, 1951, Joe wrote to Chairman Gillette via the wire services:

To take it upon yourself to hire a horde of investigators and spend tens of thousands of dollars without any authorization to do so from the Senate is labeling your elections sub-committee as even more dishonest than was the Tydings committee.

Again on December 19:

You and every member of your sub-committee who is responsible for spending vast amounts of money . . . on matters not concerned with elections, is just as dishonest as though he or she picked the pockets of the taxpayers.

On March 21, 1952, he wrote to the Senate Rules Committee:

As you know, I wrote Senator Gillette, chairman of the sub-committee, that I considered this a completely dishonest handling of taxpayers' money. . . . The staff's scurrilous report, which consisted of cleverly twisted and distorted facts, was then leaked to the left-wing elements of the press.

Joe was referring to a scoop reporting the staff's confidential findings, published in the Providence *Journal* — a Republican newspaper.

But the McCarthy mail continued pouring into the sub-committee — c/o the Associated Press, United Press, and International News Service. Most of the letters were addressed to Chairman Gillette, but some were sent to other committee members, such as a sarcastic letter to the three Democrats on the sub-committee, in which Joe wrote:

I ask you gentlemen not to be disturbed by those who point out that your committee is trying to do what the Communist Party has officially proclaimed as its No. 1 task [to defeat McCarthy]. . . . After all, you must serve the interests of the Democratic party — there is always the chance that the country may be able to survive.

By this time, Senator Mike Monroney of Oklahoma was growing weary of McCarthy's abuse and called for a showdown in the Senate. When Welker returned from his speechmaking, the sub-committee voted 4 to 1 in favor of Monroney's move; the dissenting vote, of course, was

Welker's. The question was next put up to the full Senate Rules Committee, which voted 8 to 3 for the showdown with McCarthy. The three opposing votes came from long-time McCarthy rooters: Senators Everett Dirksen of Illinois, William Jenner of Indiana, and Welker. That day a column by Doris Fleeson appeared in the Washington *Star,* reporting: "The cloakrooms have it that the sub-committee knew also that pressure involving their personal affairs was being put on members of its staff by Senator McCarthy." There was no question that Joe was against a showdown.

But when the issue reached the Senate floor on April 10, 1952, McCarthy changed his strategy. He announced that the Senate vote would not be a showdown after all, because he, too, favored a vote of confidence in the Gillette sub-committee. This was an abrupt reversal from the letters of no-confidence he had been writing to the sub-committee. But Joe explained that he had an ouster resolution of his own to introduce, and he wanted the sub-committee to investigate it with equal vigor. He therewith sent to the desk a resolution calling for an investigation of his arch-enemy, Senator William Benton of Connecticut.

Benton took note of this new development on the Senate floor. He said:

I had spent much time studying Soviet propaganda. I pointed out the tactics: the tactics of hitting and running, of never standing still, of never answering charges, of hitting, of hitting again, of running again — tactics which have so brilliantly been illustrated on the floor of the Senate this afternoon. . . . It was the Senator from Wisconsin, the skillful propagandist which all of us know him to be, who today had the floor of the Senate at 12:30 P.M. It is what he said then that will appear in the newspaper headlines this afternoon.

Sure enough, Joe's demand for an investigation of Benton had taken the headlines away from the Senate debate on McCarthy.

But the debate echoed loud and clear in the Senate chamber. Iowa's Senator Bourke Hickenlooper got the floor early in the affray, and he made a shoulder-shrugging, what's-all-the-excitement-about speech. Monroney came back with nine specific criticisms that McCarthy had leveled at the sub-committee, ranging from "spending tens of thousands of dollars" and "hiring hordes of investigators" to "picking the taxpayers' pockets." Shouted Monroney:

The payroll showed that we had two stenographers, one assistant counsel, and three special investigators. These three investigators were employed a period of approximately 45 days. They were investigating . . . also the Senatorial campaign in Ohio. So where are the "tens of thousands of dollars"? Where are the "hordes of investigators"? The record shows that $3,200 was spent for 45 days of work by three investigators, who were working on the Senatorial campaigns in three of the largest states of the Union. The junior Senator from Wisconsin had that information, although he did not appear to want to use it.

Joe charged that the Gillette sub-committee had no authority to investigate him. But Senator Carl Hayden of Arizona, the scholarly chairman of the Senate Rules Committee, had a different opinion; he told the Senate:

I have placed in the *Record* the precedents which clearly show that the jurisdiction of the former Committee of Privileges and Elections was not limited to election matters, but extended to expulsion, exclusion, censure, and other matters totally unconnected with the conduct of Senators in elections.

This brought McCarthy to his feet; and the debate was on. Here is the excerpt from the official record:

MR. McCARTHY: I hope the Senator will not misunderstand my vote against the discharge of the sub-committee as a vote of confidence in the sub-committee. I have absolutely no confidence in the majority members of the sub-committee.

MR. MONRONEY: It has been well established . . . for seventy-five years that the privileges and elections sub-committee has the jurisdiction. That is well settled by the precedents. It is so well settled, Mr. President, that even the junior Senator from Wisconsin, after traveling across the country and broadcasting and telling the country over the Associated Press and the United Press wires that the committee had no jurisdiction and that it was usurping jurisdiction, finally admitted in a press release that the committee did have jurisdiction. . . . Mr. President, let us not delude ourselves as to what this issue is all about. The issue is whether Senators have confidence in their committee and believe that it is not stealing taxpayers' money, or whether we are to have a continuation of the performance to which I have referred. . . . If the junior Senator from Wisconsin believes what he has written and what he has said across the land on every Associated Press and United Press wire, he should vote to discharge the committee.

MR. McCARTHY: After the fantastic activities of the sub-committee in the Maryland elections case, I can have no confidence in it. However, I shall vote against a discharge of the sub-committee because I feel, now that a precedent has been set in the McCarthy case, the sub-committee should follow the same precedent in the Benton case and in every other case.

MRS. SMITH: Mr. President, I was a member of the sub-committee on privileges and elections when Senator McCarthy charged on December 5, 1951, that the members of that sub-committee were "guilty of stealing" and accused them of complete dishonesty. I say to the members of the Senate that Senator McCarthy has made false accusations which he cannot and has not had the courage even to try to back up with proof. . . . Regardless of the face-saving attempts and words of Senator McCarthy at this time in trying to soften the rebuff and to confuse the issue, any Senator who votes "yea" for this resolution is saying unequivocally to the people of his state and the people of the nation that he believes that Senator McCarthy's charges are truthful and that Senators Gillette, Monroney, Hennings, Hendrickson, and Smith of Maine are guilty of complete dishonesty and of stealing. Any Senator who votes "nay" and against the resolution is voting to repudiate the McCarthy charges against Senators Gillette, Monroney, Hennings, Hendrickson, and Smith of Maine.

MR. McCARTHY: Let me say that I think it is very unfortunate that the sub-committee has come to be known as the Gillette sub-committee.

MR. GILLETTE: Yes, so do I. [Laughter.]

MR. McCARTHY: I think it is unfortunate that the country as a whole does not realize that, although the sub-committee has become known as the Gillette sub-committee, actually the Senator from Iowa has taken very little part in the investigation of the Maryland Senatorial campaign, and has had practically nothing to do with the writing of the report on that matter, and, as I understand, has had nothing to do with the investigation of me. . . . I believe that if the Senator from Iowa had been the active head of this sub-committee, better and cleaner results would have been obtained from the investigation of the Maryland Senatorial campaign.

MR. GILLETTE: I cannot agree with the conclusion of the able junior Senator from Wisconsin that if I had been privileged to be more active, the result would have been different.

MR. McCARTHY: I have so much confidence in the Senator from Iowa that I feel sure if he had been the active head of the sub-committee, he would have to be ashamed of the sub-committee's report on the Maryland Senatorial campaign, as I believe the Senator from Iowa should be ashamed of it.

MR. GILLETTE: I wish to state . . . that I, as chairman of the entire sub-committee, joined in approving the report when it was made to the full committee . . . and that report was made with the approval of the entire nine-member sub-committee. . . . It was unanimous. . . .

MR. HICKENLOOPER: I am mystified by this whole procedure today. I have not yet had it clarified. . . . I wish to make the record perfectly clear that the "stop beating your wife" technique, I say with all courtesy and kindness to the Senator from Maine, with which she interpreted a vote upon the pending question, I shall not accept as the interpretation of what my vote for or against the resolution will mean. . . .

If Senators wish to discuss their personal attitudes about the actions of the junior Senator from Wisconsin one way or the other, that is their privilege, of course.

MRS. SMITH: Will the Senator from Iowa [Mr. Hickenlooper] tell me whether he was ever accused of being a thief?

MR. HICKENLOOPER: I may say to the Senator from Maine that I am utterly sympathetic with the umbrage and justifiable objection which the Senator from Maine may entertain from a generalized statement of [McCarthy's] kind. I am utterly in sympathy with her feelings.

MRS. SMITH: I should like to ask the Senator if he thinks that McCarthy's "picking the pockets of the taxpayers" charge is a general statement. I would consider it a very specific statement and accusation. . . . I should like to ask the Senator a specific question. Was he as a member of that sub-committee ever accused of stealing tax-payers' money?

MR. HICKENLOOPER: No, I do not believe I have even been accused as a member of that sub-committee. . . .

MRS. SMITH: Would the Senator ever become calloused enough not to mind being called a thief by a fellow member of the Senate?

MR. HICKENLOOPER: I presume no person who is honorable would ever become calloused to charges of that kind. . . . I am not in-dulging in any approval or disapproval of the statement by the Senator from Wisconsin . . . but I cannot for one minute place myself in the position of being subjected to an interpretation of what my vote will be by the statement of the Senator from Maine.

MRS. SMITH: It is not a question of interpretation. It is a question of fact.

MR. HICKENLOOPER: Perhaps so. There may be differences of opinion. It seems to me that the committee . . . ought to go ahead and do their job and submit a . . . report. That is why I am mystified by this whole proceeding. If one member of the Senate can, by a letter or a statement, throw a roadblock into the operation of one of the foremost standing committees of the Senate, that is a new pro-cedure to me in the Senate. That is why I am mystified. I shall vote against the resolution because I believe the committee ought to pro-ceed, saw wood, and get its job done.

MR. HENDRICKSON: I think I can understand why this is a mystery to the distinguished Senator from Iowa [Mr. Hickenlooper]. A few moments ago he said, if I heard him right, that the target of this whole debate was the distinguished junior Senator from Wisconsin. Actually the target of this whole debate is the sub-committee on privileges and elections of the Committee on Rules and Administration. So if the Senator is looking at the improper target, naturally he is mystified.

MR. HICKENLOOPER: I perfectly understand the resentment of the individual members of the committee at receiving a highly critical, caustic letter.

MR. MONRONEY: It is not a question of the committee being dis-appointed at receiving a highly critical letter. . . .

MR. HICKENLOOPER: I think the Senator from Oklahoma [Mr. Mon-roney] is becoming hyper-sensitive. Members are constantly charged with various things of which they are not guilty. . . . The mystery is still unsolved why time was set aside, and why this proceeding is conducted in the manner in which it is being conducted. . . . I hope this is not a precedent which will govern the deliberations of the greatest deliberative body in the world.

MR. MONRONEY: . . . I should like to have the Senator from Iowa [Mr. Hickenlooper] say whether even one charge, repeated nine times, that we were stealing taxpayers' money, is a matter of "casual" criticism which one should lightly brush off. I wonder whether the Senator from Iowa agrees that we do need a little confidence in our government. I get worried about democracy sometimes. I get worried when some forces in this nation try to shake the very foundation stones of our government and try to stir up suspicion, distrust, and religious hatred, and do other things that are completely inimical to free and democratic government. We have seen the same pattern overseas, where we saw many governments fail because of these very attacks on the foundations of government by people who created doubt.

The debate was clearly going against McCarthy. But he was a shifty target; he never held still long enough to get hit; instead he set up a new target to divert the fire. In the middle of the debate, Joe shifted from the defensive to the offensive. And the most handy victim was the chief counsel of the Senate Rules Committee, Darrell St. Claire, who happened to have served once on a State Department loyalty board.

Joe charged that St. Claire "cast the deciding vote in the Posniak case, a vote finding Posniak loyal after there had been twelve separate FBI reports opposing it." (See Chapter 33 for the story of the forgery of the FBI report.) Then citing St. Claire as "an example of incompetency in the State Department," Joe went on to charge that he had been "actively assisting the staff of the sub-committee in drafting not only the Maryland election report, but also the scurrilous draft report against McCarthy." And for a while, Joe succeeded in changing the subject of the debate from McCarthy to St. Claire.

Senator after Senator jumped up to defend St. Claire. "The junior Senator from Wisconsin is completely inaccurate and completely misinformed," said Monroney. "I may say also that I resent the effort made to connect a member of a Senate committee staff with pro-Communistic tendencies. . . ." This opinion was shared by many Senators who knew St. Claire. "The name of Darrell St. Claire has been dragged into this discussion without any basis in fact whatsoever," said Senator Carl Hayden of Arizona, chairman of the Senate Rules Committee. "So far as I know," added Gillette, "he [St. Claire] had nothing whatsoever to do with the writing of any report of the sub-committee." Hendrickson agreed that St. Claire "has never had anything to do with the work of the sub-committee"; and Mrs. Smith put it even more strongly, swearing that he "never sat with the sub-committee, never had anything to do with the typing of the report or anything to do with the Maryland or the Benton resolution that I know of." Then Senator Hubert Humphrey of Minnesota rose and addressed the chair:

Mr. President, I should like to make just one observation. During all the debate, something has happened. . . . A name has been brought into the debate, the name of a man who is accused of lack of loyalty and patriotic devotion to his country, the name of Darrell St. Claire, chief clerk of the Rules Committee. Five members of the sub-committee have stated that he had nothing to do with the report. . . . But how did his name get into the debate? It was brought in by Senator McCarthy. It is improper to pass over lightly what has been done to the name and character of a fellow citizen. . . .

What are we going to do — let another man be thrown to the wolves? Here is the name of Darrell St. Claire brought on the floor of the Senate. The insinuation is made that if he had anything to do with the sub-committee report, the report would be biased.

I rise to defend him. I do not know him as a person except as he has called my office, but I submit that in this country a man is innocent until he is proved guilty. Something terrible has happened to us. We go around accusing people day after day and demanding that they prove their innocence. That is totalitarian law, not democratic law. It is Anglo-Saxon jurisprudence upside down. The Senate should assume a man's innocence until his guilt is proved — and I mean to a jury of his fellow men. It is not becoming to the United States Senate to drag in names day after day, week after week, and month after month. It is like the days of Nero when the innocent were thrown into the arena to be destroyed.

I think it is time we stated that we are not going to let people be ruined, their reputations destroyed, and their names defiled because we happen to be in the great game of American politics. If that is what politics is coming to, I am getting out.

Senator Herbert Lehman of New York echoed Humphrey's sentiments:

I have been shocked, as have many other members of this body and of the public, by attacks on individuals, constituting character assassination, by charges unfounded, ungrounded, unproved. In the past two years a policy of indicting by smear has been indulged in, and the victim has no opportunity whatsoever to defend himself. There has been a policy of trying to prove guilt by association, not only of persons, but of ideas. . . . I do not think this is a time for the Senate of the United States to pussyfoot on a matter of as tremendous importance as that which we are discussing. We are still being beset by the prevalence of distrust, suspicion, and accusations of subversion, disloyalty, and treason without foundation and without justification. I very much hope that . . . this committee [will receive] a vote of confidence.

And when the vote was finally taken, the score was 60 to 0 in favor of the sub-committee. But McCarthy did not vote; he left immediately after his attack on Darrel St. Claire to catch a plane to make an address to some college students on — among other subjects — ethics and honor in government.

49. The Feud Continues

FOR A LONG TIME, THE ACTION BETWEEN THE TWO WARRING
Senators — William Benton of Connecticut and Joseph Mc-
Carthy of Wisconsin — was limited to insults shouted from a
distance. Then Benton decided to get down off his lofty
speeches and brawl with McCarthy on his own level. The
little New Englander promised to nail Joe's hide to a high
board fence and leave it there as a warning to the next
"irresponsible demagogue" who happened along. But Joe
laughed at what he called the "puny threat" of Connecticut's
"mental midget"; and indeed, Washington ringsiders took it
for granted that when the dust had cleared away, they would
see Benton's hide — instead of McCarthy's — tacked securely
to the lumber.

But on March 18, 1952, Benton put on the brass knuckles
and charged out onto the Senate floor, lambasting McCarthy
so mercilessly that the Republicans tried to stop his speech.
Senator Styles Bridges, the minority leader, leaped to his
feet and complained that Benton's derogatory remarks about
his fellow Senator violated Senate rules. Benton was forced
to take his seat, but regained the floor again on a motion by
Senator Ernest McFarland of Arizona, the majority leader.
This byplay stirred Senator Herbert Lehman of New York
to comment that Benton had been forced to take his seat for
speaking harshly about another Senator, "and yet we protect
in every way here in the Senate a man making every kind of
accusation to the destruction of reputations and careers."

Back on his feet, Benton made no move to apologize; he explained that he was replying to a McCarthy tirade, delivered on Edward R. Murrow's television program, "See It Now." Joe had charged over television that Benton was "shouting and screaming to high heaven" about Congressional immunity though, all the while, he allegedly hid behind it himself. The Connecticut Senator repeated McCarthy's statement, then told the Senate: "What I was shouting and screaming to high heaven about — if you will pardon the quotation — was not immunity, but honesty. If Senator McCarthy wants me positioned as legally responsible he doesn't have to ask for it in court." Benton then offered to waive his Senatorial immunity and invited Joe to sue on any of the charges that he (Benton) had made in more than 30,000 words of anti-McCarthy testimony.

Joe was not in the Senate to receive the invitation, but it was forwarded to him over the news tickers. McCarthy's bluff had been called, and there was nothing for him to do but see it through. He dispatched a letter to Benton, challenging him to sign a legal statement putting his offer in writing. He wrote sarcastically:

Not being a lawyer, you may not be aware of the fact that immunity is not waived by merely so stating on the Senate floor. If you honestly are willing to waive your Senatorial immunity covering the statements made before the Gillette committee and on the Senate floor, I would appreciate your notifying me as to what time would be convenient for our attorneys to meet and draft the documents necessary for your signature in order to legally waive your immunity.

Benton fired back an answer, calling McCarthy's proposal a "grandstand gesture," and added: "My statements on the floor or elsewhere can be taken literally and at face value. If you want my signature legally to attest my statement on the floor, you have it in this letter." Joe grumbled that "Benton's letter is just another cheap, phony bluff." But Benton had drawn the line in the dust with his toe; if Joe now crossed it, the fight would be on under the shadow of the high board fence.

Five days later Joe, egged on by the crowd, stepped across the line. He filed a $2,000,000 libel-slander-conspiracy suit against Benton; it was the first time in the memory of Capitol Hill veterans that one Senator had sued another. McCarthy said in his complaint that he had been "seriously injured and damaged" and "held up to ridicule, disgrace, scorn, and obloquy," not to mention the "injury to his good name and reputation." The papers were served on Benton on April 4, 1952, giving him twenty days to file an answer. Both Senators loudly insisted that they would do their utmost to expedite the case before the fall elections.

On April 19, five days before Benton's answer was due, Joe jumped the gun and accused Benton of "stalling." On April 23, one day before the deadline, Benton filed a short answer. He contended that, in accusing McCarthy, he had only done his duty "as a citizen and a United States senator." On April 28, Joe subpoenaed Benton for a pre-trial deposition; and the stage was set in McCarthy's office. But Benton didn't like the props; he refused to testify when he caught sight of a tape recording machine, with its mechanical ear cocked in his direction. The court took a month to rule out the tape recorder and restrict the record-taking to official stenographers. Finally, on June 5, Benton marched back into Joe's office with a retinue of lawyers, aides, and newsmen.

For the next hour, the two Senators and their lawyers played a furious game of ring-around-the-rosy; then everybody got mad and quit. Both Senators accused each other of aiding the Reds. Then Joe quoted a report that New York labor leaders had pledged $50,000 to finance Benton's defense. "I hope it's true," quipped Benton; but he refused to name any contributors. "I've had many types of threats — by mail, telephone, emissaries," he explained. "Naturally, I'm

not going to expose friends of mine, who are going to help
me financially, to that kind of abuse." Joe also demanded
that Benton supply "names of Communists who were in
the State Department" while he was Assistant Secretary of
State, from 1945 to 1947. Unless he named the alleged Communists, Joe said, "it will be impossible for us to proceed."
And on that note, the proceeding abruptly ended.

Meanwhile the Gillette sub-committee, bolstered by the
60-to-0 vote of confidence from the Senate, rushed ahead
with its investigation. But if the members expected the
unanimous voice of the Senate to cow McCarthy, they were
mistaken. He refused to face the sub-committee in person,
but resumed his bombardment from off-shore. In the space
of a week, he wrote three open letters and a telegram to the
sub-committee — all uncomplimentary. But the most in-
triguing message was contained in the telegram.

Joe wired Gillette on May 8, offering to be of "all possible
assistance" in locating the sub-committee's "chief witness
against me"; but he tantalizingly withheld the name of the
witness. The next day, Joe whetted the curiosity of the press
with another kernel of information; he told reporters that
the witness was "mentally unstable." Joe laughed: "I am in
a most co-operative mood. If the sub-committee wishes to
question this witness in the asylum in which he is presently
confined, I am perfectly willing."

Three days later, on May 12, the five-man elections sub-
committee convened in the Senate caucus room to hear the
first witnesses. Four crystal chandeliers shed their glittering
light upon the scene, and reflected dazzlingly the white hair
of Chairman Gillette. A dozen white marble pillars gave
the room something of the aura of an imperial Roman court.
As usual, McCarthy did not show up — but a letter from him
did. Gillette read the letter, expressing Joe's deep regret
that the sub-committee was forced to open its public hearings "without the presence of the star witness." But Mc-

Carthy added that the mere fact that the witness had been
"committed to an institution for the criminally insane" should
not prevent the sub-committee from calling him. Senator
Tom Hennings of Missouri, his curiosity aroused, asked who
this mysterious and vital witness was; the sub-committee
counsel, John Moore, suggested that McCarthy might be
referring to a Columbus, Ohio, pre-fab house-builder, who
had suffered a series of heart attacks.

Then a parade of witnesses marched through the august
hearing room, each shedding a glint of light on the Lustron-
McCarthy romance (see Chapter 25). George McConley,
the assistant general counsel of the Reconstruction Finance
Corporation, testified that when it paid Joe $10,000 for his
housing booklet Lustron owed the government more than
$37,500,000. Carl Strandlund, Lustron's former president,
admitted under cross-examination that McCarthy had ap-
proached him on the pamphlet proposition and that "the Senator named the price — he wanted $10,000." Strandlund
considered the investment "good advertising," he said. "He
had great weight with the public," Strandlund said. "This
was not an article written by Joe Blow, but by Senator
McCarthy, vice-chairman of the Joint Committee on Housing."

It was, commented Senator Monroney dryly, "like putting
the word 'sterling' on silver."

Another witness, Lorenzo Semple, a former vice-president
of Lustron, testified that McCarthy had received $10,000 for
writing thirty-seven pages of the booklet, while the remaining fifty-nine pages had been written by a professional
writer, Maron Simon, who was paid a mere $2,000. "Do
you think that was quite fair to Mr. Simon?" asked Counsel
Moore.

While the sub-committee hearings explored the Lustron
phase of McCarthy's activities, Joe kept sending advice in
an unrelenting stream of sarcastic letters. One letter in-

formed the sub-committee that his housing pamphlet was the only profit-making enterprise that the ill-fated Lustron Corporation had ever engaged in. But Senator Monroney totted up the cost of writing, publishing, and distributing the pamphlet, subtracted the small return it had brought — and announced that the pamphlet had cost the American taxpayers $50,265.

But Joe could not be taunted into coming out from behind the mailman and testifying in person, until the sub-committee put the shoe on the other foot and announced it would hold hearings on McCarthy's resolution to expel Benton. This brought Joe out early on the morning of July 3, ready and eager to testify against his arch-critic. And for the next nine hours, diatribes fell like hail; McCarthy assailed Benton for five hours, then Benton assailed McCarthy for four.

Among other things, Joe called Benton the "chameleon from Connecticut," whose "pink-checkered career" had parralleled "the Communist Party line right down to the last period, the last comma." Senator Monroney suggested this was ridiculous on the face of it, since Benton had supported the North Atlantic Pact, the Marshall Plan, the Mutual Security Program, the defense of South Korea, and innumerable other policies violently opposed by the Communists.

Joe replied that Benton was waging "a mythical war against Communism."

"I would like to think it's stupidity," said McCarthy. "If anyone can be that stupid, I don't know."

Specifically, Joe accused Benton of "sheltering" and "harboring" persons "dangerous to America." And with this, Joe fired another buckshot-load of names. One happened to hit a spectator in the audience, an ex-State Department employee named William T. Stone. Stone rose dramatically and demanded a chance to reply to the "false, malicious, and libelous" charges against him. "I am prepared further to show," he said, "how McCarthy can distort and twist a record to turn truths into falsehoods." But Chairman Gillette already had his hands full, and asked Stone to wait until a later date.

When Benton's turn came, he suggested that Joe's performance on the witness stand was the best evidence that he ought to be kicked out of the Senate. "You have had example after example of a pattern of fraud and deceit and deception," said Benton. "I don't think you have to call any more witnesses on my resolution to expel McCarthy. . . . I think you have had the star witness today." The Connecticut Senator then called on the sub-committee to turn both his and McCarthy's testimony over to the Justice Department "for examination on the grounds of perjury."

Late that night, the Benton-McCarthy fireworks were shut off so that committee members could go home to celebrate the Fourth of July next day. And the two principals returned to their offices to fume in private. Ironically, if Joe had ever gone through the ceiling over something Benton had said, he would have come out right under Benton's desk; for Benton's office was located directly over McCarthy's. And newsmen were given to speculating on how many microphones might be concealed in the floor that divided the two antagonists.

By this time, the air was full of pre-election politics; and the Gillette sub-committee shut the door on its investigation. But the authors learned from inside sources that the committee had struck a gold mine of canceled checks, made out to McCarthy but never reported on his tax returns. It was possible that the checks could be untaxable income, such as loans or gifts; otherwise, the discovery would add up to a serious case of income-tax violation.

The evidence was kept under lock and key by the Senate Rules Committee chairman, Carl Hayden of Arizona; but one Senator, who had examined the list of canceled checks, told the authors the total was roughly $148,000. He also reported that the committee had stumbled on to a mysterious flurry on the stock market, wherein McCarthy had transacted $400,000 worth of business in the short space of three months. At this writing, the committee was waiting to get Joe's testimony on this hidden chapter in his finances. (See Chapters 38 and 39.)

Meanwhile, on the eve of the 1952 Wisconsin primary, Joe's faithful friend, Senator Herman Welker of Idaho, resigned from the Gillette sub-committee in a blaze of publicity. "I've had enough," he announced to the press. "I'm resigning from this smear committee as of this moment." He charged that the committee had been conducting the investigation so as "to smear McCarthy and whitewash Benton." Perhaps it was a coincidence in timing, but Welker's blast hit the front pages just as Wisconsin's voters were preparing to go to the polls to decide that McCarthy was to wear the GOP label for re-election to the Senate. At the same time, the Chicago *Tribune's* Senator, Everett Dirksen of Illinois, was quietly bringing pressure on all Republicans to dissociate themselves from the committee, in order to give it a strictly partisan Democratic aspect.

But in spite of the fuss and the fury, one thing was certain: the case against Senator Joe McCarthy was far from closed.

50. A Helping Hand

BY THE MIDDLE OF 1951, SENATOR JOE MCCARTHY WAS suffering from political shell shock. He had been in the thick of battle for a long time, and it was beginning to take a physical toll. Joe was getting jumpy.

One result was that he grew more and more trigger-happy. Let anything move in the political woods, and Joe would open up with his scatter-gun. He even fired short bursts at his own battlemates, including Senators Ken Wherry of Nebraska, Owen Brewster of Maine, and Robert Taft of Ohio. When Wherry stuck up for McCarthy at a Senate Rules Committee meeting, Joe snapped that he didn't need help from anyone. And later, he barked at Brewster and Taft at a strategy meeting of Republican Senators. It got so that friend and foe alike gave McCarthy a wide berth.

At this critical juncture, a grizzled, battlewise veteran appeared and offered to lead Joe out of his predicament. Shortly afterwards, Joe McCarthy and Pat McCarran set off together through a dangerous political no-man's-land. The Appleton *Post-Crescent* headlined this alliance on August 10, 1951: LET MCCARRAN UMPIRE DISPUTE, MCCARTHY SAYS. The story underneath was taken from the wires of the Associated Press. It began:

> Senator McCarran (D., Nev.) said today his Senate Internal Security sub-committee might be willing to consider the controversy over charges by Senator McCarthy (R., Wis.) of Communism in government.
>
> "We don't crave it, and are not asking for it," McCarran told a reporter, "but it might be our staff could analyze and present it."

McCarthy earlier said he was willing to let "a good Democrat" —
meaning McCarran — and his sub-committee decide who is right about
the long feud he has conducted with the State Department.

McCarthy declared he is anxious to have the McCarran sub-committee "decide the whole issue."

"All my files are open to the McCarran committee, and I hope they
can get into this in detail," McCarthy told a reporter.

Who was this man willing to help McCarthy along?

Pat McCarran was a Democratic Senator from the sparsely
populated state of Nevada. In his eighteen years in the Senate, he had risen to sixth in seniority and just about first in
power. He ruled the Senate Judiciary Committee with an
iron hand; he could block any private bill, any judicial appointment that came before Congress. This meant that no
Senator could get a judge or district attorney appointed, no
Senator could get his pet private legislation approved, without first coming to McCarran. It provided the strong-willed
Nevadan with a whip hand that he never hesitated to use.
By the same token, no top Justice Department official could
be confirmed by the Senate without coming to terms with
McCarran. His power was so great that once, when Assistant
Attorney General Peyton Ford hesitated to carry out a Mc-
Carran "request," the Nevadan cracked the whip, got Ford's
promise to do his bidding, and then, as a lesson, badgered the
nation's second highest legal official into humbling himself
and repeating like a child: "Cross my heart."

But if McCarran was first in power, he was next to last in
popularity. Washington correspondents voted him the "second worst" Senator — just one step removed from McCarthy
himself — in *Pageant's* 1951 poll. And among his colleagues, McCarran had a reputation for being a "lone wolf"
and a "little Napoleon." Though he wore the Democratic
label, his politics were closer to the extremists of the Republican Party. He was devoted to four main causes:
gambling, silver, Spain, and anti-Communism—especially the
last. He had spent hours in Madrid discussing international

politics with Dictator Franco. And at home McCarran set himself up as the foremost judge of the Americanism of his countrymen. He exercised this function through the Senate sub-committee on internal security with such a vengeance that Alan Barth was led to describe him in the *Reporter* magazine as "grand inquisitor and lord high executioner in charge of the extirpation of heresy."

From the beginning, Senator McCarthy sought to plant his own agents in positions of power on the McCarran committee. The authors of this book were kept abreast of Joe's plans by one of his own employees, who also supplied other valuable bits of information. This employee reported what Joe was up to, in a confidential memorandum dated February 8, 1951:

Robert Morris interviews witnesses for McCarthy at the University Club, NYC, of which he is a member. Bob Morris was temporarily employed by the Tydings committee when it investigated the State Department over McCarthy's charges. He has only been with McCarthy a short time. McCarthy is pushing Bob Morris for the job as counsel for the new Senate committee to be set up by McCarran to investigate subversive activities and McCarthy's charges. It is generally conceded that he is a leading candidate for the job. McCarthy is not a member of this committee, but is very close to McCarran and to Homer Ferguson, another committe member, and McCarthy boasts he will have a lot to say about what the committee does.

The employees working with McCarthy agree that he is very likable and very democratic in his relationship with them. He tells the investigators working with him not to call him Senator but to call him Joe. They are all extremely loyal to McCarthy and believe McCarthy to be a man of destiny.

Another confidential report from the same McCarthy employee revealed, nine days before it was made public, that Morris would get the job as McCarran's chief counsel. The report stated:

Morris' appointment is regarded as a victory for McCarthy. McCarthy put up a terrific fight to get this job for Robert Morris, and as a practical matter, Morris' employment as chief counsel, with the sole right to select his assistants, will give McCarthy a great deal to say about the activities of the Senate sub-committee on internal security.

The announcement came nine days later; Morris was in. As for his attitude on cleaning out Communists, he wrote a revealing article for the October 30, 1950, issue of *Freeman* magazine — an ultra-conservative magazine, financed in part by China Lobbyist Alfred Kohlberg. In the article, Morris denounced the "secret liaison between the Communists, [Owen] Lattimore, the [Tydings] sub-committee, and the Democratic administration." The only man in Washington who had ever publicly made a more sweeping and unprovable charge was Joe McCarthy.

It soon became apparent that the McCarran sub-committee was out to prove Joe's still-unproved charges. Joe pitched in and helped. As a starter, he sent his hired handyman, Don Surine, to keep a secret rendezvous in Lee, Massachusetts. The meeting was with Thomas Stotler, a young, nervous schoolteacher. His aunt, Mrs. James Markham, happened to be the caretaker of "Sunset Farm," the summer place of Edward C. Carter, former secretary-general for the Institute of Pacific Relations. On one of Stotler's visits to his aunt, he discovered several steel cabinets stacked high in a dusty corner of an old barn across the road from the Carter house. The cabinets contained the dead files of the IPR — a gold mine for McCarthy, who had called the IPR a Communist nest.

Stotler considered it his patriotic duty to notify McCarthy; and thereby began a weird chain of events. On December 21, 1950, Stotler stepped into the middle telephone booth of a row of five in the Pittsfield (Massachusetts) railroad station, and put in a collect call to Surine, in Washington. He told Surine that he would help smuggle out documents from the files. On January 4, 1951, Surine telephoned his young accomplice in Portland, Maine, and made final arrangements. Then Surine hurried to New York City and conferred with the Hearst newspapers' chief specialist on Communism, J. B. Matthews, about photostating the smuggled documents. Two days later, Surine called his boss from a pay station in a drugstore at 495 Columbus Avenue, and reported all in readiness.

Then began the delicate task of pilfering 20,000 documents from their storage place in the barn, and whisking them to Matthews' office in the Hearst building in uptown Manhattan for photostating. By February 3, over 1,800 documents had been secretly filmed. But more intrigue was afoot than the secretive Surine had bargained for; without his knowledge, he had been followed by investigators of the House Un-American Activities Committee. They knew exactly how many drawers from the locked filing cabinets had been removed from the barn and hustled to New York.

Between McCarthy and Matthews, a widening circle of confidants had also been brought in on the plot, including William Randolph Hearst, Jr., Senators Homer Ferguson of Michigan and Karl Mundt of South Dakota, and Hearst Columnists George Sokolsky and Westbrook Pegler. Sokolsky, the ex-IPR stalwart, tipped off Ed Carter about what was going on in his barn, then telephoned Robert Morris that news of the smuggled documents was all over town. The columnist called Morris again the next day, and two days later held a telephone conference with Senator Ferguson, also an ex-IPR member. By this time the grapevine was sounding the alarm; and when an agent for the House Un-American Activities Committee suddenly appeared in Matthews' office, the conspirators feared the jig was up. There was the risk that they might be charged with breaking and entering, or even possibly transporting stolen property across interstate lines. The situation clearly called for something drastic.

First, the smuggled records were spirited off the Hearst

premises and started on their way back to the Carter farm. Then McCarthy arranged with McCarran for a belated subpoena to be issued for the documents. On February 7, 1951, three men burst into the Sheraton Hotel in Pittsfield and asked for a room that would accommodate all three. They registered as Donald Surine of Washington, D.C., Thomas Stotler of Cape Elizabeth, Maine, and Frank W. Schroeder of Delaware City, Delaware. That night a howling blizzard struck town; snow, accompanied by gusty winds, swirled down for twenty-four hours. When the blizzard was at its worst, the three strangers pulled their heads down in their coat collars, leaned against the driving snow, and marched up Fourth Street to the office of the Associated Transport Company. They startled the night dispatcher, "Red" Wilbur, with a demand for a truck, a driver, and a helper.

The dispatcher was skeptical. But Frank Schroeder identified himself impressively as an investigator for the Senate sub-committee on internal security, and announced that the truck was needed at once for official business. After the red tape was untangled and the snow cleared up a bit, a truck was turned over to the three men. They called on Stotler's aunt, Mrs. James Markham, and handed her a subpoena calling for the delivery of all the "letters, papers, and documents" in the Carter barn. It was still snowing heavily as they carted the filing cabinets out of the barn, loaded them on the truck, and then drove over snow-clogged roads to New York City. There, the Treasury Department provided an armed convoy, which screamed ahead of them all the way to Washington. The next day, the nation's front pages blazoned with sensational headlines: RED PROBERS SEIZE SECRET "LATTIMORE" FILES IN FARM RAID. PROBERS PROMISE FULL STUDY OF SEIZED FILES. DARING RAID NETS I.P.R. FILES.

Then Senator Mundt made a slip which gave the show away. He told reporters about seeing evidence that Moscow had made contributions to the IPR. Asked where this evidence was located, he blunderingly remarked that he and McCarthy had studied "sample" IPR documents, which had been obtained by Don Surine. "Surine got about fifty exhibits," Mundt said, "through one of the methods used by investigators generally, without the knowledge of the IPR. I don't think I had better say just how he got them. It might get somebody into a lot of trouble." McCarthy also couldn't resist the temptation to brag a little. Talking to reporters after a speech in Racine, Wisconsin, Joe confided that Carter's barn was "crammed with documents." Then he added knowingly: "I succeeded in — I don't like to use the word 'stealing' — let's say I 'borrowed' the documents."

As for the IPR, the new secretary-general, William L. Holland, complained that the seizure was "an unnecessary and melodramatic raid . . . a cheap publicity stunt." He said the papers had been stored in the old barn to avoid storage charges, and because Carter had planned to write a history of the IPR. Nothing was said about bringing charges against Surine for his premature — and totally illegal — seizure. But the most ironic fact didn't come out until several months later: that a dozen FBI agents, at the invitation of IPR officials, had been quietly sifting through the files all during the summer of 1950—long before Surine ever "discovered" them.

Meanwhile, McCarthy had been able to cut down on his investigating staff; the McCarran committee was doing the work for him. He told the *U. S. News and World Report* in an interview, published September 7, 1951: "At the present time, we only have the regular staff. I have only one investigator, which, of course, costs me something when I send him out. But this year if I find anything of importance, I just ship it down to the McCarran committee, which I couldn't do last year."

So, although McCarran was steering the new Communist investigation, McCarthy was doing a good deal of backseat driving.

There were those who feared Pat McCarran's bite worse than Joe McCarthy's bark. The aged and ailing McCarran, a power to be reckoned with around Washington, knew how to make his power felt. Few others could get more action out of a telephone call or a whispered word or a meaningful look. Once McCarran silenced his Nevada colleague, Senator George Malone, in the middle of a speech simply by stalking across the Senate chamber and giving him a dark look. When the withering stare caught Malone's eye, he sputtered, flushed, and then sheepishly sank into his seat.

Senator McCarran had made sure he would have a clear field to investigate Communism. For a while, it looked as if he would have a rival; President Harry Truman had appointed the new Subversive Control Board, headed by Admiral Chester Nimitz, to make an "impartial investigation." But McCarran was boss of the Senate Judiciary Committee, which had to pass on the board members; and he refused to give them his okay. He explained simply that he had heard "some rather serious comments" about the nominees. And so the board languished and died, for it could not begin its work without McCarran's approval. But insiders knew that McCarran had decided to investigate McCarthy's charges himself and did not relish having a rival group of distinguished Americans stealing the show.

As usual, McCarran took his cue from McCarthy. Of all the State Department offices, Joe had singled out two for special condemnation: the Voice of America and the Far Eastern Division. He had told Washington reporters that "the easiest way to get in the Voice of America is to be a well-known Communist. Unless you have a Communistic background, you cannot qualify for a position with the Voice of America." And in a Senate speech on March 30, 1950, Joe had said:

The more deeply I delve into this subject, the more I am convinced that two distinct but at the same time interlocking areas of operations are almost completely controlled and dominated by individuals who are loyal to the ideals and designs of Communism rather than to those of the free, God-fearing half of the world. I refer to the Far Eastern Division of the State Department, and to the Voice of America.

The "Voice" was obliged to come begging for funds to McCarran, who, in addition to his other powers, headed the Senate appropriations sub-committee which controlled the State Department's purse strings. Formal hearings were held during March 1952; and McCarran, together with an elderly cantankerous colleague, Senator Kenneth McKellar of Tennessee, subjected three young State Department officials to a ferocious hazing. They were Carlisle Humelsine, the Deputy Under-Secretary of State; Edward Barrett, the Assistant Secretary of State; and Foy D. Kohler, chief of the Voice of America's broadcasting section. The hearing proceeded as follows:

MR. MCCARRAN: Will you give this committee the loyalty reports on every State Department employee connected with the Voice of America program? I want a yes or no answer.

MR. HUMELSINE: Senator, I have no individual discretion in that matter. I am under the same restriction as everyone else in the State Department on this executive order. Only the President can release those confidential records.

MR. MCCARRAN: In other words, we can't get those records.

MR. HUMELSINE: Not unless the President of the United States personally authorizes you having them.

MR. MCKELLAR: Let me give you a little advice right there. You had better tell the President to instruct you to give these things to this committee. If you don't, you're going to be in one hell of a fix. Is that clear to you?

MR. MCCARRAN: And I want to add that before I get finished, I am going to show there are people in your program who shouldn't be there. I'm going to have you all up before my Internal Security Committee for investigation.

MR. BARRETT: We welcome any investigation.

MR. MCCARRAN (turning to Barrett): I would like very much to have your background and loyalty record. I'd like to know all about you.

MR. BARRETT: That's easy. My life's an open book.

MR. McCARRAN: All right, then answer this question. Are you connected with any Socialistic or Communistic institutions?

MR. BARRETT: Of course not. I am not now and never have been. I have never belonged to any organization listed on any subversive list. During the war, I was deputy chief of psychological warfare in the Mediterranean theater, and later I became editorial director of *Newsweek* magazine.

MR. McKELLAR: What are your views on Socialism and Communism? What about fellow travelers? Are you for them or against them?

MR. BARRETT: I came to Washington to fight Communism. . . .

MR. McCARRAN (*addressing Kohler*): Whom do you know in the Russian government?

MR. KOHLER: Did you say the Russian government?

MR. McCARRAN: That's what I said. Whom do you know personally in the Russian government?

MR. KOHLER: I have no friends in the Russian government.

At a later hearing, McCarran and McCarthy joined forces to flay Brigadier General Conrad E. Snow, lifelong New Hampshire Republican and head of the State Department's loyalty-security board. During an angry colloquy with Mc-Carthy, Snow defined McCarthyism as "the making of public statements that are not based on fact."

This brought McCarran into the debate, snorting fire. "Where did you get the right to revile a member of the Senate of the United States?" he demanded. "Where did you get the authority?"

Snow replied evenly: "I am a citizen of the United States, and I am engaged in public office."

To this McCarran shouted: "That is right! You ought to be out of that office!"

But Snow kept his temper and insisted he had the right to reply when a Senator made speeches "which impugn the operation of my public office."

At the same session, McCarthy suggested that Carlisle Humelsine should be cited for contempt for refusing to give the names of employees who had resigned while under loyalty investigation. But McCarran objected: "What I do not propose to do, if I can avoid it, is to make Mr. Humelsine a whipping boy for the department."

The silver-haired, barrel-chested McCarran was noted for his drive, which impelled him to frenetic activity despite the burden of his seventy-four years and his precarious health. But he operated for the most part behind closed doors; he preferred the stealthy rather than the noisy approach. In this respect he was unlike McCarthy, who couldn't get out of the garage without honking the horn. But McCarran's long periods of silence and secrecy were interrupted by sensational outbursts. On November 21, 1951, McCarran accused the State Department of failing to oust a Czech diplomat who he charged was a trained killer. "For about six months he was given special training in Czechoslovakia in methods of silent killing," said McCarran, "involving such methods as garrotting, breaking the neck with a sudden blow, jabbing a stiletto into a vital spot, and forcible use of powerful anesthetics." But that was the last McCarran, or anyone else, ever said of the terrible Czech. McCarran never explained where he got the information (if it *was* information); and for all the public knew, this mysterious killer was still slinking down dark alleys, practicing his ugly talents. In June 1952, McCarran also tried to withdraw United States funds from the United Nations Educational, Scientific, and Cultural Organization because, he said, it "slanted at or promoted One World government" in some of its literature.

McCarran, like McCarthy, appeared to be more concerned with dissipating time and money to create one-day headlines than with building a world healthy enough, spiritually and materially, to withstand the pressures of totalitarianism.

51. A Political Issue

In colonial Virginia, a justice of the peace named Charles Lynch condemned men to the gallows without benefit of trial; and his name went down as an ugly word in the English language. In nineteenth-century Ireland, Captain Charles Boycott used such harsh methods to collect rents that the impoverished tenants banded together; their resistance took a unique form that became known as "boycott." In 1940, a Norwegian major named Vidkun Quisling helped the Nazi conquerors take over his country; his name ended up in the dictionary as a common noun meaning "traitor." Likewise, Senator Joe McCarthy gave his name to the vernacular: McCarthyism after 1950 came to mean "character assassination."

But McCarthyism was more than a word; it was an issue that assumed huge political proportions by 1952; and the Presidential contenders had to face up to it. Of all the major candidates, Senator Robert Taft of Ohio was the most equivocal. He stalked around the McCarthy issue, eying it from every angle, alternately drawing toward it, then pushing away from it. It was a strange performance for the man who had come to be known to millions of Americans as Mr. Integrity; for probably no other Senator enjoyed so wide a reputation for intellectual honesty and the courage of his convictions as Robert Taft.

At first, Taft kept aloof from McCarthy. But the Senator from Wisconsin was not the kind of person you could ignore;

you had to be "fer or agin" him — in McCarthy's pasture there was no handy fence on which to sit. And this was particularly true of Senator Taft, whose word had the influence of a papal decree with millions of Republicans. One word from Taft, and a huge bloc of Republicans would be ready to accept or reject Joe.

There are those who say that the disintegration of Taft, the Champion of Morality, began on the day he made the pronouncement that Joe was O.K., that Joe was the genuine article. There are those who say that the alluring lights of 1600 Pennsylvania Avenue got in Taft's eyes. At any rate, he came out foursquare for McCarthyism in all its meanings and shadings.

Taft was a man of strong character; and he did not succumb without a struggle, despite the massiveness of his ambition. For a period, the battle hung in the balance; some days he would publicly disown McCarthy; but on other days he would issue statements backstopping the Wisconsin Senator.

On March 23, 1950, the New York *Times* reported: "Mr. Taft told reporters that he personally had been urging Mr. McCarthy to press his prosecution 'and if one case didn't work, to bring up another.' " That same day the New York *Herald Tribune* reported: "Senator Taft said he had proffered help to Senator McCarthy and on one occasion arranged a meeting between the Wisconsin Senator and a possible informant." Also on that date the Baltimore *Sun* reported: "Taft insisted that the [Republican] party, as such, was not underwriting McCarthy's campaign against the State Department, although he personally endorsed the Wisconsin Senator's efforts."

Later Taft traveled to Maine, where he announced: "The greatest Kremlin asset in our history has been the pro-Communist group in the State Department." And Taft was among the first to defend McCarthy against the Tydings

report, calling it "of a purely political nature and . . . derogatory and insulting to Senator McCarthy." Such comments
made it look as though the political liaison between the two
Senators was firmly established. Taking note of this, the St.
Louis *Post-Dispatch* remarked in February 1951:

> Taft wants to be President. McCarthy does too, but being a younger
> man, can perhaps afford to wait. It may be that history will have to
> decide whether Taft is using McCarthy for his own purposes, or
> whether McCarthy is using Taft. The important fact today is that they
> are pulling in harness.

But gradually the groundswell of opinion against Mc-
Carthy began also to envelop Taft. Then Joe delivered his
Senate tirade against General Marshall. While other Senators lashed out at McCarthy, Senator Taft commented cautiously that he did not agree with "McCarthy's accusations
of conspiracy or treason." Having thus eased a short distance
away from Joe, Taft widened the rift by announcing on August 21, 1951, that McCarthy was simply expressing his own
views about the State Department — not the official views
of the GOP. Next month, Taft completed a 180-degree
shift. He told Spencer R. McCulloch of the St. Louis *Post-
Dispatch* that he considered McCarthy's methods "perfectly
reckless" and the content of his charges "bunk."

A few days later, the emboldened Taft told newsmen
in Des Moines that he believed McCarthy had "overstated
his charges." And he noted that McCarthy's statement that
Philip Jessup was a Red sympathizer "is not necessarily
true." As a finishing touch to the interview, Taft predicted
hopefully that McCarthyism would not be an issue in the
1952 campaign.

For Joe's part, he replied with a simple statement which
had vast undercurrents of meaning. He said: "I just don't
think Bob Taft will join the camp-following elements in
campaigning against me."

If this was a warning that even Taft could be linked with

the Communist "camp followers," he apparently took the hint. At least he began retreating from his anti-McCarthy position, and moving around the circle toward the high noon of a pro-McCarthy endorsement.

The first intimation of this came out of Taft's Georgetown neighborhood. A woman collecting money for the March of Dimes told about stopping at the Taft house. The bell was answered by Mrs. Taft's nurse, who then went into the house to pick up a contribution from the Senator and "a guest." Presently the nurse returned with five dollars from Taft and his guest, plus another three dollars from herself. The solicitor walked away; but before she had gone far, the front door of Taft's house flew open and McCarthy bounded out, loudly whistling a popular tune. He opened the door of his car parked at the curb, took a briefcase from the seat, and bounced breezily back into the house.

There were other signs of Taft's reconversion to McCarthyism. On January 21, 1952, he told an audience in Wisconsin, where he was campaigning, that the "pro-Communist policies of the State Department fully justified Joe McCarthy in his demand for an investigation." And so the bond between Robert Taft, the well-to-do son of a former President, and Joe McCarthy, the brawling back-country politician, was repaired — this time for the duration of the 1952 campaign.

But what did Joe do in return for this loyal support? Apparently nothing. His only comment on Republican candidates before the convention was to say that General Douglas MacArthur would make a wonderful President — that is, if a younger man were on the ticket with him. And by "a younger man," McCarthy did not mean Taft.

But the Taft-McCarthy friendship continued to bloom; and by convention time it was in full flower. The Taft forces, which openly controlled the convention machinery, scheduled McCarthy for a main speech. And when his turn came on the afternoon of July 9, Taft's hand-picked tem-

porary chairman, Walter Hallanan, introduced McCarthy as
"Wisconsin's fighting Marine," maligned for his courage in
"exposing the traitors in our government."

Joe strode to the rostrum to the strains of the Marine
hymn, "The Halls of Montezuma." The galleries gave him a
rousing hand; and a bunch of delegates, wearing Taft but-
tons, paraded in front of the hall, holding aloft fish-shaped
placards. These were supposed to represent red herrings,
and bore the names "Acheson," "Hiss," and "Lattimore." Joe
started off his speech by praising General MacArthur as
"the greatest American that was ever born." He then went
into his regular act, flailing away at the usual targets and
gushing about the "blood and agony and tears" of the
mothers and wives "who shall go so deep into the valley
of darkness and despair" on account of the Korean war. Next
morning, the New York *Times* commented:

At precisely 3:21 P.M. yesterday, Eastern daylight-saving time, the
Republican convention in Chicago reached rock bottom. This was
when Senator Joseph R. McCarthy of Wisconsin, traducer of reputations and mudslinger extraordinary, sponsor (under the libel-proof
privileges of the Senate) of the incredible charge that General
George C. Marshall has been part of a "conspiracy so immense and
an infamy so black as to dwarf any previous such venture in the
history of man," mounted the rostrum to address the assembled delegates. He did so at the explicit invitation of the Republican National
Committee, tendered by it for reasons best known to itself.

This is the low point. From now on the course must certainly be
upward.

As it turned out, the Republican convention did not
nominate McCarthy's friend, Senator Robert Taft, but chose
instead one of his targets, General Dwight Eisenhower.
Three times in the speech against General Marshall, Joe had
accused Eisenhower, in effect, of knowingly participating in
the "conspiracy" to help Russia dominate the world (see
Chapter 36). And just before the convention, Joe had circulated the whisper that Eisenhower, while president of

Columbia University, had coddled a nest of Communists on the campus. But these past suspicions did not prevent McCarthy from announcing his full support of Eisenhower, once he was nominated.

Ike, for his part, wasn't so quick to endorse McCarthy. Privately, the GOP nominee let it be known that he had no use for McCarthy; he even gave his approval for Paul Hoffman, one of his ex-campaign managers, to testify against Joe — this in spite of the fact that McCarthy, a Republican, was fighting for his political life against Senator William Benton, a Democrat. Hoffman, taking the witness stand with Ike's blessing, described Joe's charges against General Marshall as "fantastically false." As for Joe's attempts to discredit the Marshall Plan, Hoffman said: "Senator McCarthy either has not got the facts or has deliberately misrepresented the situation."

All this disturbed the peace of mind of the Republican National Chairman, Arthur Summerfield; he could not have the party's Presidential candidate campaigning, in effect, against one of the party's Senatorial candidates. So Summerfield rushed around to see Eisenhower and begged him to support all Republican candidates, including McCarthy; the GOP chairman argued that Ike couldn't go around denouncing all the Republicans he disagreed with. So Eisenhower promised to swallow the McCarthy pill in the name of party loyalty.

But Ike had trouble reconciling party loyalty with his feelings about McCarthy; so he ended up coming out both for and against McCarthy. On the one hand, Eisenhower announced he would back all the GOP nominees for Congress, including McCarthy. "I believe in party responsibility," he said. But on the other hand, he made it plain how he felt about the Senator from Wisconsin. Replying to questions about McCarthy, Ike declared stoutly that he wouldn't "campaign or give blanket indorsement" to anyone who clearly violated his ideas "of what is decent, right, just and fair." He specifically defended General Marshall, declaring: "There is absolutely no disloyalty in General Marshall's soul." He added fiercely: "George Marshall is one of the patriots of this country — a man of real selflessness." Then, in a direct slap at McCarthy, Ike said: "I have no patience with anyone who can find in his [Marshall's] record of service to this country cause for criticism."

As for Joe, he chose to be big about the matter, and promised to support Eisenhower, regardless of whether the General backed him. "I know," complained Joe, "that every one of those writers and radio commentators who have long supported the Truman-Acheson-Lattimore triumvirate will every day try to needle Eisenhower into making a statement against McCarthy. I hope they don't succeed in drawing him into an untenable position."

But the man in the untenable position was Joe McCarthy; he was supporting for the Presidency a man who he had implied was pro-Communist. In fact, according to Joe's logic, Eisenhower was following the orders of the jailed Communist Party secretary, Gus Hall. For Ike had clearly denounced McCarthyism; and Joe had a special quotation for the benefit of such heretics. He was fond of quoting Gus Hall as saying: "I urge all Communist Party members, and all anti-Fascists, to yield second place to none in the fight to rid our country of the Fascist poison of McCarthyism." Then Joe would follow this quotation with a statement that those who criticized him were following Communist Party orders (see Appendix, page 413).

If Joe followed his past reasoning, Eisenhower would now be a fellow traveler of the Communists. And that would make an Eisenhower supporter, such as Joe McCarthy, a *fellow*-fellow traveler.

52. The McCarthy Methods

SENATOR RUSSELL LONG, THE ABLE SON OF THE LATE LOUISIANA "Kingfish," Huey P. Long, told the Senate in 1950: "The day of the demagogue is over." But even as he spoke, Joe McCarthy was riding up and down the land, preaching that the United States was being sold down the river by its own leaders. And thousands of troubled citizens agreed and applauded.

The reaction at Fort Atkinson, Wisconsin, was typical. Joe was the big Saturday-night attraction at the town auditorium; and he packed the townfolks in. They went wild over his speech. Cries of "Give 'em hell, Joe," spiced up the porridge of clapping and whistling. Afterwards, the Spring Valley *Sun* reported in its April 12, 1951, issue:

> When Joe McCarthy had finished Saturday night, there were few skeptics in the jammed auditorium. We were in a position to witness perhaps 400 of the 700 in the audience. Only two remained seated. The rest rose as one person, clapping and cheering. Among them were four able Fort Atkinson industrialists, two competent Fort Atkinson labor leaders, and half a dozen loyal Democrats.

How can a man with no special training, with an awkward manner, a rough voice, and an unsophisticated appearance, successfully cast a spell over almost every large audience he addresses? One reason is his very lack of the typical demagogue's qualities. People are convinced by the look of perspiring sincerity on his face, by the awkward, ringing delivery, by the heavy fist-pounding on the rostrum. Joe

"becomes the object of a systematic campaign of character assassination." But he promises: "No matter how much McCarthy bleeds, the job will continue until we have had a thorough house cleaning." These are typical of quotations that crop up frequently in his speeches.

Joe always arrives for a speech a few minutes late, accompanied in Wisconsin by his balding bodyguard-agent-manager, Otis Gomillion. By the time McCarthy reaches the meeting hall, he has often brought his mind and body to just the right pitch by not eating for four or five hours and by taking a couple of quick shots of whiskey. "I take two or three, depending on how I feel," he says. "The nourishment keeps me going." Once the speech begins, Joe's most valued prop is the bulging briefcase, carefully placed on the floor or a chair beside him. From time to time during the talk, Joe will bend over to take out an affidavit, a transcript, or some other document. These are equipped with large tabs for quick access; but McCarthy finds it more effective to rummage around in the bag for a minute or two before coming up with the correct "proof." It gives the impression that the bag is overflowing with documentary evidence.

Usually the crowd is with Joe, and anyone who raises a critical voice is hooted down. Roy Evans of Dallas, Texas, tried it during a question-and-answer period, and here is his account of what happened:

McCarthy was pleased with himself. You could see it on his face. He said this was the first time he had spoken in some time that Communists had not been at the door with leaflets. The people cheered and believed what he had said. . . .

Looking down at his watch, the Senator signaled that he was tired of the questioning. It looked very likely that I wouldn't get to ask my question. I rushed to the front of the auditorium. I had to know how he would answer.

"Senator, one more question!"

The Senator appeared uneasy.

"Senator, I would like to know what truth you see in the statement made by one of your Republican colleagues, Margaret Chase Smith — I do not believe you can call her Communistic or stupid: 'Some of the demagogues who shout loudest about Communism and who smear anyone who disagrees with them by calling him a Red are the foremost disciples of the Big Lie. They can be just as great a danger — ' "

"Are you making a speech or asking a question?" asked the Senator. This was the cue for the crowd, which had been quite still, to stomp and roar for me to sit down.

"Are you afraid of free speech?" I asked. Another roar from the crowd.

"Next question," said the Senator. The crowd bellowed at me, and the Senator smiled greasily. I walked back to my seat.

But, now and then, an entire audience will be hostile; then Joe turns on the audience furiously. On April 10, 1952, when he was hissed by the girls of Smith College in Northampton, Massachusetts, he shouted angrily at them: "Hiss — that word sounds familiar." But Joe can take boos and jeers better than ridicule; when a University of Wisconsin audience started laughing at him, he went completely to pieces.

Joe is not so much a cold, calculating Machiavelli as a fast-talking super-salesman. "The two best things that have happened to the country for a long time are Senator McCarthy and Hadacol," remarked a hearing-aid salesman, discussing Joe in the bar of Appleton's Conway Hotel. He was paying tribute, as one salesman to another, to Joe's glib line and convincing air. And when it comes to the gimmicks of modern salesmanship, Joe has gone the experts one better; he has invented the technique of calling a press conference in order to announce the calling of another press conference. This method was described by Richard Rovere in the *New Yorker* magazine on May 13, 1950:

McCarthy will bring in the reporters in the morning by notifying their offices that he has something important to disclose. When they arrive, he will disclose that he has called them together to alert them for an afternoon press conference, at which he will have something breathless to reveal. This announcement makes the afternoon papers. The breathtaking revelations, if there are any, make the newspapers of the following morning. If, as is often the case, he has nothing of news value to announce, he has at least profited by the afternoon head-lines.

Joe has also refined to an art the technique of the old patent-medicine "pitchers." He describes in terrible tones the country's afflictions which his product will cure or prevent; he plays on the fears, troubles, anxieties, and griefs of his audience. He draws a word picture of the impending doom which will fall at any time unless some drastic measure is taken; and the listener soon gets the impression that support of McCarthy is the "drastic measure" they must take.

For example, Joe tolled a warning in November 1950: "One of the greatest disasters in American history is in the making." He did not elaborate; but by December 1950 the approaching catastrophe loomed larger. Joe said: "Day by day and hour by hour the situation grows more black." One month later he was saying: "Every thinking American knows that there will be neither a Democrat nor a Republican party if the sellout continues and the Communists win out." Two months went by, and in March 1951 Joe warned: "Unless we chart a foreign policy which is truly by and for America and free civilization, there may well be recorded in the corridors of time the epitaph of all Western civilization." By the next month, April, the danger was almost upon us: "The next six, eight, ten months can well determine whether this nation lives or dies." As for the cure, Joe made it clear that the people should kick out the "traitors" and put red-blooded McCarthyites in charge of their affairs. Or, as he put it another way: "If you again want vast millions of mothers and wives going deep into the valley of darkness and despair — then vote Democrat!"

About a year after McCarthy had launched his campaign against Reds-in-government, he began to be *for* virtue as well as *against* sin. Gradually more and more references to "Western civilization" and to God and religion appeared in his speeches. In a welcome-home demonstration at the new athletic park in Manawa, Wisconsin, Joe addressed the townspeople from a speaker's stand on the baseball diamond. Suddenly he lowered his voice almost to a whisper, and in his most folksy manner said: "There are two fundamental truths of religion: there is a God who is eternal, and each and every one of you has a soul which is immortal." From there, Joe jumped into the main part of his speech. He called Secretary of State Acheson a traitor and said he had proof that our foreign policy was being directed from the Kremlin. Near the end of the speech, he remarked that his anti-Communist crusade was not political.

The implication was clear: the campaign was religious. God and Joe, with the voters' help, would emerge victorious.

53. The Multiple Lie

IT WAS NINE O'CLOCK ON THE MORNING OF AUGUST 15, 1950; and already fifty thousand visitors had assembled around the black-and-white tar-paper house outside Necedah, Wisconsin. The devout, the skeptical, and the curious arrived by train, by bus, and by car; and they hurried across the fields of half-grown wheat and alfalfa to join the crowd. For Mrs. Mary Ann Van Hoof, who lived in the tar-paper house, had announced that she would receive her seventh visit from the Virgin Mary at noon.

The multitude grew more restless as the morning wore on. Some prayed quietly or recited their rosaries; others, more commercial-minded, set up soda-pop stands and sold out in two hours; but most just stood around, staring and craning. Finally, at five minutes to twelve, a gaunt, worn farm woman emerged from the house and knelt before a small shrine. She remained transfixed for ten minutes, gazing heavenward. Then she arose, walked to a waiting microphone, and began repeating to the crowd what the Blessed Virgin had told her.

The crowd had seen nothing. But many believed that Mrs. Van Hoof had beheld a heavenly vision; and they believed the words she spoke came from the Mother of God. "The beginning of a horrible time is coming right now," the farm woman said in a low, trembling voice into the public-address system. "Your papers, your press don't give you the truth . . . the time is here when we must save ourselves . . . black clouds are coming." The words went on; but they were rambling and indistinct. Then a clarifying whisper buzzed through the crowd; the garbled message, according to this ear-to-ear report, was: fight Communism and clean the Reds out of the State Department.

But the message did not come from heaven; it came from two of Senator Joe McCarthy's supporters, who were circulating through the crowd, spreading the word. The resourceful McCarthy was getting in a quiet plug for his campaign; the gathering of thousands of Wisconsin voters in one spot had been more than he could resist.

So it is with Joe; no occasion is too big, no stratagem too small, if it will further the cause of McCarthy. His publicity tricks are well known, but his basic techniques are not so obvious. His political friend of the 1930's, Jerry Jolin, may have dropped a clue when he told the authors that Joe used to study the masterwork of Naziism, Hitler's *Mein Kampf*. In that book, Hitler told about his favorite technique, "the Big Lie." He defined this as a falsehood so large and round, so grandly conceived and boldly set forth, so imaginative and impressive, that people would mistake it for truth.

It may be unfair to say that McCarthy deliberately embraced this poisonous dropping from an envenomed pen. And yet the record shows that he has followed the Big Lie technique. The St. Louis *Post-Dispatch* — included by editors on the list of the nation's "ten best" newspapers — put it this way on February 18, 1951:

There is nothing secret about McCarthy's operations. He follows a simple totalitarian formula simple to imitate. How to do it was best expressed by Hitler, whose doctrine is followed daily by Communist propagandists and often by McCarthy. Since, as Benton told the Senate, it seems likely that "a new and worse siege of irresponsibility lies ahead of us," it may be useful to recall what Hitler said in his book, *Mein Kampf*:

"The greatness of the lie is always a certain factor in being believed; at the bottom of their hearts, the great masses of a people are more likely to be misled than to be consciously and deliberately bad, and in the primitive simplicity of their minds, they are more easily victimized by a large than by a small lie. . . . Some part of even the boldest lie is sure to stick."

McCarthy has been calling Secretary of State Dean Acheson the "Red Dean of Fashion," which is, of course, nonsensical. But Hitler also said: "The receptive ability of the masses is very limited, their understanding small; on the other hand, they have a great power of forgetting. This being so, all effective propaganda must be brought out in the form of slogans until the very last man is enabled to comprehend what is meant by any slogan."

McCarthy has also frequently employed another technique. It goes like this: "It appears that (name of person) never actually signed up as a member of the Communist Party, and never paid dues . . . " That is the same as saying McCarthy does not eat human flesh. Yet it may ruin a man's reputation.

Ever since Joe McCarthy, star rookie in the Manawa hot-stove league, amazed the townspeople with the tall tales and the ready "facts" which he used to win his arguments, he has played fast and loose with the truth. McCarthy has gone Hitler one better; where Hitler depended upon the "Big Lie," McCarthy has added a new twist. He buttresses one falsehood with another, spraying out small untruths in a long stream, and constantly spinning from one lie to another, thus preventing the public from keeping up with the pace. Richard Rovere, writing in the *New Yorker* magazine, called this technique "the multiple untruth." What he meant by this was set forth in the April 22, 1950, issue:

The "multiple untruth" need not be a particularly large untruth, but can be instead a long series of loosely related untruths, or a single untruth with many facets. In either case, the whole is composed of so many parts that anyone wishing to set the record straight will discover that it is utterly impossible to keep all the elements of the falsehood in mind at the same time. Anyone making the attempt may seize upon a few selected statements and show them to be false, but doing this may leave the impression that only the statements selected are false and the rest true.

An even greater advantage of the "multiple untruth" is that statements shown to be false can still be repeated over and over again with impunity, because no one will remember which statements have been disproved and which ones haven't. Haldore Hanson . . . proved to the satisfaction of everyone present that McCarthy, in his testimony, had flagrantly misquoted from a book Hanson wrote eleven years ago. Two days later, when McCarthy took the Senate floor, he read into the record exactly the same misquotation Hanson had corrected before the committee.

In the same speech, McCarthy professed to be quoting from a letter written several years ago by Owen Lattimore to Joseph Barnes. . . . Several Senators rose from their seats to ask if McCarthy wasn't being unfair in quoting parts of the letter out of context. . . . But the truth of the matter, and a truth that hasn't caught up with McCarthy and probably never will, is that he wasn't quoting out of context, because he simply wasn't quoting. The most charitable description of what he was doing is "paraphrasing," and that's carrying charity pretty far.

It is next to impossible to keep up with all the lies that have tumbled from McCarthy's mouth. Some are reported in this book as they fit into the McCarthy story; others are so complex that the reader might get lost in the verbiage if an attempt were made to untangle the truth from the entwining falsehoods. Still other McCarthy lies are impossible to doublecheck, such as Joe's unlikely story of his conversations with ex-Secretary of Defense James Forrestal. Joe quotes Forrestal as sharing his views, and as saying of McCarthy's targets: "McCarthy, those men are not incompetent or stupid. They are crafty and brilliant. If they were merely stupid, they would make a mistake in our favor once in a while." Forrestal, long since dead, can hardly deny the quote — but his diary mentions no meetings with McCarthy.

Joe even went so far as to document his untruths, as in the case of the forged FBI report (see Chapter 33). In his Wheeling, West Virginia speech, he swore that he held "here in my hand a list of 205" known State Department Reds. It turned out that he held no list of any kind in his hand, but borrowed the figure from a dead letter that had already been investigated (see Chapter 28). Again, when McCarthy rose in the Senate in April 1950 and read from a sheet of paper that he claimed was a letter from Owen Lattimore to Joseph Barnes, he waved the so-called letter and invited his fellow Senators to come to his desk and read it for themselves. To McCarthy's surprise, Senator Herbert Lehman of New York accepted the invitation; but Joe refused to show it to him and brushed him aside. When the actual letter was finally made public, it did not read at all as McCarthy had "quoted" it; he had invented a text all his own. And on a television broadcast of March 16, 1952, Joe claimed to be reading from a statement given by Senator William Benton to the Senate elections sub-committee. He held up "a document" and "quoted" what he said was a note at the head of the text: "No part of this must be used by the press until I have become immune as I testified." The next week, the television network was forced to report that not a word of this had appeared on the Benton statement; Joe had made it all up.

If Joe was not particular about his own veracity, he did have a plan for curing untruthfulness in others. "It would be a good idea," he told the Associated Press on December 21, 1951, "to have all government employees and officials in sensitive jobs submit to lie-detector tests."

Side by side with Joe's trail of lies was a parallel trail of special laws. For instance:

(1) Until McCarthy came along, it was a felony in Wisconsin for a judge to run for another political office. Then he arranged with his friends in the state legislature to change the law the year before he made his first bid for the U. S. Senate. It remained a violation of the state constitution. (See Chapter 20.) But Joe was safe; it was no longer a jail offense.

In other cases, legislation favorable to McCarthy's interests was blocked before it became law:

(2) After setting his sights on Senator Robert La Follette's Senate seat, McCarthy tried to keep "Young Bob" out of the Republican primary by promoting a law that would have barred him on account of his affiliation with the old Wisconsin Progressive Party. This tricky legislation was carefully steered through the legislature, but was vetoed by the Governor.

(3) Joe's tax troubles (see Chapters 38 and 39) caused him so much embarrassment that he persuaded his friends to introduce a bill closing the state income-tax returns to the public. The bill came close to passing in its original form, but was finally watered down to provide merely that a person must pay one dollar to inspect a tax return and must state his reason for examining it.

(4) Because McCarthy was disturbed over too many inquiries into his past, he persuaded State Senator Warren Knowles to slip a secrecy bill through the Wisconsin legislature. This would have made a newsman liable for damages if he invaded the "legal right of privacy" by asking too many questions; and it probably would have prevented the writing of this book. But Wisconsin's newspapers caught the bill in time to stop it.

Other special laws have been passed or proposed to prevent another McCarthy from following too closely in his footsteps:

(5) Judge McCarthy's circuit court gained a modest reputation as a "little Reno" because of the "quickie divorces" he handed out (see Chapter 13). But after a couple of these easy divorces turned out to be political favors, the scandal burst in the press; and the state legislature passed two laws tightening up Wisconsin's divorce proceedings.

(6) In the 1950 elections, McCarthy invaded Maryland

to campaign against his political enemy, Senator Millard Tydings. One campaign trick that Joe pulled was the composite photograph showing Democrat Tydings and Communist Earl Browder posing chummily together (see Chapter 44). This fake photograph brought such a storm down on McCarthy's head that two bills were introduced in the 1951 Wisconsin legislature for the purpose of outlawing composite photographs.

(7) Joe's assaults on private reputations from the vantage point of the Senate floor have also stimulated special legislation, both in Wisconsin and Washington. Several bills are pending that would give redress to any citizen who is slandered by a Senator under the cloak of Congressional immunity.

In the past, McCarthy has managed to outdistance the lively skeletons from his closet; but at the time of this writing they are running hard on his heels.

54. The Presidential Bug... and McCarthy's Party-line Record on Foreign Policy

SENATOR JOE MCCARTHY SHOUTED AND TRUMPETED AROUND his political Jericho until the walls of opposition came tumbling down. And his clamor paid off at the polls.

What was the explanation? In these politically turbulent times, many voters were accustomed to hyperbole; politicians were granted a certain license to stretch the truth; and Joe's blowing was accepted as the usual exaggeration. The populace also had a perverse affection for a brawler; and they only became more defiant as the hurricanes of national denunciation roared around Joe's head. But Joe, himself, probably offered the most likely explanation; he announced that his large vote was an endorsement of "my campaign to rid the government of subversive forces." To many people, McCarthy symbolized the fight against Communism; they still accepted him at face value.

But the big question lay not so much in the past as in the future. Joe was not the kind who let political moss grow under his feet. He never stood still for his opposition to catch up with him; he was always poising for the next jump. And on June 25, 1952, he told a reporter for the Washington *Daily News*: "Leavenworth Federal Penitentiary won't hold all the officials I'll send there if I become head of the Special Investigation Committee in 1953." He predicted that the Republican Party would win control of the Senate and said it meant "that McCarthy, as the ranking Republican member of the Committee, will become chairman."

But even this was not the limit of his ambition; through the haze, another goal began to take shape. From Little Chute, Wisconsin, came a report that Joe had boasted to a small group of Catholic war veterans that he would become the nation's first Catholic President. And a former friend, interviewed by one of the authors, claimed that Joe had once told her: "I'll end up either in the White House or in jail."

For a while, it looked as if he might even make the bid in 1952; at least this was the word that leaked out from his political coterie. But before Joe took a high flyer into the political stratosphere, he usually sent up a trial balloon. And Wisconsin politicians had come to watch a local column-ist — John Wyngaard — as the McCarthy weathervane.

Thus there was a great stir among the politicians when Wyngaard's daily column reported on October 9, 1951, that McCarthy "has been importuned by some of his admirers around the country to enter his name in a few of the early state Presidential preference primaries." The columnist ex-plained cautiously that this would give McCarthy a chance to test the Communist issue. "Some of his friends seem to feel," wrote Wyngaard, "that should he enter several of the early primaries — Oregon, Nebraska, New Hampshire, and Wisconsin are among the possibilities — he might solid-ify party attitude on the issue he has developed and that has not yet been accepted by many elements of his own political party." Wyngaard then weighed Joe's thinking on this daring move, which the politicians took as coming straight from the McCarthy pipeline:

Should [McCarthy] decide to list his name as a candidate for the Presidential nomination and then lose, it would probably have a disastrous effect upon his candidacy for Senator in his home state immediately afterward. Even the bare announcement of such a plan would be detrimental — giving his critics an opportunity to say that his Communist-hunting exploits were calculated solely for his own political aggrandizement.

Conversely, the reward would be great should he make such an adventurous jump and be successful. It would instantly still the clamors in his own party against him and his methods and his targets. It would undoubtedly make him a figure of some influence at the nominating convention.

McCarthy's career to date has not been distinguished by the caution of his approach. While there is nothing to indicate that McCarthy intends to make the biggest jump of his spectacular political life, those who have followed him closely know also that they will not be surprised if such a decision comes.

But before Joe could carry out any wild scheme to run for President, he found himself up to his neck in political hot water. His Senate seat was threatened by a move to expel him; and Senate investigators were digging dangerously deep into his financial dealings. So Joe devoted the 1952 political season to watching out for his own neck. But after his strong showing at the polls in September 1952, he was free to dream again. And in 1956, he could take a long shot at the Presidency without risking his Senate seat.

As the cornerstone of his political future, McCarthy surrounded himself with devoted workers. He screened his staff carefully; if it came to a choice between ability and loyalty, he always chose loyalty. Take, for example, the case of Mary Tom Savage, receptionist and typist. Mary Tom first met McCarthy at a Young Republican affair in 1950 at Chicago's LaSalle Hotel. After delivering the feature address, Joe hurried off to keep another appointment. But Mary Tom was so touched by his philippics that she ran down the hall after him with tears in her eyes. When she caught up with him, she explained that she just wanted to tell him how wonderful his speech had been. Joe took her name and address on the spot; and within two weeks, she got a phone call from him, offering her a job in his Washington office.

Occasionally, Joe got into trouble with the Post Office for reading other people's mail. The first instance was a letter from John Hebal of the University of Minnesota to Miles McMillin, a political reporter for the Madison *Capital Times*. At a meeting on March 15, 1952, Joe fished the letter out of his briefcase and read it to his audience. This was the first McMillin had heard of it; he had never received the letter. Annoyed at having his mail delivered to Mc-Carthy, the reporter protested to the Post Office. But the postal authorities, not anxious to tangle with McCarthy, found no evidence that the letter had been swiped while under their jurisdiction. "There are laws," said McMillin, "that cover the stealing, the opening, and the publishing of other peoples' mail. And there are laws covering the receipt of stolen property." But the laws didn't seem to apply to McCarthy.

Thus encouraged, Joe pulled the same trick again. In a pre-trial encounter over the McCarthy-Benton law suit, Joe's lawyer produced a letter from Robert Fleming, a Milwaukee *Journal* reporter, to Stan Allen, Benton's administrative assistant. In this case, the letter had reached its destination. But before its arrival, it had been torn open, stapled together again, and marked: "Opened by mistake." Remarked Allen ruefully: "McCarthy seems to have a strange affinity for other people's mail."

But this wasn't the end of Joe's difficulties with the Post Office. Next, he was caught using his free mailing privileges to advertise his book *McCarthyism: The Fight for America*. This was also against the law, which restricts free postage to official business only and strictly forbids commercialism. But when it came to the postal laws, Joe was still living recklessly. He mailed out reprints of a favorable book review in large brown manila envelopes marked "Public document

— Free." The reprints had been taken from the magazine *The Freeman;* and the back page was taken up with an advertisement of the magazine, inviting subscriptions at $5 a year and offering additional reprints of the book review for ten cents a copy.

As for an issue, Joe was content to keep harping on the subject of spies in our midst. He had come a long way as the anti-Communist crusader; and there was no reason to switch to an untried issue. But when it came to opposing the Communists, McCarthy's speeches were much more impressive than his record. Joseph Alsop had this to say in his column about the foreign policy of Senators Joe McCarthy, Bob Taft, and Ken Wherry:

Let the test be a tabulation of the key votes of the three Senators on the great post-war measure of foreign policy, and especially of their votes on key amendments by which bills can be nullified. Unless I am gravely mistaken, such a tabulation will show that these three Senators, and most of the others who joined them in the present clamor, have voted the straight Communist Party line on every major issue of foreign policy, as laid down in the *Daily Worker,* ever since the war.

Washington's foremost fact-finding organization, *Congressional Quarterly,* has done a research job on the McCarthy record for this book.* The record bears out Alsop's contention in cold, hard fact. In 1950, Joe voted down the line with New York's Congressman Vito Marcantonio, the lone pro-Communist spokesman in Congress, against the Point Four program to aid underdeveloped foreign nations. He also voted for a $100,000,000 cut in foreign military aid; against a $3,945,000 boost for the Voice of America; for the McClelland amendment to restrict the expenditure of ECA funds; for a $500,000,000 cut in foreign aid; and again for another $250,000,000 cut. McCarthy stayed away when the

---

* For the complete voting record, see the reports of the *Congressional Quarterly,* available at most public libraries.

over-all foreign aid bill came up for final vote, but he finally registered a reluctant "yea" in favor of the military-aid bill.

In the following year, 1951, Joe's votes followed the same pattern. He voted for two Dirksen amendments to reduce foreign aid, first by $500,000,000, then by $250,000,000. He voted against the Kefauver amendment to increase military aid by $249,650,000, but for the Dworshak amendment to cut military aid by $37,000,000. On the final count, he voted for the military-aid bill he had tried to trim — then turned around and voted against the conference report which adjusted the differences between the Senate and House versions.

When this legislative score was added up, Joe had voted — with the two exceptions — the straight Communist line on foreign policy. But the more he voted with the Communists abroad, the louder he shouted against them at home. Sometimes, however, his investigators were kept so busy spying on Joe's political enemies that they had little time left for investigating Communists.

Many books have been written about Communism; but this is the first book-length treatment of McCarthyism. The authors acknowledge their limitations; they are not historians; and the scholarly treatment of the baffling post-war phenomenon called McCarthyism must await a detached academician. The authors are journalists; and theirs is a book of journalism — reporters' notes on McCarthy, the man, the Senator, and the "ism." Theirs was the job to put down on paper what kind of person he was and what he did.

Sociologists may deal in the future with a field the authors have barely explored — the varied and multicolored responses of the American people to the McCarthy sideshow. How they reacted — and why — is perhaps even more interesting than the phenomenon itself, for without public ridicule and response, McCarthy would have never become the Senator and there would have been no "ism."

McCarthy, himself a man of extremes, inspired others to extremes. He was the object of adulation and of hatred. People found it difficult to be objective about him. His charges either roused them to blind enthusiasm or touched them with fear and filled them with hatred.

There can be no doubt that the greatest threat to America today is Soviet Communism.

In McCarthyism, the problem is a moral one — the means versus the ends. Many who detested Communism could not bring themselves to adopt or sanction the methods McCarthy used. Others who hated Communism forgave the means for what they considered the ends — though the facts herein show that McCarthy never accomplished what he said he would do.

There were those who used their hatred of Communism primarily as a camouflage for attacking everyone who spoke up for the Bill of Rights and for the great moral values of the American heritage. They bore the characteristics of native totalitarianism; some of them had been on the side of the Nazis and the Fascists more than a decade before; and they reveled in McCarthy's methods. Intimidation, threats, mud-slinging were the weapons they understood.

But there were those also whose contempt for McCarthy's totalitarian-like methods led them to believe him as great a danger as the Communists themselves. The similarity of the methods confused them to the actual nature of the Soviet threat — a threat which was not only national but international, and backed by enormous resources and manpower.

There was an important group of American intellectuals who had concentrated on the Soviet threat since the days of the Bolshevik Revolution. They had never been among the so-called "practical" people who tried to get along with Russia. They warned that Russia was bent on world conquest many years before Joseph McCarthy, for one, frankly accepted Communist support in his first race for the Senate. To these people whose warnings were ignored for decades, it was galling to have a roughneck politician taking up the cudgels against Communism, and do it in such a way — with attacks on American civil liberties — that the public was only further confused.

Some of them forgot that "good" ends are not won by "bad" means and, in their zeal, could not bring themselves to denounce the Senator's methods. Instead they were silent, or argued that McCarthyism was a phantom conjured up by other intellectuals who could not see the danger of Communism because of their concern for Fascism.

Still others were fearful that the American public would lose its perspective on the Communist threat if it dealt seriously with McCarthyism—and these people therefore tried to reduce McCarthy to a mere incident on the American scene, a little man of no real threat. The usually penetrating *Commentary* magazine stated in September 1952 that McCarthy "remains in the popular mind an unreliable, second-string blowhard; his only support as a great national figure is from the fascinated fears of the intelligentsia." This somewhat patronizing comment by a favorite magazine of many intellectuals reached many *Commentary* subscribers (it was also given a million-and-a-half circulation in two full pages in *Time*) the same day that the nation was stunned by McCarthy's record-shattering primary-election victory.

But to most defenders of historic liberal values, McCarthyism — although smaller in scope and terror — was, like Communism, a hole in the dike of freedom. To them any demagogue whose methods were totalitarian was an enemy — whether or not he shouted in the name of liberty. It was a difficult road for the thoughtful American. The problem was on the one hand to acknowledge that there was, in Soviet Communism — as there has always been throughout history in any totalitarian regime — a threat to the basic freedom of all men; to try to swing the balance of the world away from dictatorships and toward democracy; and at the same time to use the methods of democracy so that freedom would be preserved.

55. The Age of Accusation

In MID-CENTURY, THE NATION WAS FILLED WITH A STRANGE, un-American malaise, compounded of personal insecurity, economic doubts, and anti-Communist fears. The causes for these feelings were real, the solutions slow and beset with temporary failures. Because the problems were complicated, so were the solutions. But a growing number of Americans sought simple answers and looked for strong leaders who would *tell* them what to do. The impersonality of the times made them seek personal explanations. All these things Senator Joe McCarthy understood; and he supplied the Communist issue as both the problem and the solution.

Too many people wanted quick yes-or-no answers to the troubles that confronted the nation; thus they created a market for the hate-peddlers, 'the myth-mongers, and the fear-spreaders. These merchants of doom peddled phony eyeglasses, which transformed the exciting world of colorful reality into a grim, distorted world of Red and white. They were the either-ors, the totalitarian-minded, who were forever unable to see human society as it was, many-hued and changing, but could see it only in terms of great, inevitable Armageddons. They were the rabble-rousers, offering push-button, yes-or-no answers.

But if they were able to discolor the facts and cloud the outlook, it was because too many people took their information in small, sugared capsules. They expected their news mediums to entertain before informing; they scanned the headlines with only half an eye, listened to the news broadcasts with half an ear. In February 1951, the New York *Times* published the following facts: that a third of a sample of voters were unable to identify Secretary of State Dean Acheson; that only 58 per cent knew what the "cold war" meant; that only 36 per cent knew the meaning of "welfare state"; that only 5 per cent could define Point Four; that only 25 out of every 100 voters were reasonably well informed; but that the large figure of 79 per cent of those queried had heard charges of "Communists in the State Department." And at the University of Wisconsin, a journalism instructor asked 43 third-year students what position Owen Lattimore had held in the State Department. Only 13 gave the correct answer: no position.

In this subterranean world of half-light, Joe McCarthy could paint his weird distortions and present them as the true picture. It was easy to believe him. He was in some ways the apotheosis of the American success story. He was a country boy who had refused to live and die in a small corner of America; and the dizzy, incredible pace of his rise to power was impressive. Pressures seemed to build up in McCarthy until they became so strong that they broke out in the form of bold, brash action — a "plunge." And his plunges were usually successful; he lurched forward with tremendous surges.

Joe's spectacular skyrocket was powered by the pressures of the times: the doubts, the fears, the confusions. He was the biggest flash in a skyful of lesser fireworks; and many couldn't see beyond the fireworks into the firmament. But if McCarthy obscured the vision of some, the fault was not all his. Archibald MacLeish, after watching McCarthy's meteoric trail, philosophized:

No, it is not the irresistible spread of Communism over the earth, or some Phoenix change in Russia, which has altered us . . . from a

THE AGE OF ACCUSATION

people who believed the future was our future to a people who talk
of fighting for survival. . . . The real change, as always, is neither
in our stars nor in our enemies, but in ourselves. It is not that Russia
is all at once ten times more dangerous, but that we see her so. It is
not that the Marxist dialectic has proved the inevitability of its
triumph, but that we do not believe, as we once did, in the inevitable
triumph of the dialectic of freedom. . . .

McCarthy is not the author of the decay in American confidence.
On the contrary, it is the decay in American confidence which made
McCarthy possible. . . . Merely to be against Communism is not an
offensive. It is not even a policy. . . .

Everything depends upon our undertaking again the achievement
of the American dream of a truly free, a truly democratic society in
which men shall be equal in opportunity, equal before the law, not
in word only but in fact; a society in which the inexhaustible human
resources of a great and intelligent people may be released for the
creative labor which is the dignity of human life. Until we undertake
that task we shall not regain the sense of national purpose which is
our present and fatal lack. Until we have accomplished some part at
least of what we propose, we cannot recapture from the Communists
the political and social initiative which we must have to win the
struggle for the future.

But if the doctrine of doom and disaster had been sim-
mering all along, Joe McCarthy brought it to a boil. Others
had whispered that the Kremlin was spinning its web in
Washington, that the nation's policy-makers were dopes
and dupes of Moscow — but McCarthy swelled the whisper
into a roar. He pulled the cork out of the bottle, and great
purple clouds of oratory swirled up in the nation's greatest
deliberative body. He made Communism the hottest domestic issue of the decade; he made it more popular for the
people's elected representatives to make charges than to
make laws. For McCarthy demonstrated a simple political
fact: charges made headlines, which made publicity, which
made votes, which made power. William H. Hessler caught
the spirit of the times in an article in the June 6, 1950, issue
of the *Reporter* magazine. He wrote:

The presses roar by day and night; the newsboys cry on thousands of street corners across the nation their garbled, laconic distillations of monumental untruths uttered in Congress. Small men of great ambition address a jury of 150 millions of people, impaneled by their common fears. Small people besmirch the reputations of those who are eminent and therefore vulnerable. The immunity designed to ensure courageous debate becomes a shield for cowardice, and reaches down through editors and headline writers to newsboys, covering them all as they play their diverse roles in the ordeal.

So in the topsy-turvy land of American politics at the turn of the half-century, the quiet, sincere, competent men in Congress were often elbowed aside; and their calmer counsel was apt to be drowned out in the general hubbub. The New York *Times*'s Capitol Hill expert, William S. White, watched this condition developing, and was impelled to write:

The Age of Accusation and the Era of Profound Ill-Feeling now grimly enwrap the capital of the greatest power in the world, the home of a lost tolerance and the center of a compassion that now is receding in memory. The square, massive, sad memorial to Abraham Lincoln, the rounded, softer, and more pleasing pile that commemorates Thomas Jefferson — physically these remain, white and cold and lifeless. . . .

Washington is not alone the seat of Western power. It is the seat also of a kind of trial by fire. . . . Men in the State Department trim their reports and their views in fear of the present, or of another, Senator McCarthy. Men in other bureaus, who ordinarily would be dealing hard-headedly in hard goods (like munitions), trim their activities. . . .

There is the evolution of the Congressional investigation into what, in all disinterest, must be called all too often a kind of pitiless inquisition in which, to put it plainly, the accused is licked before he starts. . . . Congressional inquiries have for the most part become punitive rather than fact-finding. In the real sense, the verdict is in before the evidence begins.

But even this unhappy position has so far taken into account only the official judges — the committee bench. There is yet a jury, a jury of a whole nation; the man in the bar, the housewife peering at the television around the top of the automatic dishwasher; a large, inchoate group of citizens of whom it can hardly be said that their one purpose and preoccupation is to return what is called a "true verdict." . . . It is said that these verdicts of national pseudo-juries do not convict for felonies before law. Perhaps they put no man in jail; sometimes they take away only his job, his life work, and his honor.

The decisions of the American people had also come to hold a fearful importance for the rest of the world. The problems were too deep, too vital for snap-finger solutions; but McCarthy delved into his patent-medicine kit and came up with cure-all, easy-to-take remedies. He would reduce the military budget, but at the same time strengthen defense; he would curtail foreign aid, but at the same time bolster our allies. In Asia, he would rely on the weak and corruption-ridden Chinese Nationalists against the march of Communism; in Europe, he would duck down behind the Germans and the Spaniards. For Americans, he offered more security at less sacrifice.

And so Joe barged into the Great Debate over mutual security during the early, hectic days of 1951. For two afternoons, he slouched over his desk, composing foreign policy. The product was an amendment to utilize "the military and other resources of western Germany and Spain." He would pull the Americans out, and leave the fate of Europe in the hands of the "tens of thousands of Germans and Spaniards who are willing to fight against Communist aggression." Joe showed the same confidence in the Chinese Nationalists, who once already had been driven into the sea by the Communists; and he joined in the clamor to turn Chiang Kai-shek's armies loose again on the Chinese mainland. And on August 8, 1951, with the Korean war still blowing hot and cold, Joe announced: "I believe Congress will, and should, cut back on the military program." Two months later, he voted against the foreign-aid bill, including both military and economic assistance to our allies.

This was the line of the semi-isolationist clique; and if Joe liked it, so did Moscow. For a man who enjoyed quoting

Communist sources against his enemies, McCarthy should have been chagrined at what the Reds had to say about his foreign-policy ideas. For example, when the McCarthy-backing Chicago *Tribune* argued that "with far less money for defense than has been appropriated, and probably without resort to the draft, this country can feel secure," Andrei Vishinsky quoted the editorial approvingly at the United Nations meeting in Paris. And on February 2, 1952, the Communist mouthpiece *Pravda* devoted a large proportion of its newsprint to quoting from and praising Herbert Hoover's speech calling for a retreat to isolationism.

No matter how McCarthy and his ilk tried to disguise it, their security-without-sacrifice doctrine was nothing but retreat, budget cut after budget cut, from the world-wide fight against Communism. Harvard Professor Arthur Schlesinger, Jr., called the advocates of this policy the "New Isolationists." Writing in the May 1952 issue of the *Atlantic Monthly*, Schlesinger suggested:

How are the New Isolationists to get around the fact that their proposals are greeted with loud cheers in the Kremlin? Somehow they must cover their retreat; and what better way to do so than by raising a great outcry about the supposed dangers of Communism within our own country? Such a sham battle at home might well distract attention from the stealthy desertion of our allies abroad. And the outcry would have the further incidental advantage of putting frightened liberals out of action and of smearing the whole movement for domestic reform.

I do not suggest that these affairs arranged themselves in the minds of the New Isolationists in quite this Machiavellian way. Still, anyone advocating policies which benefit Communism abroad and win the approbation of *Pravda* might well be tempted to justify himself to his constituents by redoubling his zeal to extirpate Communism at home. This, surely, is the powerful logic of the alliance between Taft and McCarthy. The simple fact is that Taft cannot repudiate McCarthy, because he needs him too much. McCarthyism is an indispensable part of the New Isolationism. Without McCarthyism the New Isolationism would be almost indistinguishable from a policy of appeasement.

The authors of this book have taken a long, hard look at the life and record of McCarthy. To those who would give him credit for arousing America to the danger of Communism, the authors would say: they were convinced that Communism was a dangerous threat to democratic freedom long before McCarthy came down the pike, and so was America; their resources were ranged against the Communists years before McCarthy raised his voice in the halls of Congress. To those who think McCarthy has caught some spies, the authors offer the facts — he hasn't. They would point out that, on the whole, McCarthy has instead aided the cause of Communism, whose technique is to confuse, frighten, and divide a nation, to smear the innocent, to intimidate the weak and cow the strong, to stifle freedom of expression and assembly, to judge men guilty until proved innocent, to purge 'the ranks of all but the conforming and the conscienceless. Communism's tactics are to convince the free world that it cannot win, that the Red power is invincible. This is McCarthy's secret weapon. His, too, is a fifth column of fear.

Only a strong, vital, and confident democracy can combat totalitarianism, for Fascist and Communist promises are empty; their "ideals" are false. McCarthyism would weaken democracy by striking at its roots in the hearts of free men.

Two decades ago a black economic sickness rolled over the nation. A politician with a glib tongue strode out of the Louisiana swamps into the United States Senate. Huey Long sought power. He got it — by bluster, intimidation, threats, lies. Long, in his crude way, tried to do some badly needed things; but he knifed democracy. This brought flocking to him such men as Gerald L. K. Smith and Joseph Kamp, who hovered over his victim — and who screamed "Communist!" at every critic of the Senator. Huey cried that

America must choose either his way or disaster. "A movement like mine has to come. . . . It's the only stop-gap to Communism," he said — using the totalitarian "either-or" argument.

Today in the crisis of fear that Soviet tyranny has brought to America, another demagogue with a glib tongue harangues the Senate — this time a power-hungry politician from the north country of Wisconsin. The weapons are the same: bluster, intimidation, threats, lies. McCarthy in his crude way has tried to do *some* badly needed things. But his knife has sunk deep into democracy. Again the Gerald L. K. Smiths and Joseph Kamps instinctively recognize their own kind, and they are hovering again over democracy. McCarthy cries that America must choose between his way and disaster. And even some of the Senator's camp-following "intellectuals" have swallowed the line that the nation must support McCarthy if it rejects Hiss.

Two decades before, the nation in its good sense rejected this intellectually bankrupt "either-or" line — and repudiated *both* demagogue and disaster. In fact, Huey Long's son, Russell, now himself a Senator, has firmly rejected demagogic extremes and is building a sturdy reputation as a progressive, responsible legislator.

Today the same native good sense is stirring throughout the nation. America is beginning to recover from its initial panic. Quietly and resolutely the nation is solving its present crisis — as it did before — in the American way; the decent way; the democratic way. The nation is stronger than McCarthy knows. It is resisting the Soviet threat — with concrete measures that *McCarthy has opposed*. The nation is moving forward once again toward full democracy.

APPENDIX

Pros and Cons

DURING SENATOR MCCARTHY'S MOST TURBULENT YEARS, 1950-52, probably more words flowed over the dam about McCarthyism than any other political subject. And from this torrent of comment, the authors have selected representative pros and cons as a measure of public opinion.

THE PRESS

As for the press, the tide of opinion ran against McCarthy; even those who approved of his stated motives usually took care to denounce his methods. A typical sampling was taken by Jack Olsen, a Washington correspondent for the American Broadcasting Company, on August 21, 1951. He sent out questionnaires on the Wisconsin Senator to the Capital press corps. He got back 211 replies; most gave well-thought-out evaluations of McCarthy; and for every friendly evaluation that came in, eight were critical.

It was perhaps significant that few of the newsmen signed their names. One reporter, who had classified McCarthy as "a disgrace to the nation," added in a postscript: "The fact that I prefer not to sign this is one evidence of the harm McCarthy has done to our country." An Associated Press reporter wrote: "McCarthy must surely represent to Moscow an asset fully as valuable as the one they lost when Fuchs was jailed. Fuchs stole our bomb. McCarthy can and is delivering our heart. I know what I am saying. I was in Europe as a foreign correspondent from 1940 to 1949. I saw the morally confused delivered — in full, physical strength — to both Fascism and Communism. Take away our moral superiority (that's my definition of democracy) and we have nothing left to fight for, and won't fight. America is not land and factories and railroads and a standard of living. It is the most nearly perfect *way* of living yet devised. McCarthy does not belong to it. Even so, to defeat him without losing to him, we must defeat him legally and ethically." The A.P. man signed his name but added: "As I work for the A.P., I can't let you use my name."

Another unsigned reply said: "McCarthy is as dangerous as a Goebbels, a Vishinsky or a Thorez. He has debased his high office and should be stripped of it." Another: "I feel that the sum total of the hardship, the misery, the confusion and bitterness McCarthy has caused by his limitless ambition and egomania is beyond atonement by any one man." Another: "Whoever thinks a Hitler or a Stalin can't rise in America had better take a second look at the methods of Joe McCarthy. La Follette underestimated him and got defeated for the Senate. Tydings underestimated him and lost his seat. Who was it that said if America is ever conquered by a dictator, it will be from within — in the guise of Americanism?" And yet another: "It is not simply the tactics McCarthy uses, although these violate every precept of American justice and fair play; but even worse, the fact that he is totally insincere. He lies, not with the fervor of the impassioned believer in a cause, but with the cool cynicism and surpassing skill of the consciously dishonest mountebank. He is a very dangerous man because he has in common with the Communists a complete amorality which does not even require a noble end to justify an ignoble means."

But here and there, a few pro-McCarthy replies bobbed

up. One that was not signed stated: "McCarthy has performed a duty as a Senator that those lacking guts to do it themselves now decry. He has been rough, yes; but the job wasn't one for silk-gloved hands. He has used a sledgehammer because in his judgment, I should imagine, he thought a tackhammer wasn't heavy enough. It is my humble opinion that McCarthy rendered an unmatched service to the public and in rendering it he is distinctly a credit to the Senate; this at a time when direct action rather than pussyfooting and weasel words was needed."

It is possible that the questionnaire reached McCarthy's own office; one of the unsigned replies was typed on navy-blue ribbon of the same shade that McCarthy's secretaries have used to address his mail; it was written in Joe's own unrestrained style, using many of his pet names and phrases; and characteristically, it began with an attack on the network conducting the poll. "I think it highly inappropriate, to say the least, for the news department of the American Broadcasting Company to conduct such a campaign as this one obviously is," the anonymous reply began. "McCarthy is no more of a disgrace to the Senate than any of your left-wing bleeding hearts — Elmer Davis, Drew Pearson — virtually every news commentator in the employ of ABC. So long as Davis, Pearson and the rest of the left-wingers continue their own brand of distortion and misinformation, there will be a real job for the McCarthys. Such a poll as the one being conducted here, obviously aimed at discrediting McCarthy and helping remove him from the Senate, raises the question of the fitness of ABC's so-called news department to even report the news, much less comment on it. Joe McCarthy at least is honest enough not to try to hide behind the claim of objectivity — which your Elmer Davises, Drew Pearsons and other self-anointed pious commentators do."

Here is a cross-section of what the national press has said about McCarthy, in answer to the ABC questionnaire and on other occasions. (For editorial comment by the nation's "ten best" newspapers — as determined by a nationwide poll of editors — see Chapter 43.)

PRO

Walter Trohan, Chicago Tribune: "There are no grounds for Mc-Carthy's removal [from the Senate] except the blatherings of Sen. Benton and the phony pious incantations of characters like Sen. Margaret Chase Smith and Sen. Hendrickson. Benton, Smith and Hendrickson all have a vested interest in smearing McCarthy because they are linked with his disclosures." (August, 1951)

Parker LaMoore, Scripps-Howard papers: "McCarthyism, so called, was an inevitable reaction to the failure or refusal of the Administration to purge itself of disloyal and untrustworthy elements, particularly in the State Department. By dramatizing this issue, Senator McCarthy has performed a distinct public service." (August, 1951)

Gould Lincoln, Washington Evening Star: "What do you think the State department would be like and would be doing if there had been no McCarthy?" (August, 1951)

Constantine Brown, Washington Evening Star columnist: "Senator Joseph McCarthy rendered a signal service to the American people by drawing their attention to the subversives in government, some of whom are still in responsible positions. Only nine of those

CON

Cabell Phillips, New York Times: "McCarthy is about the most conspicuous and unequivocal discredit to the Senate of this century. His crime of using his privileged position and Congressional immunity to spread terror and doubt among the people and to persecute his political enemies is an infinitely more sinister one than any of the traditional forms of graft and corruption. These, after all, are in the American tradition; we know how to cope with them. Intellectual and spiritual sabotage — for which the short name is McCarthyism — is the corrosive sort of affliction that feeds on itself. And there is no antidote for it — not yet." (August, 1951)

Richard L. Strout, Christian Science Monitor: "I think McCarthy should be ousted for abusing the necessary privilege of Senatorial immunity and introducing into American politics — at a time of extreme global danger — the Hitler technique of the Big Lie." (August, 1951)

Kenneth Scheibel, Gannett News Service: "I think Sen. McCarthy has been a discredit to himself, to the state and people he represents, to the Senate and to the sincere fight being made by true Americans — both in and out of

PRO

mentioned by him in 1950 have been so far eliminated. The idea of expelling him from the Senate because of these activities — and because he exposed Tydings' attempted whitewash — is preposterous." (August, 1951)

Freeman Magazine: "That no politician since Goliath ever had such a uniformly bad press is only half the frightful story; the truly appalling phenomenon is the irrationality of the college-educated mob that has descended upon Joseph R. McCarthy. . . . Suppose Mr. McCarthy were indeed the cad the 'respectable' press makes him out to be; would this, in the name of Horace Greeley, justify the cataclysmic eruptions that, for almost a year now, have emanated from all the better-appointed editorial offices of Manhattan and Washington, D. C? It must be something in Mr. McCarthy's personal makeup. He possesses, it seems, a sort of animal, negative-pole magnetism which repels alumni of Harvard, Princeton and Yale. And we think we know what it is: this young man is constitutionally incapable of deference to social status. And so the irrepressible young man goes on with his job—a politician's job, mind you, which means that he sometimes has evidence and sometimes none." (December, 1951)

CON

government — against Communism." (August, 1951)

Garnett D. Horner, Washington Evening Star: "Since McCarthy is succeeding much more than any Communist-label campaign could in destroying confidence in the U. S. government—obviously a prime Communist objective — could it be that he is the prize dupe of some devious Communist mastermind?" (August, 1951)

Collier's Magazine: "It looked for awhile as if Senator Joseph McCarthy were going to disprove the prevalent notion that the presence of smoke is a pretty sure sign of fire. . . . The Senator has failed to turn up a single Communist in the State department. . . . He has injured American prestige, undoubtedly hampered diplomatic relations and otherwise played a reckless, dangerous game from behind his shield of Congressional immunity. He has embarrassed his party and confused the whole country without revealing anything of significance through his own efforts. *Collier's* thinks he deserves the critical blast of editorial comment that most of the press has given him." (July 15, 1950)

Life Magazine: "We deplore the wild and irresponsible behavior of Sen. Joseph McCarthy. It is right to fight Communism; it is wrong, wicked to smear people indiscriminately. . . . It is wrong when millions of Americans lose their decent sense of judgment and are ready to believe any charge leveled against anybody, regardless of proof." (April 10, 1950)

Life Magazine: ". . . sin brings us back to McCarthyism. That's sin all right — at least according to the rules we were taught. But what kind of sin is it? Churchmen sometimes speak of 'venial' sins and 'mortal' sins. Without consulting the moral theologians, we'd classify McCarthyism as a venial sin. Communism is a mortal sin. Contemporarily, Communism is the Great Sin Against Humanity." (September 8, 1952)

Saturday Evening Post: "All in all, we wish the judicial attitude could have intruded upon Sen. McCarthy's enthusiasms. Because he was careless with his definitions, the vestiges of Red espionage here are likely to gain some valuable time." (May 2, 1950)

The New Leader: "Now is the time to rout out communism and McCarthyism through methods — and men — which will be a credit to democracy." (June 10, 1950)

CATHOLICS

As a Catholic, McCarthy won the early support of Catholic leaders who were inclined to view his campaign as part of the fight against religion's avowed enemy: Soviet Communism. But gradually, this support was withdrawn; and many Catholics who at first commended McCarthy began to condemn him. The climax came at the annual meeting of the nation's Catholic bishops on November 16, 1951; without mentioning McCarthy by name, the bishops struck him with an ecclesiastical bolt. "Those who are selected for offices by their fellowmen," they declared jointly, "are entrusted with grave responsibilities. They have been selected not for self-enrichment but for conscientious public service. In their speech and in their actions they are bound by the same laws of justice and charity which bind private individuals in every other sphere of human activity. Dishonesty, slander, detraction and defamation of character are as truly transgressions of God's commandments when resorted to by men in political life as they are for all other men. . . . There are not two standards of morality. . . . One and the same standard prohibits false statements about private individuals, and false statements about members of minority groups and races."

But other Catholics were less subtle; they referred to McCarthyism by its proper name. Here, in microcosm, is how Joe's fellow Catholics regarded him:

PRO

The Rev. Leopold Braun, a Catholic priest who was for 12 years a chaplain for Americans in Russia: "Senator McCarthy's position on Communism is entirely defendable." (October 22, 1950)

The Tablet (Brooklyn diocesan weekly): "The critics of Senator McCarthy never criticize Hiss; they never utter a protest over Acheson and the pro-Reds and the perverts of the State Department, or the Rosenbergs and other thieves of A-bomb formulas. . . . Their one object is to shut up, to destroy, the Wisconsin Senator, for then no one else will have the courage to stand up and expose the Reds and pro-Reds who infil-

CON

Commonweal, national lay Catholic weekly: "Another McCarthy-type attack is objectionable, because the Senator's tactics are completely irresponsible. And his supporters are not making much effort to hide their political motives. This is, in our judgment, demagoguery; a shameless, ruthless exploitation of innuendo that may yet rip apart the fabric of our foreign policy." (February 1, 1951)

Francis Downing, associate editor of *Commonweal*: "The voice of McCarthy was abroad in the land, and it was, as it was in the beginning, a poisoned and fearful thing. It went on forever making un-

PRO

trate the government; no one will
have the courage to take the abuse
and fight back . . ." (August 30,
1952)

CON

proved charges, forever irresponsible, forever merely free of libel;
it went on exploiting the insecure,
the anxious, the confused, the
afraid. It went on attacking Hiss,
assaulting Acheson, attacking perverts, attacking unnamed Communists, attacking Yalta, praising
MacArthur as if he were God and
McCarthy had invented him; it
went on, the voice, and it harassed the discontented, and it
assigned guilt, and it called
names, and it laid blame; and it
talked to the emotions. In every
case where it made foreign policy
an issue, it won. We have known
demagogues in our political history, but this is a special kind —
an evil kind; it adds falseness to
the already false, it represents the
other side of the election coin.
It is the spurious and the counterfeit. It would be legal nowhere
in any world where reason was
and where intelligence was operative. Yet men took it as though
it were legal tender and had value
and was clean and bright and
new, and had been minted honestly." (February, 1951)

Commonweal: "Hysteria tends to
breed counter-hysteria, and over-
statement and extreme partisan-
ship on both sides of the Mc-
Carthy debate have helped
matters not at all. In some danger of being overlooked in the
heat of the argument has been a
very practical fact: whatever else
may be said about Senator McCarthy's tactics, it should be obvious
by now that they do not work.

PRO

CON

CON

Concealing membership in the Communist party in order to work for the Government is an offense punishable under law. Senator McCarthy continues to make speeches, but where is the evidence that would produce indictments by the Grand Jury?

"Despite this failure in operation, what has come to be called McCarthyism is itself a genuine threat. A real danger exists that the smear technique and the sly innuendo will come to be accepted as normal tools of statesmanship, that the blanket accusation and the careless charge will become routine elements in any political campaign." (August 22, 1952)

Commonweal: "The man and his approach to political problems of the day have an undeniably wide appeal. He is a hero to thousands, and the fact that his record brands him as something less than a knight in shining armor is not likely to shatter their loyalty. For many, nothing in the self-damning McCarthy record makes much difference; they are willing to accept their hero even as a heel. They will admit, for instance, that maybe he overdid it when he branded George Marshall as a traitor, that maybe a number of innocent people were hurt during the McCarthy crusade, that it may be true that Joe doesn't always stick with the truth, that his replies to factual critics are rarely if ever straightforward and direct, that perhaps Joe's respect for the

PRO

CON

democratic processes is not as keen as it might be — you will get admissions like this from the Mc-Carthy partisans if you press hard enough. But the admissions don't really mean much.

"What most Americans find repulsive in McCarthy's record, his defenders gently speak of as Joe's 'mistakes.' General Marshall publicly branded as a traitor after a lifetime of service to his country — a 'mistake'! The wholesale calumniation of innocent government workers — a 'mistake'! The faked composite photo showing Senator Tydings and Earl Browder together (circulated in Maryland when Tydings was up for re-election) — another 'mistake'! Every politico should be allowed a certain margin for error, but Joe's 'mistakes' are of a kind that the penny catechism has harsher words for. Oddly enough, those who take an indulgent attitude toward McCarthy's 'mistakes' are often the same people who have no tolerance for genuine errors of judgment." (September 12, 1952)

Graham Greene, British author and Catholic layman: "The United States seemed prepared to take on Stalin, but not McCarthyism." (February 19, 1952)

James A. Eldridge, lecturer at the Catholic Bernard Sheil School for Social Studies in Chicago: "Senator McCarthy's shotgun methods have not yet produced a single Communist, but they have smeared the reputation of able,

PRO   *CON*

conscientious public servants. . . . Furthermore, McCarthy's personal attacks upon Mr. Acheson have created the division and distrust which I am sure is very helpful to the Soviets." (May 16, 1950)

America, national Jesuit weekly: "We ought to be very careful . . . not to identify ourselves too closely with anti-Communists like Senator McCarthy." (June 5, 1950)

OTHER RELIGIOUS LEADERS

The comments of other religions ran about the same as those of Catholics. For example, the Northern Baptists of the United States, holding forth in convention at Boston on May 26, 1950, passed a resolution denouncing "campaigns of character assassination." And in Joe's home state, the executive head of the Wisconsin Council of Churches, Ellis H. Dana, said that "methods of McCarthyism can never be justified" despite an "understandable condition of doubt about Communistic infiltration in government. I wish to repudiate the kind of leadership which has been using a technique of brazen half-truths, sly innuendoes and reprehensible character assassination." Israel Goldstein, speaking as president of the American Jewish Congress, declared on June 14, 1952: "If Thomas Jefferson were alive today, I imagine he would be called un-American by the McCarran-McCarthy adherents and probably be denied a passport to travel abroad on the ground that it would not be in the interests of the United States. . . . There is a spirit of inquisition abroad in the land, which affects teachers, artists, men and women in all walks of life, including scientists and social servants."

VETERANS

But if Joe was frowned on by the nation's church leaders, he was more popular among his fellow veterans. On April 8, 1950, the Marine Corps League awarded McCarthy its "Americanism" award at Passaic, New Jersey — but not without a voice of protest from Irving L. Stein, the League's judge advocate in New York. He objected: "Senator McCarthy has demonstrated that he should be the last considered for such a great honor. We are ashamed that Senator McCarthy, a fellow Marine, vilifies decent Americans while he himself hides behind a wall of immunity." But four months later, the Military Order of the Purple Heart followed suit and presented McCarthy with another "Americanism" award, citing "his courageous effort to rid our country of radicals, subversives and Communists." Meanwhile, McCarthy got in trouble with some of the veterans in his home state; he delivered such a violent harangue at Wisconsin's 1950 American Legion convention that the 1951 convention passed a resolution, interpreted as a slap at him; the resolution banned politicians from making political speeches at Legion conventions. And on August 31, 1951, Kenneth L. Greenquist, Wisconsin commander of the American Legion, warned all state posts against having political speakers, after he learned that McCarthy was scheduled to speak at two of the posts. Here are some typical comments on McCarthy by spokesmen for veterans:

PRO

Jerome Host, former Wisconsin commander of the American Legion: "The confidence of the American people in our State department will not be restored until vital changes are made. The Tydings committee was guilty of

CON

Charles C. Ralls, national commander, Veterans of Foreign Wars: "[McCarthy's] methods hurt those of us who are sincerely fighting the Communists. I'm afraid all McCarthy is interested in is making a big name for him-

PRO

white-washing the charges of Senator Joe McCarthy." (July 25, 1951)

Edgar C. Bundy, former Air Force captain, speaking to the Daughters of the American Revolution in Madison, Wisconsin: "It is men like Senator McCarthy, whose statements have been, in the main, completely with foundation, who realize the perils of these [Communist-front] organizations. McCarthy had the courage to bring the story out, even though he cannot substantiate his claims at present." (March 13, 1950)

CON

self. He should forget about the publicity." (April 5, 1951)

L. D. Hale, Wisconsin commander, Marine Corps League: "I kept McCarthy away from our 1950 convention. . . . I have agreed fully with those who felt certain officers were supporting McCarthy so vigorously that they weren't considering the good of the organization." (October 7, 1951)

National Planning Committee of the American Veterans Committee: "McCarthy has been guilty of doing more than any other un-American force to bring world scorn, domestic obloquy and general disgrace upon the Senate. He accepted without a word of protest, much less any public disclaimer, the support of the Communist party in Wisconsin — which means that of the Communist party of the United States, which undoubtedly cleared such action with the Kremlin — in his candidacy for Senator." (June 5, 1950)

EDUCATORS

Among prominent educators there was little approval of McCarthy. Few apparently let their concern over the Communist problem stampede them into an endorsement of McCarthyism. Here are a few typical quotes:

PRO

Kenneth Colegrove, professor of political science, Northwestern University, Evanston, Ill.: "McCarthy has been made the victim

CON

Dr. John Lapp, former director of the social science department at Marquette University, the Jesuit college attended by McCarthy:

PRO

of 'one of the most vicious smear campaigns in American history.'"
(From a pamphlet quoted in *The Washington Religious Review*, May 19, 1952, which reported that the following men endorsed it: Dr. James W. Fifield, Jr., national director of "Spiritual Mobilization"; Dr. Norman Vincent Peale, Marble Presbyterian Church, New York; Dean Clarence Manion of the University of Notre Dame Law School; Dr. Roscoe Pound, dean emeritus of Harvard Law School.)

CON

"The greatest menace to liberty we've had in a long time is McCarthyism . . . McCarthy will be blown sky high when people wake up to what he has done." (March 22, 1951)

John TePoorten, co-ordinator of Wisconsin's vocational schools: "A certain irresponsible U. S. Senator from this state is going up and down the country defaming people he disagrees with by calling them Communists, without any proof or foundation for his charges." (March 15, 1951)

Carl Auerbach, professor of law, University of Wisconsin: "Senator McCarthy would like to have us believe that anyone opposed to him must be on the side of the Communists. And the Communists would like to have us believe that anyone opposed to them must be on Senator McCarthy's side. In this way, each gives aid and comfort to the other. . . No justification exists for taking either of these two positions; supporting either endangers the very ends for which people of good will everywhere are struggling. Why should we be forced to choose either Senator McCarthy or the Communists, when devotion to the democratic cause demands that we fight them both? . . . We must oppose the use of lies, calumny, and slander as political weapons whether used by the Communists or Senator McCarthy." (April 1, 1952)

LABOR LEADERS

Like the educators, the nation's labor leaders were prac- tically unanimous in their opposition to McCarthy. The Neenah-Menasha Trades and Labor Council, near Joe's home town, even went so far as to call upon the Wisconsin State Federation of Labor to institute a recall petition against McCarthy. And on April 21, 1951, the Wisconsin State CIO Legislative Conference declared formally: "Senator Mc- Carthy has soiled the reputation of the state of Wisconsin by slanderous statements against distinguished citizens, by irresponsible actions and a total disregard for ethical and moral decency." Here are statements showing how typical labor leaders regarded McCarthy:

PRO

CON

Herbert Steffes, Wisconsin CIO president: " 'If Joe McCarthy isn't a Communist, he is cheating them out of dues.' I made this state- ment at the 1951 C.I.O. conven- tion in Milwaukee, and now I say it again — without Senatorial im- munity. . . .

"I have seen both the Com- munists and Joe McCarthy in ac- tion. It wasn't until 1946 that the true trade unionists drove the Communists from the control of the Wisconsin C.I.O.; but by that time the Communists had helped to defeat a great public servant, the liberal Robert M. La Follette, senior Senator from Wisconsin. They contributed to his defeat by indirectly supporting McCarthy, urging the thousands of C.I.O. members in our state to vote against La Follette. McCarthy has not disappointed this scheming

PRO   *CON*

clique. His actions on and off the floor of the Senate have tended to destroy our faith in democratic government.

"McCarthy's voting record negates every effort that has been designed to stop the growth of world communism. He voted against the Marshall Plan, against giving aid and assistance to governmental plans for stopping communism in Europe. . . ." (Quoted in *The Nation*, August 30, 1952)

George A. Haberman, president of the Wisconsin State Federation of Labor: "Most federation members, like myself, are opposed to the reelection of Senator McCarthy for these reasons: he has failed to represent the majority of his constituents; he has ruined Wisconsin's fine tradition of excellent United States representation and progressive legislation; he has shamed the people of the state by his unscrupulous methods, his frequent tax troubles, his vicious attacks on defenseless people, and his reputation for engaging in public brawls. Wisconsin people . . . are contemptuous of a person who makes irresponsible attacks on fellow-citizens while hiding behind his Senatorial immunity." (Quoted in *The Nation*, August 30, 1952)

Theodore R. Kurtz, secretary, Wisconsin Industrial Union Council (CIO): "If he [McCarthy] were seriously interested in stopping communism, it is logical to presume he would have voted for

PRO

CON

measures designed to destroy it. He has done the opposite. His vote was *against* the Point Four program, *against* the Benton European aid amendment to encourage the development of free trade unions, *for* the vicious Dirksen amendment which would have seriously crippled our European aid program . . . McCarthy has bred intolerance, and distrust. His words say he is anti-Communist. His actions belie his words." (Quoted in *The Nation,* August 30, 1952)

Paper Maker, official organ for the International Brotherhood of Paper Makers: "McCarthy appears wide open to the charges that he has seriously damaged the nation's reputation by depicting us as a nation of hysterical witch hunters. On this score, we slam one right back into Joe McCarthy's teeth. For his actions in this modern inquisition, we label him America's worst security risk." (May 15, 1950)

REPUBLICANS

But the storm of controversy over Joe McCarthy was nowhere more violent than inside his own political party. In Washington, many Republican leaders regarded him as a black sheep but didn't exactly know what to do about him. However, a few raised their voices against him. At home, McCarthy found more support from his fellow Republicans. On May 7, 1950, the Wisconsin Young Republican convention passed a resolution endorsing McCarthy and demanding continuation of his "investigation" of Communists. And on July 7, 1951, McCarthy delivered the main address at the 1951 state Republican convention and received a tremendous ovation. Two young delegates, State Assemblyman Arthur Peterson and Methodist Minister Al Eliason, were physically manhandled when they attempted to oppose a resolution commending McCarthy. The resolution, passed over their opposition, praised McCarthy's "outstanding service to the United States in facing the Communist issue and awakening the American people." This was echoed by the Shawano County Republican organization, in McCarthy's home district, which unanimously backed his charges against the State Department and complimented him for "compelling Dean Acheson and State Department Security chief John Peurifoy to kick out 92 perverts from the State department."

But one rebellious group of young Republicans, the executive committee of the Marathon County Young Republican Club, came out against McCarthy. After five hours of debate, a resolution was adopted declaring: "We reaffirm our belief in the traditional concept of American justice that no man is guilty until proved so beyond any reasonable doubt." This set off a series of resolutions among Young Republican Clubs throughout the state, reaffirming their allegiance to McCarthy. In the Senator's home town, the Appleton club passed a resolution praising him; the vote was 52 to 25 with nine abstentions. The Winnebago County club commended Joe for his "outstanding service to the American people in spearheading the drive to rid our country of traitorous elements"; and the Crawford club praised him for his "hard-fisted Americanism, his enthusiasm for truth and his eradication of Communism in government." Here is what some leading Republicans have said about him, both in and out of Wisconsin:

PRO

Thomas E. Coleman, Wisconsin Republican "boss" and Senator Robert Taft's 1952 campaign manager: "McCarthy thinks you can't do anything without taking vigorous action — and so do I. McCarthy believed that there was Communist influence in the government. So do I, and most of the people." (February 10, 1951)

Harold Stassen, former Governor of Minnesota and Presidential candidate in 1948 and 1952: "I do not wish to pass on the individual things McCarthy has done and said, but I do believe that Senator McCarthy is a patriotic Marine veteran of World War II, and I can understand how a man who has seen his buddies killed in World War II in the Pacific, would feel intensely about Communists in this government." (September 27, 1951)

Guy Gabrielson, Republican National Chairman: "The American people should be proud of what the Senator has done. McCarthy has brought out to the American people the tremendous infiltration of pinks and fellow travelers in our government." (February 2, 1952)

Congressman Charles Kersten of Wisconsin: "McCarthy's campaign will result in a net substantial good to America. Top State department officials hold the destiny of our nation and of our nation's children in their hands. In the present life and death struggle with world Communism, we can-

CON

Republican Senators Thye of Minnesota, Ives of New York, Smith of Maine, Aiken of Vermont, Tobey of New Hampshire, Morse of Oregon and Hendrickson of New Jersey: "Certain elements of the Republican Party have materially added to this [national] confusion . . . through the selfish political exploitation of fear, bigotry, ignorance and intolerance . . . It is high time that we all stopped being tools and victims of totalitarian techniques — techniques that if continued here unchecked, will surely end what we have come to cherish as the American way of life." (June 1, 1950)

Senator Alexander Wiley of Wisconsin, McCarthy's Senate colleague: "I do not want to see the Republican party attempt to climb to power by an unprincipled policy of pouring venom on individuals, by personalities, rather than by calm, reasoned analysis of issues and principles. We Americans can, and must, get rid of the incompetents, the security risks, the disloyal individuals in government — but we can do so in the traditional American way." (June 26, 1952)

Senator Henry Cabot Lodge of Massachusetts: "A loyalty investigation must never allow itself to be used to carry out some hidden purpose of creating a political result here at home, regardless of whether or not such a result injures the country." (April 23, 1950) [NOTE: *On Sept. 19, 1952, in the middle of the fight for re-*

PRO

not have questionable characters in that high and important post." (October 2, 1951)

CON

election, Lodge endorsed McCarthy's re-election.]

Governor J. Bracken Lee of Utah: "McCarthy is a symbol of the problem of low standards of public conduct. McCarthy has made some big mistakes. I can't condone making statements without knowing whether they are true. Instead of unsupported accusations of Communism, he might better have said that some people have acted like Communists. . . . We Republicans certainly must have our own house in order." (October 2, 1951)

Arthur Peterson, Republican State Assemblyman from Prescott, Wisconsin: "Joe McCarthy has not fooled the unscrupulous and the self-seeking — his pattern of action is too familiar to them; they know to what depths a man will sink to attain his own aims and to further his own ambitions. We do have subversive elements working in our nation which we must expose and expel, but, because of McCarthy's wild charges, people are beginning to believe that there is no danger at all. It is like the story of the boy who cried 'wolf' once too often." (September 3, 1951)

Senator Margaret Chase Smith of Maine: "I am not proud of the way in which the senate has been made a publicity forum for irresponsible sensationalism. I am not proud of the reckless abandon in which unproved charges have been hurled. . . . I don't like the way the senate has been made a

PRO

CON

rendezvous for vilification, for selfish political gain at the sacrifice of individual reputations and national unity. I am not proud of the way we smear outsiders from the floor of the senate and hide behind the cloak of immunity.... The American people are sick and tired of being afraid to speak their minds lest they be politically smeared as 'Communist' or 'Fascist.' I don't want to see the Republican Party ride to political victory on the four horsemen of calumny — fear, ignorance, bigotry and smear. In fact, I doubt, if the Republican Party could ..."

Former Gov. Charles A. Sprague of Oregon (Republican), editor and publisher of *The Oregon Statesman:* "If the Republican Party is to endorse McCarthyism it deserves to be laid in a grave both wide and deep."

Senator Wayne Morse of Oregon: "I'm still waiting for the first case when Senator McCarthy can establish his burden of proof. I want proof — not accusations; I want proof — not smear; I want proof — not character assassination."

DEMOCRATS

Except for Senator Pat McCarran of Nevada, McCarthy got little sympathy from the Democrats. They were slow in replying; but President Harry Truman, himself, led the counter-attack. On March 30, 1950, he called McCarthy "an asset to the Kremlin." And again on August 14, 1951, the President denounced the "hate-mongers and character-assassins" who, he said, were doing their best to make the American people "so hysterical that no one will stand up to them for fear of being called a Communist." The cry was taken up by Democrats from Wisconsin, where Democratic Leader James E. Doyle described McCarthy as "this puny man who has snatched a moment of cheap notoriety at the risk of his country's security," to Washington, D. C., where Senator William Benton of Connecticut called on the Senate to expel McCarthy. Here are examples of what the Democrats have said about McCarthy and McCarthyism:

PRO

CON

Governor Adlai Stevenson of Illinois: "Perhaps this hysterical form of putrid slander not only escapes tar and feathers, but actually flourishes, because it satisfies a deep craving to reduce the vast menace of world Communism to comprehensible and manageable proportions. Indeed, the apoplectic quality of our anti-Communism, its very violence, makes it the more difficult for us to analyze and understand Communism's attractive power, and thus to combat it." (June 15, 1950)

Gov. Adlai Stevenson: "[McCarthyism] has become a trade mark of a new breed of political demagogue who carelessly impugns the loyalty of patriotic men, and shouts dire forebodings of a treacherous doom for America and all her cherished institutions. . . . We have all witnessed the stifling, choking effect of McCarthyism, the paralysis of initiative, the discouragement and intimidation that follow in its wake and inhibit the bold, imaginative thought and discussion that is the

PRO

CON

anvil of policy." (Quoted in *The Progressive,* Sept. 1952)

Senator Estes Kefauver of Tennessee: "McCarthyism represents one of the greatest threats to our nation today and to our freedom. Due to this guilt-by-association technique and smear technique used for political purposes, McCarthyism is forcing a lot of our people into conformity of thinking. I think McCarthyism is one of the greatest problems facing America today. . . . We, of course, must be vigilant and uncompromising to ferret out and destroy any subversive elements in our Government, and we have loyalty boards and the FBI to do that job." (March 20, 1952)

Congressman Richard Bolling of Missouri: "The purpose of McCarthyism is not to fight Communism but to get publicity, power and prestige for Senator McCarthy. Do not be fooled. McCarthyism is not a crusade against Communism. McCarthyism is irresponsible and unsubstantiated attacks against individuals who are at a disadvantage in defending themselves." (October 2, 1951)

Secretary of Agriculture Charles Brannan: "It's about time some of those crying loudest against Communism took time to join the team that is really fighting Communism in a realistic way, instead of actually tearing down the very bulwarks we are building up against it." (July 9, 1951)

Conrad E. Snow, chairman of the State Department's Loyalty Secur-

PRO

CON

ity Board: "McCarthy's statement that where there is smoke there's fire is erroneous. . . . There is no excuse for mistaking dust for smoke. The dust in the present case is created by one man, tramping about the nation and making, over and over again, the same baseless and disproved accusations." (February 11, 1952)

Senator Blair Moody of Michigan: "McCarthyism is not a one-man effort but a deliberate attack by a group of Republicans to undermine for political reasons our foreign policy — which is fighting Communism."

PROFESSIONAL AGITATORS

Among the first to leap on the soap-box and exercise their lungs over McCarthyism were the professional hate-mongers and rabble-rousers of both the red end and the black end of the political spectrum. The Communists denounced McCarthy daily; and McCarthy eagerly clipped all the bad things they said about him. He was fond of waving these clippings (and especially the Gus Hall quotation below) before the public as "proof" that all who dare to criticize him "follow the order issued by the Communist Party — to discredit and destroy McCarthy." (He even used this language against St. Louis Banker Towner Phelan. Phelan had written an article for the ultra-conservative, pro-McCarthy magazine *The Freeman,* in which the banker lamented that McCarthy's "unethical tactics" had "hurt the anti-Communist cause.")

Time and again Joe McCarthy finds himself cornered by the truth. He has only one tactic. He never answers the *facts.* He cracks a blackjack down on the head of critics of

the type in the pages ABOVE, RIGHT. The blackjack is the accusation that the critics "follow the orders" of his gutter-level
enemies BELOW, RIGHT. If this line of reasoning were true,
then McCarthy would be forced to admit that his supporters
of the type in the pages ABOVE, LEFT "follow the orders" of his
gutter-level supporters BELOW, LEFT. Of course both arguments are utter nonsense, and the authors hope this tabulation will help clarify the air for both critics and supporters.

PRO

The Cross and The Flag, edited by
the anti-Semitic agitator, *Gerald
L. K. Smith:* "We are reprinting
another of Senator McCarthy's
speeches in this issue. This fearless young statesman constitutes
one of the most hopeful signs that
has appeared on the horizon. . . .
He has increased in knowledge
and in courage, and promises to
be one of the most influential and
valuable men in our nation. The
new 1951 Congress offers this
courageous statesman the opportunity of his lifetime to fulfill his
ideals, substantiate his charges
and help save his America." (December, 1950)

Gerald L. K. Smith: "Senator
Joseph McCarthy exposes Reds.
They call him a 'liar' and a
'character assassin' and a 'smear
artist.' Then times passes, investigations take place, documents are
dug up, and it turns out that
McCarthy is right. This is the
formula by which the fearless
Wisconsin Senator is rising to a
position of great prominence and
respect in the life of the American
people." (From *The Cross and
The Flag*, April, 1952)

CON

Gus Hall, Communist Party secretary, now in jail: "I urge all Communist Party members, and all
anti-Fascists, to yield second place
to none in the fight to rid our
country of the Fascist poison of
McCarthyism."

Daily Worker, official Communist
newspaper: "McCarthy today is
regarded by many people, maybe
by a majority, as a clumsy but
dangerous clown. But it is possible that at some time in the
future the ravings of McCarthy,
together with the irresponsible
charges of the UnAmerican Activities Committee, will provide the
'evidence' upon which labor leaders, Negro leaders and progressive
persons from all walks of life,
will go to jail." (March 22, 1950)

Philip Frankfeld, convicted Communist: "Defeat McCarthyism or
face the threat of political annihi-
lation. . . . At all times, remember
the fact that the main enemy is
McCarthyism." (In a pamphlet
published in November, 1950)

Political Affairs, official Communist Party "doctrinal" organ: "Truman's acts feed the growth of

PRO

Upton Close, well-known Axis apologist, whose anti-Semitism has kept him off the major networks: "Anyone who opposes McCarthy is giving aid and comfort to the enemies of the Republic." (From Associated Press dispatch in *The New York Times,* September 1, 1952)

Closer Ups, the news letter published by *Upton Close:* "It is to be hoped that every voter at the polls will remember that the Administration which condemned McCarthy for inaccuracy and irresponsibility, participated in a conspiracy to lie to the public. . . . The anti-McCarthyites, the defenders of Acheson, and the breakers-up of our large patriotic organization are an interlocking group." (March 10, 1952)

Conde McGinley, editor and publisher of *Common Sense,* which recently characterized General Eisenhower as a "Marxist stooge": "Those Americans who wish to live as free men and enjoy Christian worship as they see best, should thank our good Lord for such a man as Joe McCarthy. Senator McCarthy, like all other leaders who had the courage to challenge Marxism, is now attacked by Marxists and their dupes and hatchetmen. Only a few Communists are allowed to admit that they belong to the Communist party and, actually, none have carried cards since 1945. Those 55,000 admitted Communist Party members are only shock troops for the Marxist-

CON

McCarthyism.* . . . the vast majority of the American people still do not see through Truman's demagogy. One of the principal reasons for this is his pretense of fighting McCarthyism in defense of the Bill of Rights, even as he goes about destroying those rights . . . wide sections of the labor movement under Rightwing leadership and sections of the Negro people under reformist [democratic, anti-communist] influence either do not see or are as yet unwilling to speak out against the Smith Act, which is the keystone in the Administration's effort to destroy the Bill of Rights and clamp fascism upon the land." (October, 1951; article by Michael Bianca)

Political Affairs: "McCarthyism is the *ultimate* expression of the reactionary policies of the Truman bi-partisan administration. It exemplifies the process in the present stage of history of how reaction leads to greater reaction. Vito Marcantonio, chairman of the American Labor Party, aptly describes McCarthyism as 'the Frankenstein created by Truman' . . . we can and must demonstrate that it is the reactionary policies of the *Truman government in power* that contribute to the extremism of McCarthyism

---

* This became one of the favorite arguments of "respectable" apologists for McCarthy during the 1952 election campaigns. This would make them—under McCarthy's line of reasoning — "fellow travelers of the Communists."

PRO

Zionists who are the brains and directors of Communism while posing as loving, respectable men and philanthropists." (April 1, 1950)

The National Wage Earner, racist and foremost labor-baiting monthly in the country: "Senator Joseph R. McCarthy, in the opinion of the WEC, has done more than any other man in the past twenty years to preserve our freedoms. How much he is feared by the Labor Bosses can be gauged by the ferocity and constancy of the attack by smear goons on the air and in the press. How much influence he has in the United States today among the people who cast the vote, may be gauged by the fact that every candidate for office that Senator McCarthy opposed was soundly beaten last November. It would not surprise the experts if this valiant leader became next President of these United States." (February, 1951)

Jessie W. Jenkins, only woman leader of Ku Klux Klan: "Despite the awful fact of the powerful Leftist coalition having betrayed our government, as Senator McCarthy has so nobly undertaken to show us, HOPING TO AROUSE PUBLIC OPINION AND ACTION — we must surely have a good 100 million GOOD Americans ready to rise to the challenge." (From *Your Pocket Atom Bomb,* 1950)

Joseph P. Kamp, Nazi-endorsed propagandist and currently vice-

CON

and make it so dangerous. We can thus more effectively demonstrate that you cannot fight McCarthyism merely as a 'lunatic fringe' and stand silent in the face of government-inspired Smith Act prosecutions. . . . Thus it is the interweaving of the Truman policies and McCarthyism with its contradictions that have, with the weapons of terror and demagogy, blanketed the nation in a smog of fear and confusion and speeded up the tempo of fascization." (October, 1951; article by George Blake)

Daily Worker: "One contradiction in Governor Stevenson's speech to the American Legion Convention on August 27 was his subtle advocacy of McCarthyism while attacking McCarthy. The Democratic Party nominee said that 'the denial of the right to hold ideas that are different — the freedom of a man to think as he pleases' cannot be justified, 'cannot be cloaked in the shining armor of rectitude and of righteousness.' He appealed for 'free enterprise for the mind.' He lashed out at the attacks on General Marshall, which were initiated by Senator McCarthy, and he denounced this kind of patriotism as 'the last refuge of scoundrels.' But before the echo of these words had died away, Stevenson was telling the Legion delegates that 'there can be no secure place . . . in our public life' for Americans who are Communists. Thus, the Democratic

PRO

chairman of the "Constitutional Education League": "May God sustain Senator Joe McCarthy! . . . Nobody in years has given the entrenched Fair Deal-New Deal pressure group in Washington such a battle as has Joe McCarthy, with his forthright assault upon Communists in the State Department. . . . McCarthy revealed dismaying qualities of fearless courage and persistence." (From *It Isn't safe To Be An American*, copyright, Constitutional Educational League, Inc., 1950)

CON

Party nominee was criticizing not the aims of McCarthy, but his methods. It was Stevenson's 'charming way' of saying he would try to do what McCarthy and Nixon are doing, but in a different way, perhaps a more 'charming' way, as the Truman Administration is doing." (Columnist John Pittman; September 2, 1952)

Index

NOTE — q. = *quoted*

417

Marshall Plan, 3, 216, 247, 249, 337, 356, 404
Martin, Attorney General, 70 q.
Marxism, 414
Maryland, 289, 370; campaign, 296 ff., 315, 322, 326, 327, 329
Matthews, Secretary of the Navy Francis, 165, 168, 171, 248
Matthews, J. B., 313, 344
Mauston, Wis., 27
Mayflower Hotel, 193
McCarran, Senator Pat, 216, 219, 340 q., 341 ff., 347 ff., 348-49 q., 399, 409
McCarran sub-committee, 316, 341 ff., 346
McCarthy, Bridget, 7, 12
McCarthy, Howard, 10, 251, 252
McCarthy, Olive, 9 q., 11, 18, 69, 250
McCarthy, Timothy, 7, 8, 11, 12, 21 q., 252
McCarthy, William, 252
McCarthyism, 288, 291, 293, 251, 257, 259, 278, 279, 386, 389, 392, 394, 395, 396, 402, 410, 411, 413, 414, 415
McCarthyism: The Fight for America, 64, 221, 375
McClelland amendment, 376
McCormick, Colonel Robert R., 111 q., 112, 290, 293 f., 297
McCulloch, Spencer R., 353
McFarland, Senator Ernest, 332
McGinley, Conde, 414-15 q.
McGovern, Professor William, 218
McGrath, J. Howard, 210
McGraw, James, 313
McKellar, Senator Kenneth, 348 q., 349 q.
McKinnon, Arlo, 75
McMahon, Father, 26
McMahon, Senator Brien, 181 q., 185, 209
McMillin, Miles, 120 q., 375 q.
McMurray, Professor Howard, 101, 105, 107 q., 109 q., 113, 117
McPherson, Aimee Semple, 106
Menominie, Wis., 87

Mesta, Perle, 166
Metropolitan Club, 193
Middle East, 138 f.
Mikolajczyk, Stanislaw, 283
Military Order of the Purple Heart, 61, 400
Miller, Ruth McCormick ("Bazy"), 297, 298, 299 q., 305
Milwaukee (Wis.), 20, 53, 75, 78, 82, 96, 102, 103, 107, 109, 144, 226, 248, 256, 274, 403; CIO, 274; City Council, 27; Common Council, 144; County Republican Women's Club, 94; Journal, 28, 50 q., 54 q., 55 q., 74 q., 79 q., 83-84 q., 85 q., 103 q., 104-05 q., 109, 112 q., 113 q., 114 q., 271, 273 f., 286, 289 q., 376 f.; League of Women Voters, 69; Retail Food Dealers, 274; Sentinel, 20 f.; Society of Accountants, 90
Minnesota, 407; University of, 375
Missouri, 247
Mondovi, Wis., 87
Mongols, 217
Monroney, Senator Mike, 304, 320, 323, 325-26 q., 328 q., 329-30 q., 336 q., 337
Montgomery, Jean, 285
Moody, Senator Blair, 412 q.
Moore, Ewell, 302, 304
Moore, John, 336 q.
Morehouse, Commander Albert K., 62
Morris, Robert, 219, 297, 342 f., 344
Morse, Senator Wayne, 115, 151 q., 194, 209, 407 q., 409 q.
Morton, George R., 117
Moscow, 223, 271, 383, 386, 389
Mow, P. T., 194
Munda, 59
Mundt, Senator Karl, 184, 344, 345-46 q.
Mundy, Cornelius, 205, 297, 298 q.
Munn, Major E. E., 64 q.
Munsey Trust Company, 135
Murdock Hotel, 35
Murphy, Arnold F., 56 q.
Murphy, John Harold, 74

221, 223, 225, 230, 232, 243, 249,
268, 270, 277, 278, 283 f., 296,
315, 316, 329, 335, 342, 347 f.,
348, 349, 350, 352, 353, 354, 366,
368, 382, 384, 392, 393, 395, 400,
406, 407, 411
Stearns, Perry, 82, 117-18 q.
Steele, John, 282
Steffes, Herbert, 403-04 q.
Stein, Gunther, 284
Stein, Irving L., 400 q.
Steinle, Circuit Judge Roland J., 73
Stettinius, Edward, 239
Stevenson, Governor Adlai, 410-11
q., 415
Stimson, Henry, 239
Stone, William T., 337-38 q.
Stotler, Thomas, 343, 345
Strandlund, Carl, 152, 153, 154, 155
Strout, Richard L., 284, 285, 392 q.
Subversive Control Board, 347
Sulgrave Club, 275
Summerfield, Arthur, 356
"Sunset Farm," 343
Superior, Wis., 73, 87
Surine, Donald A., 196, 197 q., 198
q., 221, 237, 238, 262, 302, 303,
304, 310, 311, 312, 343, 344, 345,
346
Susteren, Urban P. Van, 4 q., 51 q.,
62, 74, 116
Sweden, 249
Swift, Rev. Wesley, 309, 310
Switzerland, 199, 200, 201
Swope, Gerard, 227
Syracuse *Post-Standard*, 286

Taber, Congressman John, 189
Tablet, 395-96 q.
Taft, Senator Robert A., 115, 138 q.,
151, 204, 278, 316, 351 ff., 352-53
q., 354 ff., 376, 386, 407
Taft-Ellender-Wagner bill, 144, 146,
151
Tankersley, Garvin E., 298
Tankersley, "Bazy" Miller. *See*
Miller
Tehan, Robert E., 109
TePoorten, John, 402 q.

Thorez, 390
Thorp, Wis., 87
Thorpe, Brigadier General G. Elliot,
216
Throne, David, 89 q.
Thye, Senator, 407 q.
Tibbetts, J. L., 254 q.
Time, 227, 236-37 q., 250 q., 277
q., 278-79 q., 286, 379
Tobey, Senator Charles, 131-32 q.,
141, 142 q., 146 q., 150, 407 q.
Tobin, Secretary of Labor Maurice
J., 269, 270
Todd, Bill, 146 q.
Tokyo, 234
Toledo, 261; *Blade*, 270
Treasury, Department of the, 189,
345
Trippe, Juan, 227
Trohan, Walter, 392 q.
Truman, President Harry, 93, 129,
151, 166, 168, 214, 233, 236, 237,
247, 248, 249, 288, 347, 357, 360,
409-10 q., 413-16
Truman Doctrine, 240
Two Rivers, Wis., 86
Tydings, Senator Millard, 167 q.,
170 q., 175, 208, 231, 248, 295 ff.,
315, 316, 317, 360, 371, 390, 393,
398
Tydings committee, 314 q., 315 q.,
321, 342, 400

Underhill Country School, 9
United Nations, 93, 223, 225, 226,
230, 232, 233, 247, 386; Commis-
sion on the Status of Women, 204;
Educational, Scientific, and Cul-
tural Organization, 350
United Press, 269, 282, 283, 323, 326
University Club, 342
Unmuth, Marty, 91 q.
U. S. Navy, 165
U. S. News and World Report, 308
q., 346 q.
U. S. Savings and Loan League, 143
U. S. Supreme Court, 159
Utica, N. Y., 224, 229
Utley, Mrs. Freda, 215